ULTIMATE
THINGS

ULTIMATE THINGS

An Introduction to
JEWISH AND CHRISTIAN
APOCALYPTIC LITERATURE

GREG CAREY

CHALICE
PRESS

ST. LOUIS, MISSOURI

Cover art: FotoSearch
Cover and interior design: Elizabeth Wright

Visit Chalice Press on the World Wide Web at
www.chalicepress.com

10 9 8 7 6 5 4 3 2 1   05 06 07 08 09 10

Library of Congress Cataloging–in–Publication Data

Carey, Greg, 1965-
Ultimate things : an introduction to Jewish and Christian apocalyptic
   literature / Greg Carey.
     p. cm.
   Includes bibliographical references
   ISBN-10: 0-827238-03-7
   ISBN-13: 978-0-827238-03-9
     (pbk. : alk. paper)
1. Apocalyptic literature—History and criticism. I. Title.
   BS646.C37 2005
   220'.046–dc22

                                                    2005003649

CONTENTS

Preface   vii

Abbreviations   xi

Introduction: Encountering Apocalyptic Discourse   1

1. The Earliest Apocalypses: 1 Enoch and Daniel   19

2. Emerging Apocalyptic Discourse in the Hebrew Scriptures   50

3. Interpreting the Times: Jewish Apocalyptic Discourse beyond the
   Apocalypses   69

4. The Gospels and Jesus   102

5. The Pauline Epistles   125

6. Responses to Tragedy: Jewish Apocalypses after 70 C.E.   147

7. Christian Historical Apocalypses   179

8. Christian Ascents: What Are They Good For?   207

9. Epilogue: Legacies and Prospects   228

Notes   245

Bibliography   263

PREFACE

As an introduction to apocalyptic discourse in early Judaism and Christianity, this book invites two audiences. It aims to engage students and instructors in intermediate to advanced undergraduate and seminary courses on apocalyptic literature. It also seeks to interest the Bible students who want to delve a bit deeper into an area of scripture where they have interest, perhaps even intense interest, but not much information.

Much of the material presented here, and especially the angles from which I approach particular subjects, have emerged from my own teaching experiences and so should be helpful to the college or seminary student and instructor. I have also imagined a broad audience, people who have read the Bible, perhaps even taken a course in it, but who do not pursue biblical studies as a professional discipline. I hope this book will introduce this audience to the richness of ancient Jewish and Christian apocalyptic discourse: its spiritual imagination, its theological creativity, its literary artistry, and its worldly engagement.

My own students continually find themselves captured by a host of provocative questions that emerge from this literature. Who's to say which questions are "central" and which are "peripheral"? Yet after a few years of teaching, I've learned to expect some questions that routinely interest people. And yes, some of them still snag my own curiosity as well. As a result, I've set apart some "boxed" discussions throughout the chapters to address these discrete topics. Some teachers and students may wish to explore these topics in depth, or perhaps some individual readers will do so on their own.

In addition to this general audience, I want to contribute to my field, the academic study of early Jewish and Christian apocalyptic discourse. These chapters do not so much advance a thesis as they promote a way of reading apocalyptic texts. Historical critical scholarship has traditionally taken a somewhat "archaeological" approach to these texts, digging beneath the surface to uncover the sources of their ideas to reveal the histories of their composition and the nature of their relationships to other literary sources. This book continually relies on the results and proposals such scholarship has generated. All of us seek to understand how, why, and in what context people composed these books.

I am interested in reading these texts somewhat differently, perhaps even with a sort of naive curiosity. As a *religious person,* as someone who wonders about God and the world, I value these texts as conversation partners. Thus, I want to call attention to their theological and cultural creativity, to the distinctive ways that they interpret their religious traditions and respond to pressing questions. As a *reader of literature,* I do not want to emphasize these texts as products of redaction or as sources of abstract ideas, which they are, but I want to experience them as literature, to explore their literary and rhetorical design, to engage them as a sort of holy poetry. As a *social person,* I wish to engage these texts as interventions in the lives of early Jewish and Christian communities, promoting certain ways of being, believing, and acting while opposing others. We might appreciate these religious, literary, and social dimensions of ancient apocalyptic discourse as constructive theology, poetry, and rhetoric. When we hold these categories in mind, we may find ourselves surprised by our own engagement with the creativity, religious passion, and social engagement expressed in these ancient texts. We may even wonder as they stretch our religious and cultural horizons. That has been my experience, and I hope that similar testimonies from students reflect more than brazen flattery.

I'm not aware of another book quite like this one in which a single author looks at the broad range of early Jewish and Christian apocalyptic literature, including texts from beyond the body of formal apocalypses. In comparison with volumes in which individual scholars deal with their special fields of research, or anthologies to which teams of scholars make individual contributions, my approach has obvious weaknesses. Yet I believe it has its strengths as well.

In any case, the scope of this project has intimidated me. It isn't possible to discuss every relevant text, though I have attempted to introduce a large and representative selection. As with most surveys, I rely heavily on the hard labor of people who know a lot more about 3 Baruch, for example, than I ever will. In many, many cases, I relied on translations. And yet in every chapter I seek to present fresh interpretations of these ancient texts, from small insights concerning literary devices or rhetorical design to larger arguments concerning their overall function or motivation. Without overloading the pages with scholarly apparatus or jargon, I have sought to acknowledge my many debts and to demonstrate my engagement with the range of contemporary scholarly opinion.

Throughout this volume I rely on publicly accessible translations so that readers may consult the texts for themselves. Unless I indicate otherwise, I make particularly generous use of the *New Revised Standard Version Bible,* James H. Charlesworth's two-volume *The Old Testament Pseudepigrapha,* Florentino García Martínez's *The Dead Sea Scrolls Translated:*

The Qumran Texts in English, and J. K. Elliott's *The Apocryphal New Testament.* Quotations from other sources or translations of my own are indicated in the text and in notes. In general, I have followed the style format of the Society of Biblical Literature, with one exception. Reflecting my commitment to set aside a book's canonical status for the purposes of understanding it in its ancient literary, historical, and religious contexts, I do not marginalize ancient Jewish and Christian non-canonical texts by italicizing their titles.

Lots of people have earned my gratitude by contributing their ideas, their critical readings, and their support. The administration, trustees, and faculty of Lancaster Theological Seminary have offered their faithful support, including the spring 2003 sabbatical that empowered me to complete this manuscript. I'm especially grateful to Jon Berquist, the editor who first encouraged and supported this project. He may not know this, but without him I never would have believed I could have pulled this off. Having taken over the manuscript near its completion, Trent Butler has been exceedingly gracious with his comments, suggestions, and kindness.

In addition to my former spouse, Laura Carey, and my Mom, Barbara Akin Pace, other friends have read portions of the manuscript: my Lancaster Seminary colleague Julia M. O'Brien, to whom I'll never adequately express my personal and professional gratitude; Lancaster students Andrea Brown and Fritz Ackerman, who generously provided their wisdom and skill; Stephen Cooper of Franklin and Marshall College, a new friend and keen scholar; Rev. Dr. Chris Ayers of Charlotte's radically progressive Wedgewood Baptist Church; Courtney Harvey, a college student and Lancaster Seminary staff member who's brighter and more gifted than any mortal has a right to be; and the students at Rhodes College, Winthrop University, and Lancaster Theological Seminary—students make their teachers, and I'll never know how many of the insights in these pages I've stolen from them. Tim Van Meter, another Lancaster colleague, has contributed theological and cultural observations. I'm also grateful for the wisdom and encouragement of Catherine A. Hastings and Dean Clemmer of Lancaster's Samaritan Counseling Center. Thanks as well to the congregations of Highland Presbyterian Church of Lancaster, Pennsylvania, and Eastminster Presbyterian Church of York, Pennsylvania, whose pastors, Rev. Dr. Larry Chottiner and Rev. Jim Crawford, have invited me to lecture and teach on this topic.

Finally, to my two daughters, Erin Summers Carey and Emily Hope Carey, I dedicate this book. Young as they are (ten and six when this book sees print), they embody the power of vision. When these young women see a future, they start living it out right away. They may envision the perfect birthday party or encounter a new role model, and off they go to mold their parents and change their world so as to grow their hopes into experience. Compassion and a hunger for justice mark their clear—and articulate—passion. This book has brought sacrifices for them, as much as it has for Laura and for me. In the meantime, their ability to demonstrate love, their willingness to take risks, and their gift for creating laughter enrich my life with joy. I love you, E and Em.

ABBREVIATIONS

Primary Sources

In addition to the standard abbreviations for works from the Bible and the Apocrypha, the following abbreviations appear for other ancient works.

1 En	1 Enoch
11QTemple	Temple Scroll (Qumran)
1Q28a	Rule of the Congregation (Qumran)
1QH	Thanksgiving Hymns (Qumran)
1QM (War)	War Scroll (Qumran)
1QpHab	Habakkuk Pesher (Qumran)
1QS	Community Rule (Qumran)
2 Bar	2 Baruch
3 Bar	3 Baruch
3Q15	Copper Scroll (Qumran)
4Q186	4QHoroscope (Qumran)
4Q242	Prayer of Nabonidus (Qumran)
4Q243	Pseudo-Daniel (Qumran)
4Q244	Pseudo-Daniel (Qumran)
4Q245	Pseudo-Daniel (Qumran)
4Q521	Messianic Apocalypse (Qumran)
4QMMT	Halakhic Letter (Qumran)
Ant.	Josephus, *Antiquities*
Apoc Paul	Apocalypse of Paul
Apoc Abr	Apocalypse of Abraham
Apoc Peter	Apocalypse of Peter
Asc Isa	Ascension of Isaiah
b. Hag.	*Tractate Hagigah*, Babylonian Talmud
b. Sanh.	*Tractate Sanhedrin*, Babylonian Talmud
CD	Damascus Covenant (Qumran)

Herm.	Shepherd of Hermas
Jub	Jubilees
Lam. Rab.	*Lamentations Rabbah*
m. Hag.	*Tractate Hagigah,* Mishnah
Man.	Shepherd of Hermas, Mandates
Sib Or	Sibylline Oracle(s)
Sim.	Shepherd of Hermas, Similitudes
t. Hag.	*Tractate Hagigah* (Tosefta)
t. Sanh.	*Tractate Sanhedrin* (Tosefta)
T. Ben.	Testament of Benjamin
T. Dan	Testament of Dan
T. Jos.	Testament of Joseph
T. Jud.	Testament of Judah
T. Lev.	Testament of Levi
T. Naph.	Testament of Naphtali
T. Sim.	Testament of Simeon
T. Zeb.	Testament of Zebulun
Vis.	Shepherd of Hermas, Visions
War	Josephus, *Jewish War*
y. Hag.	*Tractate Hagigah* (Jerusalem Talmud)
y. Ta ͨan.	*Tractate Ta ͨanit* (Jerusalem Talmud)

Secondary Sources

AB	Anchor Bible
ABD	*Anchor Bible Dictionary*
ABRL	Anchor Bible Reference Library
ACNT	Augsburg Commentary on the New Testament
AMWNE	*Apocalypticism in the Mediterranean World and the Near East* (ed. David Hellholm)
AOT	*Apocryphal Old Testament* (ed. H. F. D. Sparks)
BibInt	*Biblical Interpretation*
BNTC	Black's New Testament Commentaries
BR	*Biblical Research*
CBQ	*Catholic Biblical Quarterly*
CBQMS	Catholic Biblical Quarterly Monograph Series
CRINT	Compendia rerum iudaicarum ad Novum Testamentum
EDB	*Eerdmans Dictionary of the Bible*
ESCJ	Studies in Christianity and Judaism
GNS	Good News Studies
HSM	Harvard Semitic Monographs
HTR	*Harvard Theological Review*
ICC	International Critical Commentary
IDBSup	Interpreter's Dictionary of the Bible: Supplementary Volume

Int	*Interpretation*
JAAR	*Journal of the American Academy of Religion*
JBL	*Journal of Biblical Literature*
JECS	*Journal of Early Christian Studies*
JQRMS	Jewish Quarterly Review Monograph Series
JSJSup	Journal for the Study of Judaism: Supplement Series
JSPSup	Journal for the Study of the Pseudepigrapha: Supplement Series
LCL	Loeb Classical Library
LEC	Library of Early Christianity
NIB	*New Interpreter's Bible*
NICNT	New International Commentary on the New Testament
NIGTC	New International Greek Testament Commentary
NovTSup	Supplements to Novum Testamentum
NTA	*New Testament Apocrypha* (ed. Wilhelm Schneemelcher)
NTS	*New Testament Studies*
OTL	Old Testament Library
OTP	*Old Testament Pseudepigrapha* (ed. James H. Charlesworth)
OtSt	*Oudtestamentische Studiën*
SBLDS	Society of Biblical Literature Dissertation Series
SBLSP	*Society of Biblical Literature Seminar Papers*
SBLSymS	Society of Biblical Literature Symposium Series
SJLA	Studies in Judaism in Late Antiquity
SNTMS	Society for New Testament Studies Monograph Series
StABH	Studies in American Biblical Hermeneutics
SVTP	Studia in Veteris Testamenti pseudepigraphica
TDNT	*Theological Dictionary of the New Testament* (ed. G. Kittel and G. Friedrich)
WBC	Word Biblical Commentary

INTRODUCTION

Encountering Apocalyptic Discourse

"There is nothing better than imagining other worlds," [Baudolino] said, "to forget the painful one we live in. At least so I thought then. I hadn't realized that, imagining other worlds, you end up changing this one."[1]

One of Umberto Eco's most brilliant characters, Baudolino possesses two remarkable gifts: he can learn any language within minutes, and he is a great liar. Not only do people believe Baudolino's lies, his lies also turn out to become true. Baudolino's effectiveness as a liar arises not so much out of a desire to deceive people as from an acute perception of what people want to believe. Thus, when he finds himself in danger or when friends face a crisis, Baudolino intervenes with just the right lie. Everyone wants to believe his lie, and so it becomes true. Even when Baudolino concocts an entirely fictional empire, his compelling vision inspires a movement to go and find it. So by imagining other worlds, Baudolino transforms his own.

The Roots of Apocalyptic Discourse

Likewise, apocalyptic discourse pushes the boundaries of the imagination, yet it also emerges from the common human longing to reconfigure the world. It addresses questions that we begin to ask in our childhood and that hound us throughout our lives. Is the world headed in any particular direction? Does justice win out in the end, or does history lack purpose? How does one account for disaster when meaning seems absent? What realities lie beyond the world as we ordinarily perceive it, and how might those realities influence our world? What is death, and what, if anything, follows it? Every child asks questions like these, and though we may stop asking them aloud as we age, we never actually grow out of them. For early Jews and Christians, apocalyptic discourse provided a rich context in which to pursue these challenges.

The Perplexity Roused by Apocalyptic Discourse

Despite the nearly universal appeal of these questions, the ancient apocalyptic literatures of Judaism and Christianity typically perplex modern readers. In North America, "apocalyptic" and "apocalypse" have come to imply little more than a vague sense of the catastrophic, evoking nuclear, biological, or environmental threats to human survival. The continuing influence of television "prophecy teachers," who argue that books such as Daniel and Revelation point to the imminence of the coming end and the final judgment, associates apocalyptic literature with a pessimistic view of history. Perhaps even more seriously, their influence has caused mainstream interpreters and large segments of popular culture to view apocalyptic texts with suspicion, in many cases avoiding them altogether. As I complete this manuscript, I recall the many conversations—on airplanes, at reunions, or even at the mall—in which people have asked me about my research interests in apocalyptic literature, only to fall into awkward silence as they fumbled helplessly for something appropriate to say.

That awkwardness disappears when people encounter apocalyptic literature on their own, whether in academic, churchly, or other contexts. For while modern persons may not adopt all of the answers proposed by the ancient apocalyptic writers—nor could we—those common questions concerning justice, fate, and otherworldly realities still compel our attention. The answers to questions such as these defy analytical attempts to answer them. We may propose hypothetical answers, but of course those hypotheses are not subject to testing. Because the scientific method is largely foreign to ancient apocalyptic discourse,[2] ancient Jews and Christians turned to other ways of knowing. Naturally curious about their world and its workings, ancient persons searched the stars, studied the weather, investigated the earth's most basic elements, and searched for a greater order to account for their observations. To account for their findings, they also turned to their most basic cultural models: biological processes such as childbirth and death, the cycles of the seasons, common machines, and the administration of empires, courtrooms, and households. In particular, they appealed to *revelation*, divinely revealed mysteries otherwise unavailable to mortals. (Indeed, our word *apocalyptic* derives from the Greek *apokalypsis*, which means "revelation.")

Apocalyptic Modes of Discourse

Ironically, revealed truth involves two apparently contradictory modes of discourse. At one level apocalyptic discourse reflects remarkable *innovation*, as people imagined—perhaps through extraordinary mystical experiences and certainly through creative speculation—the ultimate realities that shaped human experience and destiny. For in apocalyptic literature we encounter particular ideas for the first time in Jewish literature, concepts without which rabbinic Judaism and Christianity could not have emerged as we know them. For example, we find expectation that history hurtles toward a final judgment, hope for victory over death through a resurrection, and a cosmos populated by powerful spiritual beings who serve good and evil purposes. Thus, early Jewish and Christian apocalyptic discourse demonstrates significant religious creativity, so much so that its influence on Western culture defies exaggeration.

At another level, however, apocalyptic discourse relies on *authority*.[3] When the apocalyptic authors introduce these innovative ideas, they cannot draw on scriptural or institutional sanction. Their alternative sources of authority include spectacular and mystical revelations. Such revelations identify the classical apocalypses such as 1 Enoch, Daniel, and Revelation, in which a visionary travels into the heavenly realms, encounters heavenly mysteries, and wonders at the revealed future.

The Jewish apocalypses and related literature often appeal to heroes from Israel's sacred history, attributing their visions to figures such as Enoch, Abraham, Moses, and Ezra. Likewise, Christian apocalypses draw on the authority of Isaiah, Peter, and Paul. Apocalyptic discourse offers unverifiable claims about the realms of heaven and hell, life beyond death, and history's ultimate future. Claims such as these naturally provoke the question, "How do you know?"[4] In reply, apocalyptic discourse necessarily appeals to authority, whether related through the narration of a vision, passed down by tradition, appealed to directly by the visionaries themselves, or expressed through creative biblical interpretation.

Apocalyptic Discourse: Its Topics and Modes of Address

What makes apocalyptic literature distinctive from other discourses? The answer largely involves two features: its characteristic topics and the ways in which it presents itself to its audiences. In other words, apocalyptic literatures characteristically turn to identifiable basic concerns or *topics,* while they also employ sets of standard literary devices or *modes of address.*

In the past, scholars talked about apocalyptic literature as if its meaning were obvious. This approach needed revision, in large part because people generally relied on the best known literary apocalypses–Daniel and Revelation–to inform their understanding of apocalyptic literature as a whole. Thus, the term *apocalyptic* could be applied to any literature that involved the expectation that God would intervene at the end of time to judge the wicked and redeem the righteous. Unfortunately, this strategy caused people to overlook some features that are common to a wide range of apocalyptic literatures but that are absent in Daniel and Revelation. For example, many texts reflect more interest in heavenly mysteries such as explorations of the heavenly and hellish realms than in the course of history.

In the last thirty years or so, biblical scholars have begun to clarify what we mean when we discuss things apocalyptic. Each of the following terms has enhanced the precision with which we study apocalyptic literature.

- An *apocalypse* denotes a literary text that belongs to a particular literary genre. According to the most widely accepted definition, "'Apocalypse' is a genre of revelatory literature with a narrative framework, in which a revelation is mediated by an otherworldly being to a human recipient, disclosing a transcendent reality which is both temporal, insofar as it envisages eschatological salvation, and spatial, insofar as it involves another, supernatural world."[5] In short, an apocalypse almost always includes (a) a revelation (b) by a supernatural being (c) to a human recipient concerning (d) cosmic mysteries or the future.[6]
- *Apocalyptic eschatology* involves the sort of beliefs one typically finds in apocalypses and related literature. Scholars use the word *eschatology* (which derives from the Greek *eschaton*, or "end") in relation to ultimate things, such as the resolution of history or the fate of the soul. At its most basic level, apocalyptic eschatology expresses the expectation that God will intervene so that "the adverse conditions of the present world would end in judgment of the wicked and vindication of the righteous, thereby ushering in a new era of prosperity and peace."[7] In other words, apocalyptic eschatology holds a pessimistic view of the human condition that requires decisive divine action for its resolution.
- *Apocalypticism* functions to describe social contexts in which apocalyptic eschatology flourishes, becoming the dominant ideology of a given group.[8]

Each of these terms has helped scholars to clarify what we mean when we describe apocalyptic texts, beliefs, or movements. Yet the terms also have certain limitations. For example, the group that developed the classic definition of an apocalypse realized that their definition did not include an understanding of the genre's literary or social function: What do apocalypses *do*? Thus, the group added the following words to the definition—"intended to interpret present earthly circumstances in light of the supernatural world and of the future, and to influence both the understanding and the behavior of the audience by means of divine authority"—but this modification has proved too vague to be of much help.[9]

As we shall see, the various apocalypses address widely diverse social contexts, and they do so for a broad array of social ends. Some apocalypses advocate new ideas or practices, as in Daniel, which argues for the resurrection of the dead. But others call for a return to traditional values. Likewise, the eschatologies of various apocalypses differ both in their assumptions concerning the present world and in how they imagine its resolution, while apocalyptic movements emerge in contexts as diverse as medieval peasant rebellions and affluent conservative North American Christianity. In short, the remarkable variety of apocalyptic texts, beliefs, and social phenomena demands our attempts at precision even as it defies our efforts to advance valid generalizations.

To reflect this tension, I tend to use an additional term, *apocalyptic discourse*. The invocation of discourse as a category of study represents an attempt to bring together the literary, ideological, and social dimensions of apocalyptic language. Contemporary students of culture and literature employ the term *discourse* to indicate how meaning is constructed in social contexts.[10] Over time, human groups build recognizable networks of linguistic conventions, cultural assumptions, and social relationships that function as traditions. In effect, they create their own worlds of truth, so that they function as common sense.[11] For example, we might speak of the discourses of privacy, according to which some societies designate certain realms of experience as subject to public scrutiny but others, particularly sex or religion, as private matters. And we might note how different societies have adopted radically divergent logics concerning privacy.[12]

With respect to ancient Jewish and Christian apocalyptic discourse, literary texts provide our primary resources. Though the results of archaeological and historical research continue to deepen our understanding of the people who produced these literatures, their specific social settings largely remain a matter of conjecture. Over time, apocalyptic discourse eventually cultivated logics of its own. If the book of Daniel, for example, has to argue for the resurrection of the dead as a religious innovation, by the time of Jesus some Jewish groups (such as the Pharisees) believe in the resurrection while others (such as the Sadducees) do not. And while Paul struggles to help his audiences understand the resurrection in letters such as 1 Corinthians and 1 Thessalonians, its sacred logic seems self-evident to him. *Of course* the risen dead have bodies, Paul insists. (How could they not?) But *obviously* those bodies must not be identical to the decaying flesh in which we now live; they must be "spiritual bodies" (1 Cor. 15:35–54; cf. 1 Thess. 5:23).

We recognize a discourse, then, by its rhetorical configuration, according to which certain *topics* accrue particular force in shaping people's imaginations and in moving them to adopt particular views and patterns of conduct. *Topics* (or *topoi,* in the technical language of rhetorical criticism) amount to "recurring themes in discourse and patterns of reasoning."[13] In other words, the topics of a given discourse are the conventional concerns, values, and modes of argumentation that form the basis of its social logic.[14] As I understand it,

> Apocalyptic discourse refers to the constellation of apocalyptic topics as they function in larger early Jewish and Christian literary and social contexts. Thus, apocalyptic discourse should be treated as a flexible set of resources that early Jews and Christians could employ for a variety of persuasive tasks.[15]

Thus, apocalyptic discourse involves the intersection of ideas, values, and social contexts that empowered the texts we will study in this book.

While the nature, history, background, and persuasive aims of these texts often differ markedly from one another, they all participate in the social logic of apocalyptic discourse.

Varieties of Apocalyptic Phenomena

Before we move on to discuss the topics of apocalyptic discourse, we may reflect on an additional benefit this category offers. The formal categories of apocalypse, apocalyptic eschatology, and apocalypticism do not account for the varieties of apocalyptic phenomena we encounter. For example, in his letter to the Galatians, Paul appeals to his "apocalypse" as a source of his uniquely authoritative gospel. Apparently he is describing his vision of the risen Jesus, to which he alludes in 1 Corinthians 15:8 and which serves as the basis for Luke's famous account of his vision on the Damascus Road (Acts 9:1–9; 22:6–11; 26:12–18). However, Paul's apocalypse is not a literary text, but an experience. Nor does his apocalypse convey a specific eschatological system; rather, it communicates a mission to proclaim the revelation of Jesus, as Paul attests in Galatians 1:15–17. Nor does his apocalypse belong to an identifiable apocalyptic movement, for we know little about Paul's specific social affiliations prior to his experience with the early Jesus movements. Neither a literary apocalypse nor a clear case of apocalyptic eschatology or apocalypticism, Paul's "apocalypse" requires a more flexible category for reflection and analysis. Or consider the pronouncement of Luke's Jesus–"I watched Satan fall from heaven like a flash of lightning" (10:18)–which transcends the categories of genre and end-time speculation while its social context is lost to us.

Topics of Apocalyptic Discourse

The *topics* of apocalyptic discourse provide both its distinctiveness and its energy. These topics include not merely subjects but also literary conventions, such as the modes by which apocalyptic texts address their audiences. No discussion is likely to exhaust these topics, nor should one expect all of these topics to appear in every instance of apocalyptic discourse. Instead, the following topics simply sketch the rough contours of apocalyptic discourse. Like looking at a map before moving to a new city, being familiar with these topics prepares us to recognize the distinctive ways in which these features play out in particular texts.[16]

1. Perhaps the most distinctive trait of apocalyptic discourse is its interest in *alternative worlds,* whether in terms of *time* (such as the age to come) or *space* (as in the heavenly realms).[17] In other words, apocalyptic discourse refuses to acknowledge the present world of perception and experience as the ultimate reality. Instead it looks toward an alternative reality in which righteousness prospers while evil is either punished or abolished. Many apocalyptic texts reflect keen interest

in both historical and cosmic matters. Scholars continue to debate whether we should interpret the end-time and otherworldly visions to represent literal expectations concerning those realities or whether a more figurative approach is appropriate, yet the texts share the expectation that the way things seem to be in this realm does not reflect their ultimate resolution.

2. *Visions and/or auditions* addressed to the visionary by God provide the ultimate source for apocalyptic revelation. As defined above, all the classical literary apocalypses are narrations of such visions. The description of these mystical experiences often identifies them with dreams or trances. Normally, these experiences are accompanied by traumatic physical manifestations such as fear, trembling, prostration, and exhaustion. Legends concerning these experiences demonstrate both their authenticity and the virtue or piety of the visionary.[18] (Scholars continue to debate whether the classical apocalypses derived from authentic visionary experiences; I tend to emphasize their creative literary character.) Some texts beyond the classical apocalypses appeal to such revelations, whereas many other instances of apocalyptic discourse may presuppose them. For example, belief in the resurrection, final judgment, messianic age, or afterlife eventually became commonplace, so that people could appeal to these values without narrating a revelatory experience. Ultimately, however, claims regarding such expectations may have rested on revealed truth that had been passed down in some form of literature or tradition.

3. *Heavenly intermediaries,* particularly angels and occasionally even the deity, serve as guides and interpreters for these visions and auditions. Such dialogue sometimes provides the basic literary form for an apocalypse, while other apocalypses resemble the narration of a tour, with a heavenly being functioning as the tour guide. These intermediaries explain and clarify the vision's significance for the audience, and they also provide an opportunity for the visionary to advance the pressing questions that motivate the apocalypse as a whole. In the formal apocalypses we also encounter other heavenly voices—often choruses of heavenly beings—that comment on the significance of what the audience "sees."

4. Intense *symbolism* is a prominent feature of apocalyptic discourse, particularly of the formal apocalypses. These symbols, while obscure at best to most modern readers, typically draw on earlier traditions and archaic cultural myths, with which ancient audiences may have been familiar. In drawing on such powerful cultural resources, apocalyptic discourse links deeply-held values to historical and contemporary persons or institutions. For example, historically-oriented apocalyptic literature often depicts foreign imperial powers in the form of primeval monsters. Such intense symbolism also

intensifies the persuasive effect of the apocalypses, as it empowers a sense of literary license, enabling apocalyptic authors to explore fantasy and metaphor. "Visions," claims one of Umberto Eco's characters, "are like dreams, where things are transformed into one another."[19]

5. *Pseudonymity,* the attribution of a literary work to a fictitious author, characterizes all of the classical apocalypses, with the exceptions of the book of Revelation and the Shepherd of Hermas. The apocalypses draw on prominent heroes from antiquity, who often carry mystical associations as well, to deliver their revelations. In many cases the identity of the visionary–and the traditions associated with that person–contributes vital color to the meaning of a given apocalypse. So prevalent is this device, that in many cases it probably functioned as a literary convention rather than as an attempt at forgery, though clear instances of forgery appear as well. For example, one of the earliest apocalypses, 1 Enoch, is attributed to a mysterious person from Earth's primeval history.

6. *Cosmic catastrophe* always precedes ultimate deliverance in the historically oriented apocalyptic traditions. These portents include war, violence, apostasy, persecution against the righteous, and even cosmic distress. They almost always imply suffering for the faithful, though they often affect all people. Because many apocalyptic traditions identify the end times with the time of their own composition, traditions concerning tribulation often provide a sense of meaning and order to a present or anticipated crisis. Again, whether the topic of tribulation functions literally or figuratively remains open to speculation.

7. *Dualism* provides the ideological lens through which apocalyptic discourse evaluates people, institutions, events, and even time. For example, mortals as well as heavenly beings come in two flavors: the righteous (saints, holy ones, just) and the wicked (sinners, rebellious ones). People live in the present (evil) age, anticipating the age to come or the heavenly realm. Rarely, though occasionally, does apocalyptic discourse account for the possibility of persons who fall between these two ends of the spectrum. More frequently, apocalyptic discourse calls people to repentance, allowing for the possibility that people might move from one category to another. The early Christian Shepherd of Hermas, for example, investigates those persons who carry flaws and how they may find salvation. On the other hand, the early Christian book of Revelation invites some members of its audience to repent, but it explicitly denies that people outside the churches might likewise find mercy.

8. *Determinism* involves the expectation that the course of history has been set by God–or at least that God already knows its outcome.

Determinism may function at a cosmic level, announcing the fates of heavenly powers or major political forces. Or it may work at the level of individual mortals, whose judgment is already assured. Scholars have often exaggerated apocalyptic determinism: Apocalyptic discourse typically aims at moving audiences to repentance or toward more demanding levels of faithfulness, which implies a measure of openness in the cosmic plan that depends on human responses.

9. *Judgment and the afterlife* represent key concerns for many apocalyptic texts. These topics attach themselves to both otherworldly and historical apocalyptic discourses, and they play themselves out in a variety of ways, as they raise fascinating questions. For example, do only the righteous survive the grave, or do the wicked also rise to face judgment? Do people move to their ultimate fate immediately upon their deaths, do they move to an intermediate state, or do they simply rest? What, exactly, survives death–the soul, the body, or some transformed self–and what happens to the body in the resurrection? Do the saints become angels, or do they simply retain their status as humans? All of these questions also serve multiple rhetorical ends: promises of the afterlife and threats of judgment can at once inspire faithfulness in the present, comfort those who lack hope, or even frighten people toward repentance.[20]

10. *Ex eventu prophecy* (prophecy after the fact) results from the combination of pseudonymity with determinism. The vision of Daniel 10–12, especially chapters 10–11, provides an excellent example. Though the book of Daniel is set in the sixth century B.C.E., these chapters accurately narrate the history of Israel up until about 167 B.C.E. The period between 167 and 164 B.C.E., which is the climax of the vision, is largely inaccurate, as we will see in chapter 1. This period just happens to correspond to the initial stages of the Maccabean Revolt against Seleucid rule in Judea. Thus, we know (a) that the book is pseudonymous (no sixth-century Daniel could have written it) and (b) that it was written sometime during the Maccabean Crisis, for its accuracy ends at this point. *Ex eventu prophecy* serves a variety of purposes in apocalyptic literature. It demonstrates the authenticity and authority of the text as a whole. After all, if some of a text's predictions have already come to pass, then one may expect the others to prove accurate as well.[21] *Ex eventu prophecy* also lends a sense of order to the overall flow of history. If apocalyptic literature attempts to give meaning to history during difficult times, then *ex eventu prophecy* finds patterns of meaning in current and past events.

11. *Cosmic speculation* distinguishes some apocalyptic texts from others that convey a stronger interest in history. Thus, many apocalyptic texts reveal the identity and activities of the sun, moon, and stars,

including explanations for natural phenomena such as the rising and setting of the sun, the passing of the seasons, and the origins of storms and other remarkable events. Other texts reflect a great interest in heavenly beings, describing the roles and names of angels and other cosmic mysteries. Like *ex eventu prophecy,* such cosmic speculation subordinates the apparent disorder of the present to a larger cosmic order. And like *ex eventu prophecy,* cosmic revelations enhance the visionary's status as one who has received extraordinary privilege to investigate realms from which mortals are excluded. Moreover, these revelations justify certain kinds of technical arguments, such as which is the correct calendar, according to which religious observances may conform to the heavenly models. (The calendar represented a major point of contention among some ancient groups.)

These eleven topics merely represent a starting place. They reflect some of the most prominent resources for apocalyptic discourse, but they fall far short of a definition, even shorter of an exhaustive catalogue. For that matter, individual apocalyptic texts include some but not all of these features. Nevertheless, discussion of the phenomenon requires some sense of its contours. As John J. Collins insists, "The use of the term ["apocalyptic"] should be controlled by analogy with the apocalyptic texts, and not allowed to float freely as an intuitive 'theological construct.'"[22]

Apocalyptic Discourse: Its Contexts

Much of the research on apocalyptic literature involves its origins. In this context, two particular questions have emerged. First, what cultural resources supplied the ideas that came to distinguish apocalyptic literature? Second, in what social contexts did it flourish? Here, we can recall the cautious rule of Martin Dibelius: "we cannot interpret every trustee of the inheritance as a relative of the testator."[23] In other words, no one can fully trace a cultural development's imaginative resources, as if a phenomenon such as apocalyptic discourse emerged from simple lines of influence. Rather, new cultural formations adapt existing cultural resources—ideas, literary forms, rituals, and the like—to their own contexts, often with surprising results.

Yet in past decades scholars worked intensely to identify the primary inspirations for apocalyptic literature, with *wisdom* and *prophetic* discourses among the foremost contenders. Wisdom discourse, usually associated with royal administrations, priestly establishments, and other elite scribal institutions, pondered the fundamental workings of creation. It could embrace ancient sciences, such as astrology and cosmology, as well as conventional morality. According to wisdom discourse, God has created an orderly cosmos. By knowing its fundamental principles, communities may live in harmony with the world. Biblical books such as Proverbs, Job, and Ecclesiastes come to mind. When scholars have invoked prophetic discourse, however, typically they have envisioned figures such as Amos and Micah, who represented ordinary people in their struggle for justice. According to a prophetic worldview, for justice to prevail, things must change. While this presentation surely oversimplifies the conventional debate, it does point out the stakes involved: People link wisdom discourse to the conventional desire for order, while associating prophetic discourse with more revolutionary impulses.[24]

Indeed, both wisdom and prophetic concerns appear in apocalyptic texts, and often even within single texts. The book of Daniel locates its hero among a circle of young court servants. This recalls the wisdom traditions associated with Joseph, who interpreted dreams in the Egyptian court. First Enoch's interest in astronomy exemplifies early human scientific reasoning, while both Fourth Ezra and Second Baruch press the theoretical question of God's responsibility for the presence of injustice. Moreover, numerous apocalyptic texts point to the "wisdom" of following God's ways and of understanding particular revelations.

On the other hand, prophetic conventions such as conversations with heavenly beings and symbolic visions abound in apocalyptic discourse, while many apocalyptic texts share the prophets' concern regarding world affairs. The book of Revelation identifies itself as a "prophecy" and locates its author among circles of competing and complementary prophets.

Beyond wisdom and prophecy, we can easily propose other cultural resources for apocalyptic discourse. A wide range of ancient literature—from Mesopotamia, Egypt, Greece, and Rome—features oracular experiences, bizarre monsters, and tours of the realms of the dead. Dualistic thinking flourished not only in the Persian traditions now known to us as Zoroastrianism, but in Greek philosophy as well, so that good and evil could be absolutely opposed to each other, as could the spiritual and the fleshly.

Unlike most modern societies, in which valuable knowledge is supposed to be shared, ancient Mediterranean cultures emphasized the value of mystery. Esoteric knowledge required revelation to the privileged few, a tradition reflected not only in apocalyptic literature but also in gnostic movements within Judaism and Christianity and in the popular mystery cults.[25] The genius of apocalyptic discourse, which it shared with other forms of sacred imagination in the ancient world, was its ability to *reveal secrets*. That is, apocalyptic discourse brought its audience into otherwise inaccessible mysteries concerning the future and the heavenly realms. In short, apocalyptic discourse drew on a broad range of ancient literary conventions, philosophical ideas, sacred beliefs, and popular sensibilities.

Models for Interpreting Apocalyptic Discourse

Many people immediately associate "apocalyptic" with the world's imminent—and catastrophic—end. Even people who pay little attention to the Bible and its related texts have some familiarity with the popular end-time prophecy teachers. Naturally they assume that apocalyptic literature involves literal predictions of the world's demise. As a result, some people expect apocalyptic literature to be bizarre, vengeful, mysterious, or even irrelevant.

Were the apocalyptic authors indeed attempting to predict history's climatic details? In those apocalyptic texts that reflect no interest in historical outcomes, the answer is a clear no. In other texts that narrate event by event scenarios for the final moments, perhaps the answer is yes. Yet I would suggest that what John J. Collins has named "the apocalyptic imagination"[26] far transcends the mundane world of prediction. Instead, apocalyptic discourse provides a remarkably flexible set of resources for interpreting the significance of the present and for luring people and communities toward alternative futures.

If *prediction* does not determine our interest in apocalyptic discourse, what alternative categories might prove helpful? I propose three: constructive theology, poetry, and rhetoric.

First, we might consider *constructive theology*. Contemporary theologians emphasize the inevitability that discourse concerning holy things requires acts of the imagination. Interpretations of God, for example, by necessity follow indirect paths, taking the form of metaphors or analogies rather than categorical assertions. God is not a parent in any ordinary sense, though God may perhaps resemble parents–and differ from them–in significant ways. The point, of course, is that language concerning sacred matters involves degrees of relative adequacy and inadequacy. Moreover, theological reflection requires the invention of new models and the reassessment of traditional ones, so that contemporary theologians emphasize the creative and artistic dimensions of their work.

Likewise, apocalyptic discourse inhabits the realms of imagination, of comparison, symbol, and vision. Our appreciation of a text such as the Shepherd of Hermas, which features the image of the church as a tower built from the blocks of individual human lives, leads us to explore the artistic dimensions of this metaphor. Obviously God is not building a tower out of human beings, but how does this image shape readers' imaginations about what God is doing in the world and how mortals "fit" into God's work? We might note how the image embodies a corporate if not institutional notion of the church. Individuals seek to win inclusion on the basis of their faithfulness, though Hermas portrays such inclusion in terms of how one fits into a corporate whole. Consider how Hermas' tower differs from God's house in John 14, in which one hopes to dwell immediately with Jesus, or from Jesus' speech to the criminal on the cross, "*today* you will be *with me* in Paradise" (Lk. 23:43).

The creative dimension of apocalyptic discourse implies that *how* things are described matters–not literally, but in terms of the dispositions and behaviors these descriptions foster. One might compare the Qumran War Scroll (1QM) with Revelation 12. Both texts depict a violent conflict between the holy people and their enemies. Yet in the War Scroll, God's people form a holy army, while Revelation 12 portrays a woman and her infant son. The contrast between the formidable army and the vulnerable mother and child could hardly be clearer, one might assume. Yet careful reading reveals how much these images share in common, for both the War Scroll and Revelation emphasize the victory of the saints, while neither text details actual fighting on their part: Their respective victories result from God's sovereign action.

Second, perhaps we should consider *poetry,* for apocalyptic discourse employs the sort of dense language typical of poetic art. Evocative symbols, images, and allusions animate the apocalyptic visions. Astral powers fall from the sky; holy people walk golden streets; and beasts embody the features of several animals at once. Many artists have attempted to capture the portrait of Jesus from Revelation 1:12–16, which may defy simple transfer from the conceptual to the visual imagination.

Likewise, several apocalyptic texts include idealized descriptions of the future temple or the new Jerusalem. These likewise resist literal blueprinting. The most famous of the lot is probably in the book of Revelation, according to which "the street of the city is pure gold, transparent as glass" (21:21). As hard on the imagination as transparent gold may be, Revelation's ideal city draws on earlier imagery from Ezekiel 40–48, a vision of the future temple. Let us return to Baudolino, who says,

> The problem, however, arises when you read the vision of Ezekiel. Not one measurement holds up, and so a number of pious men have admitted that Ezekiel had indeed had a vision, which is a bit like saying he had drunk too much and was seeing double.[27]

Baudolino recalls a certain Richard, who tried to build a to-scale model of this temple: "Every two minutes the entire thing collapsed."[28]

Are the books of Ezekiel and Revelation to blame, or should we fault ourselves for failing to grasp the poetic dimension of apocalyptic discourse? Like poetry, apocalyptic discourse shapes unconventional, sometimes even countercultural visions of the world. If it calls its readers to imagine the world differently, sometimes the metaphorical realm takes precedence over the literal. Like poetry, apocalyptic discourse often aims at affect rather than data, at moving its audience rather than informing them.

In addition to employing densely figurative language, apocalyptic literature often resembles poetry in another way. That is, we might call apocalyptic discourse "literary," in that it develops stock literary conventions and builds complex webs of literary allusions. Over time, certain motifs recur frequently in apocalyptic discourse. For example, visionaries typically ask questions that propel their revelations; imperial powers appear in the guise of wild beasts; certain numbers take on standard meanings; and astral powers such as the sun, moon, and stars change their appearances and behaviors. As for literary allusion, consider the continuing influence of Jeremiah, with its assurance that God will restore Zion after seventy years of captivity (25:11–12; 29:10). Daniel (9:2) and Zechariah (1:12; 7:5) likewise pick up on this motif, but Daniel–written centuries after Jeremiah and during Seleucid control of Judea–transforms the seventy years into seventy *weeks* of years, or 490 years.[29] These literary conventions and allusions indicate a certain "scholarly" dimension for some apocalyptic texts. Though all of the classical apocalypses claim to relate mystical experiences such as visions and cosmic tours–and how does one evaluate the authenticity of a mystical report?–they also rely on the hard work of people who knew and interacted with other texts.

Third, readers of apocalyptic discourse have tended to underestimate its role as *rhetoric*. Like other early Jewish and Christian texts, apocalyptic literature aims to persuade its audiences to adopt certain dispositions, believe particular things, and behave in specific ways. Although ancient texts rarely announce their specific social contexts in ways that are useful to historians, often we can sketch the general social contexts and concerns of a given text–and we can reconstruct the aims of those who wrote it and circulated it.

For example, many apocalyptic texts inspire resistance against the dominant imperial or internal powers of their day. Because they are in the Bible, Daniel and Revelation represent the two most prominent examples of this phenomenon. Both books call for faithful but nonviolent resistance, Daniel against the Seleucid Empire that derived from Alexander the Great and Revelation against the Roman Empire. Other examples apply as well, as nearly every apocalypse with a historical interest engages the dominant political forces of its day. As a result, many readers assume that apocalyptic literature originated from within oppressed communities. Indeed, even today many liberationist communities draw inspiration from Daniel and Revelation, in particular.

How exactly can an apocalypse inspire resistance? The most obvious answer is that the apocalypses offer direct rewards and punishments. They claim that God's intervention in history will bring a final judgment between the righteous and the wicked. Inclusion in the blessed future (whether on this earth or beyond) depends on one's faithful resistance against the oppressors. But there's more to it than that: Apocalyptic discourse is not only capable of imagining an alternative world, it can reinterpret the present world as well. In the wake of Jerusalem's devastation at the hands of the Romans, for example, many apocalyptic texts referred to Rome as "Babylon," the ancient empire that had destroyed the holy city almost seven hundred years earlier. The analogy makes a point. If Babylon looked fearsome in the sixth century B.C.E., like other powers it had met its end.

Nor could Roman imperial domination endure forever. The Jewish apocalypse 4 Ezra (part of 2 Esdras in the Christian apocrypha) addresses Rome's fate:

> "You, the fourth that has come, have conquered all the beasts that have gone before; and you have held sway over the world with great terror, and over all the earth with grievous oppression; and for so long you have lived on the earth with deceit. You have judged the earth, but not with truth, for you have oppressed the meek and injured the peaceable…Your insolence has come up before the Most High, and your pride to the Mighty One. The Most High has looked at his times; now they have ended, and his ages have reached completion." (2 Esd. 11:40–44)

Not only does 4 Ezra condemn Rome, it also names the Empire's offenses—terror, oppression, and deceit, not to mention blasphemous insolence—a literary act that amounted to treason. Indeed, apocalyptic discourse empowers this critique of the Empire, for it attributes this judgment of Rome not to its author but to a heavenly being, the "Lion" or Messiah (12:31–32). In other words, apocalyptic literary conventions give the author a transcendent point of view regarding Rome. However impressive the Empire may have seemed in its own time, 4 Ezra examines it from an eschatological point of view, *revealing* its wickedness and *declaring* its ultimate fate.

While texts such as 4 Ezra, Daniel, and Revelation have inspired many to identify apocalyptic discourse with oppressed communities, substantial evidence suggests that apocalyptic discourse emerged in a variety of social contexts. For example, in one of the formative studies of apocalyptic literature, Paul D. Hanson argues that apocalyptic movements emerged from a sense of social alienation.[30] However, many apocalyptic texts do not reflect a sense of immediate oppression. Indeed, some apocalyptic texts argue for institutional authority. Some early examples of emerging apocalyptic discourse, for example, reflect strong attachment to the Jerusalem Temple, rather than to the peasant masses.[31]

Even the book of Revelation, which condemns Rome for its oppressive economic practices and its war against the saints, acknowledges the mixed status of its audience. Some possess wealth (3:17–18), while others do not (2:9). Although the early ancient Jewish and Christian apocalyptic texts seem to reflect diverse social contexts, *all* of them share one common feature: a radical dissatisfaction concerning some dimension of public life. So it is not a matter of oppression in some objective sense that defines apocalyptic discourse, but rather a sense that the world has gone horribly wrong and that God must intervene to change things. As Stephen D. O'Leary has proposed, evil stands among the most ubiquitous of apocalyptic *topoi,* for almost all apocalyptic discourse concerns how God will address the evil of the present order.[32]

Instead of attributing apocalyptic discourse either to the oppressed or to their oppressors, perhaps we might try a more sociologically oriented distinction between *scribal* apocalyptic discourse and its *popular* counterpart. That is, over time apocalyptic topics achieved a degree of cultural familiarity, so that they could be appropriated in a variety of literary and cultural contexts. Thus, we encounter the "great tradition" of apocalyptic literature in grand apocalyptic works such as 1 Enoch (itself clearly the product of a literary tradition), Daniel, 4 Ezra, 2 and 3 Baruch, Jubilees, and some of the Dead Sea Scrolls. We find the "little tradition" in fragments such as sayings attributed to Jesus and in the apocalyptic teaching of Paul's epistles.

Sometimes these perspectives stood at odds with one another, as some scribal apocalypses concern themselves with maintaining proper cultic observance while Jesus and Paul apparently engaged in some level of conflict with the temple establishment. On other occasions, such as when Judea faced threats from imperial oppressors, the great and little apocalyptic traditions stood in relative solidarity.[33] This construction helps us account for the discrepancy between the relatively high literature of some apocalyptic texts and the less "literary" status of others, but it also comes with a liability. By linking Jesus and Paul to the "little tradition," this model accommodates a sophisticated form of Christian preaching that associates Christianity with liberation and Judaism with institutionalism and oppression. By way of caution, we may recall that Jesus and Paul emerged from within Jewish populism, while some Christian apocalypses demonstrate a keen fascination with maintaining communal and even institutional order.

Apocalyptic discourse is particularly rich in the scope of its imaginative resources. Paying attention to its rhetorical potential enables us to see what apocalyptic discourse can *do* in concrete social circumstances. It draws on revealed mysteries, classical cultural myths, scenes and voices from heaven, and compelling visions of the future. David A. deSilva has it just right:

> Apocalypses provide exactly what standard oratory cannot: Aristotle writes that "in deliberative oratory narrative is very rare, because no one can narrate things to come" (*Rhet.* 3.6.11), but things to come are precisely what an apocalypse is able to narrate and what, as a genre, apocalypses tend to narrate.[34]

By looking beyond the everyday world and the conventional wisdom that attends it, apocalyptic discourse seeks to reshape the imagination. It portrays a larger order when chaos seems to reign. It renames the present, identifying local elites as wicked and imperial force as beastly, and it envisions a future in which justice reigns and humankind prospers.[35]

In conclusion, apocalyptic discourse emerged in a variety of social contexts and served diverse rhetorical and social functions.[36] The book of

Revelation demonstrates this remarkable flexibility in its letters to the seven churches. Some apocalyptic texts articulate innovative doctrines, whereas others correct "mistaken" views concerning the fate of the dead or the possibility of repentance. Some develop sophisticated arguments concerning technical matters such as the correct number of days in a year or the workings of the sun, moon, and stars; others address mundane issues such as sexual morality. Some texts comfort audiences in their distress; others admonish audiences for their moral laxness. Some undermine the reigning powers of their day; others legitimate conventional power arrangements. While apocalyptic discourse eludes our efforts to limit its rhetorical potential to a single category of applications, we recognize it by its ability to configure certain recognizable topics such as judgment or the world to come toward a variety of effects.

These categories—constructive theology, poetry, and rhetoric—all underscore the creative dimension of apocalyptic discourse. As theology, apocalyptic discourse engages life's greatest questions—the nature of God, the desire for justice, the frustrations of human finitude. As poetry, it expresses the theological imagination in vivid symbols and conventional literary forms. Thus, apocalyptic rhetoric seeks to change the present world by envisioning its alternatives.

For Further Reading

Bauckham, Richard. *The Fate of the Dead: Studies on the Jewish and Christian Apocalypses*. NovTSup 93. Leiden: Brill, 1998.

Carey, Greg, and L. Gregory Bloomquist, eds. *Vision and Persuasion: Rhetorical Dimensions of Apocalyptic Discourse*. St. Louis: Chalice Press, 1999.

Collins, John J., ed. *Apocalypse: The Morphology of a Genre. Semeia* 14 (1979).

_____. *The Apocalyptic Imagination: An Introduction to Jewish Apocalyptic Literature*. 2d ed. The Biblical Resource Series. Grand Rapids, Mich.: Eerdmans, 1998.

_____, ed. *The Encyclopedia of Apocalypticism: Volume 1: The Origins of Apocalypticism in Judaism and Christianity*. New York: Continuum, 1998.

Hellholm, David, ed. *Apocalypticism in the Mediterranean World and the Near East: Proceedings of the International Colloquium on Apocalypticism, Uppsala, August 12–17, 1979*. Tübingen: Mohr-Siebeck, 1982.

Hill, Craig C. *In God's Time: The Bible and the Future*. Grand Rapids, Mich.: Eerdmans, 2002.

Murphy, Frederick J. "Introduction to Apocalyptic Literature." Pages 1–16 in *The New Interpreter's Bible: Volume 7*. Nashville: Abingdon Press, 1996.

Nickelsburg, George W. E. *Jewish Literature Between the Bible and the Mishnah*. Philadelphia: Fortress Press, 1981.

O'Leary, Stephen D. *Arguing the Apocalypse: A Theory of Millennial Rhetoric.* New York: Oxford University Press, 1994.

Rowland, Christopher. *The Open Heaven: A Study of Apocalyptic in Judaism and Early Christianity.* New York: Crossroad, 1982.

Stone, Michael E. "Apocalyptic Literature." Pages 383–441 in *Jewish Writings of the Second Temple Period.* Edited by Michael E. Stone. CRINT 2/2. Philadelphia: Fortress Press, 1984.

VanderKam, James C. *An Introduction to Early Judaism.* Grand Rapids, Mich.: Eerdmans, 2001.

Watson, Duane F., ed. *The Intertexture of Apocalyptic Discourse in the New Testament.* SBLSymS 14. Atlanta: Society of Biblical Literature, 2002.

Yarbro Collins, Adela, ed. *Early Christian Apocalypticism: Genre and Social Setting. Semeia* 36 (1986).

CHAPTER 1

The Earliest Apocalypses

1 Enoch and Daniel

The two most ancient apocalypses, 1 Enoch and Daniel, develop several ideas whose collective effect was no less than revolutionary. For the first time these ideas, which stand among the most distinctive contributions and topics of apocalyptic discourse, surface in these two works. They include:

- the expectation of a final judgment, in which God separates sinners from the righteous;
- hope for resurrection of the righteous dead to a glorious realm;
- reflection upon God's role in history, both past and future, leading to a new age of justice and deliverance; and
- speculation concerning a heavenly messianic figure–a Son of Man, Elect One, Righteous One, or Messiah–who will administer final justice upon the world.

We find these concepts nowhere else in the Jewish Scriptures–at least not explicitly. Their first known articulations occur in 1 Enoch and Daniel. Eventually these ideas became prominent among many early Jews and were essential for the formation of Christianity.

1 Enoch

A Composite Work

First Enoch presents itself as a collection of five "books," with chapters 106–7 and 108, respectively, representing two appendices. Each book originally circulated independently, and their composition may have required as much as five centuries. The books are conventionally identified as:

- the Book of the Watchers (1 Enoch 1—36; probably third century B.C.E.);
- the Similitudes (or Parables) of Enoch (1 Enoch 37—71; probably first century B.C.E. or the first century C.E., though proposed dates range to the third century C.E.);
- the Astronomical Book (or the Book of the Heavenly Luminaries; 1 Enoch 72—82; probably third century B.C.E.);
- the Book of Dreams (1 Enoch 83—90; almost certainly from 170–163 B.C.E.), which includes the Animal Apocalypse (chaps. 85–90); and
- the Epistle of Enoch (1 Enoch 91—105; second century B.C.E.), which includes the Apocalypse of Weeks (1 Enoch 91:12-17; 93:1–10;).

Languages and Texts

First Enoch is extant in its entirety only in Ethiopic manuscripts, yet the Ethiopic texts represent translations from Greek manuscripts, which themselves are translations from Aramaic. The Dead Sea Scrolls include Aramaic fragments from every section except the Similitudes of Enoch (1 Enoch 37—71), demonstrating the probability of Aramaic originals; however, they do not include a single text of 1 Enoch as a whole.[1]

Although Western Bible readers recognize the book of Daniel from their own canon, few realize the significance of 1 Enoch for the rest of the biblical tradition. Apparently, First Enoch ranked among the most treasured texts at Qumran, the community from which we have the Dead Sea Scrolls, for the site has yielded fragments of at least eleven Aramaic manuscripts from 1 Enoch along with nine manuscripts from a related work, the Book of the Giants.[2] First Enoch's appeal must have extended more broadly than a single sectarian community, though. For example, the Jewish books of Jubilees and the Testaments of the Twelve Patriarchs demonstrate significant direct reliance upon 1 Enoch. Among Christians, verses 14–15 of the New Testament epistle of Jude explicitly quote 1 Enoch 1:9, while a wide variety of other early Christian sources also quote from, allude to, or depend on 1 Enoch.[3] The early Christian theologian Tertullian apparently identified 1 Enoch as inspired scripture,[4] and the book has also found acceptance in the Bible of the Ethiopian Orthodox Church.

As we have it, 1 Enoch is a collection of five books, supplemented by two appendices. Many have noted that Enoch's "five books" parallel the traditional five books of Moses, the Pentateuch. Yet it is not entirely clear what to make of this association. Given the Law's minimal role in 1 Enoch's program, some might suggest that 1 Enoch reflects an alternative to Mosaic Judaism. That argument, however, requires making a hypothetical mountain out of a textual molehill, for Enoch never explicitly undermines the Torah. Perhaps we may simply observe the parallel between 1 Enoch and the five books of Moses, noting that in its times and places of composition, 1 Enoch certainly represents distinctive Jewish traditions. And we should acknowledge that in Judaism's emergence, some did see Enoch's status as a possible threat to that of Moses.[5]

Enoch's five books also pose a literary problem: how to assess these books' relations to one another. At some point, people began to read 1 Enoch as a single work, implying that they perceived some sort of literary unity. And yet clearly 1 Enoch evolved over time, with separate parts emerging in various contexts. Its five books reflect diverse interests, reflections on different periods and crises, and sometimes conflicting ideas. One cannot expect to find the remarkable ideas or traits of one "book" in any of the others. In this chapter I will emphasize 1 Enoch's larger patterns, but I must also acknowledge its development over time and the singularity of each of its "books."

Five Books and Two Appendices

Throughout this chapter it is necessary to identify the various "books" of 1 Enoch by title, assuming some familiarity with their basic contexts. Manuscript evidence demonstrates that these books once circulated independently of one another, though their common emphasis on Enoch and his revelations may have established their mutual association from the very beginning.

The Book of the Watchers (chaps. 1–36)

This first "book" narrates two major stories. First, it relates the story of the Watchers through an interpretation of Genesis 6:1–4. In Genesis, the "sons of God" descend from heaven to have sexual intercourse with mortal women. Their relations produce a race of giants, the Nephilim. The Genesis account leads directly to the more famous story of Noah and the flood. The Book of the Watchers draws a clear connection between the more obscure story of the Nephilim and that of the flood: The "sons of God" are angels, also called "Watchers," who "watch" over the earth (20:1). According to the book of Similitudes, they do not sleep (39:12–13; 61:12; 71:7).[6] By violating the boundaries between mortals and heavenly beings in a variety of ways, the Watchers reduce the world to chaos and provoke God to intervene by means of the flood. Enoch observes both their behavior and their judgment.

Second, the Book of the Watchers includes a tour of the cosmos, including both heavenly and hellish realms. Enoch shares his astrological and meteorological findings—establishing a solar calendar of 364 days—and sees places of blessing and judgment. He also reveals the names and identities of various heavenly beings. The entire Book of the Watchers addresses itself as a blessing to the elect in the last days (1:1) and concludes by celebrating the wonders of creation (36:4). As a result, the Watchers proposes three related arguments: (a) God's world works according to order, as born out by careful observation and especially by Enoch's revelations; (b) part of that order is judgment, because God has judged the angels and the Watchers and will judge humankind; therefore, (c) the elect should bless God.

The Similitudes of Enoch (chaps. 37–71)

The Similitudes includes three "parables" of Enoch concerning God's final judgment. These parables present not so much challenging comparisons as revealed mysteries. Because a messianic figure who overthrows the wicked and establishes righteousness figures prominently in the Similitudes, some have wondered how this section of Enoch may inform our understanding of early Christian messianic reflection. Some have also speculated that the Similitudes may be a Christian composition, though 1 Enoch 71:14 identifies *Enoch* as the Son of Man. The Similitudes also identify the wicked with the wealthy and the powerful.

The Astronomical Book (chaps. 72–82)

This book describes Enoch's tour of the heavenly realms. Particularly concerned with the sun and the moon, the Astronomical Book–like the Book of the Watchers–promotes the solar calendar. And like the Book of the Watchers, it provides the mysterious identities of various angelic beings. A certain "scientific" spirit permeates the Astronomical Book through its systematic presentation of detailed astrological information.

The Book of Dreams (chaps. 83–90)

The Dreams section encompasses two distinct visions attributed to Enoch's early life. The first vision relates the judgment of the wicked through the flood. It presumably reminds the audience that the wicked will face their own judgment. The second vision is known as the Animal Apocalypse. Including only chapters 85–90–but these are exceptionally long chapters–it reviews Israel's sacred history through a series of allegorical animal characters. The history breaks off during the reign of Antiochus IV, the Seleucid ruler whose program to impose Hellenistic cultural values on Judea led to the Maccabean Revolt. Thus, we conclude that the Animal Apocalypse was written just before or during the Revolt (perhaps 170–163 B.C.E.) and that its authors regarded these events as the eschatological tribulation. The Animal Apocalypse envisions victory for the righteous and judgment for their adversaries.

The Epistle of Enoch (chaps. 91–105)

The Epistle begins with an exhortation from Enoch to his children, that they should pursue righteousness. It then presents a letter from Enoch to all the earth's inhabitants, particularly those of the last days. Remarkably, this section includes the Apocalypse of Weeks, a review of history that is now out of order: Weeks 1–7 may be found in 93:1–10, whereas Weeks 8–10 are depicted in 91:12–17. Manuscript evidence from Qumran reveals that these passages once circulated in the correct order. The Apocalypse of Weeks prepares for admonition concerning the judgment of the rich and powerful.

First Enoch concludes with two independent traditions: Noah's portentous birth (chaps. 106–7) and a final book concerning the judgment (chap. 108).

Enoch the Visionary

The figure of Enoch provides our first example of pseudonymity in apocalyptic writing. Though one scholar has described Enoch as "a most unlikely biblical hero," perhaps the biblical Enoch offers the perfect set of attributes for an apocalyptic man of mystery: timing, exceptional righteousness, and almost unique immortality, all accentuated by a lack of narrative detail.[7] In the sixth generation from Adam, Enoch precedes the great flood (Gen. 5:18, 21–24). Both this numerical designation and Enoch's pre-deluge status identify him as a significant figure. His righteousness—he "walked with God" (Gen. 5:24)—is remarkable in its literary context, for none of the other pre-flood figures receives such praise. Moreover, that "he was no more, because God took him" places him, along with Elijah, in a two-person class of humans who escaped death by being carried up into God's dwelling. His translation further implies that Enoch has observed heavenly secrets, concerning which mere mortals may only speculate. These mysterious details encourage speculation, but the book of Genesis refuses to satisfy our curiosity. Thus, Enoch's singular biblical profile invites the continuing ingenuity of his interpreters. In that sense, Enoch possesses superior qualifications as an apocalyptic visionary.

Enoch's reputation lived on beyond the Hebrew Bible. The apocryphal wisdom book of Ben Sira includes Enoch among the "famous mortals," noting that "Enoch pleased the Lord and was taken up, an example of repentance to all generations" (Sir. 44:16), and that "Few [in the Greek versions, 'no one'] have ever been created on earth like Enoch, for he was taken up from the earth" (Sir. 49:14). The book of Jubilees notes that Enoch was the first literate man who composed an astrological book (4:16–25).[8] The New Testament book of Hebrews likewise cites Enoch as an example of faith; his ascension enabled him to escape death (11:5). In addition to 1 Enoch, two other texts—the Book of the Giants and 2 Enoch—are attributed to him. Enoch even surfaces in the Quran as a prophet and saint (19.56; 21.85).[9]

Within the work itself, Enoch's character is notoriously complex. Perhaps Enoch's most prominent trait throughout the work is his status as an intermediary, which presents several dimensions. Though obvious, his role as a mediator of revelation defies overstatement. Enoch's status as a heavenly figure who has earthly ancestors, earthly children, and an earthly history bridges the divide between mortals and the heavenly world.

Enoch relates what he has seen, heard, and even felt first-hand, providing heavenly truth that is at once authoritative and otherwise inaccessible: "None among human beings will see as I have seen" (19:3, *OTP*). Because 1 Enoch identifies itself as a blessing (1:1), sustaining this point of view throughout the work, Enoch's revealed knowledge amounts to the path of salvation. Occasionally the book insists on its own authority, claiming that Enoch receives his revelations from irrefutable sources and that he understands them (1:2). Perhaps 103:2 represents the most explicit of these claims:

> For I know this mystery; I have read the tablets of heaven and have seen the holy writings, and I have understood the writing in them; and they are inscribed concerning you. (*OTP*)

Enoch's role as mediator takes on a particular form in the Book of the Watchers (chaps. 1–36). Chapter 12 describes Enoch as "hidden" in the heavenly realms among the righteous Watchers and the Holy Ones (or perhaps the Holy Watchers). But he is called out of his hiding to go down and inform the wicked Watchers of their impending judgment. When Enoch has mediated the heavenly condemnation to the now-earthly Watchers, they then ask him to compose a prayer of forgiveness that might help them avoid their doom (chap. 13).

Unfortunately, in a vision, Enoch learns from God's own voice that these Watchers will have no peace (16:3). After all, it may be appropriate for the Watchers to intercede for mortals, but by no means should a mortal intercede for them (15:2). Thus, whereas Enoch's mediation may fail in one sense, it reveals his exalted status in the heavenly realms: the Watchers rely on him, and even God, "the Excellent and the Glorious One" (14:21, *OTP*), converses with Enoch and employs him as a messenger.

According to 1 Enoch 1:1–2, the vision blesses the elect ones in a distant generation. But the Astronomical Book, the Book of Dreams, and the Epistle all address Enoch's descendants, particularly Methuselah. In either case, Enoch's vision addresses insiders, who reside among the elect. At the same time, the work contains enough admonition as to preclude an easy comfort among its audience.

Throughout the book, Enoch demonstrates a series of responses to his revelations. Interaction with heavenly intermediaries will become a stock topic in the portrayal of apocalyptic visionaries. He experiences fear and trembling (e.g., 14:13; 60:3; 71:11); he falls prostrate before the presence of the holy (e.g., 14:23–24; 60:3; 65:4; 71:11); he seeks clarification, especially by asking questions (e.g., 21:4, 8; 27:1; 40:8; 56:2); and he blesses God (e.g., 22:14; 39:9; 71:11; 81:3). These behaviors have biblical precedents, so they are not new, but their concentration prepares the way for conventional characterization of apocalyptic visionaries.[10]

Enoch's heavenly identity takes different forms in 1 Enoch's various "books." All of them presuppose Enoch's translation to the heavenly realms, though the Book of Dreams also relates visions that came to Enoch during his childhood and just before his marriage. But the most remarkable claim concerning Enoch occurs in the Similitudes. After several meditations concerning the messianic figure (the Elect One, the Righteous One, the Son of Man, and the Messiah) and with repeated insistence that Enoch has been granted eternal life (37:4; 39:8; 70:1–3), the angel addresses Enoch himself as "Son of Man" (71:14). Are we to understand this address to identify Enoch as *the* Son of Man who comes to judge the world and deliver the righteous? Or, by "Son of Man" does the angel simply address Enoch as one mortal among others, a usage familiar especially to readers of Ezekiel?

Scholars continue to debate this question, and for good reason. If Enoch is *the* Son of Man, then the Similitudes almost certainly did not develop in Christian circles. One even wonders why 1 Enoch's Christian copyists allowed the text to stand as it is![11] Thus, we could mine the Similitudes for background material to understand early Christian messianism. And we could investigate why early Christians inserted the Similitudes into their copies of the book of Enoch. So the stakes are significant. And the evidence is difficult. Even the major translations differ as to whether or not 1 Enoch 71:14 identifies Enoch as the Son of Man.[12] Some scholars have argued that chapters 70–71 represent later additions to the Similitudes.[13] It is difficult to identify Enoch, a mortal whom God "took" to heaven, with the Similitudes' Son of Man, who has existed from before the earth's foundation.[14]

While 1 Enoch 71:14–16 addresses Enoch in the second person ("you"), 71:17–the Similitudes' final sentence–speaks of "*that* Son of Man" in the third person, perhaps distinguishing the two figures. On the other hand, "Son of Man" plays such a prominent role in the Similitudes that one would expect consistent usage. Its only clear application to a mortal occurs at 60:10, addressing Noah as "Son of Man." Moreover, the angel's continuing discourse to Enoch emphasizes Enoch's exalted status: the righteous "shall not be separated from you forever and ever and ever" (71:16, *OTP*). In short, while most scholars believe 1 Enoch 71:14 identifies Enoch himself as the Son of Man, the issue remains far from settled.

Enoch's characterization takes on different emphases in the various "books," but the continuity is just as remarkable. Enoch, the righteous mortal whom God took up into heaven, has access to heavenly mysteries and provides the source for knowledge of ultimate things. His status in the heavenly realms secured, he seeks the welfare of his descendants and of the elect in the last days. Later stages of 1 Enoch's composition exalt Enoch even higher: he is the heavenly Son of Man who will judge the world and redeem the righteous.

Mode and Process of Revelation

Because 1 Enoch is so clearly a composite work, with five books and two appendices, we expect to find discontinuities from one "book" to another. And yet in another sense 1 Enoch functions as a literary whole. For one thing, some very early Jews and Christians actually read the work as a whole. Moreover, its redactors designed the book as a literary unit, for "Through a consistent system of literary connections, allusions, and quotations, each book consciously refers to the preceding one(s)."[15] Thus, in their final form the latter four books identify themselves as Books Two, Three, Four, and (belatedly; 92:1) Five, respectively.

As Nicklesburg observes, 1 Enoch's depiction of an alternative reality contains those two basic categories of revelation: a temporal dimension and a spatial/material dimension.[16] These two dimensions form the basic model for all apocalyptic revelation: However things may appear in the realm of mortals, the ultimate reality that determines all meaning lies either in the future or in the heavenly realms.[17]

Both temporal and spatial revelations appear in 1 Enoch's earliest sections: the Watchers and the Astronomical Book. The Book of the Watchers presents a detailed tour of the cosmos, but it also begins with God's coming to judge all mortals and preserve the elect (1:2–9). While the Astronomical Book largely relates heavenly and cosmic mysteries, it also looks ahead to a "new creation" (72:1, *OTP*) and describes an eschatological tribulation (80:2–8). Historical or temporal interests, on the other hand, dominate the Similitudes, the Book of Dreams, and the Epistle of Enoch. All three of these "books" anticipate the final judgment. The Animal Apocalypse (found in the Book of Dreams) and the Apocalypse of Weeks (found in the Epistle) further evince a temporal interest by reviewing sacred history up until their own historical contexts.

First Enoch privileges no single mode of revelation, as do some other apocalypses. Instead, Enoch receives his revelations through a variety of media. Understanding precisely what sort of experience Enoch narrates often proves difficult. For example, the work introduces itself as a blessing, a parable, a vision, and a heavenly audition (1:1–2). The Similitudes introduces itself as a collection of three parables. Then it relates three revelations, yet these revelations do not accomplish what most parables do. That is, the revelations do not compare two realities in such a way that one illuminates the other. These are "parables" only in the sense that they convey heavenly mysteries.

Throughout the work dreams, visions, cosmic journeys, conversations with various heavenly beings, and visions of heavenly "tablets" or books intertwine in complex ways. Some modes of revelation encompass other literary forms, as when Enoch's dreams review Israel's history. Collectively, these diverse modes of revelation reinforce one another. First Enoch does not so much develop a linear argument for how one should live and view the world as it creates a cumulative effect of images, literary forms, and values.

Distinctive Concerns

As diverse as Enoch's five books may be, many topics are common to two or more books. Obviously, the figure of Enoch plays a prominent role in all these books, as it unifies the work as a whole. But other topics also receive development and elaboration.

JUDGMENT

Almost all apocalyptic literature imagines some sort of final judgment, in which the wicked receive punishment and the righteous blessing. Each of the five books mentions the prospect of a final judgment, though this topic clearly figures more prominently in some books than in others. Without explicitly making an argument concerning judgment, the Book of the Watchers connects the judgment of the Watchers with that of mortals.

Just as Enoch receives a sense of cosmic order from his tour of the heavens, Enoch finds moral order in the balances of cosmic judgment. In chapters 18–21 Enoch sees the judgment places of the wicked stars and Watchers. Then in chapter 22 he encounters a sort of holding place where the souls of the dead dwell until the great judgment. Even this pre-judgment state separates the righteous from the wicked. It has four realms: just one for the righteous, with three for various classes of sinners.[18] Chapters 25 and 27 continue this theme; after judgment, the righteous experience blessing, and the wicked receive torment.

If anything, judgment figures even more prominently in the Similitudes. The Similitudes develop a systematic anthropology, in which God's very own self has "separated the spirits of the people" into two classes: the righteous and the sinners (41:8). Chapter 45 explicitly envisions the scene of judgment. Sinners, held in limbo between the heavenly realms and the earth, face destruction, while the faithful dwell in a realm of light and justice. As Richard Bauckham observes, "The wicked dead are not in hell, but observe it, knowing they are condemned to it, and suffer the pain of anticipating their future punishment."[19] Judgment appears to represent the Similitudes' most prominent concern, as it spills over into other topics, such as the rich and the powerful, on the one hand, and resurrection, on the other. For resurrection brings transformation. In the resurrection age, judgment overturns the social structures by which the righteous suffer at the hands of the wicked (chaps. 50–51).

While a final judgment may figure most prominently in the Watchers and the Similitudes, every book of 1 Enoch discusses it and presupposes it. The Astronomical Book reveals a heavenly book of judgment (chap. 81), the Animal Apocalypse leads up to a judgment that includes the "sealed books" that judge the rebellious stars, the nations' angelic caretakers, and apostate Jews (90:20–27), and the Epistle of Enoch envisions fire for the wicked and justice for the righteous (91:9–17). Thus, one may argue that for 1 Enoch as a whole, judgment poses the primary concern. Whether judgment functions to provide assurance in times of crisis, as in the Watchers, or as admonition to inspire righteous conduct in the present, as in the Epistle, 1 Enoch argues that the entire cosmos, including human life, will find its just resolution.

A Future Age

Throughout 1 Enoch's historical sections stands the hope of future blessing. Although this blessing *can* arrive in the form of a blessed afterlife, 1 Enoch's books tend to emphasize a period of righteousness and refreshment. Thus, in the Apocalypse of Weeks the eighth week is the "week of righteousness," when oppressors and sinners will fall into the hands of the righteous, and the ninth week allows for freedom to pursue the path of uprightness because the wicked have departed (91:12–14, *OTP*). Likewise, the Animal Apocalypse envisions a time when all of Israel's enemies, depicted as wild birds and animals, become gentle and dwell in peace in God's house, which is "large, wide, and exceedingly full" (90:32–36, *OTP*). Even the Similitudes, which seems preoccupied with judgment, envisions a blessed messianic age as well; for example,

> I shall (also) transform the earth and make it a blessing,
> and cause my Elect One to dwell in her.
> Then those who have committed sin and crime shall not set foot in
> her. (45:5, *OTP*)

Eschatological Tribulation

We can readily imagine why apocalyptic texts include a final judgment. If a group perceives the world to be in moral disorder, then a final judgment provides one possible resolution to such injustice. We find it harder to explain why apocalyptic texts that reflect an interest in history usually envision an escalation of chaos—an eschatological tribulation—just prior to the future age of righteousness. Perhaps apocalyptic eschatology implies such a tragic view of the present order that it requires that things grow radically worse to "force" divine intervention.

Or maybe the sense of impending disorder encourages a disaffected audience to identify with its message by conveying a sense that the audience is living through history's most critical moments. First Enoch begins,

> The blessing of Enoch: with which he blessed the elect and the
> righteous who would be present on *the day of tribulation at (the time
> of) the removal of all the ungodly ones.* (1:1, *OTP,* author's emphasis)

Neither the Book of the Watchers nor the Similitudes emphasize this tribulation, though the vision of the metal mountains in chapter 52 depicts how neither precious metals nor the metals of armor or weapons will benefit anyone when the Elect One arrives. In 1 Enoch, expectation that apostasy will appear, wickedness and violence will increase, and cosmic chaos may develop is especially prominent in the historically-oriented Animal Apocalypse and the Apocalypse of Weeks.

ASTRAL AND METEOROLOGICAL PHENOMENA

First Enoch presents a strongly temporal emphasis on judgment and Israel's history, but some sections emphasize a more spatial interest. Enoch's tour of the heavens in the Astronomical Book includes instruction concerning the sun, moon, and stars, as well as the winds and storms. While his heavenly tour in the Book of the Watchers emphasizes judgment, it provides some cosmic details as well. Remarkably, even the much later and more historically-oriented Similitudes includes "the secrets of lightning and thunder, and the mysteries of the winds" (41:3, *OTP*), along with the paths of the sun and the moon.

One wonders what motivated the apocalyptic authors' interest in astral and meteorological phenomena. Simple curiosity offers one plausible explanation. One of my students, a former chemistry professor named Stock Weinstock-Collins, has noted how these sections resemble ancient "natural philosophy" in their systematic and in some ways correct descriptions of the heavens. At the same time, this sense of order may address religious as well as scientific concerns. If the cosmos makes sense, perhaps a larger order may transcend the world's violence and injustice. In the Astronomical Book, we find the even more direct purpose of arguing for the 364–day solar calendar against those priestly circles who adhered to the 360–day lunar calendar.

> On this account there are people that err; they count them…in the computation of the year: for the people make error and do not recognize them accurately; for they belong to the reckoning of the year. Truly, they are recorded forever: one in the first gate, one in the third, one in the fourth, and one in the sixth. The year is completed in three hundred and sixty-four days. (82:5–6, *OTP*)

For people who observed annual sacrifices on specified dates, the calendar was a serious matter; to get things "wrong" meant to promote at best cultic error and at worst cosmic disorder.

HEAVENLY BEINGS

Angels figure prominently throughout 1 Enoch, especially as mediators of Enoch's revelations, but 1 Enoch's first three books develop this interest more explicitly. The Book of the Watchers, of course, attempts to account for the bizarre story of Genesis 6:1–4, in which the "sons of God" procreate with mortal women to produce a race of giants, the Nephilim. Because

Genesis was sacred scripture, one easily imagines that some circles were compelled to account for what the legend does *not* say by elaborating its details. Thus, the Book of the Watchers initiates a tradition of speculation concerning these figures that influences both the Book of Dreams and the Similitudes, in addition to later sources such as Jubilees.

In addition to the interpretation of Genesis 6:1–4, 1 Enoch's treatment of the Watchers stands out for its detail and systematization. Readers new to this literature may express surprise at the myriad names assigned to these heavenly beings, good and wicked. Semyaz leads the evil Watchers (6:3, 7), of whom seventeen are named, while Azazel is the primary agent of human corruption (8:1; 9:6). Good Watchers appear as well, with specific names and purposes: Raphael, Raguel, Michael, Saraqa'el, Gabriel, and perhaps Uriel stand among them (20:1–7). The Astronomical book attributes the annual seasons to the labors of several named angels under Uriel's leadership (82:7–20). Even the Similitudes provides names both for good angels (40:1–10) and for evil ones (69:1–15). Thus, most of 1 Enoch depicts an angelic world populated with identifiable figures who fulfill specific tasks. Some of these demonstrate faithfulness to God, while others rebel.

MESSIANIC EXPECTATIONS

The most historically-oriented sections of 1 Enoch all reflect some degree of messianic expectation. Modern readers may find the terminology confusing. In addition to the familiar "Messiah" (which means, "Anointed One") or even "Son of Man," 1 Enoch often discusses the "Elect One" (or, "Chosen One") and the "Righteous One." All of these titles appear in the Similitudes, where messianic expectation is most prevalent. Messianic expectation also appears in the Animal Apocalypse and the Epistle of Enoch. In the Similitudes, the titles "Chosen One" and "Son of Man" occur most frequently.[20]

The Animal Apocalypse relates Israel's history up until the Maccabean Revolt, when the Ram, Judas Maccabeus, delivers the people with heavenly assistance. Here, we encounter two heavenly figures who deliver Israel during its time of crisis. The first is a "Man" who assists Judas and opens the books of judgment (90:14–27). This is apparently an angelic figure, as the Man is one of "those seven snow-white ones" (90:22, *OTP*), presumably angels who assist in the judgment (90:21). The second such figure, a White Bull, appears *after* the judgment (90:37–39), however. The Bull is born among the "snow-white" sheep, a genetic marvel that signals God's eschatological activity. The Bull performs a remarkable work. It draws honor from all the animals (i.e., all the Gentiles) and transforms them into snow-white cows. Thus, the Animal Apocalypse holds hope that the messianic age will bring all people into righteous standing.[21]

More explicit, though still unclear at points, is the Epistle of Enoch. In its present form, the Epistle begins with chapter 91, which includes the *conclusion* to the Apocalypse of Weeks, found in chapter 93. In an earlier form, perhaps the Epistle began with chapter 92; if so, messianic expectation introduces this fifth "book."

> (Book) five, which is written by Enoch...for all the offspring that dwell upon the earth, and for the latter generations which uphold uprightness and peace. Let not your spirit be troubled by the times, for the Holy and Great One has designated (specific) days for all things. The Righteous One shall awaken from his sleep; he shall arise and walk in the ways of righteousness; and all the way of his conduct shall be in goodness and generosity forever. He will be generous to the Righteous One, and give him eternal uprightness; he will give authority, and judge in kindness and righteousness; and they shall walk in eternal light. Sin and darkness shall perish forever, and shall no more be seen from that day forevermore. (92:1–5, *OTP*)

Here, the age of the Righteous One brings judgment as well as redemption. Like the White Bull of the Animal Apocalypse, the Righteous One judges not with harshness but with kindness and righteousness.

Messianic expectation reaches its most systematic expression in the Similitudes. The first parable introduces the Righteous One, who appears when "the congregation of the righteous" is revealed (38:1–6, *OTP*). The Righteous One reveals heavenly knowledge and judges sinners, restoring the world–and its corrupt rulers–to the saints. Though the Similitudes employ other titles for this figure, these three functions–revelation, judgment, and redemption of the righteous–remain consistent. At the resurrection, the Chosen One will dispense "secrets of wisdom,"[22] delivering a glorious age for the righteous (51:1–4; cf. chaps. 61–64).

When the Son of Man and the Messiah appear together in 1 Enoch 48, the picture grows more complicated. Again we find revelation, judgment, and redemption, and even hope for the Gentiles (48:4); but we learn other things as well. For one thing, the Son of Man is preexistent, having been named before the world's creation and hidden from eternity (48:4, 6–7). At his revelation all the earth's inhabitants will bring him worship (48:5). So exalted is he that the kings and the powerful have no hope, for "they have denied the Lord of the Spirits and his Messiah" (48:10, *OTP*). Hence, salvation depends not only upon one's righteous living, but also upon one's recognition of the Son of Man. Most readers experience surprise when the angel informs Enoch that *he* is that Son of Man from whom peace will proceed (71:14), but here, the Similitudes end, leaving unresolved major questions concerning Enoch's identity and his relationship to messianic hopes.

AFTERLIFE AND RESURRECTION

Judgment of the earth's inhabitants faces an obvious obstacle: Many of those facing judgment have died. Judgment also implies a continuing fate beyond the verdict itself. Thus, the notion of judgment implies some form of life beyond death. In 1 Enoch, and for Daniel as well, judgment requires a resurrection of the dead. The challenge for the authors of 1 Enoch, who express somewhat diverse views on the question, was straightforward: As far as we know, resurrection presented a new idea in Judaism. First Enoch and Daniel faced significant obstacles in promoting it.

Resurrection or Immortality?

Many people today believe in a life after death. Most envision this as resulting from the immortality of the human soul, a concept familiar from ancient Mediterranean religion and in popular Hindu and Buddhist thought. Thus, heroes such as Odysseus and Aeneas could visit the realm of the dead. Socrates could resolutely face his own death, expecting that death brought no evil. For him, death meant either annihilation or a migration of the soul from one realm to another (*Apology,* 40c).

The notion of resurrection can mean another thing entirely. For resurrection accepts death as what it appears to be—the end of life. In the Hebrew Bible, the dead dwell in Sheol, the pit, where God is absent and joy cannot be found. As the psalmist writes,

> I am counted among those who go down to the Pit;
> I am like those who have no help,
> like those forsaken among the dead,
>   like the slain that lie in the grave,
> like those whom you remember no more,
>   for they are cut off from your hand. (Ps. 88:4–5)

In Jewish apocalyptic thought, however, resurrection involves the restoration of life, usually in bodily form. More than mere resuscitation, resurrection involves an entirely new order of existence.

As Richard Bauckham observes, "The earliest Jewish notion of resurrection was that the dead would return from the place of the dead to life on earth."[23] Although some traditions eventually linked belief in a resurrection with belief in the soul's immortality, the earliest Jewish references to resurrection—1 Enoch and Daniel—do not. Thus, 1 Enoch 51:1 takes very seriously the need for the grave to return its physical contents: "In those days, Sheol will return all the deposits which she had received and hell will give back all that which it owes" (*OTP*).

The Epistle of Enoch reflects the struggle to establish this new idea. Just as Enoch is about to introduce the topic, he acknowledges the conventional belief concerning the righteous dead:

> But they perished and became like those who were not, and descended
> into Sheol—and their spirits too—with anguish. (102:11, *OTP*)

Then Enoch slows down to insist on the authority of his knowledge:[24]

> I now swear to you, righteous ones, by the glory of the Great One and by the glory of his kingdom, and I swear to you (even) by the Great One. For I know this mystery; I have read the tablets of heaven and have seen the holy writings, and I have understood the writing in them; and they are inscribed concerning you. For all good things, and joy and honor are prepared for and written down for the souls of those who died in righteousness. Many and good things shall be given to you— the offshoot of your labors. Your lot exceeds even that of the living ones. (103:1–3, *OTP*)

The righteous "shall shine like the lights of heaven" (104:2, *OTP*), while the wicked anticipate their judgment (104:7–8).

Whenever 1 Enoch discusses the afterlife, it presupposes that judgment separates the righteous from the wicked. The Book of the Watchers is less explicit concerning *how* the afterlife comes to be, yet it also posits a blessed existence for the righteous and torment for rebellious angels and wicked mortals. The landscape includes intermediate dwelling places that separate the righteous from the wicked until the judgment (chap. 22). Ultimately, the righteous dwell near a fragrant tree on a holy mountain (chap. 25), while the wicked suffer in an accursed valley (chap. 27).

GOD'S THRONE OR DWELLING

Enoch's heavenly tours bring him into the presence of the divine throne. This motif, the vision of the throne, did not originate with apocalyptic literature—one recalls the throne vision of Isaiah 6. First Enoch 14 initiates a pattern that becomes typical of the heavenly tours: God's throne resides in the highest heaven. Visionaries get to see the throne, and occasionally even to glimpse its owner. Occasionally, visionaries only hear a voice from the throne, or see the throne's glory, or even hear about the throne from a lesser heavenly realm. Yet Enoch gets the full treat: he sees both the throne and the Holy One.

By identifying Enoch's description of the deity in terms of "veiled anthropomorphism," Christopher Rowland underscores both the ways in which 1 Enoch refuses to portray God in concrete terms and the near necessity of relating God to the human imagination: Like mortal rulers, the Great Glory sits on a throne and with a mouth utters words that Enoch can hear and understand.[25] Enoch's vision of the heavenly temple in chapter 14 reveals "a lofty throne." Drawing upon imagery from Isaiah 6, Ezekiel 1, and perhaps 2 Kings 2, Enoch observes its brightness and glory. His report is remarkable in that while neither angels nor mortals may look upon God, "the Great Glory," Enoch at least perceives the great flames that surround God's presence. During this overwhelming experience, God speaks directly to Enoch and refuses the Watchers' appeals for mercy.[26]

Oddly, Enoch also sees God's throne in a northwestern mountain range. Although this vision shares some imagery with that in chapter 14, notably fire and stone, it also differs in significant ways. Here, the emphasis leads to a hidden place of judgment for the heavenly powers (18:6–16).[27] In chapters 24–25 Enoch sees the throne in another mountainous place, where Eden's tree of life awaits the righteous.

Although Enoch's throne visions in the Book of the Watchers receive the most attention, interest in the throne appears in two of Enoch's other books as well. The Dream Visions include a song that echoes Isaiah 66:1: the heavens are God's throne and the earth God's footstool. Yet the song transcends this conventional metaphor by insisting on something more specific:

> Your throne has not retreated from her station nor from before your presence.
> Everything you know, you see, and you hear;
> nothing exists that can be hidden from you, for everything you expose. (84:3, *OTP*)

This hint of judgment continues, as the song concludes by confessing that God's wrath will abide until the day of judgment comes (84:4). Likewise, the Animal Apocalypse includes a throne scene in which "the Lord of the sheep" opens the books of judgment (90:20–27, *OTP*).

Perhaps the most intriguing references to the throne occur in the Similitudes, where two figures share the throne. At the time of judgment the Elect One assumes the throne, (45:3; 51:3; 55:4; 61:8; 62:2–4; 69:27, 29), though the throne properly belongs to God, the "Head of Days" (47:3; 60:2; 71:7). The Similitudes insist on this, for while "the Elect One may sit on God's throne" (51:3, *OTP),* his authority properly derives from the Lord of the Spirits, who *places* the Elect One upon the throne to judge the heavenly beings (61:8).

Enoch's throne visions may involve a dimension of mystical religious experience. Eventually some Jewish mystical circles came to emphasize visions of the divine throne, and some signs of mysticism accompany Enoch, as when he simultaneously experiences hot and cold (14:13).[28] Yet this survey of references to the throne reveals the throne's more pervasive function. Throughout 1 Enoch, and not just in the Similitudes, throne visions indicate not simply God's dwelling but also judgment. The throne enhances the spirit of admonition that animates all of 1 Enoch; God's order implies orderly justice.

RULERS AND THE RICH

Some commentators have identified the topic of rulers and the rich as a central interest of 1 Enoch. Thus, 1 Enoch expresses the alienation of a group victimized by the powerful, and it articulates their hope for resistance. However, the rulers and the rich figure prominently in only two of Enoch's five books, the Similitudes and the Epistles. The topic arises repeatedly throughout the Similitudes. The righteous find salvation precisely because of their resentment toward "this world of oppression" (48:7, *OTP*). The judgment scene foregrounds "the kings and the potentates" who apparently hinder the congregation of the Chosen One (53:5-6, *OTP*). The most concentrated indictment against the powerful occurs in chapters 62-63, where "the kings, the governors, the high officials, and the landlords" are delivered "to the angels for punishments in order that vengeance shall be executed on them–oppressors of [God's] children and [God's] elect ones" (62:1, 11, *OTP*). That day brings salvation and freedom from oppression (62:13).

Enoch's Epistle also admonishes wealthy oppressors, though perhaps with an invitation for their repentance.

> Woe unto those who build oppression and injustice!...
> Woe unto those who build their houses with sin!...
> Those who amass gold and silver;
> they shall quickly be destroyed.
> Woe unto you, O rich people!
> For you have put your trust in your wealth...
> In the days of your affluence, you committed oppression...
> (94:6-9, *OTP*)

This admonition continues through chapters 94-99, warning the wealthy of the doom that results from their persecution of the righteous (95:7; 98:13-15), their use of force to coerce the weak (96:8), and their excess (98:1-2). Their judgment answers the prayers of the righteous (97:5-6). Blessing the righteous, however, Enoch promises the time when their oppressors and persecutors (95:7) shall be removed from their presence (96:1-3; 97:1-2).

While only these two "books" discuss the rulers and the wealthy explicitly, one might argue that the legends regarding the judgment of the Watchers, who became powerful by revealing the tools of oppression such as how to build weapons, offer another reinforcement of that message. Moreover, if the Watchers have priestly functions in the heavenly temple, then their sin may represent a thinly veiled condemnation of the Jerusalem priesthood.[29] The connection is explicit in 1 Enoch 67:12, where Michael pronounces: "This verdict by which the angels are being punished is itself a testimony to the kings and the rulers who control the world" (*OTP*). Likewise, 1 Enoch 64 follows the indictment of rulers and landlords with the revelation of the rebellious angels. One scene in the Similitudes strengthens this connection: The rulers observe the judgment of Azazel and the other rebellious angels, presumably as an object lesson (55:4).

Despite these associations, however, they belong only to the Similitudes. It is impossible to judge with certainty whether the Book of the Watchers, for example, also associates judgment of the angels with human oppression.

Reading 1 Enoch

Throughout our study of 1 Enoch, we have grappled with the tension between reading 1 Enoch as a literary whole and emphasizing the distinctiveness of its constituent parts. For example, messianic speculation emerges only in some books but not others, with a heavy emphasis in the Similitudes. On the other hand, only the Similitudes, the Dream Visions, and the Epistle stress human history, with reviews of Israel's history limited only to the Animal Apocalypse and the Apocalypse of Weeks. While heavenly tours occur in the ancient Book of the Watchers and the Astronomical Book, references to such esoteric knowledge in the Similitudes reveal some tradition of development and influence over time. And, of course, interest in the mystical figure of Enoch links all five books.

Our analysis of the distinctiveness and connectedness of Enoch's five books could continue indefinitely, yet in my view two consistent threads color the whole book. First, 1 Enoch reflects a sense of dissatisfaction. Whether the problem is cosmic, as in the rebellious Watchers and even natural disasters, or human, as in the oppression of some mortals by others, all of 1 Enoch reflects the tragic assessment that evil corrupts human existence in the present order.

Second, 1 Enoch also insists on order. At the cosmic level, all the astral and meteorological powers have their places, and the sun and moon track their predictable courses. Such order enables the computation of a reliable calendar. In history, the judgment of the wicked and the deliverance of the righteous demonstrate the justice of the divine order. Viewed together, these threads animate a vision of the cosmos in which apparent injustice and oppression now will meet their just resolution at God's judgment. Ultimately, as Martin Luther King, Jr., would say, "The arc of the moral universe is long but it bends toward justice."[30] Many have speculated concerning the social origins of apocalyptic literature in general and of 1 Enoch in particular. Certainly, 1 Enoch reflects concern for a disempowered body of the righteous, who are subject to the waves of international and internal violence. For these righteous ones, 1 Enoch promises salvation, whether after death or in God's future age. Naturally, then, one might assume that 1 Enoch emerged from an oppressed community.

Perhaps the search for social origins presupposes a prior question. How do we know that 1 Enoch represents any particular ancient community or movement? When we read 1 Enoch, what we have are literary texts, not archaeological finds. Although literary texts certainly emerge within social and communal contexts, those contexts do not fully determine the literature. In other words, perhaps we would do better to speak of the points of view reflected in and promoted by 1 Enoch rather than its origins. If we do so, further questions require reflection.

- How would such a disenfranchised group produce such "scholarly" literature, with its allusions to scripture and ancient Near Eastern culture and its investigations of natural science?
- How do we account for the priestly interests of 1 Enoch, particularly concerning the throne and the temple, on the one hand, and the calendar, on the other?
- And how would a marginal group not only produce literature such as 1 Enoch, which required both literacy and the expensive media of writing, but also preserve and modify it, so that it could reach its present form?

If anything, these considerations seriously compromise the notion that 1 Enoch emerges from communities of the oppressed. If the producers of 1 Enoch *perceived themselves* as alienated from their rightful status and subject to the whim of others, or if they promoted that point of view through their literature, perhaps that is enough to account for such a complex work as this. First Enoch fascinates because its multiple writers responded to their contemporary situations. They could have written legal codes or epic fictions. They could have turned to Israel's wisdom traditions or even to its literary laments. Instead, they cultivated the emerging topics that identify the books of Enoch as apocalypses. Through the figure of Enoch and his extraordinary revelations, they depicted an alternative heavenly realm and an alternative future.

Daniel

Historical Setting

Daniel has a literary setting and a historical setting. Daniel's story is set in sixth-century B.C.E. Babylon, but details in the narrative reveal that it achieved its present form during or around the Maccabean Revolt of 167–164 B.C.E.

Languages and Texts

Daniel is unique within the Hebrew Scriptures because so much of the book occurs (2:4b—7:28) in Aramaic, a language closely related to Hebrew. (Ezra 4:8—6:18; 7:12–26 are also in Aramaic.) Also, from an early date, Greek versions of Daniel included several additional legends concerning Daniel, which now are included in the Apocrypha of most modern English translations, apart from the Roman Catholic Bibles (where they appear as Dan. 3:24–40 and 13:1—14:42).

Readers who attended church school regularly as children have immediate associations with the book of Daniel. In particular, they recall stories: Daniel and his friends refusing to eat the king's diet (chap. 1), Shadrach, Meshach, and Abednego in the fiery furnace (chap. 3), and Daniel in the lion's den (chap. 6) are the most prominent. (Indeed, the popular Christian video series *Veggie Tales* includes two of these stories on separate episodes.[31]) Those who paid special attention might also recall Daniel's interpretation of the writing on the wall (chap. 5) or Daniel's identity as an interpreter of dreams (chaps. 2 and 4).

That covers chapters 1–6 of Daniel, but what about chapters 7–12? The latter half of Daniel is thoroughly apocalyptic in both literary form and topical content and is far less familiar to most readers—unless they stay up at night to watch those television preachers who are announcing and interpreting the last days. I would suggest that, despite their clear differences in content and form, Daniel's two halves belong together. Whoever created Daniel as we know it selected from the available traditions concerning a wise figure named Daniel and united those traditions to the visionary material that follows. They fused different literary media to present a consistent message that addressed the most pressing concerns of a particular time and place.

One can hardly overestimate Daniel's importance for other early Jewish and Christian literature. Within the Hebrew Scriptures, Daniel is the only book that contains an explicit expression of resurrection hope.[32] Daniel's vision of the Son of Man influences not only Christian messianism, which identifies Jesus as the Son of Man and hopes for his return on the clouds of heaven, but also Jewish apocalyptic messianism as well.[33] Allusions to and reinterpretations of Daniel's vision of the four kingdoms redound through Jewish apocalyptic literature and the book of Revelation as well.[34]

Daniel the Visionary

The most important fact about Daniel the visionary in this book is almost too obvious: Daniel is the primary character of the legends that precede his visions. At the same time, we have reasons to believe that Daniel was a familiar name in some Jewish circles before our book was completed. The book's characterization of Daniel continues beyond the legends into the visionary material as well.

The book of Ezekiel twice mentions a Daniel (or "Danel"). Ezekiel 14:14–20 includes Daniel with Noah and Job as three models of righteousness. The larger argument is that when God judges a land, even persons as righteous as these could save only themselves from devastation; they could not save even their own sons and daughters. Ezekiel 28:3 also invokes divine judgment, but in a different way. Addressed to the prince of Tyre, the passage acknowledges his wisdom but promises judgment for his arrogance. "You are indeed wiser than Daniel," but your enemies will "thrust you down to the Pit" (28:3, 8).

Ezekiel's allusions to him indicate a tradition in which Daniel (or Danel) is known as a righteous and wise man—an image consistent with the Daniel of the later apocalypse. Other Jewish legends about Daniel, including those in the Greek translations of Daniel and in the Dead Sea Scrolls, confirm this impression.[35] Moreover, certain legends in Daniel—such as the story of the lion's den—recall other ancient Near Eastern literature,[36] while the Ugaritic Aqhat tale features a wise and righteous judge named Danel.[37]

Even if the name Daniel evokes positive associations, the legends in the book of Daniel remain distinctive. Daniel, along with his colleagues Shadrach, Meshach, and Abednego, are noteworthy for their loyalty to Yahweh in the face of overwhelming imperial pressure. Enjoined to adopt a diet that violates their law, they maintain another diet. Required to worship a golden image, Daniel's friends respectfully decline. Prohibited from praying to his own god, Daniel does so anyway. In each case God delivers these faithful ones from danger. In addition to his loyalty, Daniel also possesses both wisdom and the ability to interpret dreams. On one occasion, he even describes Nebuchadnezzar's dream, which he had not seen (chap. 2). Such supernatural gifts accompany noble virtues (1:3–4), for Daniel remains diplomatic and respectful even in the worst of circumstances (e.g., 2:12–16; 6:21); he performs his duties faithfully (6:4) and demonstrates his concern for others (2:24, 49).

Daniel's story recalls the stories of Joseph from the book of Genesis. Joseph, too, found himself in a foreign court and rose from a lowly status to administer a great empire. Like Daniel, Joseph demonstrated his faithfulness to God under trying circumstances, notably his refusal to have sex with Potiphar's wife. Most importantly, like Daniel, Joseph is noted for his wisdom and his ability to interpret dreams.

The Joseph parallels further enhance Daniel's status as an authoritative visionary. But whereas Joseph moves from having dreams to interpreting them, Daniel is transformed from an interpreter to a visionary. The book's visionary material also contributes to the image of Daniel. His first vision troubles and terrifies him, but Daniel persists in requesting clarification from a heavenly attendant (7:15–16). His curiosity, a common trait of apocalyptic visionaries, enables him to transcend his fear and seek understanding.

Complementing his desire for understanding is Daniel's scholarship, as when he realizes that Jeremiah's prediction that Jerusalem would suffer seventy years of devastation required further inquiry and interpretation. This insight leads Daniel to seek revelation aggressively, and here Daniel demonstrates his piety when he fasts, prays, and confesses his people's sin. Moreover, repeated physical symptoms and reactions—trances, prostration, sickness, exhaustion, pallor, trembling—reinforce the authenticity of Daniel's revelations. As he mourns for Jerusalem, Daniel neglects himself for three weeks.

Finally, let us note that the book also includes direct claims concerning Daniel's reliability and his virtue. Daniel 10:1 features the claim that the word Daniel receives is "true" and that Daniel "understood" it. One would assume these things, yet for some reason the book insists on naming them explicitly.[38] Toward the end of the book, the angel confirms Daniel's righteousness, informing him that "you shall rise for your reward at the end of the days" (12:13).

When the book moves to Daniel's own visions in chapters 7–12, it also changes its narrative point of view. Whereas the legends of the previous chapters are related through a third-person narrator, Daniel 7:1 tells us that Daniel himself has recorded his visions. Sure enough, we encounter Daniel's own voice in the following verse. "I, Daniel," guides us through the rest of the book, though Daniel 10:20–12:4 recount the revelations spoken directly by "one in human form," probably an angel. Thus, the book of Daniel insists on the authenticity of its contents.

Throughout chapters 7–11, Daniel's revelations receive reasonably clear interpretations from his heavenly interlocutors. So despite its bizarre imagery, Daniel is a relatively open book. Its openness is reflected in the degree of agreement among scholars as to many of the book's details. Yet Daniel also reserves some knowledge, for his words remain sealed until the last days (12:4, 9). This epistemological reservation is a familiar device in apocalyptic literature (cf. 1 Enoch 1:1–2), and it invites Daniel's audience to participate in his book. After all, if they are reading it, they must be among those for whom it was written, and they must be living in those last days!

Literary Setting

The *story* of Daniel takes place in sixth-century B.C.E. Babylon. Daniel and his colleagues are exiled Jews who receive training for service in the royal court. His career spans the reigns of the Babylonian rulers Nebuchadnezzar and Belshazzar, and then the Median ruler Darius, who is apparently a fictional character. (It was Persia, and not Media, that conquered Babylon, and three Persian rulers were named Darius.) The book plays fast and loose with the historical details of its literary setting, which explains the series of Babylonian, Median, and Persian empires in chapters 7–10.[39]

Daniel's primary *historical setting*, however, clearly relates to the Maccabean Revolt, 167–164 B.C.E. No doubt, some of the material in Daniel 1–6, and perhaps even its complete form, may have developed quite a bit earlier. Parts of Daniel 7–12 may be older than others, but Daniel as a whole surfaced during this period of crisis.

The Seleucid ruler Antiochus IV, in part responding to internal Judean disputes, determined to intervene militarily. His forces took control of Jerusalem, and the temple was dedicated to Zeus. In the temple courtyard, a new altar—Daniel's "abomination that makes desolate" (11:31)—was erected, and even swine (unclean in Jewish eyes) were offered on it. Jewish primary sources such as First, Second, and Fourth Maccabees indicate that Antiochus' attempt to stamp out resistance led to the persecution of some Jews, including banning distinctive Jewish practices such as circumcision as well as imposing pagan ones (1 Macc. 1:41–50). Whether Antiochus, in fact, "outlawed" Judaism is a matter for debate, but 1 Maccabees attributes his policies to an attempt to unify his empire under one culture.

At any rate, Jews responded to his policies in a variety of ways. Some, judging Antiochus's cosmopolitanism as good for culture and commerce, supported him. Others revolted, and these eventually gained relative freedom for Judea. So momentous was their success that the holiday Hanukkah commemorates their purification and rededication of the temple. Still other Jews apparently resisted Antiochus by insisting on loyalty to their Jewish customs and laws. Some of these latter faced martyrdom.[40]

Daniel was written in response to this crisis. Scholars base this judgment on several considerations. Most prominently, Daniel 11 includes a review of history, what we call *ex eventu prophecy* ("prophecy after the fact"). Its description of "a contemptible person on whom royal majesty ha[s] not been conferred" (11:21) begins a summary of Antiochus's reign, though with a strong polemical angle of vision. The account includes the temple's profanation and the divisions within the Judean populace.

Then, at 11:40 comes a remarkable phrase, "At the time of the end," at which point the prophecy's *accuracy* simply stops. As we have seen, "At the time of the end" indicates events contemporaneous with Daniel's audience (12:4, 9). What we read here is a vision for Judea's (and Antiochus's) immediate future, including Antiochus's death. But Antiochus eventually met his death in Persia in 164 B.C.E., not between Zion and the Sea, as Daniel 11:45 anticipates. Thus, Daniel addresses Judeans who are torn by the struggles of their day. It answers one question—*What represented a faithful or prudent response to such intense pressure?*—by combining legends concerning Daniel and his colleagues with Daniel's special revelations.

May we say more about Daniel's immediate social context? Did Daniel's "author(s)" belong to an identifiable social or religious group? Did he or they have a particular audience in mind? Some scholars have looked beyond the book itself to the "Hasidim" of 1 Maccabees 2:42; 7:13. Yet Daniel does not recommend violence at all, which does not square with the Hasidim as we know them. These "pious ones" who followed the Law joined the Maccabean Revolt. They also trusted deceitful Seleucid emissaries, who massacred sixty of them at once. Other historians have found a clue for placing Daniel among the Maskilim, or "the Wise." According to Daniel 11:33, the wise understand the times and instruct the people, only to fall to violence. Yet their death may ultimately lead to their salvation (11:35; 12:3, 10). Perhaps, some wonder, Daniel represents the voice of a literary or priestly elite who seek to guide the general population in the ways of righteous—but not military—resistance.

Apocalyptic Discourse as the Language of the Oppressed?

Historians of apocalyptic literature have long asked *whose* literature it is. Historically, this concern has mattered most among those for whom Daniel and the book of Revelation, in particular, are sacred scripture. While many have marginalized or even criticized biblical apocalyptic discourse for being violent, vengeful, esoteric, or irrelevant, its advocates have often countered that apocalyptic discourse emerges from history's underdogs. Thus, the argument goes, apocalyptic literature provides a means by which people resist oppression and articulate their vision for an alternative reality. Some scholars have even distinguished between the apocalyptic literature of the oppressed and its co-optation by elites.[41]

On the one hand, the apocalypses in particular reflect intense learned, or scribal, activity. They quote and allude to other texts and legends, and they pursue specialized forms of knowledge, including astrological speculation and priestly concerns regarding temple and cult. These features discourage the attribution of Daniel's apocalyptic discourse to impoverished communities. For example, Daniel, with its traditions concerning the Babylonian court and its dream interpretations, combined with its familiarity with scripture and its concern for the temple, has often been attributed to scribal or wisdom circles. To complicate this problem, learning did not belong exclusively to the elite in the ancient world. Some persons and institutions employed literate slaves or common people as scribes and accountants.

On the other hand, Daniel also presents a case of resistance literature in that it clearly embodies an attempt by a colonized people to subvert an imperial power. Thus, while Daniel demonstrates exceptional learning, in some sense it also embodies the concerns of an oppressed group. Daniel reveals that the question of "oppression" requires specificity as to whether one points to an oppressed people, an oppressed social class, a group that experiences material deprivation, a group that experiences cultural disenfranchisement, or a group that simply protests the way things are in some form or another.

Plot and Mode of Revelation

That division between the two "halves" of Daniel is important: The legends precede the visionary material. In seeking to understand this pattern, perhaps we will benefit by stretching our imaginations, forgetting for the moment that Daniel is a book in the Bible and that we live in the twenty-first century C.E., and imagining how "new" Daniel might have appeared in its own time and place. For although Daniel stands in clear continuity with biblical traditions, both wisdom and prophetic, it also introduces relatively new literary forms and religious ideas. Daniel, with sections of 1 Enoch, stands among the earliest apocalypses, introducing new literary devices that would later become conventional. Perhaps many of Daniel's first readers would be encountering ideas such as the Son of Man, the judgment, and the resurrection for the first time. Thus, the more conventional forms of Daniel 1–6 provide a relatively smooth introduction to the visions that followed. As we shall see, those legends also model an ethical perspective for which those visions provide the justification.

Throughout the legends of chapters 1–6, a consistent pattern emerges:

a. the Judean heroes face external pressure to compromise their faithfulness to their traditions.
b. Daniel and his companions demonstrate their loyalty by refusing to abandon those traditions.
c. God delivers these heroes from danger.

For example, in chapter 1 Daniel and his friends find themselves in training for service in Nebuchadnezzar's court, but the training involves a diet that would force Daniel to "defile himself." When Daniel requests that he and his friends be excused from this diet, the palace master expresses fear: if these Judean youths do not prosper, his own head may be in peril. Daniel sagely offers a compromise: a ten-day testing period to see how well he and his companions would do simply by eating vegetables and drinking water. Sure enough, after the test, the loyal youths emerge from the test even more healthy than their peers.

The youths receive permission to continue their alternative diet. This story would amount to a common-sense argument for the superiority of Jewish dietary customs. Perhaps in part it is, but for one additional consideration: God's presence and protection frames the entire episode. When Daniel first addresses the palace master, we learn that "God allowed Daniel to receive [his] favor and compassion" (1:9). Otherwise, why would the palace master even listen to Daniel's request? After Daniel and his companions receive permission to continue with their diet, we further learn how God granted the four boys "knowledge and skill in every aspect of literature and wisdom" (1:17), with Daniel particularly gifted with insight into visions and dreams.

The same general pattern plays out in the other two legends concerning the fiery furnace and the lion's den. When Nebuchadnezzar orders universal worship of a golden statue (chap. 3) under penalty of death in the furnace, Shadrach, Meshach, and Abednego (Daniel is strangely absent) refuse, claiming that their God may be able to deliver them from the flames. When the king examines the furnace, he sees not three men but four walking around in the flames. Apparently, an angel or other heavenly being has protected the three.

Likewise, Darius signs a decree that for thirty days people may pray only to him—a law proposed by those who seek Daniel's death. Again, the law includes the penalty for those who violate it: being thrown into a den of lions (chap. 6). Yet Daniel continues to pray to his own God. Again, God sends an angel to protect Daniel, thereby delivering him from the lions while Daniel's accusers meet their doom in the den. One can readily imagine how these stories could have reinforced resistance during the Antiochene Crisis. They deliver a consistent message: despite external pressures to violate the Torah and despite fearsome sanctions, God will deliver those who remain faithful to the Law.

Daniel's ability to interpret dreams also prepares for the visionary material. Nebuchadnezzar's dream of the great statue, with parts of gold, silver, bronze, iron, and finally iron and clay, amounts to an apocalyptic review of history (chap. 2). Each part corresponds to a successive dominant empire up until the days of Daniel's audience: Babylon, Media, Persia, and Greece. A great stone smashes these empires and becomes a great mountain, representing the rule of God.

Nebuchadnezzar's later dream of the great tree is also an apocalypse on a smaller scale, revealing that the king would endure a period of insanity before his restoration to health and power (chap. 4). (While no other texts suggest that Nebuchadnezzar had such an experience, a similar legend found among the Dead Sea Scrolls may reveal that such a legend did circulate in Jewish circles.) Finally, we should emphasize the keen political edge of the story of Belshazzar and the writing on the wall (chap. 5). The writing, which announces Belshazzar's own doom, appears precisely when the king uses precious items from the Jerusalem temple at a feast. This bad idea comes because the king is drunk, and it leads to the royal court's praising various gods while holding the sacred objects from Zion. This legend recalls one of Antiochus's most notorious actions, in which he plundered the temple of its sacred objects (1 Macc. 1:20–23), thus directing a barbed critique of Antiochus and his empire.

The book of Daniel is far from an arbitrary patchwork. These two blocks of material—the legends of Daniel and his friends and the visions of the kings—reveal a consistent program that prepares for Daniel's own visions in chapters 7–12. The legends inspire faithful resistance to pagan pressures, whereas the dreams explore the borders of apocalyptic revelation. In particular, Nebuchadnezzar's dream in chapter 2 prepares the way for what will become a common motif of apocalyptic literature: the review of four successive kingdoms.

Those four kingdoms resurface in Daniel's first night vision of the bizarre beasts (chap. 7). Fearsome though the beasts appear—and the fourth beast is by far the most dreadful—the vision leads to a sudden resolution. The Ancient One (literally, "Ancient of Days") appears on his throne; judgment commences; and the fourth beast meets destruction. The vision also includes "one like a Son of Man" (literal translation) who arrives on the clouds, presents himself before the Ancient One, and receives an everlasting dominion over all the earth.

This first vision precisely fulfills the functions of an historical apocalypse, for it "reveals" in two different ways. Obviously, it reveals an envisioned future, one in which evil empires meet their ends and God's reign, administered through this Son of Man, finally manifests itself.

But a more subtle, subversive "revelation" is at work as well, for the vision—and its later interpretation by the heavenly attendant—interprets not only the *course* of history but also its *nature*. This fourth beast is indeed fearsome, and so is the "Little Horn" that emerges from it to usurp power. Daniel reveals the Little Horn's "arrogance" three times (7:8, 11, 20)—once immediately before the Ancient One's appearance, once immediately after, and finally in the heavenly attendant's interpretation. Daniel also reserves some information about the Little Horn until *after* its destruction. Though it "seemed greater than the others" (7:20), it also makes war against the saints and prevails against them for a set period (7:25), until the Ancient of Days' intervention.

These literary strategies dramatically *reveal* two things about the Little Horn:

a. While it may appear mighty, its claims amount to sheer arrogance.
b. While its power may have seemed victorious, its limits were set in history, with the Ancient One's judgment standing as the ultimate boundary.

This message, or revelation, fits perfectly in Daniel's context, in which Antiochus Epiphanes, who had indeed emerged from among the heirs to Alexander the Great's empire, was at war with the Judeans. Antiochus had committed acts that his Judean opponents regarded as blasphemy. In this sense Daniel exemplifies the creative potential of apocalyptic discourse to interpret the present by re-imagining the apparent realities such as empires and their rulers and by envisioning a transcendent reality such as the advent of the Ancient of Days.

Daniel's introduction of the "one like a human being [in Aramaic, son of man]" (7:13) no doubt inspired some early Jews, such as those who composed the Similitudes of Enoch, as well as early Christians, who identified Jesus as *the* Son of Man. In those later traditions, the link between Son of Man imagery and messianic expectations has crystallized. Yet we must claim fewer certainties regarding his enigmatic appearance in Daniel. Daniel's Son of Man stands in contrast to the arrogant "Little Horn," though it is unclear whether this comparison involves

a. competing individuals, so that the Son of Man usurps the Little Horn to gain dominion, or

  b. a description of a "human" Judahite empire as opposed to the "beastly" empire of Antiochus. (Biblical literature occasionally personifies Israel as a whole in the form of an individual.)

The first option includes other possibilities as well: Is the Son of Man a cipher for Judas Maccabeus, who defeated Antiochus; for some other present or human leader; or for some heavenly figure? In Daniel 7:18 "the holy ones of the Most High" receive the kingdom forever, a factor that encourages us to see Daniel's Son of Man as a corporate personification. Certainty remains elusive.[42]

Daniel's second vision, the Ram and the Goat, also presents a review of history (chap. 8). The Ram, with its two-horned depiction of Median and Persian power, meets its end under the hooves of the Goat. Gabriel, who interprets the vision for Daniel, explains what the Goat represents: "the king of Greece" (8:21), from which four smaller empires emerge (8:22). The pattern is familiar: from one of those four empires ("horns") emerges a Little Horn that acts arrogantly, even to the point of disrupting the temple offerings and attacking the holy people (8:9–12, 23–25). Again, the pattern of vision followed by interpretation allows Daniel to reinforce the message. The vision twice emphasizes the Little Horn's fate: His power shall endure for 1,150 days (8:14),[43] and "he shall be broken, and not by human hands" (8:25).

Between his second and third revelations Daniel offers an extended prayer on behalf of the people (9:1–19). In one sense, this prayer simply sets up his third revelation. It begins with Daniel's reflection upon Jeremiah's prophecy that Jerusalem's fate would last for seventy years (9:1–2; Jer. 25:11–12; 29:10; cf. 2 Chr. 36:21), and in Daniel's third revelation Gabriel explains that Jeremiah had signified not seventy years but seventy *weeks* of years (9:24–27). Thus, Jerusalem's desolation continues through the crisis that Daniel is addressing.

But the prayer does more than simply clear the way for this innovation, a task the book could have accomplished simply by introducing Gabriel at the moment of Daniel's reflection. It also instills a theological set of values through which one may interpret both the past and the present. Daniel devotes the bulk of the prayer to a lament and confession: God's people have met their "present" crisis on account of their faithlessness. Daniel also presses God to forgive Jerusalem and restore its people. In this way, Daniel adds a particular edge to its interpretation of the Antiochene Crisis. Following the pattern of the biblical Deuteronomistic History, Daniel attributes Israel's woes to its collective apostasy. While Antiochus remains the clear villain, Judea must still seek faithfulness for God's blessing to be realized.

Gabriel's speech in Daniel 9:22–27 introduces the mode of revelation that continues through to the end of the book. Whereas heavenly agents have previously spoken to interpret what Daniel has seen, here Daniel receives explicit and direct instruction from a heavenly being. Daniel's final revelation, consisting of the bulk of chapters 10–12, relates such a vision: "one in human form" simply tells Daniel what is to happen. This "word" (10:1) does not stand alone, for it also is introduced as a "vision" (10:1) in the form of a mystical experience that follows a period of fasting. Yet the "word" Daniel receives reveals a straightforward course of history that includes the emergence and dissolution of Alexander's Macedonian empire and the rise of that "contemptible person," Antiochus IV, and his persecution of the faithful.

The narrative pauses to assess Antiochus's character: he acts as he pleases; he exalts himself above all the gods; and he relies upon his own force and prosperity. He disregards all human concerns, except that he rewards those who show him loyalty and pay tribute (11:36–39).

Daniel 11:40 stands as the watershed for this review of history, preparing the way for the book's closing exhortations. The verse turns from the immediate past and known present of the Antiochene Crisis to predictions concerning Antiochus's fate. At this point, Daniel's review of history turns decidedly unhistorical: Daniel expects Antiochus's death "between the sea and the beautiful holy mountain" (11:45), that is, between the Mediterranean and Zion, but Antiochus actually died in Persia. But that is not the point. *Daniel 11:40 transforms current events from a genuine crisis in the life of Judea into the ultimate eschatological conflict.* It sketches the line between current events to the anticipated future as "the time of the end" and looks ahead to "that time" when Michael, Israel's angelic protector, will deliver the people. "That time" includes eschatological tribulation, resurrection, and judgment (12:1–3).

The flow of the narrative breaks up as Daniel draws to a close. Daniel hears additional information about those last days–how long they will last and how people will respond (12:10). It is impossible to figure out how three-and-a-half years ("a time, two times, and half a time," 12:7) relates to 1,290 or 1,335 days (12:12–13)!–and how people will respond (12:10). Daniel also receives personal instruction: He is to keep his book secret until "the time of the end" (12:4, 9), and he is to rest in the assurance that in the end he will rise for his reward (12:9, 13). Thus, in its closing the apocalypse reemphasizes its most characteristic literary strategy: The book speaks to the eschatological present from the ancient past.

Reading Daniel

For many who know Daniel and its stories as familiar and sacred scripture an act of willful imagination is required to grasp just how innovative this work must have been in its historical contexts. Admittedly, Daniel's producers did not invent the apocalypse as a literary genre, nor were they the first to review history in schematic form. Nor is it likely that Daniel introduced brand-new theological or religious ideas, such as the resurrection and judgment. Yet for Daniel's readers, these literary forms and ideas were by no means established. More likely, they were either new or subject to criticism and debate. Daniel's literary accomplishment is to combine emerging literary forms and religious sensibilities into a coherent whole that addressed the most pressing concerns of its day.

Two of Daniel's innovations go hand in hand (11:40–12:3). First, assuming that Daniel's ancient readers grasped the thinly-veiled references to Antiochus and their own crisis, imagine their response to Daniel 11:40: "At the time of the end..." This tiny insertion invests the present distress with cosmic significance, as it invites Daniel's audience to see themselves as living in the last days. The effect must have been something similar to that of the contemporary popular "prophecy teachers" who inspire their own audiences toward eschatological urgency. In theory at least, living in such a momentous time raises the stakes for all human endeavors.

Second, Daniel immediately ties this end-time sensibility to the themes of resurrection and judgment. For Daniel, judgment involves not simply God's cosmic and social administration of justice to the nations; it also discriminates among individuals, even in Israel. Although it has its antecedents in prophetic literature (notably Ezek. 18:1–32; Jer. 31:29–30), this level of discrimination is not the common view portrayed in scripture. Instead, it stands as one of the innovations of apocalyptic discourse. For Daniel, the stakes are enormous, amounting to the difference between "everlasting life" in which one shines like the stars and "everlasting contempt" (12:2–3). Not only are these the last days, Daniel insists, but one's response to the present crisis determines one's eternal fate.

On a larger scale, Daniel's union of legendary material with apocalyptic visions allows the book to model resistance to imperial pressure, then to provide the revealed knowledge that justifies such resistance. During the Antiochene Crisis, several options confronted Judea's inhabitants. They could

1. find ways to accommodate themselves to Antiochus's program
2. risk martyrdom by refusing to do so while hoping to remain in secret
3. rebel

Different persons pursued each of these options. Daniel's legends present an alternative other way: Daniel and his colleagues do not *seek* attention, but neither do they *avoid* it. Instead, they remain faithful to their Jewish practices, and God delivers them from danger. As we have seen, some elements of the stories of Daniel's first half not only present an alternative response to Antiochus, they also foreshadow the revelatory material to follow. We see Daniel as an interpreter of dreams, some of which reveal the fate of empires, preparing for Daniel's major role in the second half of the book.

By the time we reach chapter 7, Daniel has demonstrated faithful but nonviolent resistance. One might say that the visionary material explains why such resistance makes sense, over and again portraying the judgment of Antiochus and his empire and the restoration of God's people. The apocalyptic material also enables a form of revelatory analysis, depicting Antiochus's arrogance and violence in both symbolic form and through the instruction of heavenly beings. Daniel does not, however, propose a program for life after Antiochus.[44]

Fearsome though Antiochus may be, those who remain faithful await his sure destruction. In the meantime, they may rely on God's protection or hope for the resurrection.

FOR FURTHER READING

Black, Matthew, in consultation with James C. VanderKam. *The Book of Enoch or 1 Enoch: A New English Edition with Commentary and Textual Notes.* Leiden: Brill, 1985.

Collins, John J. Daniel. *A Commentary on the Book of Daniel.* Hermeneia. Minneapolis: Fortress Press, 1993.

Collins, John J., and Peter W. Flint, eds. *The Book of Daniel: Composition and Reception.* 2 vols. Leiden: Brill, 2001.

Fewell, Dana Nolan. *Circle of Sovereignty: Plotting Politics in the Book of Daniel.* Nashville: Abingdon Press, 1991.

Nickelsburg, George W. E. *1 Enoch 1: A Commentary on the Book of 1 Enoch, Chapters 1–36; 81–108.* Hermeneia. Minneapolis: Fortress Press, 2001.

VanderKam, James C. *Enoch: A Man for All Generations.* Studies on Personalities of the Old Testament. Columbia: University of South Carolina Press, 1995.

CHAPTER 2

Emerging Apocalyptic Discourse in the Hebrew Scriptures

Apocalyptic discourse did not surface overnight but emerged from within complex streams of prophetic, wisdom, and mystical discourses. While the sources that poured into apocalyptic discourse included what are now biblical texts, other ingredients ensured the solution's eventual richness. Now that we have encountered the earliest instances of classical apocalyptic literature in 1 Enoch and Daniel, we may look back in time to examples of less fully developed apocalyptic discourse, from which 1 Enoch and Daniel both drew inspiration.

Traditionally scholars have identified several biblical texts as examples of "proto-apocalyptic literature." Indeed, certain sections of Ezekiel, Zechariah, Joel, and Isaiah feature clusters of the topics and literary devices that we identify with apocalyptic discourse. A close look at these texts reveals how apocalyptic ideas emerged from attempts to shape attitudes, beliefs, and behaviors through acts of religious and social imagination.

Within the Hebrew canon, we find these examples of emergent apocalyptic discourse among the prophets. Many interpreters have traced apocalyptic discourse to a development within prophetic literature, suggesting that the discontinuity between the prophetic literature and apocalyptic discourse lies in their disposition toward the world. According to this view, the classical prophets hoped for transformation within the present social order, but the apocalyptic visionaries held a fundamentally fatalistic view of the human condition. Excluded from access to power and speaking on behalf of Jerusalem's oppressed, the proto-apocalyptic writers essentially gave up on history. They therefore believed that salvation must lie beyond the powers of human societies and institutions, that human wholeness required a dramatic intervention by God.

Paul D. Hanson, whose influential work set the tone for later studies, traces the emergence of proto-apocalyptic eschatology to a conflict for power within sixth-century Jerusalem.[1] Hanson characterizes the matter as a conflict between "visionary" and "pragmatic" elements to control the temple cult. According to Hanson, the visionary dimensions of prophecy had always grounded themselves in social reality, taking the "historical realm...as a realm of primary divine activity."[2] But the victory of priestly elements pushed their more prophetic counterparts away from reality toward the transcendent realm of "apocalyptic dreams." Fortunately, Hanson maintains, those alienated and oppressed classes managed to sustain their contact with this-worldly concerns, so that proto-apocalyptic literature did not wander into the realm of irrelevance.[3]

One of the linchpins of Hanson's reconstruction is his association of apocalyptic literature with oppressed groups in and around Jerusalem. But more recent research has demonstrated that the evidence is far less clear. As Philip R. Davies points out, "It is hard...to find very many apocalypses which clearly point to such authors."[4] Many scholars, such as Stephen L. Cook, have located *some* of the earliest proto-apocalyptic texts among "central-priestly" in-groups rather than among the oppressed. Instead, proto-apocalyptic literature apparently surfaces in a variety of social conditions.[5] Jon L. Berquist suggests a setting quite the opposite to Hanson's theory. Berquist traces the sophisticated literary forms and international consciousness of apocalyptic discourse, along with its disaffection toward the most wealthy and powerful, to "middle-class scribes and government officials" within Jerusalem.[6]

Thus, rather than giving up on the world, the prophetic texts we will study in this chapter reflect intense engagement with this-worldly concerns. Moreover, we cannot assume that apocalyptic topics emerged solely as a development within the conventions of prophetic literature. These prophetic texts by no means represent the sole sources of apocalyptic discourse, nor do they develop a sufficient base for the diverse range of apocalyptic topics that eventually evolves. Topics such as a final judgment for individuals, the resurrection of the dead, and interest in righteous and wicked angels do not emerge within this proto-apocalyptic literature. As John J. Collins wisely cautions, "While prophecy may indeed be the single most important source on which the apocalypticists drew, the tendency to assimilate apocalyptic literature to the more familiar world of the prophets risks losing sight of its stranger mythological and cosmological components."[7] Thus, apocalyptic discourse may sustain continuity with the biblical prophets, but we may not reduce it to a simple development—or degeneration—within the prophetic tradition.

Ezekiel

Set in the period surrounding Jerusalem's fall to the Babylonians in 587/586 B.C.E., Ezekiel poses a multidimensional response to that crisis and to the exile of Jewish elites to Babylon. Indeed, Ezekiel himself may have been among the first of those elites to be deported, as early as 593. Ezekiel begins by pronouncing judgment against Israel (chaps. 1–24), then moves to judgment against the nations (chaps. 25–32), and finally turns to proclaim hope for the people (chaps. 33–48).[8]

While Ezekiel bears witness to the emergence of some important apocalyptic topics, it also served as a source document for apocalyptic reflection. The book shows keen interest in the temple and the priesthood, specifically the Zadokite priesthood.[9] Ezekiel's identification with the priestly elites, reflected in his interest in cultic matters and in his early deportation to Babylon, is critical for locating the book in a plausible social context.[10]

Ezekiel faced a monumental theological challenge. Judah's religion, or Yahwism, had come to emphasize the land, the temple, and the Holy City–all of which were lost to Ezekiel and his colleagues in exile. In particular, many people believed those symbols to be inviolable, that God would preserve them eternally. At least, this had become the official view. Yet Ezekiel saw the dissolution of these symbols when the Babylonians finally destroyed Jerusalem. Amid such disorientation Ezekiel articulated a theological vision in which the people could worship Yahweh without being in the land, without the temple cult, and far from the Holy City. His vision addressed both the present, by insisting that Yahweh's presence transcended geographical boundaries, and the future, by looking ahead to Zion's restoration.[11]

"The Likeness of God's Glory"

Ezekiel begins with a fascinating superscription:

> In the thirtieth year, in the fourth month, on the fifth day of the month, as I was among the exiles by the river Chebar, the heavens were opened, and I saw visions of God. (1:1)

This beginning sounds very much like it belongs among full-blown apocalypses such as 1 Enoch and Daniel. But it is unlikely that Ezekiel drew from those traditions; rather, Ezekiel's beginning inspired later apocalyptic writers who saw the heavens open at the inauguration of their visions. At the same time, along with the heavenly throne vision in Isaiah 6, Ezekiel's experience stands out within the prophetic literature on account of its direct access to the heavenly realms and to the divine presence.

What Ezekiel then sees defies the left-brained imagination; one could not draw the vision in any representative fashion. Ezekiel sees "something like" four dazzling living creatures (1:5): Each of these creatures possesses a wheel. Spirit-empowered, the four wheels go wherever the living creatures go. In a dome above the creatures Ezekiel sees a throne upon which sits a human-like figure, clothed with a fiery splendor. Appropriately, Ezekiel falls on his face.

But what does it mean? With extreme caution Ezekiel names this vision "the appearance of the likeness of the glory of the LORD" (1:28). Here, we encounter the language of absolute holiness, a reality mortals cannot claim to represent adequately. Most scholars regard this vision as a theophany. That is, Ezekiel actually describes a vision of God's throne upon which the deity sits. The throne indicates sovereignty, as does the chariot, but combined they represent something else: The glory of YWHW that resided in the temple's most holy place is mobile. Israel's God is not confined to a particular place; instead, YHWH's mobility indicates his identity as a trans-local deity. In Ezekiel's vision, the throne meets the prophet even outside the boundaries of Israel. In a later vision, or set of visions (chaps. 8–11), Ezekiel observes abominations in the temple, the temple's destruction, and the departure of the divine glory from the temple. This scene (10:15–22) explicitly recalls Ezekiel's first vision of the throne in chapter 1. It is followed by assurance of Israel's future salvation (11:14–21). Thus, God's enthroned glory provides both condemnation and comfort: condemnation because Jerusalem's immediate fate is sealed, but comfort in that God promises to restore the people after their dispossession.

Ezekiel's vision of the throne chariot stands among the most dramatic scenes in scripture, and in some ways it has been among the most influential. Christopher Rowland has demonstrated how Isaiah 6 and Ezekiel 1 influence other visions of the heavenly realms, including 1 Enoch 14 and Revelation 4. Moreover, Rowland shows how the entrance before the divine presence at the throne-chariot becomes a primary goal in some Jewish mystical circles, particularly what we call *merkabah* mysticism.[12] Indeed, one of the most prominent motifs in apocalyptic literature involves the ascent through the levels of heaven to God's dwelling place.

"Son of Man"

In addressing Ezekiel, God repeatedly (ninety-three times) uses the phrase, "Son of Man."[13] As if it were the appropriate way for sacred beings to address mortals, the phrase really means no more than, "mortal," as some modern translations render it. Yet we have seen how in both Daniel and in the Similitudes of Enoch, "Son of Man" takes on highly esoteric meanings in apocalyptic discourse, to the degree that Jesus apparently identified himself by it—or at least the gospel authors attribute it to him. Ezekiel's so prominent designation as Son of Man likely influenced later apocalyptic writers, with the term eventually growing to include aspects of Israel's deliverance from oppression, divine judgment and rule, and messianic expectation. We have seen this development in 1 Enoch and in

Daniel, and it recurs in 4 Ezra, a Jewish apocalypse from around 100 C.E. The New Testament gospels take up this image, applying Son of Man as a messianic title for Jesus.

Life from Dry Bones

No less memorable than the vision of the throne, Ezekiel's vision of the valley of the dry bones also foreshadows the classical apocalypses (37:1–14). The scene begins with two indicators of ecstatic experience: "The hand of the LORD" comes upon Ezekiel,[14] and "by the spirit of the LORD" God transports Ezekiel to the valley. When Ezekiel sees the bones, God asks, "Son of Man, can these bones live?" Ezekiel replies, "O Lord GOD, you know" (37:3). God instructs the prophet to prophesy to the bones, announcing their new life. Then the bones come together, with sinews, flesh, and skin. Again, God instructs Ezekiel to speak, commanding the wind to give breath and life to the bones, which then stand. Finally, God commands Ezekiel to pronounce this prophecy:

> "Thus says the Lord GOD: I am going to open your graves, and bring you up from your graves, O my people; and I will bring you back to the land of Israel." (37:12)

This proclamation remains controversial among scholars: Is Ezekiel announcing the resurrection of the dead, or is he simply proclaiming a miraculous restoration of Israel through a vivid metaphor?[15] In any case, one easily imagines how this proclamation may have fostered speculation concerning the resurrection of the dead among later readers. And one readily sees the emergence of hope that all Israel will somehow be restored.

An Eschatological Battle

The book of Revelation famously draws upon Ezekiel 38–39 with its invasion by Gog and Gog's destruction. Apart from popular prophecy teachers, who in the twentieth century associated Gog with the Soviet Union, few readers have claimed certainty as to what the book means by "Gog, of the land of Magog." Whereas some scholars have suggested that this oracle was inserted into Ezekiel at a later date, that conclusion presupposes that Ezekiel could not have participated in apocalyptic discourse. (Either the book was too early, or Ezekiel's elite status would have ruled out apocalyptic interests.)[16] But several stylistic and thematic factors demonstrate this section's continuity with the rest of Ezekiel.[17]

The passage envisions an eschatological battle in which Israel faces foes from all directions. Most remarkably, these enemies act not on their own but because God forces them to do so. Thus, the battle that ensues amounts to God's precipitous disposal of Israel's enemies. The battle will be enormous; Israel will devote seven months to burying the corpses of its enemies, and that with help from scavengers. At the war's end, God will restore Israel, gathering its people from all the lands of the earth and promising them eternal protection. In this final age, God's spirit will be poured out upon Israel.

Whereas many modern readers associate apocalyptic literature with the end of the world, the Gog pronouncements offer an instructive alternative. Gog's defeat represents a dramatic divine intervention in history. Under ordinary circumstances no one could imagine how, after dispersal by the Assyrians and then the Babylonians, the entire nation of Israel could ever be gathered back to the land. That vision demands no less than a miracle. Although Israel's salvation marks the end of *a* world, it does not define the end of *the* world. Rather, Ezekiel envisions the *end* of Israel's world of vulnerability and dispersion and the *beginning* of a world of peace and righteousness.

Heavenly Temple, Heavenly Priesthood

When the LORD's hand returns to Ezekiel, he finds himself transported once again–this time to Zion, the high mountain in the south (40:1–2). He meets a man "whose appearance shone like bronze" (40:3) and who carries a cord and a rod for measuring. An extensive tour of the temple follows, complete with detailed measurements (chaps. 40–42). After the temple has been measured, Ezekiel is taken to the east gate, where the book returns full circle: The prophet watches as the glory of the LORD returns to fill the temple (43:1–5). Then the LORD's voice instructs Ezekiel that God will continually dwell within Israel again and commissions Ezekiel to describe the temple to Israel. This description (43:13–46:24) includes the restoration of the Zadokite priests (44:15–31) among other cultic regulations. Finally, Ezekiel sees streams flowing from under the temple to nourish the land (47:1–12) and new boundary definitions for the land.

Modern readers may wonder why Ezekiel devotes such detail to a structure that exists only in the imagination. Notoriously, no technology could build a structure to Ezekiel's specifications![18] So, Ezekiel is not planning for the future in some literal sense. At the same time, his vision of the temple could serve at least two possible functions.

First, it includes some specific information concerning the legacy–and the privileges–of the Zadokite priesthood as well as an ideal distribution of the land. For example, the passage elevates the Zadokites above other priests, who are simply named "Levites."[19] So even by means of an imaginative vision, Ezekiel may promote certain social points of view at the expense of others.

Second, the passage offers a means of *visualizing* an alternative future with Israel restored to the land and God present in its midst. Throughout apocalyptic literature, such specific visualizations–of the temple, the Holy City, the land, heaven and hell, or even orders of battle–likewise enable their audiences to imagine how things might be different than they presently are.

Reading Apocalyptic Discourse in Ezekiel

Having encountered books such as 1 Enoch and Daniel, contemporary readers have the gift of hindsight. In retrospect, we may perceive how Ezekiel shapes the resources of emergent apocalyptic discourse to address the concerns of its own day.

- Later apocalypses may draw upon Ezekiel's vision of the divine throne, but Ezekiel employs it to address the major question of its own day: Israel's God can accompany the people wherever they go.
- The valley of the dry bones may not express a full-blown view of resurrection, but it dramatically portrays the dramatic potential for God's intervention to restore new life to Israel.
- Gog's offensive against Israel may not bring about the end of one world and the advent of the next, but it does reach beyond history to present Israel's vulnerability—and its salvation—in cosmic perspective.
- While we will find echoes of Ezekiel's depiction of the temple in the book of Revelation's New Jerusalem and in the Shepherd of Hermas's tower, Ezekiel empowers its audience to visualize a glory that transcends its present distress.

Ezekiel features several topoi and motifs that we will encounter in later apocalyptic discourse. Vividly symbolic revelations require interpretations by heavenly figures. Solutions to Judah's crises lie beyond ordinary history in God's resurrection of the people and in the battle against Gog and Magog. Visions of an ideal temple and an ideal priesthood overshadow contemporary chaos. And Ezekiel's Son of Man language and resurrection imagery foreshadow prominent themes in later apocalyptic literature.

Zechariah

Interpreters routinely distinguish between Zechariah 1–8 and Zechariah 9–14. Typically, scholars date chapters 1–8, or First Zechariah, to the early Persian period, perhaps as early as 520–518 B.C.E. Chapters 9–14, or Second Zechariah, have proven more difficult to place in time, though possibly as early as about 450 B.C.E.

Significantly, many interpreters judge the messages of First and Second Zechariah to be completely contradictory, claiming that whereas First Zechariah emphasizes the value of the priesthood and temple cult, one finds a much less optimistic evaluation of a temple-centered society in Second Zechariah. In short, while First Zechariah apparently promotes the cult as a both the means to and the measure of Israel's prosperity, Second Zechariah regards the cult with suspicion.

This distinction between Zechariah's two "parts" often impinges upon how scholars reconstruct the origins of apocalyptic discourse. In particular, the *literary form* of the visions in chapters 1–8 resembles that of the classical apocalyptic visions, while the *content* of chapters 9–14 has more in common with later apocalyptic eschatology.[20] The question is, does it make sense to apply the "apocalyptic" label to Zechariah's later section (chaps. 9–14) but not to the visions in the first section (chaps. 1–8)?

If the distinction between Zechariah's two major parts discourages us from reading the book as a literary whole, another factor complicates things even more. In the Hebrew canon, Zechariah does not stand alone as an independent work, but instead it is part of the Book of the Twelve (what Christians often call the Minor Prophets). According to many contemporary reconstructions, the editorial activity that produced Zechariah occurred not simply to this book alone but as part of a larger process involving the entire Book of the Twelve.[21] Our studies require situating books such as Zechariah in a plausible historical framework. Nevertheless, our particular interests also involve examining how apocalyptic discourse shaped and empowered Zechariah's overall message, how apocalyptic topics and forms contributed to the book's apparent persuasive aims. Thus, we will begin by engaging Zechariah inductively and sequentially (from beginning to end), keeping the critical distinctions between First and Second Zechariah in mind but not limiting our conversation to that framework.

Visions of the Word

Zechariah begins with a fairly generic proclamation, calling for the people to recall how Israel had suffered because it had violated its covenant with YHWH and to repent of their wickedness (1:1–6). Quickly, however, the book takes a new turn, as "the word of the LORD" comes to the prophet in a series of eight night visions (1:7–6:8). A second series of oracles begins at 6:8 and continues through 8:23. These latter oracles begin with variations on the formula, "the word of the LORD came..."

The night visions resemble those of the apocalypses in several ways:

a. They employ symbols that either do not occur in the ordinary course of events (such as a flying scroll [5:1–4] or the basket with a leaden cover and a woman inside it [5:5–11]) or symbols that carry allegorical significance (such as the four horns and the four smiths [1:18–21] or the lamp stand and the olive trees [4:1–14]).

b. The visions enable the prophet to see how events transpire in the heavenly realms. For example, he overhears conversations among heavenly beings (1:13; 2:4–5; 3:1–10; 6:1–8).

c. The visions reflect some interest in heavenly beings whose activities impinge upon earthly affairs, including the Satan and the four winds.

d. Some visions include conversations in which the prophet receives instructions or interpretations of what he has seen. As Julia O'Brien notes, "although earlier prophets such as Amos also saw visions, the presence of a divine interpreter for the visions of Zechariah marks an important step on the way to books such as Daniel."[22]

The visions all proclaim hope for the restoration of Jerusalem's glory, with a particular interest in priestly and cultic matters. One vision legitimates the high priest Joshua (3:1–10), while another promises success for Zerubbabel's efforts to rebuild the temple (4:6–10). Moreover, oracles within this collection name Zerubbabel the "Branch," likely indicating some sort of messianic identity associated with Davidic ancestry (3:8; 4:6–10, 14; 6:12–14).

After these eight night visions, Zechariah 6:9–8:23 turns to the "Word of the LORD" oracles. These oracles reflect Zechariah's emphasis on the restoration of Jerusalem. As in Ezekiel, Zechariah envisions the reconstitution of the people, gathering the exiles "from the east country and from the west country" to live in Jerusalem (6:15; 8:7–8). Beyond that, Zechariah's vision also embraces all the nations, who will congregate in Jerusalem to worship its god (8:20–23; cf. 2:11):

> In those days ten men from nations of every language shall take hold of a Jew [or, Judean], grasping his garment and saying, "Let us go with you, for we have heard that God is with you." (8:23)

Oracles of Zion and Its Neighbors

A lot of things change with the transition to Second Zechariah. Most obviously, the literary form changes from "the word of the LORD" to direct oracles from 9:1 through 11:3. Also, a new poetic form occurs at 9:1, in which characteristic Hebrew parallelism dominates. In this common literary pattern, ideas and images receive both emphasis and elaboration by means of repetition with variation. For example,

> Therefore the people wander like sheep;
>   they suffer for lack of a shepherd. (10:2)

While the literary form of First Zechariah often resembled that of the classical apocalypses, First Zechariah's content was more mundane, involving the restoration of Zion. Second Zechariah's literary form may be more traditional, but its content is more strongly eschatological, envisioning YHWH's direct and decisive intervention that transcends ordinary historical possibilities.

For example, Zechariah 9:1–11:3 features oracles of God's judgments against Israel's neighbors to the north and of restoration for Zion. YHWH appears as the Divine Warrior who "encamps" (9:8) against the enemy and whose arrow resembles lightning (9:14). The LORD promises to make Judah strong in battle. All of these—judgment against the enemies, the Divine Warrior, and Judah's strength—reflect traditional prophetic motifs. Yet the LORD also proclaims the reconstitution of the scattered people of Ephraim, that is, of all Israel (10:7–12). This reflects a thoroughly eschatological vision, as the former Israel had been destroyed forever.

Chapters 9–11 also direct invective against Judah's "shepherds" and "leaders" (10:3). Thus, while earlier sections of Zechariah portray Zion's leaders in a positive light, these oracles do not. Shepherd imagery takes a new twist at Zechariah 11:4–17. Notoriously tortured,[23] the logic of the passage identifies the prophet as "shepherd of the flock doomed to slaughter" (11:4). Taking the two staffs of Favor and Unity, Zechariah tends the sheep, only to eliminate three other shepherds (whose identities are lost to us) and eventually to break both staffs, indicating the chasm that alienates Zion from blessing. For now God raises up a shepherd whose aims are exploitation and death. As David L. Petersen writes, "Yahweh cedes power to malevolent human rulers."[24]

"That Day"

Zechariah 12–14 turns to more direct eschatological discourse. Like Ezekiel 38–39, it imagines the nations of the earth coming against Jerusalem. This eschatological conflict, or "that day," will lead to a Judean victory. Even the feeblest among the Judeans will fight as David did (12:8). The victory, however, follows devastation for Zion: "The city shall be taken and the houses looted and the women raped." While its enemies carry half of the population into exile, the other half find themselves cut off from the city (14:2). Only at that point does God intervene to deliver Zion. YHWH's appearance applies the full intensity of apocalyptic imagery. God stands on the Mount of Olives, which splits in two. The people flee through the new chasm. The heavenly beings accompany God's arrival. Cold and darkness disappear, and living waters flow from the Holy City. All these signs portend God's arrival as king (14:4–9). Having faced a hideous plague at God's hand, the enemies who survive eventually acknowledge Zion's God. They visit Jerusalem once a year to worship (14:16–19), even if unwillingly. Thus, holiness pervades even the most mundane items, such as cooking pots (14:20–21).

Why does Zechariah turn to such dramatic and even bizarre imagery at this point? And why must Zion suffer such great tribulation before its deliverance? Sure answers to such pointed questions remain elusive, if not impossible, yet we might consider Zechariah's eschatological scenario more along the lines of poetry than of futuristic prediction.

Zechariah 12–14, at least, presses a far less optimistic view of social conditions than does First Zechariah. Jerusalem's salvation requires no less than a dramatic and sudden divine intervention. For instance, as in the days of Moses and Joshua, the people play no role in attaining their own victory. All action belongs to God. Perhaps this vision reflects a profound sense of Zion's powerlessness, an acknowledgment that internal and external forces have rendered it incapable of caring for itself. In the ordinary flow of history, one expects such societies to suffer the violence and degradation that Zechariah depicts. However, YHWH's faithfulness to Zion cannot allow the city to face total dissolution again. Zechariah's oracles transform the logic of Zion's vulnerability and God's faithfulness into a vivid series of images.

Reading Apocalyptic Discourse in Zechariah

No doubt, the editorial patches in Zechariah's fabric are easily spotted. First Zechariah demonstrates a positive view of the temple leadership, while Second Zechariah faults the shepherds for their faulty guidance. While First Zechariah employs recognizably apocalyptic literary motifs, Second Zechariah's content reflects a more distinctively apocalyptic eschatology. Moreover, neither First nor Second Zechariah demonstrates smooth literary unity in its own right. The esoteric visions of chapters 1–6 don't blend easily with the more traditional prophetic material of chapters 7 and 8. Both clash dramatically with the poetic parallelism we encounter in chapter 9. In Zechariah 11:4–14:21 a coherent pattern eludes our inspection. Moreover, divergent points of view regarding Zion's future and its leaders call attention to these literary seams. Are things getting better or worse? Ought the leaders be trusted?

Nevertheless, emerging apocalyptic discourse unites the book. A fundamental concern for Zion's salvation extends throughout every section of the book. For example, the Divine Warrior oracles of Zechariah 9:1–11:3 share with the "that day" passages in chapters 12–14 a fundamental sense that Zion's ultimate welfare depends on God. The visions of Zechariah 1–6 anticipate a resplendent new temple in Zion, with holy leaders and holy people, thus sharing with chapter 14 the vision of Zion's glory. Admittedly, the optimism of First Zechariah, according to which God works through present historical circumstances and identifiable figures to bring Zion's new age, is entirely absent in Second Zechariah. Transcending these contrasts, however, we see in Zechariah the ability of apocalyptic discourse to adapt over time. With respect to a single given concern–Jerusalem's salvation–circumstances change from the priestly optimism of First Zechariah to Second Zechariah's worthless shepherd. Yet through the flexibility of emerging apocalyptic discourse, Zechariah continually affirms a hope for the restoration of peace and holiness in Zion.

Joel

The little book of Joel becomes a big deal in early Christian literature, precisely because of one passage with strong apocalyptic resonances:

Then afterward
　I will pour out my spirit on all flesh;

> your sons and your daughters shall prophesy,
>> your old men shall dream dreams,
>> and your young men shall see visions.
> Even on the male and female slaves,
>> in those days, I will pour out my spirit.

> I will show portents in the heavens and on the earth, blood and
> fire and columns of smoke. The sun shall be turned to darkness,
> and the moon to blood, before the great and terrible day of the
> LORD comes. Then everyone who calls on the name of the LORD
> shall be saved; for in Mount Zion and in Jerusalem there shall be
> those who escape, as the LORD has said, and among the survivors
> shall be those whom the LORD calls. (2:28–32)

Early Christian interpreters found two major uses for this passage. First,
it proclaimed an eschatological age marked by prophetic and visionary
activity. In the book of Acts, for example, Peter recites part of the passage
to interpret the manifestations of the Spirit at Pentecost (2:16–21). Likewise,
Paul, who testifies to prophetic activity within the churches, interprets such
dramatic signs of the Spirit among his congregations as demonstrations of
their authentic religious experience (e.g., 1 Cor. 2:4–5; 4:20; Gal. 3:2; 1
Thess. 1:5). Second, while Joel's imagery of heavenly portents reflects a
stock eschatological motif (cf. Isa 13:10; 24:4; Ezek. 32:7–8), Jesus'
apocalyptic discourses (Mk. 13:24–25; Mt. 24:29; Lk. 21:25) and the book
of Revelation employ this imagery as well.[25]

Reading Joel as a Whole

As with Ezekiel and Zechariah, scholars have emphasized Joel's
apparent internal divisions. As Ronald K. Simkins puts it, "The first part
[1:1–2:27] focuses on a natural catastrophe that is presently devastating
Judah, whereas the second [2:28–3:21] deals with Yahweh's future judgment
on the foreign peoples who have oppressed the people of Judah."[26] Indeed,
the book's first lines evoke a sense of wonder concerning the effects of a
locust swarm that has devastated local agriculture:

> Has such a thing happened in your days,
>> or in the days of your ancestors? (1:2)

In a calamity that people will describe to their children and grandchildren
(1:3), one wave of locusts after another has left the land desolate.

> What the cutting locust left,
>> the swarming locust has eaten.
> What the swarming locust left,
>> the hopping locust has eaten,

and what the hopping locust left,
>   the destroying locust has eaten. (1:4)

Such a plague posed an absolute threat for an agrarian society. Such times often provoke the sort of religious reflection we find in Joel. The prophet interprets the plague as a sign that "the day of the LORD is near" (1:15; 2:1). He calls for heightened religious observances, including fasting, self-abasement, and collective prayer (1:13–14). More to the point, he exhorts the people toward repentance (2:12–17), in hopes that YHWH will return blessing to the land. Clearly, Joel sees the calamity as a sign of judgment, a common reaction, and he hopes that religious renewal will forestall God's wrath.

At Joel 2:18, however, the book's tone changes dramatically. Up to this point Joel has looked ahead, hoping that the people's repentance would soften God's hand and bring an end to their suffering. But here (2:18–27), the prophet begins to narrate Zion's salvation as an accomplished fact. God has extended mercy to the people, and God is delivering necessities such as "grain, wine, and oil" (2:19), various fruits (2:22), and even rain (2:23). "You shall eat in plenty," God promises (2:26), as the plague has run its course. In this section Joel encourages its audience to move from tenuous hope to assured certainty.

The shift in perspective represented by Joel 2:18–27 takes another turn at 2:28. From this point the book looks ahead to "afterward" (2:28) and "those days [and] that time" (3:1) when Judah and Jerusalem find restoration. Joel clearly has moved into the language of eschatology at this point, for here we find several characteristic motifs of apocalyptic eschatology:

a. an age of the spirit, marked by prophecy and visions
b. cosmic disorder, followed by auspicious signs in the natural order
c. judgment against the nations, accompanied by war
d. an alternative future, featuring a new age of safety and holiness for Zion

In short, the prophet's message has transcended the immediate crisis brought by the locusts. It proclaims hope that YHWH's faithfulness and compassion will bring not only an end to the plague but will also bring Zion's final salvation.

Reading Joel

By emphasizing what we might call Joel's point of view with respect to the question of Zion's salvation, we have identified three major movements: (1) an examination of the present calamity, with hope for future deliverance (1:1–2:17); (2) assurance that God's salvation will emerge from pity for the people (2:18–27); and (3) eschatological confidence in Jerusalem's final salvation (2:28–3:21). Remarkably, these movements create an overall literary impression that transcends the apparent division (at Joel 2:28) emphasized by many commentators, for the shift from hope to assurance occurs *before* the more apocalyptically oriented material at 2:28. Instead, such confidence begins in 2:18–27. The eschatological blessings that follow simply complete the book's overall trajectory in a way that would be familiar to readers of Daniel, the Apocalypse of Weeks, or the Animal Apocalypse. Joel interprets the present crisis as the eschatological tribulation. In that moment the prophet cries out for repentance, which (he is certain) will bring about Zion's eschatological blessings.

Moreover, apocalyptic interests combine with priestly interests to further unify the book.[27] From the outset, Joel interprets the locust swarms as an eschatological crisis, a sign that "the day of the LORD" is at hand. Never before, and never again, could there be such a force (2:2). Like the eschatological invaders of chapter 3, the book portrays the swarm of locusts as an invading horde as well:

> Like warriors they charge,
> like soldiers they scale the wall. (2:7; cf. 2:1–10)

In reply to both forces, the locusts and the military invaders, YWHW intervenes as the Divine Warrior (2:11; 3:16–17). At the same time, Joel reflects a priestly concern for the temple cult. Both foes—the locusts and the invaders—threaten not only the people's safety but also the performance of offerings and sacrifices. If the grain and wine harvests fail, then the grain and drink offerings are also cut off (1:9–10). Moreover, the people's repentance takes the form of corporate worship led by the priests (1:13–14; 2:15–17).[28] When God defeats the nations, then the people will know that God dwells on the holy mountain and that Jerusalem is holy (3:17).

These signs of unity do not rule out the likelihood that Joel is a composite work. Yet they also reveal two things about Joel and its relationship to emerging apocalyptic discourse.

First, no layer of Joel is free from eschatological reflection. The book takes the locust plague as a sign of eschatological crisis. As apocalyptic discourse develops, we will observe a tendency to interpret a current challenge as marking the culmination of history.[29]

Second, Joel reveals how apocalyptic discourse can adapt texts and even recollections of history to address continuing concerns in the life of a people. Whoever brought Joel to its present form worked hard to foster a sense of literary movement and unity. In doing so, they created a work that models how apocalyptic discourse can transform a present crisis into an opportunity for repentance. They crafted the familiar strategy by which apocalyptic topics at once challenge their audiences to renewed faithfulness and at the same time proclaim comfort and assurance.

Isaiah 24–27

The book of Isaiah stands first among the literary prophets of the Bible. Perhaps its very length influenced this location, but Isaiah also has exerted the greatest influence on the Bible's readers, perhaps especially for Christians.[30] Evidently, the book also provoked serious reflection even during its own period of composition, for people kept adding to it over the centuries. According to most scholars, First Isaiah (chaps. 1–39) has its roots in the eighth century B.C.E.; Second Isaiah (chaps. 40–55), in the sixth century; and Third Isaiah (chaps. 56–66), perhaps in the fifth.

Yet within First Isaiah, chapters 24–27, often called the "Isaiah Apocalypse," seem to come from another world. These chapters include oracles concerning the devastation of the entire earth, judgment against heavenly beings, Zion's eschatological banquet, combat against mythological monsters, and Israel's ultimate salvation. In short, we find the sort of material one expects to find, not in an eighth-century B.C.E. prophetic book, but in apocalyptic literature from much later. Thus, Paul D. Hanson identifies these chapters as an example of "early apocalyptic" literature, as opposed to the "proto-apocalyptic literature" we have been discussing.[31] Almost all scholars agree that these chapters represent a later addition to the larger book, though proposed dates for them range from the eighth to the second centuries B.C.E.[32]

Isaiah's Influence in Apocalyptic Discourse

Before we proceed to the so-called Isaiah Apocalypse, we should note two features of Isaiah as a whole. Isaiah's throne vision (6:1–13) clearly inspired later apocalyptic writers. Isaiah reports that "I saw the Lord" seated on a throne in the heavenly temple. He hears two heavenly voices, that of a seraph, who cleanses the prophet from impurity, and that of God, who commissions him to proclaim a message that the people will fail to comprehend. Several aspects of this vision resonate in later apocalyptic literature.

First, many apocalypses depict God's heavenly throne, often in the highest of a series of heavens. Ordinarily, the visionary does not see the divine person, but quite often they do hear God's voice.

Second, the notion that a heavenly temple corresponds to the Jerusalem Temple also appears in later apocalyptic discourse. (The New Testament epistle to the Hebrews offers one prominent example.)

Third, conversations with heavenly beings are so prominent among the apocalypses that the genre's standard definition includes "a revelation mediated by an otherworldly being to a human recipient."[33]

Fourth, many apocalypses include commissions for the visionary to call the people to repentance. This motif relates to a fifth: Isaiah expects his message to fail, a pessimistic outlook on the immediate future that one finds throughout apocalyptic discourse. Indeed, Isaiah 6:9–13 presents a far more pessimistic view of the people's response than do many apocalypses.

Another way in which the book of Isaiah has influenced apocalyptic discourse involves its hope for Jerusalem. In particular, Second and Third Isaiah emphasize how salvation centers around the holy mountain. For example, the LORD's comfort for Zion (51:3) is accompanied by cosmic portents:

> Lift up your eyes to the heavens,
>> and look at the earth beneath;
> for the heavens will vanish like smoke,
>> the earth will wear out like a garment,
>> and those who live on it will die like gnats;
> but my salvation will be forever,
>> and my deliverance will never be ended. (51:6)

Likewise, Third Isaiah characterizes Zion's new birth through the imagery of labor pains–another stock motif of apocalyptic discourse. Who, the prophet asks, ever saw a nation emerge "in one day" (66:6–9)? In the end, this new Zion becomes the center of the earth's worship. While the corpses of those who resisted God present a continuing witness to divine judgment (66:24), a new day emerges:

> For as the new heavens and the new earth,
>> which I will make,
> shall remain before me, says the LORD;
>> so shall your descendants and your name remain.
> From new moon to new moon,
>> and from sabbath to sabbath,
> all flesh shall come to worship before me,
> says the LORD. (66:22–23)

Apocalyptic Motifs in the "Isaiah Apocalypse"

In its present form Isaiah 24–27 follows, and perhaps concludes, Isaiah's oracles against the nations of chapters 12–23.[34] Yet both First Isaiah as a whole and the Isaiah Apocalypse have emerged from complicated compositional histories, so that neither the larger work nor this smaller section presents a continuous flow of ideas or perspectives.

The larger current of First Isaiah begins with a section emphasizing Isaiah's prophetic call and ministry, with a message of judgment against Israel, the Northern Kingdom, accompanied by oracles of Israel's future restoration (chaps. 1–12). Next come a series of oracles against Israel's neighbors (chaps. 12–23), the Isaiah Apocalypse (chaps. 24–27), oracles of woe for Israel, Judah, Assyria, and Egypt (chaps. 28–31), another series of oracles of judgment and redemption (chaps. 32–35), and finally legends concerning Isaiah's activities during and after the Assyrian siege of Jerusalem (chaps. 36–39). Thus, First Isaiah itself hardly presents a unified focus or ideological point of view.[35]

Yet contemporary readers also struggle to find unity even within chapters 24–27. These chapters move from oracles of judgment against the earth and even against rebellious heavenly beings to praise for God's salvation, from a vision of God's banquet for all peoples to judgment against the Moabites, and from Judah's song celebrating the Holy City to the vacillation between Zion's suffering and the assurance of its salvation. Many find themselves disoriented by the jostling point of view.[36]

Within these chapters, however, we find a variety of motifs that emerge frequently in later apocalyptic discourse. The section begins with a proclamation of *cosmic destruction*, as God is about to lay waste to the earth, twisting its very surface (24:1; cf. 24:1–23). This eschatological crisis extends even to the *judgment of heavenly beings*, in which the imprisonment and punishment of the "host of heaven" corresponds both to that of the "kings of the earth" and to the debasement of astral bodies such as the sun and the moon (24:21–23). Even the chaos monsters, Leviathan and the Dragon, meet their end (27:1). Yet the vision of Zion's salvation also transcends the ordinary, for it involves not only a rich *banquet* for all peoples (25:6), but also a *final end to death and suffering* (25:7–8; cf. 26:19). Thus, in its content and conceptualization the Isaiah Apocalypse unmistakably anticipates the development of similar motifs in a wide range of apocalyptic literature.

Moreover, while the Isaiah Apocalypse may jump from one image or point of view to another, perhaps in a larger sense it does promote a consistent perspective. As Donald C. Polaski points out, the effect of the whole precludes any possibility for life outside Zion, while it attributes to the Holy City both divine protection and eternal provision. Isaiah 24–27 erases all other places, people, and perspectives as unreal possibilities. Outside Zion lie only filth (25:10) and death (26:14). Zion, however, embodies the center of God's reign, a site of universal healing and pilgrimage, and a safe destiny for the righteous.[37]

Concluding Observations

Classical apocalypses such as 1 Enoch and Daniel testify to the emergence of a new literary form, the apocalypse. Yet a host of basic topics, interests, images, ideas, and literary devices that eventually come to define the apocalypses already have their antecedents in biblical prophetic literature. Their presence poses several significant implications.

First, apocalyptic discourse did not simply break onto the scene of Judean religion in a single moment. Rather, apocalyptic discourse emerged from a much richer variety of ancient discourses, among which biblical prophecy represents one important example. Those who bred and cultivated apocalyptic discourse, then, participated in a verdant cultural context. Their work represents not a decisive break with earlier forms of religious engagement, nor would it have been foreign to their neighbors; rather, apocalyptic discourse posed one viable way for imagining God's activity in the world among others.

Second, we may expect to find apocalyptic discourse beyond the classical apocalypses. Although this point may seem obvious, scholars have tended to elevate the classical apocalypses above other types of apocalyptic literature, so that understandings of concepts such as "apocalyptic eschatology" and "apocalypticism" depend too strongly on those "pure" examples of apocalyptic thought. Apocalypses such as 1 Enoch and Daniel are neither the source nor the central defining point of apocalyptic discourse. Instead, we must conclude that they embody possible concrescences that develop out of a larger flow of discursive resources.

Third, the continual conversation between apocalyptic literatures, biblical books, and other texts merits our continuing attention. Biblical scholars today invoke a technical concept, *intertextuality,* in two somewhat contradictory ways. Some scholars apply intertextuality only to cases in which one literary text shows demonstrable dependence on other texts. This may appear through outright citation or explicit allusion, or through more subtle forms of interaction. Other readers assume a much more diffuse notion of intertextual engagement, involving "the larger cultural webs in which texts are intertwined, and in which we read them."[38] This second model appreciates the impossibility of tracing the cultural antecedents of given cultural phenomena such as the literary texts we are studying or their effects. Thus, while many apocalyptic texts demonstrate clear connections with earlier biblical and extrabiblical books, in other cases the links may forever evade controlled comparisons. While some apocalyptic texts apparently privilege the Bible and seek to reinterpret or expand upon biblical texts, we do well to recall how fluid apocalyptic discourses must have been in ancient Jewish and Christian circles.

Fourth, while Zion represents the symbolic center of the prophetic texts we have been studying in this chapter, their theological innovations, literary modes, and persuasive functions differ. Zechariah 1–6 presents dramatic symbolic visions that require interpretation, whereas Joel and Isaiah 24–27 do not. Ezekiel and Isaiah present visions of the divine throne, but Zechariah and Joel do not. Isaiah 24–27 proclaims the destruction of Israel's enemies directly; Ezekiel portrays a mythological battle between the armies of God and God's enemies; and Joel draws on a catastrophic locust plague to characterize the enemies. One could easily multiply these examples, but the fundamental point is clear: From its earliest stages, apocalyptic discourse emerged as a flexible resource for imagining God, the world, and the holy people. It could adapt itself to a variety of circumstances, and it could serve diverse, sometimes even conflicting, ends.

For Further Reading

Blenkinsopp, Joseph. *A History of Prophecy in Israel*. Rev. ed. Louisville: Westminster John Knox Press, 1996.

Cook, Stephen L. *Prophecy and Apocalypticism: The Postexilic Social Setting*. Minneapolis: Fortress Press, 1995.

Darr, Katheryn Pfisterer. "The Book of Ezekiel" *NIB*, 6.1073–1607.

Hanson, Paul D. *The Dawn of Apocalyptic: The Historical and Sociological Roots of Jewish Apocalyptic Eschatology*. Rev. ed. Philadelphia: Fortress Press, 1979.

O'Brien, Julia. *Nahum, Habakkuk, Zephaniah, Haggai, Zechariah, Malachi*. Abingdon Old Testament Commentaries. Nashville: Abingdon Press, 2004.

Tigchelaar, Eibert J. C. *Prophets of Old and the Day of the End: Zechariah, the Book of the Watchers, and Apocalyptic*. OtSt 35. Leiden: Brill, 1996.

CHAPTER 3

Interpreting the Times

Jewish Apocalyptic Discourse beyond the Apocalypses

While Daniel and 1 Enoch represent our earliest expressions of "full-blown" apocalyptic discourse, apocalyptic topics figure prominently in a wide variety of early Jewish literature. We find these topics in diverse literary forms and collections, including retellings of biblical stories (such as Jubilees), additional legends concerning biblical figures (such as Testaments of the Twelve Patriarchs and Testament of Moses), expressions of community life and worship (as we see in many of the Dead Sea Scrolls), and oracular literature (such as the Sibylline Oracles). We could add to this list indefinitely, but these five bodies of literature stand out for the degree to which they participate in apocalyptic discourse. At the same time, these texts employ apocalyptic discourse to address very different concerns and to diverse persuasive ends.

Jubilees

Date

Manuscript evidence from Qumran suggests a date in the mid-second century B.C.E.

Languages and Texts

Western readers have had access to Jubilees in Ethiopic since the mid-nineteenth century, with manuscripts in Latin, Syriac, and Greek appearing later. However, at least fifteen Hebrew fragments of Jubilees were discovered at Qumran, indicating that Jubilees was probably composed in Hebrew.[1]

Selectively and creatively, the Book of Jubilees retells the biblical story from creation through the commandment concerning the Sabbath, corresponding to biblical material from Genesis 1 to Exodus 24. It divides the history it narrates into fifty successive forty-nine year periods, or jubilees. But Jubilees is not properly a summary, nor is it a condensation or even a creative adaptation of biblical narrative. Rather, in its literary form Jubilees presents itself as a revelation.

When Moses goes up to Mount Sinai after the people of Israel escape slavery, YHWH reveals to him "what (was) in the beginning and what will occur (in the future), the account of the division of all the days of the Law and the testimony" (1:4, *OTP*). Oddly, God commands Moses to write down the revelation (1:26), but then the "angel of the presence" also receives instruction to inscribe it into sacred tablets, from which the angel dictates to Moses (1:27–29).[2] Thus, if Jubilees did not devote so much attention to a straightforward narrative of legends concerning the past, we could easily include it as an apocalypse.

Jubilees apparently carried strong influence in its own day. To this day, Jubilees appears in the canon of the Ethiopian Abyssinian Church. The number of fragments found at Qumran, plus a direct citation in one Qumran document (CD 16:3–4),[3] suggests that Jubilees was highly regarded in that community. One of the Qumran texts, the Temple Scroll (11QTemple), basically picks up the retelling of biblical narrative where Jubilees leaves off. Jubilees shares some traditions with Testaments of the Twelve Patriarchs, and it provides the oldest testimony to several traditions that occur in the New Testament and some later Jewish and Christian literature.[4]

Framework and Functions

By beginning with a prologue and legends concerning the book's origins, Jubilees instructs its audience as to how it should be read. The prologue, which amounts to a long title, introduces "The Account of the Division of Days of the Law" which God had delivered to Moses on the mountain. Although much of Jubilees is devoted to narrative material, this prologue sets forth the book's major concerns, the relationship between calendar and cult. Likewise, the Lord's speech to Moses in 1:1–18 establishes the book's revelatory character.

Not only does God prepare Moses to receive the revelation to follow but the passage also "predicts" Israel's history from Moses' day to Israel's apostasy and fall, and eventually to the people's future restoration. Moses receives his revelation from an angel (1:27–29). Thus, the authority of Jubilees' ongoing emphasis regarding the calendar resides in its identity as a revelatory report.

Throughout the story we encounter editorial strategies and narrative insertions that either add drama to biblical accounts or stress key points.

For example, the narrative begins with the six days of creation and the Sabbath. While Genesis builds its way up to seven days and the teaching concerning the Sabbath (Gen. 2:3), in Jubilees the creation story begins by stating directly that creation took six days, followed by the institution of the Sabbath on the seventh day (2:1). Jubilees' account of the created works begins not with light (Gen. 1:2–5) but with the heavens, the earth, the waters, and the angelic hosts–"seven great works" in all on that first day (Jub. 2:2–3, *OTP*). Then, Jubilees devotes a lengthy discussion to Sabbath observance at the end of the creation story (2:17–33).

George W. E. Nickelsburg has noted that most of Jubilees' narrative insertions perform one of four functions:

1. connect religious festivals with the 364-day solar calendar
2. show the patriarchs of Israel following the Torah in detail (remarkably, given that they precede Moses' reception of the Law)
3. express commands and admonitions through the mouths of the patriarchs (often directed expressly at their sons)
4. provide commentaries as to how to live in observance of the Torah (*halakah*)[5]

These various functions reflect how remarkably fluid the notions of scripture and interpretation were for Jubilees' authors. At one level they assume the authority of the biblical story, expressly appealing to the Torah's binding force. But then again, they feel free to edit that story through creative additions and revisions, as if to render that Torah more specific and more convincing.

Concerns

One might wonder why someone would go to the trouble of retelling a story that already was well told and well received. It is not as if Jubilees sets out to correct the biblical narrative, nor does Jubilees simply adapt or condense it. Rather, Jubilees consistently employs the basic biblical plotline to promote several specific emphases.

CALENDAR AND SABBATH

As we have seen in 1 Enoch's Book of the Watchers and its Astronomical Book, the calendar sometimes provoked substantial concern. (Apparently, the calendar presented a major concern at Qumran as well.) Like 1 Enoch and several Qumran documents, Jubilees promotes the 364-day solar calendar. However, the Jerusalem temple authorities apparently relied upon a luni-solar calendar, which required the insertion of an additional month in three of every nineteen years.[6]

Disagreements concerning the calendar transcended mere speculation. They engaged the fundamental alignment of the people with the sacred order. An incorrect calendar would have implied that the people's sacrifices and observances were also incorrect and perhaps even detrimental. Moreover, if the people disagreed concerning the calendar, then a rift could have spread through the social fabric, as families and groups pursued important observances at different times.[7]

Indeed, Jubilees connects the correct calendar to other cultic concerns, indicating the significant stakes in this debate. Moreover, it traces the correct calendar beyond Moses to the patriarchal age. Whereas the festivals had been celebrated correctly in the heavenly realms before Moses, Moses himself institutes their proper observance among mortals. An essential part of his faithful observance involves the 364-day solar calendar, which provides regular intervals of thirteen weeks between the four major festivals. This sequence reflects the solar calendar's regularity; it establishes exactly fifty-two weeks, so that festivals and Sabbaths may occur on precisely the same days year after year (cf. Jub. 6:17–38). As Jubilees insists,

> if they are transgressed, and they do not observe them according to his commandment, then they will corrupt all of their (fixed) times, and the years will be moved from within this (order), and they will transgress their ordinances. (6:33, *OTP*)

Jubilees enhances its direct teaching concerning days, months, years, and the calendar through its constant references to periods of time, especially in measures of jubilees.

SACRIFICES AND OTHER OBSERVANCES

Closely tied to the correct calendar is the proper observance of sacrifices, festivals, and other rites. Together these interests reflect a strong cultic or priestly orientation. The very creation of the sun enables "days, sabbaths, months, feast (days), years, sabbaths of years, jubilees, and…all of the (appointed) times of the years" (2:9, *OTP*). Conversely, improprieties concerning the proper calendar and observances define Israel's apostasy (1:10–14), a failure that leads to idolatry.

Jubilees assigns permanence to cultic matters. Long before Moses, even Abraham observes tithes (13:25–27), instructs his son Isaac how to perform sacrifices (21:5–26), and observes annual festivals (22:1–2). This pattern of pre-Moses observance continues throughout Jubilees, to the degree that God ordains even the Levitical priesthood during the patriarchal age (30:18–20). Like the calendrical controversies, this editorial insertion engages active debates from the second century B.C.E. concerning the legitimacy of the priesthood. For that matter, Levi and Judah, the patriarchs whose legacies continue in early Judaism, receive Isaac's special blessing (31:9–20), and Levi begins his priestly activities during his father Jacob's life (32:3–9). Jubilees' pre-Moses Torah observance is somewhat tempered, however, by its recognition that the Law had yet to be delivered during the patriarchal age. Thus, when Reuben has intercourse with Jacob's concubine Bilhah, the two escape execution because the Law had not yet been revealed (33:15–16).

JUDGMENT AND THE FUTURE AGE

Like the Book of the Watchers, Jubilees traces human sin to those angels whose intercourse with mortal women brought disorder upon the earth. This disorder leads to judgment as the earth's fitting and final end (4:23; 5:10). And yet the fall is not absolute. Rather than insisting on original sin, Jubilees claims that God has instilled in all created beings "a new and righteous nature so that they might not sin in all their nature forever" (5:12, *OTP*). Thus, Jubilees rejects an outright tragic determinism that portrays human beings as entirely trapped in sin. Instead, the book insists that judgment depends on one's actual choices to obey or disobey God's ways (5:13–16).

Despite this open-ended anthropology, or understanding of humankind, Jubilees espouses a negative view of the present, accompanied by hope for a redeemed future. Jubilees relates that even "if a man will live a jubilee and a half [seventy-three or seventy-four years], they will say about him, 'He prolonged his life, but the majority of his days were suffering and anxiety and affliction'" (23:12, *OTP*). Moreover, Jubilees anticipates an evil generation that pollutes the most holy place and brings upon itself a divine plague (23:14–25), to be followed by a return to faithfulness and a new age of blessing (23:26–31). As James C. VanderKam observes, Jubilees hopes for a continuing life for the righteous, who will experience joy forever (23:30). "Their bones will rest in the earth," while "their spirits will increase joy" (23:31, *OTP*).[8] That new age of blessing, even a new creation, marks Jubilees' eschatological hope. As God says, when the people turn to God,

> with all my heart and with all my soul I shall transplant them as a righteous plant. And they will be a blessing and not a curse. And they will be the head and not the tail. And I shall build my sanctuary in their midst, and I shall dwell with them. (1:16–17, *OTP*)

HEAVENLY BEINGS

Even more than its eschatology of judgment and restoration, perhaps Jubilees' intense interest in heavenly beings most strongly identifies it among contemporary apocalyptic literature. Not only does Jubilees relate the legend of the Watchers who mate with mortal women, but it also notes how some of them performed righteousness while others wrought chaos (cf. 4:15, 21–22).

Jubilees assigns two names to the evil Watchers' chief, even in a single passage (10:7–13): The name Mastema occurs more frequently than does Satan. Mastema actively plots to test Abraham, a plot that results in Mastema's shame when Abraham actually prepares to offer his son Isaac (17:15–18:13). Even then, Mastema poses a continuing threat to the faithful (19:28; 48:9), though in the blessed age "there will be no Satan and no evil (one)" (23:29, *OTP*). Although Mastema remains a threat, his days are numbered. These beliefs anticipate the future portrayal of Satan, who rules the demons until his defeat in the last days.

In Jubilees angels can be friends or foes. Circumcision, which distinguishes Israel from its neighbors, also reflects Israel's distinctive relationship to the angels. God assigns angels to Gentile nations, but those angels merely provide the occasion for misguided worship, or idolatry. Other angels and spirits guard Israel from such dangers (15:27–32). So although Jubilees may not exhibit as much interest in naming each of the prominent angels and their functions, it clearly reflects an interest in heavenly beings, their past and current activities, and their roles in shaping the fates of mortals.

IDENTITY, IDOLATRY, AND GENTILES

Like other Jewish traditions concerning Abraham, Jubilees emphasizes the idolatrous culture of his childhood and his discovery of faith in one God (11:3–5, 16–17; 12:1–21; 21:3–5).[9] As Israel's preeminent ancestor, Abraham defines Jewish identity by means of contrast with other population groups. Jubilees insists on rigid ethnic boundaries, so much so that it prescribes execution by stoning for any man who seeks to give his daughter in marriage to a Gentile (30:7–17). Jubilees further envisions a period in which Israel will rule over all the nations (31:18–20; 32:16–19).

All of these themes–identity, idolatry, and Gentiles–mutually reinforce one another. Thus, Jubilees' repeated admonitions concerning idolatry also define ethnic purity. This pattern emerges clearly when Abraham blesses Jacob, commanding him, "Separate yourself from the gentiles, and do not eat with them, and do not perform deeds like theirs. And do not become associates of theirs" (22:16, *OTP*). After all, the Gentiles offer sacrifices to the dead and worship demons; their judgment is so impaired that they proclaim trees as gods and stones as savior. So dangerous is their company, Abraham warns that to marry a Canaanite would bring calamity. Such idolatrous ones are hated by God and doomed to Sheol, the pit of death (22:16–23).

Two mysterious allusions to the "Kittim" occur in Jubilees. We find this term in a variety of biblical and extrabiblical texts, including some of the Dead Sea Scrolls. It usually refers to peoples who live across the sea, that is, the Mediterranean. In particular, the Kittim come to indicate the Mediterranean powers that threaten Judean autonomy, the Greek and Roman empires. Jubilees 24:28–29 curses the Philistines with destruction from the Kittim, whereas 37:9–10 includes the Kittim among the mercenaries Esau hires in preparation for battle against Jacob. So although the references to the Kittim play only a minor role in Jubilees, their presence contributes to the book's larger sense of ethnic identity and perhaps even vulnerability. Indeed, while it is possible that Jubilees emphasizes its warnings against idolatry and assimilation merely because these represent distinctive Jewish values, it is even more likely that cultural accommodation represents a live issue among those who first produced and read the book.

SEXUAL ETHICS

Jubilees stands among our earliest witnesses to sexual asceticism in Jewish literature. The Hebrew Scriptures generally promote both sexual pleasure and procreation. By the emergence of the common era, however, we find a much less optimistic view of human sexual expression in many texts, including the early Christian gospels and letters of Paul.[10] Jubilees promotes this more restrictive view, with an emphasis upon celibacy. For example, when Rebecca instructs Jacob regarding finding a wife, Jacob remarks, "Behold, O mother, I am nine weeks of [i.e., sixty-three] years old. And I have not known or touched or been betrothed to any woman" (25:4, *OTP*). He also recalls his father Abraham's instruction "regarding lust and fornication" (25:7, *OTP*).

Likewise, Moses relates instruction concerning the dangers of fornication, which represents the greatest sin that threatens Israel's safety (33:18–20). Such concern regarding sexual boundaries naturally reinforces Jubilees' interest in ethnic boundaries in general, as it restricts sexual activity to narrowly prescribed relationships, thus addressing perceived risks to Judean ethnic–and therefore religious–purity.

Reading Jubilees

Jubilees adapts the biblical narrative to advance two major concerns. The first, which is relatively obvious, involves the sacred calendar and other cultic matters. In this sense, Jubilees promotes getting things right so that the people may align themselves with the sacred order. Thus, Jubilees inserts allusions to sacred time, to the observance of Torah even before its revelation, and to the preeminence of Levi and Judah to construct this larger sacred framework.

The second concern involves the identity and faithfulness of the people. Contemporary readers, recovering from centuries of genocide, may find this program objectionable. The prospect of judgment, combined with an emphasis on ethnic and sexual boundaries, emphasizes purity above inclusion. Yet Jubilees emerged not from an imperial power but from a group among whom some believed their very identity was at stake. Increasing Greek cultural influence (i.e., Hellenization), combined with innovations (some would call them idolatrous) in the Jerusalem cult had created a defining moment in the development of Judaism. With the land of Israel no longer representing a fulfillment of God's promises to Abraham, Jubilees turns to fulfillment through Abraham's descendants, the people of Israel.[11] Jubilees responds by designing boundaries to protect Judean culture and identity. This cultural pressure created an impossible dilemma, a tension between two competing sets of values: protection of a small regional culture versus toleration and openness within that culture. Jubilees chooses the first option at the expense of the second.

The body of Jubilees may not read like an apocalypse, but the book's logic depends on apocalyptic literary conventions. With the biblical narrative already a known quantity, how does one construct an authoritative retelling of that story that addresses one's contemporary concerns? Jubilees responds to this dilemma by presenting itself as a revelation that spans from history's beginning and even into the future. Jubilees also employs the topic of the heavenly intermediary who dictates its contents to Moses. Furthermore, the book's persistent interest in heavenly beings and its hope for a new age of salvation lend additional weight to its instruction concerning ethnic, social, and sexual boundaries.

Testaments of the Twelve Patriarchs

Date

In its current form, Testaments of the Twelve Patriarchs includes Christian material. This requires a date in the first or second century C.E. Other evidence, including possibly parallel passages in Qumran manuscripts, suggests an earlier Jewish layer that may be as old as the second century B.C.E.[12] In my view, the elevated status of Levi and Judah likely reflects an early Jewish layer, though clear Christian editorial activity has been at work.

Languages and Texts

The oldest witnesses to the Testaments are in Greek, though Armenian, Slavonic, Serbian, and Latin manuscripts, as well as Hebrew and Aramaic fragments, are also known. Most scholars believe the Greek text to be original, as it depends upon the LXX, but speculation remains as to the possibility of an earlier Hebrew or Aramaic foundation.[13]

Note Regarding Citation

For the purposes of citation, each of the Testaments is treated as a single work, beginning with its own chapter 1.

The Testaments of the Twelve Patriarchs consist precisely of what the name indicates, final addresses by each of Jacob's sons to his own descendants. Though the Testaments of Levi and Judah are significantly longer than the others, the Testaments share a common structure and common interests:

a. an introduction
b. narratives concerning the patriarch's life
c. ethical exhortation, usually tied to the narrative
d. predictions of the future, usually involving a cycle of apostasy, punishment, and renewal

    e. a brief second exhortation

    f. the patriarch's death and burial[14]

Scholars continue to debate the Testaments' origins. Everyone agrees that they include Christian material. A messiah receives the Spirit as the heavens open upon him (T. Jud. 24:1–2; cf. Mt. 3:16; Mk. 1:10), and a virgin from Judah gives birth to an unblemished lamb (T. Jos. 19:8).[15] In addition, we also find significant points of contact between the Testaments and the New Testament epistle of James.[16] But how does one account for this Christian material in the midst of traditional Jewish traditions? Some would argue that the Testaments were composed by Jewish authors and then edited by Christians; others maintain that the Testaments originated in a Christian context.[17]

The Testament of Levi

While eschatological material occurs in all twelve Testaments, only the Testament of Levi represents a full literary apocalypse. With the help of an angelic interpreter, Levi receives a vision, complete with an open heaven and a tour of the seven heavens (chaps. 2–5). A second vision testifies to Levi's priestly anointing (chap. 8). Smaller mini-apocalypses also occur in Testament of Naphtali 5–6 and Testament of Joseph 19, both of which "predict" the history of the twelve tribes.

A unique introduction reveals the Testament of Levi's eschatological focus. The testament involves all that his sons would do and experience "until the day of judgment" (1:1, *OTP*). Though Levi enjoys good health, it is "revealed" to him that his own death is approaching (1:1–2). Just as Levi begins the narrative of his own life, a sharp interruption breaks in, with familiar apocalyptic features. Levi, having received a "spirit of understanding" (2:3, *OTP*), grieves and prays concerning sinful humanity. As he falls into sleep, he suddenly finds himself on a high mountain with an angel calling him up into the heavens.

This first vision immediately certifies Levi's own visionary authority. The angel promises that Levi will "stand near the Lord" and that he will be God's priest and will disclose God's mysteries to mortals. While Levi will reveal Israel's future redeemer, he and Judah will reveal God to mortals (2:1–12). The vision features Levi's tour of the heavens, which is somewhat irregular, especially given a complicated textual and editorial history. Chapter 2 apparently narrates three heavens, though chapter 3 enumerates seven heavens; the number of heavens remains a matter of dispute among scholars.[18] In their present form, the seven heavens move from a place of punishment to the highest heaven in which the Great Glory dwells, with each heaven increasingly glorious as one ascends.[19]

Levi's second vision at once affirms his priestly ordination and at the same time circumscribes its duration. Seven heavenly men prepare Levi for his office by anointing, cleansing, and clothing him. They then declare that his posterity shall be divided into three "lots," of which the third "shall be granted a new name, because from Judah a king will arise and shall found a new priesthood in accord with the gentile model and for all nations" (8:14, *OTP*). This messianic hint prepares the way for later developments in the Testament, for Levi announces that his descendants will "act impiously" (14:1, *OTP*). Eventually, they will provoke the destruction of the sanctuary, the scattering of the people, and finally, the emergence of a "new priest" (18:2, *OTP*), a messiah who will bring judgment and righteousness (chaps. 18–19).

The Testament sketches an apparently contradictory portrait of Levi's sons and their activities. On the one hand, they receive eternal benediction, but on the other, they come to abuse their power and even to oppose the messiah (4:4; 10:2).[20] Perhaps the presence of Christian editorial insertions (*interpolations*) explains part of this pattern, but the larger pattern of blessing and apostasy is common to all the Testaments, not unique to Levi's.

The Testaments and Other Apocalyptic Texts

In narrating events from the patriarchs' careers, the Testaments necessarily elaborate upon material from the book of Genesis. But they also reflect awareness of 1 Enoch, to which they sometimes refer explicitly (T. Sim. 5:4; T. Lev. 10:5; 14:1; 16:1 [in some mss.]; T. Jud. 18:1; T. Zeb. 3:4 [some mss.]; T. Dan 5:6; T. Naph. 4:1; T. Ben. 9:1). They also develop common interests with Jubilees, such as the exaltation of Levi and Judah, biographical details of those two patriarchs, the tradition of war between Esau and Jacob, and some limited interest in identifying time in units of jubilees.[21] To be sure, there are differences. For example, while 1 Enoch largely neglects the Torah, perhaps even to displace its authority, the Testaments insist upon the Law. Nevertheless, although we cannot trace all of the sources that inspired them, the Testaments of the Twelve Patriarchs surely participated in the larger literary interchange of early apocalyptic literature.

Apocalyptic Discourse and Anthropology

In a fundamental sense, the Testaments of the Twelve Patriarchs represent a detailed anthropology, or analysis of human nature. Each of the Testaments addresses a particular virtue or vice such as envy, arrogance, courage, simplicity, and so forth, then expounds upon the value of these principles and analyzes the threats to them. Beyond simply elaborating upon these virtues and vices, the Testaments also offer analyses of human nature and behavior, and apocalyptic discourse contributes mightily to this effort.

Throughout the Testaments, the doctrines of Two Ways and Two Spirits account for the people's behavior. People may align themselves with either good or evil (Two Ways), while competing spiritual forces vie for their obedience (Two Spirits). The first Testament, that of Reuben, begins with reflection on two sets of seven opposed spirits: On one side stand life, seeing, hearing, smell, speech, taste and "procreation and intercourse," while on the other lurk promiscuity, insatiability, strife, flattery and trickery, arrogance, lying, and injustice (2:1–9, *OTP*). As the Testament of Asher describes it,

> God has granted two ways to the [children of mortals], two mind-sets, two lines of action, two models, and two goals. Accordingly, everything is in pairs, the one over against the other. The two ways are good and evil; concerning them are two dispositions within our breasts that choose between them. (1:3–5, *OTP*)

Asher goes on to explain that once a person pursues a particular path, the spirit of that path begins to gain the upper hand. If one chooses evil, "driving out the good," one is "overmastered by Beliar the devil," who turns even good intentions to evil ends (1:6–9, author's trans.). Thus, the Testaments draw upon one of the most basic topics of apocalyptic discourse, dualism, to distinguish between two kinds of people and two kinds of supernatural beings.

Apocalyptic Eschatology

The testaments also develop other characteristic apocalyptic topics. Their literary form implies the strategy of *ex eventu* prophecy, with the patriarchs looking ahead into Israel's future. They foresee apostasy followed by tribulation, judgment, and resurrection. In the meantime, angelic and demonic forces, including Beliar or Satan, struggle to control human beings and their affairs. The Testament of Judah exhibits this weaving of apocalyptic topics. It insists on the struggle between the Two Spirits (20:1–5); forecasts division, apostasy, and destruction within Israel (22:1–23:5); and envisions the arrival of a messianic "Star from Jacob" to bring peace, judge the nations, and establish God's rule (24:1–6, *OTP*). Then Judah describes the resurrection of the patriarchs, which makes possible the miraculous reconstitution of Israel's twelve tribes. This marks an age free from sin and Beliar and full of joy and prosperity (25:1–5).[22] In response to this revelation, Judah insists, the proper path is to obey the Law, for it is the source of hope (26:1). At this point, Judah dies.

We find all these topics scattered throughout the Testaments.

Reading the Testaments as Apocalyptic Discourse

As we have seen, apocalyptic topics such as dualism, reviews of history, interest in heavenly beings, judgment, messianic expectation, and resurrection contribute prominently to the Testaments. Moreover, the Testaments also include at least four mini-apocalypses: Testament of Levi

2–5, Testament of Levi 8, Testament of Naphtali 5–6, and Testament of Joseph 19. The Testaments draw upon the books of Enoch and share interests with Jubilees. So, clearly the Testaments of the Twelve Patriarchs rightly belong in the flow of early apocalyptic discourse.

Yet the Testaments do not belong with the literary genre of the apocalypses, nor is apocalyptic discourse their primary interest or characteristic. Rather, apocalyptic topics serve larger purposes. The Testaments' primary concerns involve anthropological reflection that leads to moral exhortation. Their analysis of human nature, the influence of good and evil spirits, and Israel's story of apostasy and renewal indicate the pressures that undermine righteous living. And their teachings concerning resurrection, judgment, and the messiah insist on the urgency of faithful living in the present.

The Testament of Moses

Date

The Testament of Moses was written not long after the death of Herod the Great in 4 B.C.E., though proposals vary. Many believe the Testament reflects two distinct stages of composition, one during the Antiochene Crisis of 167–164 B.C.E. (chaps. 1–5, 8–10) and one during the first century C.E. (chaps. 6–7).[23]

Languages and Texts

The sole ancient copy of the Testament of Moses is a Latin manuscript from the sixth century C.E. The text appears to derive from a Greek translation of an even earlier Hebrew or Aramaic original.[24]

The Testament of Moses, sometimes called the Assumption of Moses, employs the apocalyptic topic of an *ex eventu* (before-the-fact) prophecy. It presents Israel's sacred story up to the first century C.E., as delivered by Moses to Joshua. As such, it embodies an alternative to Deuteronomy 31–34, a collection of Moses' final discourses and traditions concerning Moses and Joshua. The Testament offers very little by way of introduction to this information, nor does it involve visions or auditions, as apocalypses do. As Moses entrusts Israel's leadership to Joshua, he lays out the future in a straightforward fashion.

Naturally, the Testament's review of history emphasizes certain critical periods, alternating between high and low moments. Chapter 2 briefly narrates how the people establish themselves in the land, with a sanctuary in God's appointed place; how the twelve tribes will divide into two kingdoms; and yet also how the people will fall away into idolatry. Chapter 3 slows down to describe Jerusalem's destruction at the hands of the Babylonians and how that crisis provoked the people's repentance, while chapter 4 envisions their return to the land under Persian administration. Things decline again in chapter 5, as the people return to idolatry, with the rise of "a wanton king" who is not a priest, probably the thirty-four-year rule of Herod the Great, who expresses God's judgment through his cruel administration (6:2–6, *OTP*).[25] Herod's heirs follow, as does their conquest by a ruler from the west, which leads to Jerusalem's devastation (6:7–9).

If we wish to locate the social and political perspective of the Testament, our interest will gravitate to chapter 7, which proclaims that after the temple's partial destruction "the times will quickly come to an end" (7:1, *OTP*). Indeed, in the wake of Herod's death, rebellion and disorder spread throughout Palestine. The conditions spelled out in Testament of Moses 6:9 came to pass when Varus, the Roman governor of Syria, intervened with force: Thousands of Jews were crucified, and in the violence a part of the temple was destroyed by fire.

As we have seen, reviews of history frequently identify their own times with the eschatological crisis. Thus, the characterization of that crisis reflects the point of view advanced by the text. A condemnation of Israel's oppressive leaders (7:3–10) follows the violence of Varus's intervention; then the text becomes illegible for two lines.[26] A surprising interruption occurs in chapters 8–9, which we shall discuss below. Without those chapters, the review of history progresses neatly until the chaos that followed Herod's death. And at chapter 10 the Testament breaks into a song of eschatological celebration. In other words, history according to the Testament of Moses culminates in the confusion ensuing after Herod's reign.

Yet Testament of Moses does not promote a concrete political agenda. It indicts the priestly and royal leaders of Judea, but it does not side with the Romans. Indeed, its only political or social program amounts to faithfulness to the Law. Instead of a political solution, it looks ahead to the establishment of God's realm, which will appear "throughout [the] whole creation" (10:1, *OTP*). Accompanied by cosmic portents and the devil's end, this kingdom brings Israel's vindication. Rather than hoping in some particular political party or historical process for this salvation, the Testament simply inspires hope among the faithful. In his closing statement Moses declares:

> All of the supports of the canopy of heaven, created and declared good by God, are indeed under the ring of his right hand. Therefore, those who truly fulfill the commandments of God will flourish and will finish the good way, but those who sin by disregarding the commandments will deprive themselves of the good things which were declared before. (12:9–11, *OTP*)

Thus, while rejecting Israel's internal leadership, the Testament replaces it not with an alternative power base but with individual faithfulness and its eschatological reward.[27]

If we skip from the end of chapter 7 to the beginning of chapter 10, the Testament of Moses progresses smoothly. Beginning with Israel's entry into the land, the review of history comes to the last days just after Varus's suppression of public disorder. However, chapters 8–9 clearly appeal to events that occurred during the Antiochene Crisis of 167–164 B.C.E., when Judeans suffered torture and execution over issues such as diet and circumcision. How does one account for this abrupt transition? Has the manuscript tradition been corrupted, so that chapters 8–9 have been displaced from their proper location? Did someone do a sloppy job of editing? Or, perhaps, did the final editors use Antiochus's suppression of Judaism as a means of providing commentary on the leadership of their own day? All of these suggestions have found support among scholars, and the issue is significant for understanding how and when the Testament was composed.

Despite uncertainty concerning the Testament of Moses' composition history, our appreciation for the role of apocalyptic discourse in the Testament does not depend on the resolution of such questions. The Testament adapts a prominent literary form of apocalyptic discourse, the *ex eventu* review of history. It also applies apocalyptic eschatology as it envisions a future age of salvation. Both of these resources come together to encourage a particular worldview: While Israel's leaders bring suffering rather than healing and while external forces such as Rome appear to determine Israel's fate, the faithful may rest in the assurance that God's reign will break out. Then they will find their reward.

The Dead Sea Scrolls

Glamour rarely comes to biblical studies as it did in 1947. In that year three Bedouin shepherds discovered some clay jars in a cave near a Palestinian site called Qumran. Two days later, one of them returned to the cave to find three scrolls—a copy of Isaiah, a text now known as the Manual of Discipline or the Community Rule (1QS), and a commentary on Habakkuk (1QpHab). Four more scrolls were later discovered in the cave, and a local antiquities dealer purchased the collection of seven. Then followed a genuine cloak-and-dagger saga of detection, evasion, and even diplomacy, as the scrolls passed hands from the antiquities dealer to a Syrian Orthodox metropolitan and to scholars from the newly formed state of Israel and from the United States. Eventually, they all came under the control of the State of Israel.

This story makes for fascinating reading in its own right, but it is only the beginning.[28] Eventually, eleven Qumran caves yielded literally thousands of manuscripts and fragments. Ranging from copies of biblical books and other previously known texts, to commentaries and psalms, to more narrow sectarian documents, the Dead Sea Scrolls amount to the greatest archaeological find in the history of biblical studies. Despite controversies concerning the texts, their interpretation, and their social and historical contexts, their contents represent essential knowledge for students of Jewish and Christian origins.

Although our interests do not allow a full introduction to the Qumran scrolls, some background information is essential. About one-eighth of the manuscripts are biblical texts. The Scrolls have more copies of Psalms, Deuteronomy, and Isaiah than of any other literary works. In addition, the Scrolls include Aramaic translations, or Targums, of Leviticus and Job.[29] Other scrolls include copies of books from the Apocrypha (extrabiblical books included in some Christian canons) and the Pseudepigrapha (other extrabiblical books), notably 1 Enoch and Jubilees.

The finds also revealed fragments of otherwise unknown expansions and adaptations of biblical texts. Finally, a wide variety of new texts also surfaced, including commentaries on biblical texts, documents devoted to community governance, liturgical pieces, and eschatological works.[30]

The People behind the Scrolls

Scholars offer conflicting assessments of the people who copied and treasured these texts. Archaeological work at Qumran has uncovered what once was a small but vibrant community that lived in the desert near the Dead Sea. Nearly everyone agrees that the community's buildings date from the second century B.C.E. and that they were destroyed—perhaps by the Romans during the First Jewish Revolt—around 68 C.E. This period roughly corresponds to the interval between the Maccabean Revolt and the end of the First Jewish Revolt against Rome. The period proved critical for the emergence of Judaism as we know it, as various groups competed for authority and influence in politics, religion, and economics. It also matches the period in which apocalyptic discourse began to flourish.

Beyond dating, important questions remain. What may we conclude on the basis of the archaeological evidence from Qumran? How did the Scrolls relate to the community there? (The people who lived at Qumran may or may not have composed any given scroll, and a particular scroll may or may not reflect the community's point of view at any given time.) May we correlate external sources with Qumran's archaeological and textual evidence to draw conclusions regarding the people behind the Scrolls?

Though debate continues, most scholars identify the Qumran community with an elusive group called the Essenes. We would know nothing about the Essenes, apart from some fairly obscure passages from Pliny the Elder, a Roman politician and natural scientist; Philo, a Jewish philosopher and cultural critic from Alexandria; Josephus, a military leader and administrator in the First Jewish Revolt who wrote about Judaism late in that century; and perhaps Dio Chrysostom, a famous philosopher and orator who lived in Rome but traveled widely. All these sources derive from about 50–115 C.E. Obscure as these sources may be, collectively they present plausible parallels to Qumran's archaeological and textual evidence.[31]

   a. Pliny and Dio (cited by Synesius of Cyrene around 400 C.E.)[32] locate the Essenes on the Dead Sea's west side. Pliny describes them as a community of celibate men who attract new members by their austere lifestyle, and he notes that the nearby city of Engedi has already–like Jerusalem–been destroyed (*Natural History*, 5.73).

   b. Philo describes a group of about four thousand men who seek to live in holiness and purity apart from the Jerusalem Temple system. Their ascetic sensibilities draw them into small villages, and they live simply, refusing to participate in war even through commerce in weapons and the like. They abandon philosophy for the study of Torah, and they benefit the rest of society through their example and by teaching in the synagogues. Demonstrating high regard for one another, they share property and condemn slavery (*Every Good Man Is Free*, 12.75–87).

   c. Josephus, who notes that the Essenes attribute all events to fate and do not participate in the temple sacrifices, also emphasizes their distinctive lifestyle and evident virtue. They abstain from sexual relations with women but adopt children. Like Philo, Josephus emphasizes their interest in purity, their sharing of communal goods, and their gathering in several small living communities. Josephus also adds particular dimensions of their communal life, including ritual bathing, prayer, a common meal, a rigorous initiation process, and severe discipline. As for doctrine, they believe that their soul transcends the limitations of the body. Finally, Josephus notes "another order" of Essenes who share these values, except that they marry (*Ant.* 18.18–22; *War* 2.119–61).

The total picture we derive from these sources corresponds fairly well to some of the architectural and textual evidence from Qumran. The Qumran community clearly isolated itself from the larger society. Its prominent bathing pools and a dining hall confirm the impression that its members participated in ritual bathing and communal meals. Remains from a nearby cemetery are almost exclusively male, with a few skeletons of women and children located at some distance from the rest. Moreover, the two most prominent sectarian documents from Qumran attest to somewhat divergent circumstances: the Community Rule (1QS) envisions a single community of men, whereas the Damascus Covenant (CD) describes related villages that include married persons.

These differences by no means rule out continuity, as they perhaps represent stages in the evolution of the Qumran community or distinct groups within that community. Moreover, these same documents attest to common values that we have encountered in the external witnesses–intense community discipline and simplicity of lifestyle–whereas the diversity of the Qumran libraries indicates an interest in Torah and other holy writings.

In summary, we may draw several probable conclusions regarding the Qumran community. It was *sectarian,* in that it had withdrawn from the larger flow of society, including the Jerusalem Temple establishment. It was *ascetic,* in that it emphasized purity and perhaps even celibacy, along with rigorous initiation processes and harsh internal discipline. It was *group-oriented,* with a strong sense of sharing and participation. It was *scholarly* in its devotion to the study and security of sacred texts. And it was *priestly* in its intense reaction to Jerusalem. As we shall see, it participated in *apocalyptic discourse* in significant ways.

Apocalyptic Texts at Qumran

Scholars have long identified apocalyptic interests in the Qumran community, but among the documents unique to Qumran only two texts, one relatively intact and one available only in fragments, resemble the classical apocalypses. Neither of the two describes the sort of revelatory encounter that distinguishes the apocalypses, but both devote themselves to visions of ultimate things: the eschatological conflict in the War Scroll (1QM) and the New Jerusalem in a variety of related fragments. In addition, the famous Temple Scroll (11QTemple) and Copper Scroll (3Q15) feature esoteric contents that recall passages such as Ezekiel 40–48, with its detailed description of an idealized Zion. And the Rule of the Congregation (1Q28a) details how the faithful must live in the last days.

The case for apocalypticism's influence at Qumran goes far beyond these few texts, for the Qumran finds also include copies of 1 Enoch, Daniel, and Jubilees, and apocalyptic topics figure prominently in other documents. Moreover, the Qumran discoveries reveal how 1 Enoch, Daniel, and Jubilees influenced the community there. For not only did the community preserve those texts, their own literature also cites, quotes, or alludes to them as well.[33] While our attention to these documents does illuminate the sort of apocalypticism that may have shaped life at Qumran, we also do well to study those apocalyptic documents that are, so far as we know, unique to the Scrolls.

THE WAR SCROLL

The War Scroll (also known as the War Rule) begins, "For the Instructor: The Rule of the War."[34] It envisions an attack by the "sons of light" against the "sons of darkness," who represent the "army of Belial." These enemies represent biblical Israel's traditional neighbors and sometime enemies, in addition to the "Kittim," those foreigners who rule over the land. The war culminates in the absolute destruction of those enemies–"with no remnant remaining"–and of the Kittim's rule (1:1–7).

Who are those "sons of light"? Their introduction progresses from the general to the specific: "The sons of Levi, the sons of Judah and the sons of Benjamin, *the exiled of the desert...*" (1:2, author's emphasis). Clearly, the sons of light represent the Qumran community, who understand themselves to be excluded from the Jerusalem establishment. As a faithful remnant, their struggle takes on cosmic proportions. Holy angels fight alongside the sons of light, but wicked angels also assist their enemies. The conflict's ultimate resolution, then, lies in the hands of God. Empowered by God, the holy army drives out all enemies over a period of forty years.

Remarkably, the War Scroll does not so much envision this conflict as it prescribes the holy behavior necessary for its conduct.[35] Led by priests and purified by sacrifices, the holy company divides into divisions and other units—requiring far more soldiers than were available at Qumran. Trumpets pronounce orders, and banners proclaim the holy identity of the army's units. Although the Scroll does detail military procedures, these tactics bear no real-life relevance. For example, column six describes an attack that begins by launching javelins, but its true interest resides in what the warriors inscribe on the weapons' points. Moreover, the second half of the Scroll presents songs of praise to God.

One wonders—and many scholars have done so—why someone would produce a scroll such as this.[36] I consider it unlikely that the War Scroll articulates an actual military plan or that people ever studied it as such. Instead, while the War Scroll does not narrate a vision, it functions as one. That is, it creates space in which people could imagine themselves as agents in an eschatological conflict, as a righteous remnant fighting alongside the angels. Such a vision could enhance a sense of community solidarity, empower individuals and the group to continue their current counter-cultural practices, and inspire hope for their eventual vindication.

Visions of the New Jerusalem and the Temple Scroll (11QTemple)

Likewise, Visions of the New Jerusalem and the Temple Scroll (11QTemple) construct an alternative reality through visualization. Like Ezekiel 40–48 and Revelation 21, the New Jerusalem fragments offer a detailed portrayal of the holy city and its temple, including measurements and, in some fragments, descriptions of its bejeweled surfaces. Like their parallels in Ezekiel and Revelation, these descriptions represent an idealized vision rather than a description of Jerusalem as anyone actually found it. The Temple Scroll, which begins with Moses' instructions to the people (cf. Ex. 34),[37] also details the lavishness of the envisioned temple, complete with measurements, precious metals, and priestly garments. Echoing Moses' discourses from the Pentateuch, especially Deuteronomy, the scroll also provides detailed instructions for the performance of sacrifices and the execution of laws. Like Deuteronomy, it promises the people's security in the land as a reward for obedience.

Again, such descriptions encourage their audiences to participate in hope by visualizing this transcendent reality for themselves. Certain gospel hymns from today's church offer an instructive parallel. Borrowing from Revelation's descriptions of pearly gates and golden streets, these songs require the audience to sing along, visualizing a glorious future in which their own faithfulness will meet its reward.

THE COPPER SCROLL (3Q15)

The Copper Scroll (3Q15) continues to defy explanation. Named because of its unique material–it really is inscribed in copper and had to be cut into sections before scholars could read it–the Copper Scroll names sixty-four locations in which astonishing amounts of treasure have been hidden. For example:

> In the channel which is on the road to the east of Beth-Achsar, to the East of Achzar: tithe-vessels and books and a bar of silver. In the outer valley, in the middle of the pen, in the stone, dig for seventeen cubits under it: silver and gold, seventeen talents. (8:1–7)

Enticed by such extravagant riches, scholars have set out–and failed–to unearth the treasures.[38] We cannot know for certain who composed the Copper Scroll or why. Perhaps the Scroll actually records the locations at which Judeans hid precious items from the temple as the Romans advanced upon the Holy City during the First Jewish Revolt. Or perhaps the Scroll testifies to some sacred imagination, now lost to us. It may–or it may not– have anything to do with apocalyptic discourse, but it certainly promises the revelation of a great mystery.

RULE OF THE CONGREGATION (1Q28A)

One more text, the Rule of the Congregation (1Q28a), presents straightforward instruction for "the congregation of Israel in the final days" (1:1). Representing a clearly sectarian mentality, the document specifies its commitment to the Zadokite priesthood while it addresses "the men of the covenant who have turned away from the path of the people" (1:2–3). The scroll begins with instructions for how to bring up and initiate young men, including a period of intense apprenticeship between the ages of twenty and twenty-five. At its conclusion, the Rule also envisions an eschatological meal, at which "the Messiah of Israel" and the priest preside. Despite its eschatological introduction and conclusion, the body of the rule lacks a clear eschatological emphasis. This pattern likely indicates a community in which people could *assume* apocalyptic topics such as the last days, messianic hope, and the eschatological banquet, so that these topics provide the framework for community regulation. The Rule shows no need to argue for or repeat these themes.

Apocalyptic Topics at Qumran

The Rule of the Congregation reveals how apocalyptic ideas can play a central role even in texts that do not share the form of the classical apocalypses. Likewise, careful study of significant Qumran documents reveals a host of assumptions about human beings, the supernatural order, and history that are grounded in apocalyptic discourse.[39]

ANTHROPOLOGICAL DUALISM

Anthropological dualism, the notion that individuals are either fundamentally righteous or wicked, perhaps due to the influence of righteous and wicked forces, permeates Qumran's sectarian literature. While the Qumran sectarians seek perfection—and the penalties for even relatively minor errors are severe—they also recognize their own imperfection, as several of their psalms praise God for God's forgiveness (cf. 1QS 1:24–2:1). Yet despite such gratitude, the Community Rule (1QS) reflects the community's sense that it embodies a righteous minority in a wicked world. The Rule proclaims the familiar doctrine of the Two Spirits. The spirits of truth and injustice compete in human hearts, with righteousness winning in some but wickedness in others. God has ordained this situation until the end times, "For God has sorted them into equal parts until the appointed end and the new creation" (4:25).

> In these lies the history of all men; in their (two) divisions all armies have a share by their generations; in their paths they walk; every deed they do falls into their divisions, dependent on what might be the birthright of the man, great or small, for all eternal time. For God has sorted them into equal parts until the last day and has put an everlasting loathing between their divisions…God, in the mysteries of his knowledge and in the wisdom of his glory, has determined an end to the existence of deceit and on the occasion of his visitation he will obliterate it for ever. (4:15–19)

Thus, the "men of the Community" withdraw from the sinful masses to pursue the life of rigorous righteousness.

Modern readers may wonder how the Qumran sectarians could have been so confident in their abilities to discriminate between the righteous and the wicked. Indeed, the Community Rule even promotes hatred and contempt for the "men of the pit" (cf. 9:21–22). Their communal ethos is simple: to love all the sons of light, each one according to his lot in God's plan, and to detest all the sons of darkness, each one in accordance with his blame in God's vindication. (1:9–11)

Yet two factors might mitigate our surprise at such moral certitude. For one thing, the boundaries between the Qumran community and the rest of the world could hardly have been more clear. The community members had volunteered for this life, had endured a rigorous initiation process, and had submitted to stringent disciplinary codes. Some evidence suggests that they considered themselves to have been exiled to this state. In short, they cultivated a remarkable sense of communal identity. Moreover, ancient persons believed that *who* a person was could be seen in *how* he looked. At Qumran we find evidence for this assumption among a collection of horoscopes:

> And his thighs are long and slender, and the toes of his feet are slender and long. And he is in the second position [astrologically, of course!]. His spirit has six (parts) in the house of light and three in the pit of darkness. (4Q186 2:5–8)

And,

> And his teeth are of differing lengths. The fingers of his hand are stumpy. His thighs are fat and each one covered in hair. His spirit has eight (parts) in the house [of darkness] and one in the house of light. (4Q186 3:3–6)

DETERMINISM

Combined with the doctrine of the Two Spirits, characterizations such as these highlight the *determinism* of the Qumran community. The major sectarian documents, the Community Rule (1QS) and the Damascus Document (CD), play upon the tension between the human capacity to choose good or evil and the sense that human destinies have already been set by supernatural forces. People simply are who they are, so that their appearance reflects their character. The Thanksgiving Hymns (1QH) reflect this conviction:

> You [O God] have fashioned every spirit
> and [...]
> and the judgment of all their deeds. (9:9)

And,

> You have shared out their [mortals'] tasks in all their generations...
> And in the wisdom of your knowledge
> you have determined their course
> before they came to exist. (9:16, 19)

Thus, God has already determined the nature of mortals, and as a result even their ultimate judgment already stands set.

INTEREST IN HEAVENLY BEINGS

The Qumran community's anthropological dualism relates intimately to its *interest in heavenly beings.* The children of light live among the righteous angels, while wicked angels accompany their adversaries.[40] The Community Rule merges anthropological and cosmological dualism, attributing divisions among mortals to the struggles among their supernatural counterparts.

> [God] created man [*sic*] to rule the world and placed within him two spirits so that he would walk with them until the moment of his visitation: they are the spirits of truth and of deceit. In the hand of the Prince of Lights is dominion over all the sons of justice; they walk on paths of light. And in the hand of the Angel of Darkness is total dominion over the sons of deceit; they walk on paths of darkness. Due to the Angel of Darkness all the sons of justice stray...However, the God of Israel and the angel of his truth assist all the sons of light. (3:17–25)

The cosmic dualism expressed here is relatively mild, for God remains the sole creator and ultimate power over the cosmos. (In some ancient systems, such as Zoroastrianism, the forces of good lack such sovereignty.) Still, Qumran's dualism is also thorough, as the powers of good and evil struggle against each other until the last days.

In similar fashion the Scrolls' other major rulebook, the Damascus Covenant (CD), attributes the rise of Aaron and Moses to the "prince of lights," but the emergence of Moses' opponent Jannes and his brother to the devil, Belial (5:18–19). Likewise, Belial rules over the hearts of sinners (12:2).[41] Belial also figures prominently in a variety of scrolls, including the War Scroll, in which he leads Israel's enemies. Although the Scrolls do not devote close attention to Belial's identity or his works, the influence of 1 Enoch and Jubilees—with their traditions concerning the Watchers who descend from heaven to create chaos among mortals—probably stands behind his role as the chief supernatural agent of evil.

LAST DAYS AND THE MESSIANIC HOPE

With respect to the course of history, the Scrolls repeatedly emphasize the *last days,* which certainly include conflict and judgment. Beyond that, the specific eschatological beliefs of the Qumran community remain sketchy at best. Only one text, the Halakhic Letter (4QMMT), expresses the conviction that the last days have already begun.[42] Some of the Scrolls attest to a messianic hope. The Community Rule (1QS 9:11; cf. the messianic banquet in 1Q28a 2:11–12) curiously ventures the possibility of *two* messiahs, a Messiah of Aaron (a priestly messiah) and a Messiah of Israel (perhaps a David-like ruler?). We may never know how widespread or influential was this expectation. Nor do the Scrolls detail the hope of resurrection, though they occasionally do relate the future condemnation of the wicked (e.g., 1QS 4:11–14). One text from the Community Rule, however, envisions the "everlasting possession" of the saints, who "inherit…the lot of the holy ones" (11:7–8).[43] This identification with the "holy ones" suggests a possible exaltation of the righteous to share in the status of the righteous angels. It also resonates with certain aspects of 1 Enoch (104:2) and Daniel (12:3), which suggest the glorification of the holy people. At the same time, visions of the New Jerusalem suggest a future in which God restores the holy people to a new creation, a purified Holy City that transcends the ages.

Reflections on the Dead Sea Scrolls

Apocalyptic discourse played a formative role within the Qumran community. We see this in the documents they preserved, such as 1 Enoch, Daniel, and Jubilees, as well as in those compositions that apparently derive from Qumran itself. Yet synthesizing this vast and diverse literature to construct a unified picture of apocalyptic eschatology at Qumran remains a challenge. At a minimum, we find both apocalyptic compositions and apocalyptic themes. The apocalyptic compositions include the War Scroll, Visions of the New Jerusalem, and possibly others that envision eschatological conflict and the ultimate order to follow. Apocalyptic themes including anthropological and cosmological dualism, interest in heavenly beings, determinism, and the last things are scattered widely throughout the Dead Sea Scrolls.

Our generalizations on the basis of this diffuse data require caution. It seems, however, that at Qumran apocalyptic discourse fused with a strongly sectarian outlook to make sense of a chaotic world. Driven to the desert by will or by compulsion, the Qumranites experienced dissonance between what they "knew" to be true and what they saw with their eyes. They, the righteous remnant, found themselves excluded from power, even within the small Roman colonial systems of ancient Judea. Their standards of cultic propriety and moral righteousness did not apply even in the temple. Apocalyptic discourse enabled them to construct an understanding of themselves and of the world that made sense of such discouraging data. So long as they endured, these "children of light" lived among the angels, their continuing faithfulness would lead eventually to vindication in the eschatological conflict, and they expected to experience transformation in the heavenly realms.

The Sibylline Oracles

Date

In their present form, the Sibylline Oracles date from the sixth century C.E., but they incorporate material from as early as the second century B.C.E.

Language and Texts

The Sibylline Oracles have been preserved in several Greek manuscripts, mostly from the fourteenth and fifteenth centuries. Two manuscript families contain Books 1–8, while a third contains Books 9–10 (which basically duplicate Books 6 and 4, respectively) and Books 11–14. These books are well attested by quotations among early Christian authors.[44]

Drawing their literary inspiration not from scripture but from Greco-Roman religious traditions, the Sibylline Oracles stand alone within the body of Jewish and Christian revelatory literature by so overtly adapting pagan literary forms. Still, John J. Collins observes:

> ...both Jews and Christians propagated oracles in the name of the sibyl because of her reputation in the pagan world. But in the process they changed the kind of oracles attributed to the sibyl, and thereby extended her reputation long after the gods of antiquity had faded away.[45]

In Greco-Roman antiquity the sibyls were aged women who possessed prophetic gifts and delivered their oracles in the first person. In the *Aeneid,* Virgil testifies to the Sibyl's wildness and ferocity (6.1–155), as did the philosopher Heraclitus:

> The sibyl, with frenzied lips, uttering words mirthless, unembellished, unperfumed yet reaches to a thousand years with her voice through the god (from Plutarch, *de Pythiae oraculis* 6 397A).[46]

References to the sibyls date as far back as 500 b.c.e., and traditions concerning them go back even farther.[47] Their oracles typically involved public and political matters, including wars, political events, natural disasters, and recommendations regarding the introduction of new cults.[48] Eventually, traditions about individual sibyls clustered around particular cities, along with records of their oracles. These records attained a fairly standard literary form. Unfortunately, very few of these records survive.

For Romans, the Sibyl at Cumae drew particular attention. In the *Aeneid,* Aeneas travels there to learn his duties and his destiny (6.1–155). The Roman Sibylline Books, ostensibly oracles from the Sibyl of Cumae purchased by the Roman king Tarquin, offered specific advice for a variety of social concerns. Two (later ten) appointed priests guarded this collection, which they would consult during times of public discernment or crisis. For example, when an epidemic was devastating the city, Roman authorities consulted the Books, which recommended a banquet in honor of the gods (Livy, *History* 5.13.5–8). To end another plague, the Books called for the introduction of the healing cult of Asclepius (Livy, *History* 10.47.6–7; *Summaries* 11).[49] Thus, the Roman Sibylline Books achieved the status of influential public documents that could address specific exigencies in the public life. A fire destroyed the collection in 83 B.C.E., though a new collection superseded it.[50]

The traditions concerning the sibyls clearly attracted the attention of some Jews and Christians, so that Clement of Alexandria (d. 215 C.E.) claimed that the Sibyl received her revelations from God, not "humanly" (*Stromata* 1.172). In the sixth century C.E., a Christian editor collected the twelve Sibylline Oracles, which became the influential collection we know today. The Prologue to the collection acknowledges that the sibyls spoke by inspiration, but it also insists that the sibylline books testify to Christ. The Prologue also concludes with a sibyl's hymn to God, which demonstrates the ultimate source of their revelation. Only books 6 and 7 represent thoroughly Christian compositions, though Christian interpolations occur throughout the collection. Oracles 3–5 remain distinctly Jewish, and they testify to the concerns of Jews who lived in different areas of the ancient Mediterranean and at different times.

BOOK 3

Book 3 reveals several characteristics of the Sibylline Oracles as a whole. Like the entire collection, Book 3 displays its own composite nature, incorporating several literary sources from diverse points in time. It further demonstrates the Sibyllines' capacity to address a variety of interests, seemingly at once. And it employs diverse literary strategies to accomplish its ends.

Denied rest because God continues to vex her spirit, the Sibyl proclaims God's greatness (3:1–45). Then she gets down to business, specifying the conditions that will bring about the heavenly rule:

> But when Rome will also rule over Egypt
> guiding it toward a single goal, then indeed the most great kingdom
> of the immortal king will become manifest over men.
> For a holy prince will come to gain sway over the scepters of the
> earth forever, as time presses on. (3:46–50, *OTP*)

This passage reflects the challenges involved in reading Book 3, for it promises to reveal more about the book's context and aims than it actually does. For example, we may easily trace the passage to a particular period and location. Rome's conquest of Egypt occurred in 31 B.C.E., and the specific interest in Egypt suggests that the oracle may have emerged from Jewish circles there, perhaps in Alexandria. However, immediately following this passage comes an allusion to a later time, the period after Nero's reign (3:63–74).[51] (Nero died in 68 C.E., long after Rome's conquest of Egypt.) In line 75 the setting returns to the first century B.C.E., to Cleopatra's reign.

The perspective changes yet again in line 97, which launches what may be the main body of Book 3. According to John J. Collins, lines 97–349 and 489–829 address the concerns of Jews living in second-century B.C.E. Egypt. In short, by line 97 we have already visited three different periods of history.

Such conflicting allusions indicate that Book 3 has emerged through a complicated process of growth and redaction. From one point of view, these shifts of perspective and emphasis provoke disorientation. If Book 3 has a connecting logic, it is by no means linear. Yet we might also identify topical threads that surface throughout the Book and lend some sense of coherence.

First, Book 3 reveals a keen interest in history, particularly with Rome and Egypt. Its major *ex eventu* review of history begins with the Tower of Babel (98–109) and then develops a succession of world empires (110–95). This scheme begins with the primeval Titans, narrates Egypt's prominence in two different ages, and culminates with Rome. The review's focus returns to Egypt when it looks ahead to an age of salvation, which accompanies the "seventh reign" of "a king of Egypt, who will be of the Greeks by race" (192–93, *OTP*, cf. 652–56). In addition to its reviews of history, Book 3's historical focus also involves woes against the nations, accusing them of idolatry and sexual immortality. From Ethiopia to Assyria, and from Babylon to Rome, these woes are—according to the view of their day—global in scope. Thus, whoever composed Book 3 not only knew the contours of Mediterranean legend and history, they also had their eye on current world affairs.

Second, the Book's historical outlook assumes and promotes a fairly conventional apocalyptic eschatology. Eschatological distress precedes the age of divine intervention, when God sends a "King from the sun" to bring salvation (636–56, *OTP*). God's judgment presents two dimensions: the destructive annihilation of human beings and the natural order (635–51; 669–701; 796–808) on the one hand, and an age of blessing on the other (741–95). Obviously, judgment brings deliverance for the righteous (703–31), but it remains unclear whether there is hope for people who are not Jews. One passage envisions global annihilation:

> And God will speak, with a great voice,
> to the entire ignorant empty-minded people, and
> judgment will come upon them from the great God, and all will
>   perish
> at the hand of the Immortal. (669–72, *OTP*)

But another promises hope for some, but apparently not all, mortals:

> When indeed this fated day also reaches its consummation
> and the judgment of immortal God comes upon mortals,
> a great judgment and dominion will come upon men.

For the all-bearing earth will give the most excellent unlimited fruit
   to mortals…
King will be friend to king to the end of the age.
The Immortal in the starry heaven will put in effect
a common law for men throughout the whole earth
for all that is done among wretched mortals.
For he himself alone is God and there is no other,
and he himself will burn with fire a race of grievous men.
   (741–45; 756–61, *OTP*)

Third, the eschatological vision also emphasizes distinctive Jewish interests. Twice the Sibyl stops to praise Jews (218–94; 573–600), "a race of most righteous people" (219, author's trans.) and "a sacred race of pious people" (573, author's trans.). She reviews Israel's history from Abraham to Moses through the exile and the return. Two particular concerns–the Law and the temple–most prominently embody Book 3's vision for Israel. For example, the Book attributes Israel's destruction at the hands of the Assyrians and Babylonians to its neglect of the Law, particularly its participation in idolatry. Conversely, in praising Jews the Sibyl praises their "sharing in the righteousness of the law of the Most High" (580, *OTP*).

When the Book looks ahead to the last days, however, its focus turns to the temple. One sign of the eschatological tribulation will be an attack against the temple, which provokes God's intervention (663–68). Likewise, the temple stands at the center of Book 3's vision of salvation:

But the [children] of the great God will all live
peacefully around the Temple, rejoicing in these things
which the Creator, just judge and sole ruler, will give. (702–4, *OTP*)

In the blessed age the temple draws not only Jews but all people to worship God.

From every land they will bring incense and gifts
to the house of the great God. There will be no other
house among [mortals], even for future generations to know,
except the one which God gave to faithful [people] to honor.
   (772–75, *OTP*)

Fourth, Egyptian politics play a critical role in this eschatological vision. The Sibyl links the Jews' destiny to the reign of a particular Egyptian king.

Every kind of deceit will be found among them
until the seventh reign, when
a king of Egypt, who will be of the Greeks by race, will rule.
And then the people of the great God will again be strong
who will be guides in life for all mortals. (191–95, *OTP;* cf. 318; 608)

Some observations: (1) This king must be one of the Ptolemies, the Greek rulers who inherited Alexander the Great's Egyptian holdings. (2) If salvation comes with the seventh Ptolemaic king, that person will be difficult to identify, as the Seleucid line becomes complicated during the second century B.C.E. We ought also to consider the arrival of the "King from the sun" in lines 636–56 (*OTP*): Under God's guidance, this ruler puts an end to war. Because lines 314–18 also predict that war and suffering cease with the seventh king's reign, the seventh king and the king from the sun likely represent the same historical figure, probably either Ptolemy VI Philometor or Ptolemy VII Neos Philopetor.[52] Although we may not be able to identify which Ptolemy the Sibyl has in mind, we may draw a more general conclusion. Book 3 places its hope in an Egyptian ruler whom God appoints to bring about the peace that marks Israel's salvation. His role almost amounts to a messianic vocation; as with Cyrus, God's "messiah" (anointed one) in Isaiah 45:1, God uses this king to deliver Israel.

By no means was such royal eschatology unique to Judaism. Indeed, in coming decades Rome promoted its own messianic eschatology of sorts, just as Egypt had endowed its rulers with divine identity and functions. So Book 3's proclamation of the king from the sun belongs in that context. It authorizes Egypt's present or coming king with divine blessing.

What can we say about Book 3? With the Law, the temple, and the Jewish people at the center of its value system, it remains intensely engaged with the social and political forces of its day. It employs apocalyptic eschatology to encourage—rather than discourage—hope in the present political order. Its worldview does not imply an anti-Gentile stance; rather, it judges the nations with a view toward their relationships with Jewish communities and whether their practices conform to the Law. Despite the evils of Roman power, Book 3 hopes in Egypt's present or coming ruler, whose reign will inaugurate the age of peace, prosperity, and righteousness. Ironically, it takes an Egyptian ruler to restore Zion to its proper place at the center of the sacred order.

From a literary point of view, Book 3 presents a lot of problems. Not only does it incorporate material from diverse periods, it also fails to present that material in any sort of chronological or sequential order. One might attribute this apparent disorder to casual or even sloppy redaction; indeed, that conclusion is quite plausible. Perhaps Book 3's various editors devoted themselves to ensuring that the right content made its way into the book rather than to developing a coherent literary structure or point of view.

Yet we might adopt an alternative reading strategy. Its literary movement is certainly not progressive—but it is repetitive and cumulative. For example, twice praise of Jews is framed by condemnations of the nations. Thus, Jewish virtue is defined by pagan vices. This pattern fosters a certain reiterative effect, as if the Book could confirm the certainty and order of its claims by articulating them over and over again.

Theologically, Book 3 insists on God's sovereignty. Its adoption of the Sibyl as a vehicle of revelation implies that God can reveal truth even through traditionally pagan media. Further, it suggests that pagans implicitly recognize Israel's God. Perhaps most importantly, Book 3 asserts that God works through all the processes of human history. Not only does God judge at the end, but God also directs the paths of rulers in the present.

BOOK 5

But come, hear my woeful history of the Latin race.
First of all, indeed, after the death of the kings
of Egypt, all of whom the evenhanded earth took under,
and after the citizen of Pella [Alexander the Great], to whom
all the East and prosperous West were subjected. (1–5, *OTP*)

Thus begins Book 5 of the Sibylline Oracles, straightforwardly indicating its own political point of view. Valuing especially the legacy of Egypt, as well as Alexander's Ptolemaic successors, Book 5 presents Rome as a menace. This initial review of history (1–51) begins with the conquests of Julius Caesar and continues through the reign of Lucius Verus, who died in 169 C.E.[53] Thus, we conclude that Book 5 derives from Egyptian Jewish circles in the second century C.E. and is animated by anti-Roman sentiment.

Book 5's anti-Roman polemic is most vivid in three passages. Lines 160–78 announce catastrophe for Italy, "because of which many holy faithful Hebrews and a true people perished" (160–61, *OTP*) and condemn Rome for its blasphemous claim, "I alone am" (173, *OTP*), which of course parodies the divine name of Exodus 3:14. According to this passage, Rome, "unclean in all things" (168, *OTP*), will sit by the Tiber's banks in mourning (169–70). In the more extended polemic of verses 386–413, two primary charges against Rome stand out: sexual immorality and devastation of the temple "by an impious hand" (399, *OTP*). And lines 434–46 identify Rome with Babylon—as do 4 Ezra, 2 and 3 Baruch, and the book of Revelation—announcing its own "bitter reckoning" (446, *OTP*).

THE NERO LEGEND

For modern readers, Book 5's condemnation of Rome takes an apparently bizarre turn with its references to the Emperor Nero, who died in 68 C.E. (93–110, 137–54, 214–27, 231, 361–85). Nero takes the role of the eschatological adversary, who "in the last time" (361, *OTP*) brings the final war, after which Jews will finally have peace. So notorious was Nero's career that it burned itself into the imaginations of Jews and Christians for decades. Blaming Christians for Rome's catastrophic fire of 64 C.E., Nero made a spectacle of them—crucifying some, feeding others to hungry dogs, and burning others alive, using their bodies as torches. Of course, although the First Jewish

Revolt that ended with Jerusalem's devastation concluded after Nero's death, it began under his watch.

Somehow a Nero *redivivus* legend emerged, according to which Nero returned from the dead to wreak havoc upon God's people. (As we shall see, this legend contributes to the book of Revelation's characterization of the Beast, and it also appears in Asc. Isa. 4:1–14.) In the Sibyllines, Nero appears as an eschatological adversary not only in Book 5 but also in 3:53–74; 4:119–22; 8:68–72, 139–68; 12:78–94.[54]

Several clues, especially in lines 137–54, indicate the presence of the Nero legend. According to line 142, this Roman king destroys his mother, while line 143 describes his flight from Babylon. Nero apparently ordered the assassination of his mother, and his own suicide occurred as he sought to escape his enemies in Rome. Line 145 indicts the king for having "laid hands on the womb" (*OTP*). Nero killed his second wife Poppaea by kicking her in the stomach while she was pregnant.[55] Line 150 blames the king for Jerusalem's fall; although Nero did not preside over the city's conquest, Roman forces did conquer most of Judea during his reign. Finally, lines 147–49 appeal to what had become a prominent part of the legend, Nero's flight to Parthia. For decades after his death, imposters appeared in the East posing as Nero. Why the Nero legend figured so prominently among Jews, Christians, and indeed others as well, and why Nero looms so heavily over the Sibylline Books, remain a matter for speculation.

Perhaps Rome's judgment is so important because Book 5 regards Rome as the primary obstacle to Jewish salvation. The emperor Nero returns from the dead to wage a final war, after which the "wise people" who remain find themselves at peace (384–85). The elevation of the Jews includes the recognition of their moral and religious excellence, so that even their enemies find themselves converted:

> No longer will the unclean foot of Greeks
> revel around your land but they will have a mind in their breasts
>   that conforms to your laws. (264–65, *OTP*)

These prophecies for Judea's deliverance (247–85, 328–32) require divine intervention in the form of a savior, a "blessed man [who] came from the expanses of heaven" (414–33, *OTP*). Judging humankind, this man destroys every city except for Jerusalem, which he recreates so that it shines more brightly than the stars, sun, and moon. Free of sin and corruption, the holy city basks in God's glory. Book 5 does not offer more details regarding this savior figure or his deeds, and it abstains from messianic language, but it does appear to express some sort of messianic hope. In contrast to the promised king of Book 3, this savior is not an Egyptian ruler. His origins lie in the heavenly realms.

Like Book 3, Book 5 spells out a fairly conventional apocalyptic eschatology. For example, tumult precedes deliverance (361–85, 447–84). Still, we find a minor difference. Book 5 offers hope for the conversion of the nations, particularly Egypt, which turns away from its false gods to the "true God" and establishes a temple in God's honor (484–511; cf. 264–65). Thus, Book 5 also holds Jewish symbols such as the Law and the temple at the center of its value system. Although it awaits Rome's doom, it also extends hope that all peoples might come to acknowledge Israel's God. Book 5 does not, however, find hope in present political conditions. While Book 3 awaits the seventh Egyptian king, Book 5 can envision the age of salvation coming only from a heavenly figure.

BOOK 4

"People of boastful Asia and Europe, give ear" (1, *OTP*). Right away the Sibyl's address inveighs against idolatry and blesses those who love the one "great God," reminding mortals of God's impending judgment (1–48). However, the body of Book 4 turns to a review of history, rehearsing the familiar scheme of the four empires from the Assyrians to the Medes to the Persians to Alexander's Macedonians, and finally to the great eschatological empire, Rome. The Sibyl proclaims Jerusalem's fall, associating it with Nero's escape (115–29). Rome's war against the holy people provokes God's wrath (135–36). This eschatological crisis, accompanied by war and apostasy, threatens God's destruction of the entire human race.

Presenting such a dire threat, Book 4 calls mortals to repentance. If human beings will cease from their violence and turn to God, God will withhold the coming wrath (162–70). If not, then the entire eschatological scenario stands as a threat: cosmic destruction followed by the resurrection of all people to face a final judgment. Book 4, then, interprets Jerusalem's fall as the final eschatological warning, and it offers mortals two options: suffering and judgment, on the one hand, or repentance that leads to "spirit and life and favor" (189, *OTP*), on the other.

In its eschatology Book 4 differs from Books 3 and 5 in remarkable ways. It holds no hope for a savior figure or for any social or political process that does not involve repentance. Its emphasis lies not with Jerusalem's restoration but with hope for the next life, presenting resurrection and judgment as humankind's ultimate fate. While Book 4 remains interested in the currents of history, it exchanges genuine engagement in those processes for individualized piety.

Reading the Sibylline Oracles

Through their very literary form, the Sibylline Oracles develop an intriguing argument. Jews and Christians in the ancient world frequently maintained that all people had access to divine knowledge. Even pagans, insisted Philo, had advanced far enough to "value and honor" the Torah (*De Vita Mosis* 2.17).[56] Paul, at once a Jew and a Christian, censures pagans for neglecting the divine truths that God had made available to them, while he maintains that some pagans do uphold the Law in some sense (Rom. 1:19; 2:26–29). Likewise, though the Sibylline Oracles may insist on the superiority of symbols such as the temple and the holy people, they also imply that God has spoken through the sibyl. By placing Jewish and Christian revelation in the sibyl's mouth, so to speak, they portray the universal accessibility of divine revelation. Even pagan oracles, according to the Sibylline books, reveal God's truth.

In both form and content, then, the Sibylline Oracles demonstrate intense engagement with the Gentile world. Book 3 begins on precisely this point, as the sibyl scolds mortals for failing to recognize their creator (8–45). Book 3 also expects Jerusalem's salvation to come through an Egyptian ruler. Although Book 5 places no such hope in ordinary political developments, offering only the most withering view of Rome, it also extends hope for the nations' salvation. Book 4, on the other hand, directly addresses Gentiles at the literary level, but that is simply a literary device. Its contents reveal a primarily Jewish audience, whom it calls to renewed faithfulness.

The precondition for such engagement with the larger currents of politics and history lies in the Sibyllines' primary theological conviction: God is sovereign. God works through all the processes of human life, including imperial intrigue and war. Such optimism is restrained, however, by a conventional apocalyptic eschatology, as the Sibyllines expect tribulation to precede salvation. The understandings of that salvation differ. Book 3 foregrounds a renewed Jerusalem, as does Book 5, but Book 5 also extends hope for the Gentiles' conversion. By way of contrast, Book 4 looks beyond the currents of history to the otherworldly post-resurrection salvation of individuals.

Conclusion

In this chapter we have surveyed a wide range of texts. Jubilees and the Testaments retell and elaborate upon the familiar biblical narratives, while the Sibylline Oracles present direct revelations. The Qumran finds themselves include wildly diverse texts, including visions of the great eschatological battle, the New Jerusalem and the ideal temple, ideals for community discipline, and the treasure map of the Copper Scroll.

If these texts embody diverse literary forms, how much more do they reflect divergent contexts and motivations. We encounter community standards, cultic details, and moral exhortation. We meet overt political critique as well as principled rejections of political engagement. We find eschatological expectation ranging from end-time conflict to idealized holy spaces. We even perceive conflicting assessments of Israel's Gentile neighbors, ranging from hopeful engagement to pessimistic withdrawal.

Despite their differences, all these texts participate in apocalyptic discourse. None of them fit the generic boundaries of the classical apocalypses. Yet they all draw upon stock apocalyptic literary devices and topical concerns to advance their respective interests. In the varied means by which they adapt apocalyptic topics to such diverse ends, these texts demonstrate the rich flexibility of apocalyptic discourse to adapt itself to multiple literary forms and socio-religious purposes.

FOR FURTHER READING

Collins, John J. *Apocalypticism in the Dead Sea Scrolls*. Literature of the Dead Sea Scrolls. New York: Routledge, 1997.

_____. *Seers, Sibyls and Sages in Hellenistic-Roman Judaism*. JSJSup 54. Leiden: Brill, 1997.

Kugler, Robert A. *The Testaments of the Twelve Patriarchs*. Guides to Apocrypha and Pseudepigrapha. Sheffield: Sheffield Academic Press, 2001.

Nickelsburg, George W. E., ed. *Studies on the Testament of Moses*. Septuagint and Cognate Studies 4. Cambridge, Mass.: Society of Biblical Literature, 1973.

Parke, H. W. *Sibyls and Sibylline Prophecy in Classical Antiquity*. Edited by B. C. McGing. New York: Routledge, 1988.

Tromp, Johannes. *The Assumption of Moses: A Critical Edition with Commentary*. SVTP 10. Leiden: Brill, 1993.

VanderKam, James C. *The Book of Jubilees*. Guides to Apocrypha and Pseudepigrapha. Sheffield: Sheffield Academic Press, 2001.

CHAPTER 4

The Gospels and Jesus

The New Testament begins with four gospels, four stories about Jesus, his activities, his teachings, and his fate. Although we have access to twenty or so other gospels, most scholars believe those four canonical gospels represent the earliest stories of Jesus to which we have access. Among the others, only one–the Gospel of Thomas–likely contains traditions that may reveal early stages of Jesus' authentic teaching. Given what we have learned so far about the emergence of apocalyptic discourse in ancient Judaism, we would expect eschatology to play a large role in the career of Jesus and in the earliest texts that relate his story and his teaching. Sure enough, it does. Apocalyptic topics and eschatological teachings represent a major emphasis of all four New Testament gospels, while Thomas's rejection of such speculation demonstrates that eschatology was an inescapable topic among early Christian circles.

Yet these gospels do not embody straightforward accounts of Jesus' career. For when we read the gospels, we find that they all reveal two stories, not just one. Obviously, the gospels narrate events in the past; that is, they relate stories about the career and teachings of Jesus. At the same time, however, each of the gospels also reflects the stories of early Christian communities. Because the gospels were all composed one or more generations after the career of Jesus, the experiences and perspectives of those early Christians inevitably shape the ways in which those stories are told. The gospels almost certainly were written

- after Christianity had moved from being a Jewish messianic sect to a new religious movement that included Gentiles
- after Christianity had spread throughout much of the Mediterranean world
- after Christian groups had developed serious rifts with some non-Christian Jewish groups

- after–or, in the case of Mark, possibly just before–the collapse of the First Jewish Revolt against Rome and the destruction of the Jerusalem Temple
- most importantly, after Jesus had himself become an object of worship

In telling about Jesus, then, the gospels reflect the concerns of their own eras as well. Through their stories, they engage questions:

1. How should Christian groups organize themselves, and who are Jesus' most authoritative followers?
2. How should Jews and Gentiles relate to one another?
3. How should Christian groups relate to their non-Christian Jewish neighbors and to the Roman civil authorities?
4. What are appropriate and inappropriate ways in which to understand Jesus and his significance?

That the gospels embody diverse perspectives on Jesus' teachings and career should not surprise us. We all tell history from the point on view of the present, not the past. For example, one of the most trying things a white Southerner can do is to investigate how his or her parents and elders perceived and responded to the civil rights movement.[1] Thus, while the canonical gospels display a significant measure of continuity with one another, each of them also shapes its own distinctive portrait of Jesus.

For our purposes, one question is critical: How do the gospels treat apocalyptic discourse? The canonical gospels–especially the synoptic gospels, that is, Matthew, Mark, and Luke–strongly associate Jesus with apocalyptic motifs. Jesus is baptized by an apocalyptically-oriented preacher in the Jordan River. Soon after that, he is sustained by angels and tempted by Satan in the desert. During his ministry, he often combats demons. He preaches the present and coming reign of God. His teaching includes parables that depict scenes of eschatological judgment. In extended discourses he teaches his disciples about the future advent of the Son of Man. Finally, God raises Jesus from the dead, and resurrection is a thoroughly apocalyptic concept. From beginning to end, apocalyptic motifs shape the stories of Jesus.

But does the New Testament–and do the synoptic gospels in particular–convey the truth about Jesus? If indeed the synoptics themselves emphasize apocalyptic eschatology, could it be that Jesus himself did not possess such a mindset? Moreover, might other early Christian gospels–the gospels of John and Thomas, in particular–reflect the non-apocalyptic trajectories among the earliest Jesus movements? Within the synoptics themselves might we find traces of an emerging apocalypticism that may have developed after–not during–Jesus' career?

Here, we face three related sets of issues. First, we should carefully assess the role and nature of apocalyptic discourse in the synoptic gospels–individually and as a group. Second, we must look into non-apocalyptic or anti-apocalyptic traditions in the gospels of John and Thomas. And third, we must consider how Jesus himself, as best we can reconstruct his career, negotiated apocalyptic discourse.

Apocalyptic Discourse in the Synoptic Gospels

When one lays out the four canonical gospels in parallel columns, it becomes apparent that three–Matthew, Mark, and Luke–share a great deal in common, while the gospel of John largely consists of material that has no parallel among the other gospels. For this reason, Matthew, Mark, and Luke are often called the synoptic (syn-optic) gospels because (a) they "see" the career of Jesus "together" in a common narrative framework, and because (b) we may observe their common vision through a tool called a synopsis of the gospels. Several helpful synopses are in print, all of which lay out parallel passages of the gospels side by side for our comparison.[2]

When we seek to explain the relationships among Matthew, Mark, and Luke–their similarities and their differences–we encounter the synoptic problem. These gospels narrate much of the same material, usually in common order and with shared vocabulary. Indeed, only a few scenes (pericopes) in Mark have no parallel in either Matthew or Luke. We call the material common among all three synoptics the Triple Tradition. At the same time, a substantial body of material (225–50 verses) is common to Matthew and Luke, but not Mark. It is called the Double Tradition. Finally, not only does each gospel include some material that is unique to itself, even the common material often takes different forms in its various retellings.

A sure explanation of the synoptic problem is not necessary for our purposes, but it helps to be aware of some basic concepts. Most scholars hold to some form of the Two-Source Hypothesis. In this model, Mark was the first of the canonical gospels and served as a common literary source for both Matthew and Luke. (This explains why almost every scene of Mark is present in Matthew or Luke, and why Matthew and Luke rarely disagree with Mark's version in the same way.) Matthew and Luke also shared a second literary source, which scholars call *Q*. (This accounts for the Double Tradition, material common to Matthew and Luke but not Mark. Q is brief for *Quelle*, which means "source" in German. Bible scholars are a creative bunch.) In brief, the Two-Source Hypothesis holds that Matthew and Luke shared two literary sources, Mark and Q. Obviously, Matthew and Luke include some of their own independent tradition as well.

As they stand, the synoptic gospels present a Jesus who lives in an apocalyptically-oriented context and proclaims a thoroughly apocalyptic message.

John the Baptist

While Matthew and Luke include genealogies of Jesus and stories of his nativity, all three synoptics begin the story of Jesus' career with his **baptism by John the Baptist**. Although the activities of the historical John are debated, the synoptics present John as baptizing people toward repentance. Two sources might enlighten our understanding of John. The Jewish historian Josephus suggests that John's baptism was primarily spiritual, involving a cleansing of the soul, but he also notes that Herod the Tetrarch viewed John as a threat to public order (*Ant.* 18.5.2). Perhaps Herod's suspicions reveal that John was more politically minded than Josephus would care to admit.

Likewise, the Manual of Discipline from Qumran cites the same passage from Isaiah (40:3–5) that the synoptics apply to John. The passage reveals that the holy community has left ungodly society for the desert to prepare the Lord's way (1QS 8:13–14). According to James C. VanderKam, the Qumran community "understood Isaiah's words *way* and *path* in a figurative sense: they were not commanded to construct a real road but to study the law and in this manner to prepare for the Lord's coming."[3] Perhaps, then, John's baptism aimed at preparing Israel for God's apocalyptic deliverance of the people from oppression. As John Dominic Crossan maintains, for John, "Baptism and message went together as the only way to obtain forgiveness of one's sins before the fire storm came." And "a Transjordanian desert location and a baptism in the Jordan, precisely the Jordan, had overtones...of political subversion."[4]

Visionary Experiences

If the synoptics associate Jesus with John's apocalyptic message, they also characterize Jesus as the recipient of the sort of **mystical and visionary experiences** that accompany apocalyptic discourse. At his baptism, Jesus sees the heavens ripping apart and the Holy Spirit descending upon him. A heavenly voice proclaims, "You are my Son, the Beloved; with you I am well pleased" (Mk. 1:11). Whereas Luke downplays the visionary aspect of this scene, Mark and Matthew describe the vision as Jesus' personal experience and the audition most likely as a public event (Mk. 1:9–11 par. Mt. 3:13–17; Lk. 3:21–22). Then follows Jesus' temptation: The same Spirit drives Jesus into the desert for forty days of temptation by Satan. Mark does not narrate the details of the temptation, but Q describes it as a conversation with Satan. According to Mark, Jesus is served by "the angels" (1:12–13), while Q reports that Jesus was famished after the forty days of fasting (Lk. 4:1–13; Mt. 4:1–11).

Luke also attributes an enigmatic saying to Jesus: "I watched Satan fall from heaven like a flash of lightning" (10:18). The statement's location within Luke is significant. Seventy of Jesus' disciples have just returned from a mission of healing and proclamation. ("The kingdom of God has come near to you" 10:9.) During mission they have been have been dependent on hospitality for food and lodging. Upon their return, the seventy proclaim, "Lord, in your name even the demons submit to us!" (10:17). Oddly enough, Jesus' reply both contributes to his characterization as a visionary and functions to downplay certain kinds of apocalyptic expectation. Jesus tells the disciples to rejoice not in their newly acquired spiritual power, but that their names are written in heaven (10:20). The notion of having one's name written in the heavenly rolls is prominent within apocalyptic literature, but its origins predate apocalyptic eschatology.[5] Here, the heavenly rolls discourage speculation that God's new age is imminent.

Combat with the Demonic

If Jesus' visionary experiences often involve Satan, **combat with Satan and the demons** also distinguishes his ministry. Satan is not prominent in the Jewish Bible/Old Testament, nor are his identity and work specified. But Satan is critical to the imaginations of most New Testament authors. This is because interest in Satan and his activity had attracted significant interest within Jewish apocalyptic discourse, a tradition inherited in early Christianity. Jesus repeatedly exorcises demons in each of the synoptics, which report such activity as characteristic of his ministry (e.g., Mk. 1:32–34; Mt. 8:16–17; Lk. 4:40–41).

Independently, Mark and Q report that Jesus' opponents charge him with collaboration with the devil. According to Mark 3:22, scribes from Jerusalem claim that Jesus was possessed by Beelzebul. In the Q version, the charge is that Jesus' exorcisms are made possible by Beelzebul (Lk. 11:15; Mt. 12:24). The synoptics all agree in linking the charge to Jesus' work as an exorcist. Luke's version is the most concise: "He casts out demons by Beelzebul, the ruler of the demons."

Jesus' reply is part of the Triple Tradition. All three synoptics agree that Jesus dismisses the charge by reducing it to absurdity: If Satan empowers Jesus' works, why would Satan allow Jesus to do good? Or how can one attribute the same activities to God and the devil?[6] (Incidentally, Paul may have disagreed, suggesting that Satan disguises himself as an angel of light [2 Cor. 11:14].) While Jesus rejects the attempt to associate him with Beelzebul, he denies neither the devil's existence nor his influence.

Apocalyptic Teaching

By all accounts, the **teaching of Jesus** in the synoptic gospels is heavily apocalyptic. Stephen J. Patterson, for example, argues that the historical Jesus *did not* promote an apocalyptic eschatology. Still, he writes of the synoptics' "view of Jesus as an apocalyptic preacher with a mission to Israel, who thought of himself as a Messiah and reflected upon the significance of his inevitable death."[7] Naturally, those who believe Jesus *did* teach an apocalyptic eschatology find most of their evidence within the synoptic traditions. As Dale C. Allison notes, the judgment of those who view Jesus in apocalyptic terms "is consistent with the Synoptics' testimony."[8] In any event, here we are discussing not the actual Jesus of history and his teachings but Jesus as he is described in Matthew, Mark, and Luke.

KINGDOM OF GOD

Sometimes the apocalyptic dimensions of the synoptics are easy to spot, but their significance is much less clear. The *kingdom of God* provides one such case. According to Mark, Jesus' ministry begins with the eschatological proclamation: "The time is fulfilled, and the kingdom of God has come near; repent, and believe in the good news" (Mk. 1:15). In Matthew, the message is, "Repent, for the kingdom of heaven has come near" (Mt. 4:17; Matthew routinely substitutes "kingdom of heaven" for Mark's "kingdom of God"). Luke does not include this particular saying, but he does report that early in his career Jesus says, "I must proclaim the good news of the kingdom of God to the other cities also; for I was sent for this purpose" (4:43). Each of these sayings is significant, as they characterize Jesus' mission in terms of his apocalyptic expectation right from the start of his ministry. Likewise, the first petition in Jesus' model prayer for the disciples is that God's kingdom will come (Mt. 6:11 par. Lk. 11:2).

But what does the kingdom of God mean? Whatever it is, it is not primarily a home in heaven, nor is it a place in one's heart.[9] The synoptic Jesus speaks of the kingdom as an alternative reality–a world in which the ordinary conventions of status and domination are overturned, but also a realm in which God's judgment is effective and tangible. For example, the parable of the laborers (Mt. 20:1–16) begins with the "real" world. Conditions are so severe that even during harvest season day laborers will wait throughout the day for work. But in the kingdom of heaven's alternative economy, everyone who needs work receives full justice–a day's wage– even if they work only a very short shift. Indeed, those who have waited all day for work receive their wages first!

One could imagine the kingdom in the parable of the laborers in present terms. In other words, here Jesus describes the kingdom as a mode of life in which people actually participate now. But other synoptic examples– such as "Your kingdom come" in the Lord's Prayer–clearly indicate a future reality. One set of examples draws upon image[s] of the eschatological banquet that derive from both Mark and Q. At Jesus' last meal with the disciples, he tells them, "Truly I tell you, I will never again drink of the fruit of the vine until that day when I drink it new in the kingdom of God" (Mk. 14:25 par. Mt. 26:29; Lk. 22:16, 18). This future expectation is reflected in a Q saying: "There will be weeping and gnashing of teeth when you see Abraham and Isaac and Jacob and all the prophets in the kingdom of God, and you yourselves thrown out. Then people will come from east and west, from north and south, and will eat in the kingdom of God" (Lk. 13:28–29 par. Mt. 8:11–12).[10] In this last instance, we see the future age as both promise and threat: people from all over the world will participate in the banquet, while others will be in torment.

This tension between present and future notions of the kingdom creates multiple possibilities. Does the kingdom refer to God's future intervention to make things right in the world? Does it have to do with living according to God's reign in the here and now, even in opposition to conventional social values? Or does it have to do with a blessed existence after death? Each of these options is distinctive. Although modern readers seek straightforward definitions, the synoptic authors apparently did not find them mutually contradictory.[11] Indeed, many early Christians–and perhaps Jesus himself–may have held all these notions at once. At any rate, the mix of kingdom sayings in the synoptics reflects what scholars call an *inaugurated eschatology*: God's reign has already broken into the world, though its full actualization is yet to come.

THE ESCHATOLOGICAL JUDGMENT

The synoptic Jesus has lots to say about an *eschatological judgment*. The Beatitudes of the Sermon on the Mount (Mt. 5:1–12) or the Sermon on the Plain (Lk. 6:20–26) presuppose an age marked by the reversal of status. How else can one bless (or congratulate) those who are hungry, whether they hunger for righteousness or for food?

More explicit pronouncements also punctuate the synoptics. Matthew's Jesus warns that confessing him as Lord does not allow one to enter the kingdom of heaven, but doing God's will does (7:21; cf. Lk. 6:46). He further insists that a final judgment will separate those (probably Gentiles) who do mercy from those who do not (25:31–46). In the Q tradition Jesus teaches that those who do not observe his teachings will be excluded at judgment (Mt. 7:22–23; Lk. 6:46–49). In both Matthew and Mark, Jesus warns that it is better to sacrifice a hand, foot, or eye in this life than for the entire self to be thrown into a fiery hell (Mk. 9:43, 45; Mt. 5:29–30). Luke's understanding of judgment may be more complicated. Sometimes Luke's Jesus alludes to a grand final judgment scene (10:13–14). In other cases he apparently assumes that after death one moves immediately to paradise or to torment (16:19–31; 23:43). At any rate, Matthew, Mark, and Luke agree in attributing to Jesus some teaching about the final judgment.

THE SON OF MAN

As we have seen, the figure of the *Son of Man* develops in early Jewish apocalyptic literature and is prominent in the synoptics. Son of Man apparently means different things in different texts–"mortal" in Ezekiel and the Psalms, an embodiment of Israel in Daniel 7, and a messianic figure who judges the world's rulers and gives light to the Gentiles in the Similitudes of Enoch (1 Enoch 37–71).[12] In the synoptics Jesus uses Son of Man to refer to himself in ordinary language, to speak of his own future suffering and resurrection (Mk. 8:31; 9:31; 10:33-34; Mt. 16:21; 17:23; 20:18-19; Lk. 9:22,44; 18:31-32), and to refer to a heavenly figure who will come to judge the world (as in Mark 13; Matthew 24; Luke 21).[13]

APOCALYPTIC PARABLES

Several of Jesus' *parables* emphasize the last judgment, at least in their synoptic form. In these short stories and vivid images Jesus communicates his vision of sacred reality. The parables begin with common scenes–lost coins, weeds, and so forth–but they almost always take a surprising turn that challenges the audience to abandon conventional notions of God and God's reign for new possibilities.

While many scholars believe the apocalyptic interests of these parables derive not from Jesus himself but from their transmission in early Christian circles, all agree that the parables as we have them are heavily invested in apocalyptic eschatology. These parables comprise a rich complex of material, with a variety of emphases and rhetorical functions. It is impossible to classify all the parables into neat, self-contained categories–this would require that every parable have only one legitimate meaning, and that modern readers could agree upon it! In any case, several apocalyptic themes do surface.

a. Some parables involve *admonition,* in that they warn how certain dispositions and behaviors will meet divine judgment. For example, the parable of the ten bridesmaids (Mt. 25:1–13) concludes, "Keep awake...for you know neither the day nor the hour," whereas the parable of the sheep and the goats (Mt. 25:31–46) envisions a final judgment based on individuals' acts of compassion.

b. Some parables offer *correction,* in revising conventional understandings of judgment. The parable of the rich man and Lazarus (Lk. 16:19–31) contradicts the assumption that wealth is a sign of divine favor, while the parable of the wheat and the weeds undermines the notion that one may confidently identify who is righteous and who is not (Mt. 13:24–30, 36–43).

c. Some parables convey a *celebratory* function, in that they exemplify God's remarkable care for human beings. The parable of the lost sheep (Mt. 18:12–13 par. Lk. 15:4–6; cf. Thomas 107) is linked with the parables of the lost coin and the prodigal in Luke 15. These parables all emphasize God's delight at the return of sinners. Likewise, the parable of the laborers in the vineyard (Mt. 20:1–16) likens God's judgment to an employer who pays everyone what they need regardless of how long they have worked. In this parable, according to W. D. Davies and Dale C. Allison, "God rewards human beings according to his [*sic*] unexpected goodness."[14]

Apocalyptic Actions

SELECTING APOSTLES

If the teachings of Jesus in the synoptics are deeply invested in apocalyptic topics, some scholars also perceive apocalyptic dimensions in his **actions.** One case involves his selection of *twelve apostles*. E. P. Sanders observes that, "although all four gospels, Acts and Paul agree that there were twelve special disciples...they do not agree precisely on their names." Although it isn't clear how many people Jesus named as apostles, exactly who they were, or whether Jesus used the number twelve symbolically (as Sanders suggests), the number twelve certainly echoed the traditional number of the tribes of Israel. Indeed, in Matthew 19:28 and Luke 22:30 Jesus tells the twelve special disciples that they will judge the twelve tribes "when the Son of Man is seated on the throne of his glory."[15]

Hope for the restoration of Israel's twelve tribes is well attested in Jewish literature of the period, indicating some degree of popular interest. Biblical Israel is characterized as the descendants of the twelve sons of Israel. Of those twelve tribes, ten had been destroyed in the Assyrian Conquest of 722 B.C.E. According to tradition, only Judah and Benjamin– perhaps with some members of the tribe of Levi–survived. The reconstitution of Israel, with its twelve tribes, would represent a miraculous divine intervention, which is precisely what some people were hoping for. Isaiah 49:6 envisions God's servant who will "raise up the tribes of Jacob," and Ezekiel 47–48 plans for the future distribution of the land among the tribes. Within apocalyptic literature, the book of Jubilees (1:15), the Psalms of Solomon (11:2–3; 17:28–31), and some of the Dead Sea Scrolls (War Scroll [1QM] 2:2–3, 7; 3:13; 5:1–2; Temple Scroll [11QT] 57:5–6) reflect this hope as well.[16] By selecting twelve apostles and appointing them as future judges over Israel's twelve tribes, Jesus recalls the eschatological hope for the ingathering of all the tribes of Israel.

ENTERING JERUSALEM AND DEMONSTRATING AT THE TEMPLE

The synoptics agree that Jesus traveled through his home region of Galilee before making one fateful journey to Judea and ultimately to Jerusalem. There, according to the synoptics, two events arouse the ire of the temple authorities, who are responsible for keeping order. Jesus makes a *dramatic entrance* into the city, and he stages some sort of *demonstration within the temple* itself (Mk. 11:1–19 par. Mt. 21:1–17; Lk. 19:28–48). If he is worried about his own survival, Jesus' timing couldn't have been worse, for his actions come as crowds were gathering to celebrate Passover. Roman authorities and temple authorities were particularly anxious during this period because pilgrims from all over the world crowd the city. Their anxiety is justified, because Passover itself carries subversive symbolic import. As they celebrate Israel's deliverance from bondage in Egypt, people can easily imagine Israel's liberation from Rome during the festival as well.

Jesus' actions certainly could arouse such revolutionary sentiments. He evokes the messianic imagery of Zechariah 9:9:

> Rejoice greatly, O daughter Zion!
>> Shout aloud, O daughter
>> Jerusalem!
> Lo, your king comes to you;
>> triumphant and victorious is he,
> humble and riding on a donkey,
>> on a colt, the foal of a donkey.

Jesus rides into the Holy City. Meanwhile, his traveling companions proclaim,

> "Hosanna! Blessed is the one who comes in the name of the Lord! Blessed is the coming kingdom of our ancestor David! Hosanna in the highest heaven!" (Mk. 11:9–10; cf. Mt. 21:9; Lk. 19:38).

After an initial survey of the temple, Jesus returns to interrupt commerce there. Although commentators disagree concerning the meaning of Jesus' temple demonstration—was it a protest against corruption, a prophetic sign of the temple's destruction?—his actions set him at odds with the temple authorities. Taken together, Jesus' entry into Jerusalem and his temple demonstration assert his messianic authority: Now, through Jesus' presence, God's rule has come to Jerusalem. Though Jesus eventually dies as a result of these initiatives, together his entry into the city and his occupation of God's house present him as Israel's king.

THE LAST MEAL AT PASSOVER

Likewise, the tradition of Jesus' *last meal* with the disciples carries eschatological significance. Matthew, Mark, and Luke alike identify the supper as a Passover meal (Mk. 14:12–25; Mt. 26:17–29; Lk. 22:7–38), the occasion when Jews celebrate Israel's deliverance from slavery in Egypt. Thus, the Passover looks *back* to God's salvation in the *past*. By Jesus' time, however, some Jews celebrated the Passover as they looked *forward* to Israel's restoration in the *future*. As we have seen, Roman forces and temple authorities took precautions during the Passover festival because it reminded Jews of their national hopes. Indeed, Josephus relates that sedition was most likely to break out during the three major festivals that attracted thousands upon thousands of pilgrims (*War* 1.88). One major incident had occurred during Passover in 4 B.C.E.

Whether deriving from the Passover tradition or not, prophetic and apocalyptic discourses commonly envision the eschatological age in terms of a great feast, or banquet. The banquet offers a particularly suitable eschatological image because it represents community and prosperity: people gather and eat a lot of good food. The Qumran community apparently practiced a sacred meal (Community Rule [1QS] 5:13–14; 6:2–23; Rule of the Congregation [1Q28a] 2:11–22; Josephus also relates that the Essenes practiced a sacred meal as a sign of God's presence among them [*War* 2.129–31]).[17]

JESUS' ASCETICISM

One of Jesus' action patterns that has often been denied or underestimated is his apparent *asceticism*. Asceticism involves "the renunciation of physical pleasures or other forms of bodily self-denial as a means of spiritual development."[18] Beyond the spiritual, however, asceticism can also embody a form of social resistance, a strategy of resistance to dominant structures of power in culture. The renunciation of bodily pleasure frees individuals and groups from conventional social networks. They can create an alternative social order without dependence on city, family, or household.[19] Such self-denial was already well known in the apocalyptic Judaism of Jesus' day, as it was practiced by some at Qumran, apparently by John the Baptist, and later by Paul.

Because Jesus and his disciples are noted for "eating and drinking" (Mk. 2:18–20; Mt. 11:16–19; Lk. 7:31–35), many scholars assume that they were not ascetics.[20] Yet the synoptics attribute some specific ascetic practices to them. Jesus and his disciples traveled from place to place, apparently relying on the generosity of others. In Jesus' own words, he "has nowhere to lay his head" (Mt. 8:20 par. Lk. 9:58). We find no hint that Jesus or his disciples enjoy sexual relations during their journeys. Indeed, Jesus notes that some become "eunuchs for the sake of the kingdom of heaven" (Mt. 19:12). Viewed in this light, an ascetic interpretation of Jesus' warning against looking at a woman with lust (Mt. 5:28) and his claim that in the resurrection there is no marriage (Mk. 12:25) seems plausible.

The Synoptic Perspective

So the synoptics unmistakably associate Jesus with apocalyptic topics. But what else may we say about their specific appropriation of the apocalyptic Jesus? As a starting point, we may say that they reflect a **post-resurrection perspective:** The apocalyptic "event" of Jesus' resurrection thoroughly tints their depiction of Jesus. Perhaps just as important, the synoptics also represent a **pre-parousia perspective:** the expectation of Jesus' glorious return frames their presentation of his apocalyptic concerns. Whatever Jesus may have said (or meant), and however he was understood by his contemporaries, the synoptics present Jesus as the Messiah whom God has raised from the dead and whose return will attend the judgment of humankind.

Jesus' Resurrection: "Event" and Significance

The canonical Christian tradition insists that after his death, Jesus appeared to his disciples. Significant variations mark the accounts of Matthew, Mark, Luke, John, and Paul (1 Cor. 15:1–8).

- The gospels all mention women who visited Jesus' tomb to find it empty. Paul does not.
- Among these sources only Mark does not *describe* an encounter between Jesus and his disciples, though Mark's story does *imply* it: at the empty tomb an angel promises that Jesus will meet them in Galilee (16:7).
- The state of the tomb varies among the traditions (except for Paul, who does not mention it).
- The sets of witnesses vary among the traditions.
- The place of the encounter varies among the traditions.
- In Luke 24 Jesus can appear suddenly and without being recognized, though the gospel insists that Jesus is flesh and bone and can eat. In John 20 Jesus can be touched, but somehow he can also appear behind closed doors. The other traditions do not speculate as to the nature of the post-resurrection Jesus.

Not only are the details of the resurrection uncertain, its very nature is also open to question. A resurrection is unknown to ordinary human experience. Thus, the resurrection—whatever may have happened—cannot be classified as a historical event. All we can say is that a variety of early Christian traditions testify that Jesus appeared alive to some of his followers after his death.

We can say much more about the *significance* of the resurrection. As we have seen, many Jews in Jesus' day hoped for a resurrection of the saints. This expectation surfaces in the book of Daniel and in a wide range of other apocalyptic sources. Among Jesus' contemporaries, it is attested at Qumran (4Q521 1:12)[21] and was shared by the Pharisees.

Though expectation of a resurrection may have been widespread, the important factors that set Jesus' resurrection apart are distinctive in two important ways.

First, other Jewish texts imagine the resurrection as a corporate event, involving all persons or at least the righteous. Jesus' resurrection involves a solitary individual.

Second, other Jewish texts connect the resurrection with the last days. Jesus' resurrection was not accompanied by an obvious change in the course of history.

Thus, early Christians faced the problem of accounting for Jesus' resurrection as a sign of the last days, even though history's objective circumstances had not changed.

Apocalyptic Motifs and the Structure of the Synoptic Stories

Beyond its impact on the direct content of Jesus' teaching and activities, apocalyptic discourse also shapes the synoptic gospels' very form. At a common level, all of the canonical gospels end with Jesus' resurrection and the disciples' anticipation of his return. Just prior to his crucifixion, Jesus' final teaching in the synoptic gospels contains his most explicit eschatological teaching concerning the Son of Man's coming. We call this Jesus' apocalyptic discourse (Mark 13; Matthew 24 [-25]; Luke 21). In addition to these commonalities, each of the synoptics also structures its stories of Jesus around apocalyptic motifs.

Mark's Apocalyptic Structure

Mark opens by announcing John's presence in the desert. With crowds gathering to repent in preparation for the coming age, John announces the arrival of the powerful one whose baptism will drench people in the Holy Spirit (1:2–8). Apocalyptic motifs continue with the baptism of Jesus, which involves both a vision and an audition. Jesus sees the heavens ripped apart and the Spirit descending upon him like a dove (1:9–11). His vision into the heavenly realms uses an interesting Greek verb, *schizo*. This verb occurs only one more time in Mark: Immediately upon Jesus' death, the curtain of the Temple rips in two (15:38). Thus, Mark frames the beginning and ending of Jesus' career with stories of tearing: Whereas Jesus' baptism transgresses the boundaries between the heavenly and earthly realms, his death opens access to the holy place of God's dwelling.[22] In short, Jesus' baptism by John leads Mark's gospel into an apocalyptic context. The motif of the heavens ripped open introduces Jesus' career, while the ripping of the temple curtain closes it.

Apocalyptic motifs also provide Mark's turning point. Here, we encounter the brief cycle in which Peter recognizes Jesus as the Messiah, Jesus predicts the Son of Man's suffering and resurrection, and Jesus admonishes a crowd that only those who have carried their own crosses will pass the final judgment when the Son of Man arrives (8:27–38). This cycle foreshadows the rest of Mark's story, which culminates in Jesus' death and resurrection and with the disciples awaiting his coming. Mark's description of the scene provides additional apocalyptic touches: A revelatory experience transforms Jesus before three of his followers, revealing his identity as God's Son. This story, the transfiguration (9:1–13), presents several apocalyptic motifs:

a. Jesus' appearance changes so that his garments become intensely white
b. two heavenly beings, Moses and Elijah, appear with him
c. a voice speaks to the disciples out of a cloud

While these devices may recall other biblical stories that do not involve apocalyptic discourse, they had also found their way into the apocalyptic discourse of the day.[23] Apparently, the transfiguration primarily testifies to Jesus' identity and authority in the light of his prediction concerning his passion and resurrection, and it employs apocalyptic images to convey this message.

MATTHEW'S AND LUKE'S APOCALYPTIC STRUCTURES

Matthew and Luke both rely on Mark's basic framework, including the baptism by John, Peter's confession of Jesus as the Messiah followed by the transfiguration, Jesus' apocalyptic discourse just prior to his arrest, and, of course, the crucifixion and resurrection. Yet Matthew and Luke, who sometimes receive credit for downplaying Mark's apocalypticism, both add apocalyptic details to shape their stories.

Matthew's introductory material consists of narratives concerning Jesus' birth. Dreams play a pivotal role in these stories. Joseph learns of Mary's pregnancy through such a revelation (1:20–21). The Magi who visit Jesus, having seen "his star" as a sign of the Messiah's birth, receive a dream that warns them not to return to King Herod, who might use their knowledge to kill the infant (2:12). Joseph, likewise, leads his family to Egypt in response to a dream (2:19–20). Dream revelations thus shape Matthew's beginning, and apocalyptic discourse enhances the gospel's ending. Upon Jesus' death, not only does the temple curtain rip apart, but also many of the righteous rise from their graves and appear in the holy city (27:51–54). The gospel itself ends by setting its epilogue within an apocalyptic context: Jesus commissions his followers to teach all peoples, promising his presence until "the end of the age" (28:20).

Luke also introduces apocalyptic discourse, though its method is radically different from Matthew's. Almost all scholars believe that the same author composed both Luke's gospel and the book of Acts, which continues the gospel's story. One can hardly overstate the significance of Acts for Luke's interpretation of Jesus' story. Again, apocalyptic motifs frame Acts. The book begins with the disciples awaiting Israel's restoration. Jesus promises a different sort of apocalyptic sign: empowerment by the Holy Spirit (1:6–8). That promise receives dramatic fulfillment on the day of Pentecost (Acts 2). Luke interprets the Spirit's descent as the fulfillment of Joel's eschatological prophecy, which would be realized "in those days" (2:16–21). According to Joel,

In the last days it will be, God declares,
that I will pour out my Spirit upon all flesh,
    and your sons and your daughters shall prophesy,
and your young men shall see visions,
    and your old men shall dream dreams.
Even upon my slaves, both men and women,
    in those days I will pour out my Spirit;
    and they shall prophesy.
And I will show portents in the heaven above
    and signs on the earth below,
blood, and fire, and smoky mist.
The sun shall be turned to darkness
    and the moon to blood,
before the coming of the Lord's great and glorious day.
Then everyone who calls on the name of the Lord shall be saved.
(Acts 2:17–21; cf. Joel 2:28-32)

Acts begins with apocalyptically-oriented expectations and manifestations, and then visions and dreams propel its plot. The inclusion of Gentiles in the churches provides one of the book's central emphases, with Peter and Paul the key figures in this process. Both Peter and Paul come to their embrace of Gentile Christianity through visionary revelations, and Luke *repeats* these accounts so as to emphasize their importance. Peter's vision of the unclean food reveals that God has declared all things–and all people–clean (10:9–11:17), whereas Paul's encounter with the risen Jesus commissions him as a missionary to the Gentiles (9:1–29; 22:3–21; 26:9–20). Without these revelations, this essential emphasis in Acts would be impossible. Other noteworthy revelations in Acts include Stephen's vision of the risen Jesus (7:55–56), the vision that prepared Ananias to receive Paul (9:10–16), the one that prepared Cornelius to meet Peter (10:3–6), Paul's vision of the Macedonian (16:9), and Paul's vision in Corinth (18:9–10). Thus, Acts continues the apocalyptic story of Jesus through the experiences of his earliest followers.

If Luke's creation of Acts as a sequel poses a radical innovation, Luke's gospel also follows Matthew's lead by using dramatic revelations to prepare the way for Jesus' arrival. Visions to his uncle (and John's father) Zechariah (1:8–20), the angel Gabriel's visit to Mary (1:26–38), and the angels' visit to the shepherds (2:8–14) all attest to his importance.

Thus, apocalyptic motifs, including dramatic revelations, provide fundamental structuring elements for each of the synoptic gospels. They introduce Jesus in apocalyptic contexts; they affirm his identity through the transfiguration; and they present his resurrection as the first event in the end-time plan. Granted, the gospels share a basic story line, but they also develop independent material. Even then, apocalyptic discourse shapes the structure of each story.

The Gospels of John and Thomas

In stark contrast to the synoptic gospels stand the gospels of John and Thomas. John and Thomas both show familiarity with apocalyptic eschatology, but they also undermine it to some degree. Indeed, one might say that while John reinterprets apocalyptic eschatology, Thomas outright rejects it. These gospels' response to early Christian apocalyptic discourse provides a fascinating study in its own right.[24]

John and Thomas Contrasted

John and Thomas could hardly be more different, both in their own historical contexts and beyond them. For modern readers, the most essential difference may be their relative familiarity. While Christians have received John's authority since the earliest stages of the canonization process, modern readers did not even have access to the text of Thomas until its discovery in 1945 at an Egyptian site called Nag Hammadi.[25] And whereas John presents a story of Jesus in narrative form, moving from his encounter with John the Baptist to his passion and resurrection like the other canonical gospels, Thomas presents a series of sayings attributed to Jesus, with minimal narrative material and no obvious arrangement. Moreover, from a literary point of view, John's Jesus talks mostly about himself, whereas Thomas's Jesus reveals that salvation comes primarily from knowing oneself and one's true nature.

Indeed, the issue of salvation represents the greatest divide between John and Thomas. Salvation in John comes through Jesus alone, while in Thomas the potential for salvation resides within the individual seeker. John emphasizes Jesus' divine identity, but Thomas reveals the divine element inherent in all persons.

Convergence Points

We must also acknowledge these gospels' points of convergence. Both John and Thomas portray a vast gap between the knowledge of those who know and those who don't. Thomas calls Jesus' sayings the "hidden sayings," while John insists that the world did not "comprehend" Jesus.[26] Such "insider knowledge" fosters a sectarian mentality according to which the few who know are superior to the masses who do not. Such privileged knowledge also indicates a certain mystical bent in John and Thomas: Both gospels affirm a living Jesus whose followers integrate elusive teaching into their sacred experience, as they embody a "present knowledge."[27] The mysticism we find in John and Thomas does not derive from apocalyptic discourse, but it shares with apocalyptic discourse this interest in sacred mysteries as they are revealed to and appropriated by privileged insiders.

The synoptic Jesus reveals the mystery of God's kingdom (Mk. 4:11 par. Mt. 13:11; Lk. 8:10), but his difficult sayings figure even more prominently in John and Thomas. Just as importantly, both gospels apparently assume some familiarity with the stories of Jesus' life, but their emphasis lies elsewhere. Thomas devotes its attention to Jesus' hidden sayings, whereas John stresses Jesus' heavenly identity as well as his teachings. With respect to John, two ancient Christian authorities from Alexandria understood this. Clement of Alexandria called John "a spiritual gospel."[28] Origen wrote that "although [John] does not always tell the truth literally, he always tells the truth spiritually," because none of the other canonical gospels "clearly spoke of [Jesus'] divinity, as John does."[29]

Eschatology in John and Thomas

With respect to eschatology, both John and Thomas diverge from the synoptic point of view. For one thing, John and Thomas agree that one's origins matter at least as much as one's destiny. Indeed, Thomas explicitly rejects end-time speculation as altogether misplaced. Thomas associates such eschatological concerns with the authoritarian church represented by Jesus' "disciples," concerns that Jesus rejects outright.

> The disciples said to Jesus, "Tell us how our end will be." Jesus said, "Have you discovered, then, the beginning, that you look for the end? For where the beginning is, there will the end be. . . Blessed is the person who will take his place in the beginning; that person will know the end and will not experience death."[30] (logion 18)

The trouble, Thomas insists, is that people seek salvation from sources outside of themselves, particularly by hoping for redemption in the end times.

Again, when the disciples ask concerning the new world and the fate of the dead, Jesus rebukes them: "What you look forward to has already come, but you do not recognize it" (51).[31] In other words, salvation has already manifested itself. To await something else only wastes energy.

John takes a more moderate stance than does Thomas with respect to apocalyptic hope. Indeed, John's Jesus repeatedly addresses the topics of judgment and the afterlife. Though he promises his followers eternal life, complete with heavenly dwelling places upon his return (14:1–7), he also locates eternal life in the present (3:36; 4:14; 5:24, 39; 6:47, 54). Indeed, eternal life consists not in life after death but in knowing God and God's Son (17:3). In short, John's gospel differs from Thomas's by acknowledging the future hope of resurrection and of Jesus' return, but it also agrees with Thomas by placing salvation in the here and now.

John's gospel includes no great eschatological discourse such as we find in the synoptics, and it rarely employs the telltale topics and signs of apocalyptic discourse. Instead, in response to early believers who expected that Jesus' Beloved Disciple would remain alive until Jesus' return, John calls them to focus on the present:

So the rumor spread in the community that this disciple would not die. Yet Jesus did not say to him that he would not die, but, "If it is my will that he remain until I come, what is that to you?" (21:23)

Likewise, when Martha laments the death of her brother Lazarus, she and Jesus have this exchange:

Jesus	Martha
Jesus said to her, "Your brother *will rise again.*"	Martha said to him, "I know that *he will rise again in the resurrection on the last day.*"
Jesus said to her, "*I am* the resurrection and the life. Those who believe in me, even though they die, will live, and *everyone who lives and believes in me will never die.* Do you believe this?"	She said to him, "Yes, Lord, I believe that you are the Messiah, the Son of God, the one coming into the world." (11:23–27)

Thus, while the believers speculate concerning the Beloved Disciple's fate, Jesus calls them to the present. While Martha expects her brother to rise "on the last day," Jesus raises him that very day.[32] His healing of Lazarus occurs only in John's gospel, and it underscores John's approach to eschatology. In response to the question, *Is salvation a present reality or a future reality?* John simply answers, *Yes.*

John and Thomas differ in that Thomas rejects eschatological speculation outright, whereas John affirms certain apocalyptic hopes. But in neither gospel does Jesus come across as an apocalyptically-oriented prophet. Both gospels agree in locating salvation in the here and now rather than in a distant future.

The Historical Jesus and Apocalyptic Discourse

The synoptic gospels associate Jesus and his followers with apocalyptic expectations such as the kingdom of God, the final judgment, and the restoration of Israel. They also link Jesus to apocalyptic visions and mystical struggles. Yet John's gospel downplays these interests, and Thomas scorns eschatological speculation altogether. For decades, most scholars have trusted the synoptic portrait, according to which Jesus stands firmly within apocalyptic traditions; yet recently, many have begun to question the synoptic accounts. The synoptic gospels, they argue, reflect the apocalyptic expectations that influenced many early Christian communities, but Thomas reveals a different possibility. What if the Jesus of history more closely resembled Thomas's Jesus than the synoptic Jesus? What if Jesus actually propounded sayings concerning living in the here and now rather than teachings concerning the coming Son of Man and the final judgment?

Technical Issues

Two technical debates attend this argument. We have space here merely to introduce them. First, while some scholars believe Thomas reflects a very ancient and independent stream of tradition concerning Jesus' teachings, others regard Thomas's traditions as much later and far more dubious.[33] The debate concerning Thomas attends another debate concerning the nature of Q, the hypothetical source that accounts for material shared by Matthew and Luke but not Mark. Some claim that Q reflects a history of transmission and editing. In this view the apocalyptic material in Q derives from later traditions that do not derive from Jesus. Like Thomas, some argue, Q's earliest layer amounted to sayings of Jesus that were free of apocalyptic discourse.[34] For these reasons, some find ancient Jesus traditions in Thomas and Q's oldest material that testify to a non-apocalyptic Jesus.

Jesus in Thomas and the Synoptics: An Example

Thomas often includes sayings that parallel material from the synoptics. Consider this one:

Thomas 92- 94[35]	Matthew 7:6–8	Luke 11:9–11
Jesus said, "Seek and you will find. Yet, what you asked Me about in former times and which I did not tell you then, now I do desire to tell, but you do not inquire after it. <Jesus said,> "Do not give what is holy to dogs, lest they throw them on the dung-heap. Do not throw the pearls to swine, lest they grind it [to bits]." Jesus said, "One who seeks will find, and [he who knocks] will be let in.	"Do not give what is holy to dogs; and do not throw your pearls before swine, or they will trample them under foot and turn and maul you. Ask, and it will be given you; search, and you will find; knock, and the door will be opened for you. For everyone who asks receives, and everyone who searches finds, and for everyone who knocks, the door will be opened."	"So I say to you, Ask, and it will be given you; search, and you will find; knock, and the door will be opened for you. For everyone who asks receives, and everyone who searches finds, and for everyone who knocks, the door will be opened. Is there anyone among you who, if your child asks for a fish, will give a snake instead of a fish?"

For Matthew and Luke (and therefore for Q), Jesus seems to be teaching about prayer. One *asks,* seeks, and knocks, and one receives. But for Thomas, prayer is absent; *no asking occurs.* Instead, one seeks and knocks. So whereas the Jesus of Q prepares his disciples to pray, Thomas's Jesus encourages self-reliant seeking. We may press this even further: in the synoptic saying, God is the source of blessing, while according to Thomas, we are on our own.

How do we account for this discrepancy? Has Thomas adapted a tradition that occurs in Matthew and Luke (or Q) and edited out the reference to prayer? Or have Matthew and Luke (or Q) added the element of prayer? Or, perhaps, do Thomas and the synoptics derive from altogether independent streams of tradition?[36]

The stakes in this debate run high, for they involve how contemporary persons understand Jesus. Those who argue for a non-apocalyptic Jesus tend to see Jesus as a countercultural sage, the sort of person who routinely undermined conventional assumptions about power and human worth. Not looking to an eschatological future, this Jesus appealed to ordinary people in the here and now, building a movement of mercy and inclusion rather than of status and power. Many persons, both within the church and beyond, gravitate toward this Jesus, who inspires contemporary social engagement.[37]

The apocalyptic Jesus may be less user-friendly. The most influential portrait of an eschatological Jesus emerged way back in 1906, with Albert Schweitzer's publication of *The Quest of the Historical Jesus.*[38] Jesus, Schweitzer maintained, makes sense only in the context of apocalyptic eschatology, which modern persons do not share. Thus, "The historical Jesus will be to our time a stranger and an enigma." For theology, Schweitzer maintained, "There is nothing more negative than the result of the critical study of the Life of Jesus."[39] Because the apocalyptic Jesus is motivated by expectations regarding God's renewal of Israel, his direct relevance for modern life—and belief—remain unclear.[40] As Bart D. Ehrman writes,

> Very few people who devote their lives to studying the historical Jesus actually *want* to find a Jesus who is completely removed from our own time. What people want…is *relevance.*[41]

Yet most scholars, myself included, still associate the historical Jesus with apocalyptic eschatology.[42] For one thing, Thomas and Q may or may not testify to an ancient layer of non-apocalyptic Jesus tradition. We do not have a reliable basis for dating Thomas, so we cannot assume that it presents earlier forms of Jesus' teachings than do the synoptics. Moreover, Thomas's outright rejection of eschatological speculation reveals that gospel's awareness of apocalyptic Jesus traditions—the very sort of material we find in its synoptic counterparts. Thus, while we cannot rule out very early layers of non-apocalyptic tradition behind Thomas, neither have they been demonstrated to exist. Instead, the Thomas we now have necessarily emerged later than traditions concerning Jesus' eschatological teachings.

At the same time, several considerations undermine the hypothesis of a non-apocalyptic layer of Q. By definition, Q is a hypothetical document. No ancient copies of Q exist. And because Q is defined in terms of material shared by Matthew and Luke but not Mark, neither do we know the full text of Q. Once again, apocalyptic discourse figures prominently in Q–as we can reconstruct it from Matthew and Luke. Hence, speculation concerning Q's earlier and later stages is just that–speculation. We should not be surprised that some experts claim that Q became *more* eschatological over time, while others argue that its later layers *downplayed* eschatological concerns.[43]

The Earliest Jesus Traditions

Having acknowledged the problems attending hypothetical stages of Thomas and Q as sources for the earliest Jesus traditions, we turn to our earliest sources for the Jesus movement: Paul's letters and the synoptic gospels (including Q as we have it). As we have seen, the synoptics consistently portray Jesus and his first followers in an eschatological context. And as we will see, so does Paul.

More to the point, the synoptics' portrait of an eschatological Jesus makes fine sense in its own context. Proclaiming repentance in preparation for the kingdom of God, John the Baptist immediately preceded Jesus. And our first evidence for Jesus' followers comes from Paul, who prepared believers for Jesus' return in victory and judgment. If Jesus began his career in the company of John the Baptist, and if the earliest Jesus communities for which we have hard evidence were awaiting Jesus' return, an apocalyptic Jesus accounts for this continuity between John the Baptist and Paul. In other words, an apocalyptic Jesus fits the context in which he emerged, and he also accounts for the early development of the movement that followed him.[44]

Although the synoptic attribution of apocalyptic eschatology to Jesus may basically reflect the sorts of things Jesus did and said, questions remain. The most basic question involves, *What was Jesus up to?* Jesus gathered disciples and traveled through Galilee and Judea, where he proclaimed the kingdom of God, taught and healed, portrayed the eschatological events in both parables and discourses, staged some sort of public disturbance in Jerusalem, and celebrated an eschatological meal with his disciples. If we interpret these activities within the context of apocalyptic eschatology, do any patterns emerge?

First, Jesus demonstrates a keen interest in Israel and its renewal. He calls twelve disciples, evoking the totality of Israel's twelve tribes. He brings the disciples to Jerusalem, where he acts as if he were Israel's king. His major apocalyptic discourses tie the temple's destruction to the last days.

Eden Seminary Bookstore
475 E. Lockwood Ave.
St. Louis, MO 63119
(314)918-2500
(314)918-2520

SALES RECEIPT

Transaction #:   68774
Account #:   1143
Date: 8/13/2013   Time: 2:49:23 PM
Cashier: 1   Register #: 1

Item	Description	Amount
000000002509	Clearance Book	$2.00
000000002509	Clearance Book	$2.00

	Sub Total	$4.00
	MO Sales Tax	$0.34
	Total	$4.34
	Cash Tendered	$20.35
	Change Cash	$16.01

* 6 8 7 7 4 *
Thank you for shopping
Eden Seminary Bookstore
We hope you'll come back soon!

So it seems that Jesus expected to reconstitute Israel, to restore and renew the covenant people.

Second, Jesus apparently believed apocalyptic signs would accompany Israel's restoration. While Jesus denied that anyone could calculate the hour of the eschatological events (Mt. 24:44 par. Lk. 12:40; Mk. 13:32 par. Mt. 24:36), he also sketched a fairly conventional scenario for them, including crises on earth and signs in the heavens.

Third, Jesus apparently shared Daniel's vision of the coming of the Son of Man to bring God's kingdom and to judge the earth's peoples. As we have seen, the title "Son of Man" figures prominently in the synoptics, where Jesus uses it to designate himself. While some scholars debate whether Jesus *actually* believed himself to be that Son of Man, as the synoptics claim, or whether Jesus expected another eschatological figure to arrive from the heavens, it seems clear that Jesus expected history to reach a decisive moment.[45]

Finally, it seems Jesus understood that his own ministry carried eschatological import. Not only was the kingdom of God on its way, but it was present in a new way in Jesus' own presence and activities. For example, Jesus proclaimed that the kingdom of God was somehow present in the here and now (Mt. 12:28 par. Lk. 11:20; Lk. 17:20–21).[46] Moreover, many of his parables concerning the kingdom lend themselves to "present" interpretations; that is, they likely describe what the kingdom of God is like now rather than what it will be like when it comes. Jesus' actions also implied that he acted the part of Israel's messiah. *He* called the twelve disciples together; *he* forgave sins; *he* marched into Jerusalem and interrupted the temple's business; and *he* hosted the eschatological banquet. Jesus believed the kingdom of God was breaking in with his ministry, and he expected to participate in its full manifestation.[47]

Such a construction of Jesus may not fit easily with many forms of devotion to him. It doesn't explicitly account for why some Christians believe Jesus died so that their sins could be forgiven. One wonders how a Jesus who two thousand years ago announced the kingdom of God and Israel's restoration would nourish a contemporary social vision. In his own context, however, people readily grasped the significance of Jesus' activities. Faced with the question of loyalty to Caesar, his reply–"Give to the emperor the things that are the emperor's, and to God the things that are God's" (Mk. 12:17 par. Mt. 22:21; Lk. 20:25)–expressed his anti-imperial sentiment. After all, because all things belong to God, what is left for Caesar? Although Jesus didn't start a revolt, his gathering of a new community, in which people shared food and hospitality with no one holding authority over others, pointed the way to an alternative path.[48]

Moreover, many interpret his challenge to the Jerusalem temple authorities as a critique of the oppression of Israel's poor by their own elite.[49] Thus, while Jesus likely proclaimed an apocalyptic message, that message also implied profound involvement with the conflicts of his day. Indeed, his message and his actions led to his political execution. All the while, Jesus' apocalyptic eschatology empowered the hope—is it misguided?—that one day good would win out over evil.[50] Perhaps, as Martin Luther King, Jr., proclaimed in his "I Have a Dream" speech, "The arc of the moral universe is long but it bends toward justice."[51]

FOR FURTHER READING

For introductions to the canonical gospels, I recommend consulting one of the standard introductions to the New Testament:

Achtemeier, Paul J., Joel B. Green, and Marianne Meye Thompson. *Introducing the New Testament: Its Literature and Theology.* Grand Rapids, Mich.: Eerdmans, 2001.

Brown, Raymond E. *An Introduction to the New Testament.* ABRL. New York: Doubleday, 1997.

Burkett, Delbert. *An Introduction to the New Testament and the Origins of Christianity.* Cambridge: Cambridge University Press, 2002.

Ehrman, Bart D. *The New Testament: A Historical Introduction to the Early Christian Writings.* 3d ed. New York: Oxford University, 2003.

Further readings for this section should include:

Allison, Dale C. *Jesus of Nazareth: Millenarian Prophet.* Minneapolis: Fortress, 1998.

Crossan, John Dominic. *The Historical Jesus: The Life of a Mediterranean Jewish Peasant.* San Francisco: HarperSanFrancisco, 1991.

_____. *Jesus: A Revolutionary Biography.* San Francisco: HarperSanFrancisco, 1994.

Fredriksen, Paula. *From Jesus to Christ: The Origins of the New Testament Images of Jesus.* 2d ed. New Haven, Conn.: Yale University Press, 2000.

Kloppenborg, John S. *The Formation of Q: Trajectories in Ancient Christian Wisdom Collections.* Studies in Antiquity and Christianity. Philadelphia: Fortress Press, 1987.

Pagels, Elaine. *Beyond Belief: The Secret Gospel of Thomas.* New York: Random House, 2003.

Patterson, Stephen J., James M. Robinson, and Hans-Gebhard Bethge. *The Fifth Gospel: The Gospel of Thomas Comes of Age.* Harrisburg, Pa.: Trinity Press International, 1998.

Powell, Mark Allan. *Jesus as a Figure in History: How Modern Historians View the Man from Galilee.* Louisville: Westminster John Knox Press, 1998.

Valantasis, Richard. *The Gospel of Thomas.* New Testament Readings. New York: Routledge, 1997.

CHAPTER 5

The Pauline Epistles

The apostle Paul was among the first to proclaim Jesus as the Messiah around the eastern rim of the Mediterranean. His accomplishments stagger the imagination. Though Paul worked during an era of relatively high mobility, the range of his travels still evokes wonder. In an age of travel by foot and by ship, with brigands and pirates along the way, his direct influence ranged from Jerusalem to Antioch in Syria, to Ephesus in Asia Minor, to Corinth in Achaia, and to Rome. In many cities Paul founded Jesus communities, or churches. In others he built strong relationships and bases of operations.

Moreover, if one takes the New Testament at face value, his influence appears overwhelming. Of the twenty-seven books in the New Testament, thirteen are attributed to Paul, two (Acts and 2 Peter) mention him directly, and another (Hebrews) has often been attributed to him. Beyond the New Testament, the literary evidence remains impressive, with noncanonical Acts of Paul, additional letters written in Paul's name, and even an influential apocalypse attributed to him. His literary influence is so great that some credit Paul with being the true inventor of Christianity, the one who took traditions concerning Jesus and turned them into a cult of mystical salvation.

Paul was important in his own day, but he was not *that* important. He did not invent devotion to the risen Jesus; rather, by his own account, others preceded him. He depended on the networks and beneficence generated by others. His letters, which have so influenced the continuing development of Christianity, reflect authentic social tension, even opposition. In many cases they may not have won over their initial audiences. And according to most scholars, several—perhaps six—of the New Testament letters attributed to Paul are pseudonymous.

Interpreting Paul

If there are diverse and conflicting interpretations of Jesus, for Paul things are hardly any different. Many factors complicate the issue, the greatest of which is the state of the evidence. The book of Acts relates a story of Paul's career, or much of it, but the accuracy of Acts as historiography is hotly contested. At some points Acts' portrait of Paul contradicts what the apostle himself wrote. Acts also portrays Paul in fairly generic terms. His speeches echo the dominant themes of the book as a whole. In form or content Paul's speeches can scarcely be distinguished from those of Peter and Stephen. Thus, it appears that although Acts recounts certain events from Paul's career, we should not rely on the book too heavily for the nuances of Paul's message or for his understanding of the events. Moreover, as mentioned above, scholars debate which of the books attributed to Paul actually derive from him. Scholars strongly affirm Paul's authorship of seven letters–Romans, 1 and 2 Corinthians, Galatians, Philippians, 1 Thessalonians, and Philemon. The authenticity of Ephesians, Colossians, and 2 Thessalonians remains disputed. And only a few scholars believe that Paul composed 1 and 2 Timothy or Titus. Because of the state of the evidence, particularly the reliability of Acts and the question of the epistles' authorship, "knowing Paul" is not a simple matter.

Thus, a balanced view of Paul and his influence is in order. For our purposes, we must engage the fundamentally apocalyptic nature of Paul's proclamation. Paul claims that he received his gospel through an apocalypse. He proclaims the resurrection of Jesus and his imminent return. Paul repeatedly reminds of God's judgment and ultimate victory. He even goes so far as to see in Jesus' resurrection the sign that God is bringing the entire cosmos to order. Just as importantly, Paul applies these apocalyptic convictions to the everyday moral life of his audiences in remarkably diverse ways.

Paul owned a rich cultural inheritance. One the one hand, he often argues for or assumes viewpoints common among the popular philosophical and religious discourses of the Greco-Roman world. Like the Cynics and the Stoics, he appeals to Greek athletic competitions as a metaphor for the struggles of the soul.[1] Like the Stoics, Paul argues that the very structure of creation reflects the nature of the Creator. Like the Platonists, Paul distinguishes between flesh and spirit, the changing and the permanent. His epistles adapt conventional Greco-Roman forms, and in them he exploits the standard devices of classical rhetoric.

On the other hand, Paul repeatedly quotes from and alludes to the Jewish Scriptures, often employing interpretive techniques prominent among Jews of the day. His letters reflect serious grappling with Jewish issues, particularly the boundaries between Jews and Gentiles and the role of Torah in shaping communal and individual life. Of course, Paul participated heavily in Jewish apocalyptic discourse, with his convictions concerning divine judgment, the resurrection of Jesus, and the resurrection of the saints.

Scholars have often expressed Paul's cultural formation in terms of "Jewish" and "Greek" elements of his thought.[2] According to this model one might trace Paul's ideas to their proper origins, often with one dimension emphasized at the expense of the other. As Abraham J. Malherbe has expressed it,

> Modern interpreters have operated on the assumption that...Paul was part of all that he had met, and that to understand him properly, it is necessary to view him in the cultural context in which he lived. As one might expect of him, however, Paul makes it difficult to decide which context, the Jewish or the Greek, we should examine in order to understand his letters better.[3]

As Malherbe points out, the trouble with this way of interpreting Paul is that in the ancient world no one encountered "Judaism" and "Hellenism" as discrete cultural streams. Rather, as a Diaspora Jew, Paul thoroughly participated in the cosmopolitan flow of ancient Mediterranean culture.

Nevertheless, distinguishing between "Jewish" and "Greek" modes of thinking can offer some help for reading Paul. For example, Paul devotes 1 Corinthians 15 to an argument for Jesus' resurrection and for the future resurrection of the righteous. This is a thoroughly Jewish apocalyptic topic, but Paul's treatment of it also reflects a preoccupation with Greco-Roman understandings of human nature and the material realm. Yes, people will be raised in bodily form, Paul argues, but at the same time their new bodies will be "spiritual" and "incorruptible." In other words, while Paul advances the apocalyptic expectation of bodily resurrection, he also assumes the Platonic distinction between the body and the soul, the transient ("corruptible") and the permanent ("incorruptible").[4] Thus, Paul accommodates his specifically Jewish apocalyptic discourse to his Greco-Roman philosophical sensibilities.

Paul the Visionary

Paul's Visions in Acts

Perhaps the most widely known tradition concerning Paul is the "conversion" story from Acts. We have discussed this tradition in chapter 4 with a view toward the role of visions in the book of Acts, but here we will look at it with respect to the role of apocalyptic discourse in the Pauline epistles. Acts narrates the experience three times, in chapters 9, 22, and 26. Traveling from Jerusalem to Damascus in his quest to persecute "any who belonged to the Way" (9:2), Paul is driven to the ground by a flash of heavenly light. He also hears the voice of the risen Jesus, who directs him to continue to Damascus, where he will learn what he is to do. In Damascus

Paul indeed encounters the disciple Ananias, who guides him into his new identity and mission.

This is clearly a revelatory experience, one that in some ways recalls the visionary reports one finds in the literary apocalypses. Perhaps its most interesting aspect involves the nature of what exactly Paul is supposed to have experienced.

a. According to Acts 9:3–7, Paul *saw* a light and *heard* a voice, but he *did not see* Jesus. Those who were with him "heard the voice but saw no one," which may imply that Paul saw Jesus.
b. In Acts 9:17 Ananias relates that Paul in fact did see Jesus.
c. The account of Acts 26 strongly resembles that of chapter 9. Paul sees the light and hears the voice, but the narrative does not relate the experience of Paul's companions. Paul describes the experience as a heavenly vision (*ouranio optasia*; 26:19).
d. In Acts 22 Paul says that he and his companions did see the light, but his companions did not heard the voice, as he did.
e. In addition to Paul's initial encounter with Jesus, Acts 16:9, 18:9–10, and 22:17–21 attribute other visionary experiences to Paul.[5]

Paul's Vision Accounts

This is how things look in Acts, but what about Paul's own accounts? Although many scholars believe Paul *does* discuss this revelatory experience, he never does so in a way that directly corroborates any of the three versions from Acts.

In 1 Corinthians 15:3–11, Paul recounts the traditions concerning Jesus' resurrection. Paul declares that the risen Jesus "appeared also to me" (15:8). Clearly, Paul claims a *vision* of the risen Jesus. But does this experience relate to the story in Acts?

Even more vexing is 2 Corinthians 12:1–10. At a literal level, Paul boasts of "visions and revelations *[optasias kai apokalypseis]* of [or from] the Lord" (12:1). But then he makes the odd move of shifting to the third person, as if the visions and revelations were not his own but someone else's:

> I know a man in Christ who fourteen years ago—whether in the body I do not know, or out of the body I do not know, God knows—was caught up into heaven. And I know such a man—whether in the body or apart from the body I do not know, God knows—that he was caught up into Paradise and heard unutterable words which it is not permissible for a mortal to speak. On behalf of such a person will I boast, but on my own behalf I will not boast, except in weaknesses. (12:2–5, author's trans.)

Those weaknesses provide the segue by which Paul reveals himself as the actual seer. Not only has Paul experienced visions and revelations, he also has learned to cope with weakness. His visions are "extraordinary" (12:7, author's trans.), but they do not elevate him beyond human limitations. Whether through the visions or through a more subtle form of experience and/or reflection, God reveals to Paul that divine power finds perfection in weakness (12:9).

Again, the question surfaces: Is there a relationship between Paul's tour of Paradise and the traditions in Acts? In this case the only overlap involves the matter of audition: Paul hears heavenly voices. Yet even here a difference appears. Acts tells us whose voice Paul hears and what the voice says, but in 2 Corinthians the words cannot be repeated. Moreover, though in Acts Paul's vision occurs in the human present and manifests itself in the physiological effect of temporary blindness, this account involves a movement, bodily or not, out of the ordinary world and into the heavenly realms. (If the third heaven and Paradise are not identical, then we have two vision reports, not one.)[6] Unless the conversation about the thorn in Paul's flesh is part of the vision, in 2 Corinthians 1:10 Paul says nothing about encountering the risen Jesus, which is the essential point both in Acts and in 1 Corinthians 15:3–11.

Scholars continue to debate whether 2 Corinthians 12 reports the same basic experience as the traditions in Acts. For our purposes, the larger point is that mystical revelations were a prominent part of Paul's religious experience. Paul himself insists that his proclamation of Jesus begins with revelatory experience. In Galatians 1:11–12, he dismisses the notion that his gospel derives from second-hand tradition, insisting that it came through a revelatory encounter.

> For I want you to know…that the gospel that was proclaimed by me is not of human origin; for I did not receive it from a human source, nor was I taught it, but I received it through a revelation *[apokalypsis]* of Jesus Christ.

Paul's claim here in Galatians is even stronger than the one in 2 Corinthians 12. Here, he bases his authority—and that of his teaching—entirely upon his own mystical experience. And to this singular apocalypse he attributes his revelation concerning Jesus. Many believe this is an allusion to the Damascus Road revelation of Acts 9.[7]

In one more instance Paul appeals to his mystical experiences, though it is easy to overlook. In Galatians 2:2, Paul claims that he visited the Jerusalem apostles "in response to a revelation" (*kata apokalypsin*). Again, Paul's point involves his authority, for while Paul has been defending his gospel against unnamed opponents, he has also been asserting his independence from other Christian authorities. Thus, he did not venture to Jerusalem because he felt a need for the approval of others; rather, he went from a position of strength in response to a mystical revelation.

To some degree, all three of these texts (1 Cor. 15:3–11; 2 Cor. 12:1–10; Gal. 1:11–12 and 2:2) reflect Paul's struggles to assert his authority among early Christian communities. The challenges may vary, but the argument is fairly consistent.

    a. In 1 Corinthians, Paul acknowledges the presence of factions among the Corinthian believers, but in chapter 15 his immediate concern is to argue for the future resurrection of the saints. Paul's claim that–like other Christian authorities–he has witnessed the risen Jesus plays a critical role in this argument. (More on this below.)

    b. In 2 Corinthians, Paul responds to challenges by persons he labels as "super-apostles" (11:5; *hyperlion apostolon*) and "false apostles" (11:13; *pseudaapostoloi*). According to Paul, these opponents wish to be equal to Paul in status but are in fact deceitful workers (11:12–13). In chapter 12 Paul's claims to extraordinary mystical experience elevate him above these opponents, while his claims that God's strength is most effective through weakness counters a pure contest of charismatic giftedness.

    c. In Galatians, Paul shows concern that some or most of his audience has adopted a teaching contrary to his own, specifically that Gentile disciples must live as Jews to be full participants in the church. He is also determined to assert his independence from the church leaders in Jerusalem.

Other signs reveal Paul's tenuous hold on authority. Only in 2 Corinthians 11 and Galatians 1 does Paul invoke the rhetoric of the "other gospel." For Paul, of course, there can be no other gospel (Gal. 1:7), so the "other gospels" he mentions at 2 Corinthians 11:4 and Galatians 1:6–7 are for him *anti*-gospels. And only in the context of such heated struggles for authority as these and that of 1 Corinthians 15 does Paul invoke his mystical experience.

Paul and the Resurrection of Jesus

Early Christian circles commonly believed that God had raised Jesus from the dead. Yet Paul most clearly articulates the significance of this belief. As we have seen, expectation for the resurrection of the righteous apparently has its roots in Jewish apocalyptic discourse. Although Jewish views on the afterlife varied considerably during this period, here we are specifically concerned with belief in the resurrection. Every instance of Jewish resurrection discourse prior to Jesus envisions a *corporate resurrection*. We find no expectation of the resurrection of a lone individual.

Of course, some Jewish texts do envision the resurrection of individuals, but always within the larger context of a corporate resurrection. For example, 2 Maccabees presents the famous account of seven brothers and their mother who were tortured and then martyred for their refusal to eat pork just prior to the Maccabean Revolt. Famously, the second brother dies with these words of resistance on his lips:

> "You accursed wretch, you dismiss us from this present life, but the King of the universe will raise us up to an everlasting renewal of life, because we have died for God's laws." (7:9)

Likewise, the fourth brother condemns the tyrant under whose hands he and his brothers are dying: "For you there will be no resurrection to life!" (7:14). These speeches reveal that 2 Maccabees envisions resurrection for all of God's people, while excluding the rest of humanity.

The speeches in 2 Maccabees demonstrate something else as well. Resurrection hopes accompanied social and political aspirations.[8] The first clear allusion to resurrection that we find in the Bible reflects this pattern:

> "At that time Michael, the great prince, the protector of your people, shall arise. There shall be a time of anguish, such as has never occurred since nations first came into existence. *But at that time your people shall be delivered,* everyone who is found written in the book. *Many of those who sleep in the dust of the earth shall awake, some to everlasting life, and some to shame and everlasting contempt.* Those who are wise shall shine like the brightness of the sky, and those who lead many to righteousness, like the stars forever and ever." (Dan. 12:1–3)

Like 2 Maccabees 7, Daniel imagines resurrection as a corporate event, though for Daniel some of the wicked are also raised to some form of judgment. But while Daniel's vision may sound otherworldly–"Those who are wise shall shine like the brightness of the sky"–it also links this hope for personal transformation to the expectation of sociopolitical reversal–"your people shall be delivered."

One could easily point to other examples, but the larger point is clear: For early Christians, the resurrection of Jesus posed a theological problem. If resurrection signals the eschatological age and if resurrection involves all the righteous, how do people make sense of the resurrection of Jesus, a solitary case? What does it mean to confess that God has raised one person, even the Messiah, from the dead?

One might object that the Bible records several stories in which individuals escape death. Enoch, as we have seen, apparently ascends into heaven without dying (Gen. 5:24), and Elijah rides up in a whirlwind (2 Kings 2:11). But these are not resurrection stories, for neither Enoch nor Elijah actually experiences death. We also find stories of people who apparently die but are restored to life. Elijah revives a widow's son in 1 Kings 17:17–24, and Elisha likewise restores the Shunammite woman's son in 2 Kings 4:32–36. In the New Testament, Jesus restores life to Jairus's daughter (Mk. 5:35–43 par. Lk. 8:49–56), a widow's son (Lk. 7:11–17), and

Lazarus (Jn. 11:1–44), and Acts attributes similar miracles to Peter and Paul (9:36–40 and 20:7–12). Yet none of these are precisely instances of resurrection, as those who are restored presumably go on to live ordinary lives–and even to age and die.

Resurrection belongs to a different order. In Paul's understanding, it involves transformation from one mode of life to another. For Jesus now resides beyond death and dwells with God in the heavenly realms (Rom. 8:34). Likewise, when Paul reflects upon the implications of the resurrection for Christ's followers, he thinks in terms of a transformed self, a "spiritual body" that is not subject to change, decay, or death (1 Cor. 15:35–57). Resurrection involves not merely the restoration of life, but a permanent and transformative event. As N. T. Wright says, for Paul

> his [Jesus'] body had not been abandoned in the tomb. Nor had it been merely resuscitated, coming back into a more or less identical life, to face death again at some point in the future. It had been transformed, changed, in an act of new creation through which it was no longer corruptible.[9]

Thus, for Paul, Jesus' resurrection presents a singular case, full of eschatological significance. First, because he understands resurrection as a corporate event, Jesus' resurrection as an individual reveals the destiny of all who are "in Christ." The risen Jesus is the "first fruits" from the dead, promising a similar future for his followers:

> But in fact Christ has been raised from the dead, the first fruits of those who have died. For since death came through a [single] human being, the resurrection of the dead has also come through a human being; for as all die in Adam, so all will be made alive in Christ. But each in his own order: Christ the first fruits, then at his coming those who belong to Christ. (1 Cor. 15:20–23)

Likewise,

> If the Spirit of him who raised Jesus from the dead dwells in you, [God] who raised Christ from the dead will give life to your mortal bodies also through [God's] Spirit that dwells in you. (Rom. 8:11; cf. 8:23)

Second, for Paul Jesus' resurrection brings not only future hope but a transformed present as well. He expresses this conviction in a variety of ways, most prominently that Christ "lives in" those who believe in him, or alternatively, that they reside "in Christ." Pauline salvation, then, includes a present dimension: The gospel embodies "God's power for those *who are being saved*" (1 Cor. 1:18, author's trans.),[10] in part because "Christ lives in me" now (Gal. 2:20, author's trans.). Likewise, "If anyone is in Christ, [they are] a new creation" (2 Cor. 5:17, author's trans.). In short, Christ's resurrection *inaugurates* the new order, and believers in Christ may participate in it in the present.

Third, for Paul, Jesus' resurrection opens the pathway to a cosmic vision. If God has raised Jesus from the dead, this simply indicates God's greater purposes for all of creation. Christ will come again to claim his people as his own and to restore order to the creation. The resurrection and return of Christ reveal that "the creator of the world will be all in all, by defeating evil and death and claiming the world as his own."[11] The resurrection even liberates the entire creation from the ordinary processes of decay (Rom. 8:21). At Jesus' return, the *parousia,* even the social and political powers that oppress humankind—every ruler, every authority, every power—are to be overturned (1 Cor. 15:24).

Jesus' resurrection and return rest at the core of Paul's proclamation of the gospel, apocalyptic through and through. As J. Christiaan Beker expressed it, "Apocalyptic is not a peripheral curiosity for Paul but the central climate and focus of his thought, as it was for most early Christian thinkers."[12] When Paul speaks of "the present evil age" (Rom. 12:2; 1 Cor. 1:20; 2:6, 8; 3:18; 2 Cor. 4:4; Gal. 1:4; cf. Eph. 1:21; 2:2; 1 Tim. 6:17; 4:10; Tit. 2:12), he implies a very different "age to come," contrasting the cosmos to the new creation (Gal. 6:14–15).[13] Jesus' death marks the end of one world order, but his resurrection inaugurates the new. In the meantime, those who are "in Christ" participate in that emerging new world both by enjoying its first fruits and by anticipating its full manifestation.

What Happens after We Die: Did Paul Change His Mind about the Afterlife?

As we have seen, early Jews and Christians held diverse views about *personal eschatology,* that is, whether one might expect life after death, how such a reality might come about, and what it would be like. Among those who held to an afterlife hope, some believed that the dead dwell in an indeterminate state until the resurrection, when the righteous would be raised to life. In this case, the fate of the wicked could be subject to judgment, or they could be expected simply to remain dead. Others believed that persons went immediately to their eternal dwelling places upon their deaths, a view that did not require a resurrection. And still others imagined an intermediate state between death and judgment.[14]

In 1 Thessalonians and 1 Corinthians, Paul apparently expresses the view that the righteous dead remain "asleep" until the parousia. Upon Christ's return, the righteous—either living or "sleeping"—are transformed into their spiritual embodiment and will dwell without change or decay forever. He also believes that the parousia is imminently at hand, even that he is among those who will be alive upon Jesus' return (1 Thess. 4:15, 17; 1 Cor. 15:51–52). We might compare this view with that reflected in Luke's gospel. There, Jesus tells the parable of the rich man and Lazarus: Immediately after death Lazarus goes to dwell in "Abraham's bosom," whereas the rich man who neglected Lazarus's needs travels to Hades and torment (16:19–31). Likewise, when one of the two men crucified alongside of Jesus asks Jesus, "Remember me when you come into your kingdom," Jesus replies, "*Today* you will be with me in Paradise" (23:42–43). Though Paul and the author of Luke share an expectation of life after death, they disagree has to how and when it happens. Paul apparently does not believe that upon death people immediately meet their fate, and he does not directly address what happens to the wicked. Luke's gospel assumes that one meets judgment or blessedness upon death, offering a specific image for what happens to the wicked.

Then we have Paul's letter to the Philippians. In contrast to 1 Thessalonians and 1 Corinthians, Paul apparently composed Philippians toward the end of his career. Reflecting upon the possibility of his own death, Paul writes:

> For to me, living is Christ and dying is gain. If I am to live in the flesh, that means fruitful labor for me; and I do not know which I prefer. I am hard pressed between the two: my desire is to depart and be with Christ, for that is far better; but to remain in the flesh is more necessary for you. (1:21–24)

Scholars have noted two differences between Paul's confession here and his claims in 1 Thessalonians and 1 Corinthians. For one thing, Paul shows much less confidence that he will remain alive at the parousia. Also, he apparently believes that he will move to a blessed existence immediately upon his death; otherwise, why should it matter *when* Paul would die?

Has Paul changed his mind? This question has vexed his interpreters to the point that one commentator simply gives up, writing that "Ultimately this matter lies in the area of mystery."[15] That same scholar proposes that perhaps Paul believed in an intermediate state of blessedness or punishment prior to the resurrection, a view held by some Jews at that time.[16] That explanation, however, is unsatisfactory, as it does not account for what Paul means when elsewhere he refers to "those who are asleep." Whatever Paul means, he certainly has not abandoned his belief in the future parousia (Phil. 1:6, 10; 2:16; 3:20–21).[17] In any case, whether Paul believes that upon their death the righteous sleep or immediately proceed to blessedness—or whether there is for him any difference between the two—remains a disputed question.

Paul and Apocalyptic Rhetoric

The resurrection and parousia may be central to Paul's preaching, but just as remarkable are the diverse ways in which he applies these convictions to particular situations. Today, people typically associate talk about the resurrection and the parousia with the sort of evangelistic preaching that uses fear to coerce people into religious conversion. Paul himself employed apocalyptic eschatology as a threat. But these convictions were core to Paul's gospel. They were far more than persuasive tools; rather, they held implications for a variety of situations.

Wayne Meeks has sketched out seven "epistolary uses" and "functions" served by Paul's apocalyptic beliefs and adapted by persons associated with him. Although this discussion diverges from Meeks, who acknowledged that his list could easily be revised or expanded, his list opens the path toward our appreciation of just how flexible apocalyptic discourse can be.[18]

1. Paul used apocalyptic discourse to *comfort* his audiences. The most famous instance is 1 Thessalonians 4:13–5:11. First Thessalonians is likely the most ancient Pauline letter that we have, and we can readily imagine the sort of situation it reflects. Apparently, Paul has proclaimed the message of the resurrection and parousia to the Thessalonians (cf. 1 Thess. 1:10), but he did not anticipate one problem. While waiting for Jesus' return, some of the Thessalonian believers have died. Have they missed out on their salvation? So Paul addresses the question directly, "Brothers [and sisters], we do not wish you to be ignorant concerning those who are asleep" (4:13, author's trans.). He replies that at the parousia those believers who have died will precede the living in joining Christ in the air. They will not miss out. "So," Paul writes, "comfort one another with these words."

> For God has destined us not for wrath but for obtaining salvation through our Lord Jesus Christ, who died for us, so that whether we are awake or asleep we may live with him. Therefore encourage one another and build up each other, as indeed you are doing. (5:9–11)

Likewise, in 1 Thessalonians 3:1–10 Paul defines the Thessalonians' suffering as part of the end-time tribulation.[19] In this case, apocalyptic discourse offers comfort, not primarily by promising a future blessing (though that is implied), but by reinterpreting the present. Paul doesn't deny the difficulty of the moment—what a foolish thing to do!—but instead he invests it with meaning. To arrive at that promised future, believers must endure distress. Difficult as it is, the present crisis actually *hastens* Jesus' return.

2. Paul can also use the resurrection/parousia discourse to *correct* his audiences. This is more precisely what's at stake in 1 Corinthians 15, where Paul argues that a future resurrection awaits Jesus' followers. But something more is at stake. For 1 Corinthians 15 represents the finishing move of a much longer argument in the epistle, in which Paul responds to various beliefs and practices held by members of his audience. Thus, Paul's discussion concerning resurrection is designed to bring to closure a debate that has many other dimensions.

Unfortunately, we do not have direct evidence for the position Paul is arguing against, so we have to read between the lines to reconstruct it. Although scholars have not reached absolute consensus on just what Paul finds objectionable among the Corinthians, it seems clear to most that a key issue is eschatology. Whereas some among the Corinthians believe that they currently possess all the blessings that Christ has to offer, Paul maintains that they are not yet as "mature" or as "complete" (*teleios*) as they think they are.[20]

> For we speak wisdom among those who are mature (*teleios*), yet it is not a wisdom whose origins are in this age, nor whose origins are in the rulers of this age, who are being done away with. (2:6, author's trans.)

Likewise,

> But when that which is perfect (*teleios*) comes, that which is partial shall cease. (13:10, author's trans.)

Especially pertinent here is the combination of completion language (*teleios*) with the Greek word *katargeo,* translated "to cease." In other words, Paul articulates what some scholars call an *eschatological reservation*: He insists that the fullness of blessing remains in the future, at Christ's return.

For Paul, this debate is not about just an arcane piece of eschatological speculation; it has important implications in the here and now. Throughout 1 Corinthians Paul admonishes members of his audience for a variety of practices that he believes are harmful or divisive. In his estimation, some of the Corinthians have been exercising their own spiritual gifts or knowledge at the expense of others. For example, while some of the Corinthians find it idolatrous to eat food that has been offered to various deities, others—on the basis of their *knowledge* (8:1)—insist upon eating such food. Paul's stance is that while such knowledge may be legitimate, neither is it complete nor is it of first importance. Also, some display their spiritual gifts in the public assembly in an apparent attempt to gain status, again at the expense of others. In the present, what matters most is not knowledge or gifts, but love (8:1; cf. 13:2). In the future, all truth will be revealed.

Paul is extremely crafty in this respect. For in the letter's greeting he congratulates the Corinthians, who

> do not lack in any spiritual gift as [they] await the revealing (*apokalypsin*) of our Lord Jesus Christ, who also will secure [them] until the end, without reproach on the day of the Lord Jesus Christ. (1:7–8, author's trans.)

So early in the letter, and keeping everything on a positive note, Paul introduces the very themes that embody issues of contention throughout the epistle. For while the Corinthians celebrate their spiritual gifts in the present, Paul insists that more remains in the end, the revealing of Jesus Christ.

3. Somewhere between comfort and correction lies *exhortation*. According to one ancient writer, exhortation amounts to the encouragement "to pursue something or to avoid something."[21] For example, in Romans 8 Paul's arresting image of the whole creation groaning in labor pains directly follows a call to live by the Spirit rather than by carnal desire.

> I consider that the sufferings of this present time are not worth comparing with the glory about to be revealed (*apokalyphthenai*) to us. For the creation waits with eager longing for the revealing (*apokalypsin*) of the children of God; for the creation was subjected to futility, not of its own will but by the will of the one who subjected it, in hope that the creation itself will be set free from its bondage to decay and will obtain the freedom of the glory of the children of God. We know that the whole creation has been groaning in labor pains until now; and not only the creation, but we ourselves, who have the first fruits of the Spirit, groan inwardly while we wait for adoption, the redemption of our bodies. (8:18–23)

Thus, one is able to endure hardship on the basis of one's eschatological hope. A better age is on the horizon.

Apparently, Paul knew apocalyptic hope as a moral resource in his own experience. For in 2 Corinthians 4:7–12 he catalogues his own suffering: Affliction, confusion, persecution, apparent defeat, and even the threat of death mark his life. But Paul also holds onto hope, for

> we know that the one who raised the Lord Jesus will raise us also with Jesus, and will bring us with you into his presence. (4:14)

The expectation for future resurrection and exaltation explains why Paul does not "lose heart" (4:16). Indeed, he expects a future reward for his present faithful suffering.

> For all of us must appear before the judgment seat of Christ, so that each may receive recompense for what has been done in the body, whether good or evil. (5:10)

This link between eschatological expectation and the call to faithfulness in the present characterizes Pauline apocalyptic exhortation. For example, the famous discussion of resurrection and parousia in 1 Thessalonians 4:13–5:11 contributes to a larger call to faithfulness. If one reads 1 Thessalonians from beginning to end, chapters 1–3 are all basically preparatory. Paul greets his audience and recalls their faithfulness. But at 1 Thessalonians 4:1, Paul moves toward exhortation:

> Finally, brothers and sisters, we ask and urge you in the Lord Jesus that, as you learned from us how you ought to live and to please God (as, in fact, you are doing), you should *do so more and more*.

Three topics follow this call:

a. discussions concerning sexual ethics
b. love within the community
c. the eschatological message of 4:13–5:11

It is almost as if Paul has written to the Thessalonians simply to keep in touch and to encourage their continuing faithfulness. Sexual ethics and community boundaries may have needed particular attention. On the other hand, discouragement regarding the fate of those who have died may have posed a potential stumbling block. For Paul's ethical exhortation to take effect, he must first respond to the grief and anxiety that have undermined the Thessalonians' zeal. Thus, Paul's teaching about the parousia may have served a larger strategy aimed at encouraging the Thessalonians to press on.

We see similar patterns scattered throughout the epistles. In 1 Corinthians 7:29–31 Paul recommends a life of celibacy; yet, knowing how demanding this call is, he reminds his audience that "the appointed time is short" and "the present form of this world is passing away." In Philippians 2:5–11 he recites what may have been an early hymn in asking his audience to emulate Christ's example of self-giving love. This hymn ends on an eschatological note: If Jesus yielded himself to the point of death, through the resurrection he has also been exalted. In the eschatological future all will recognize his preeminence (2:9–11). Likewise, Paul exhorts the Philippians to imitate *him,* reminding them that in the end Christ will transform their present bodies into glorious bodies (3:17–21). In Galatians 6:9 Paul calls the audience to persevere in doing good, for "at harvest-time" we will reap. In Romans 13:11–14 Paul follows a series of moral instructions with a reminder: "You know what time it is, how it is now the moment for you to wake from sleep. For salvation is nearer to us now than when we became believers" (13:11). Moreover, the greetings and closings of Paul's epistles occasionally combine apocalyptic topics with exhortation, as in Philippians 1:9–11 and Romans 16:17–20.

4. When Paul employs apocalyptic discourse to correct his audiences, he constructs detailed theological arguments. Sometimes he takes the less creative approach of using apocalyptic themes to *admonish* or warn them. Given Paul's reputation in some circles, this occurs perhaps less frequently than one might assume. Yet when Paul addresses the issue of divided opinions in Romans 14, he warns the audience not to pass judgment upon one another. Paul reminds them that all will acknowledge God's preeminence and that "every one of us will give an account of themselves to God" (14:12, author's trans.).

Paul invokes the same argument in 1 Corinthians 4:1–5, maintaining that his ministry is subject not to the Corinthians but to God's judgment alone. When Paul identifies lists of vices that prevent entry into the kingdom of God, as he does in 1 Corinthians 6:9–10 and Galatians 5:19–21, he is speaking of eschatological judgment (cf. 1 Cor. 15:24, 50).

5. As Meeks has observed, Pauline apocalyptic discourse could *enhance community boundaries* by defining community identity. When Paul employs the language of light and darkness, he applies an apocalyptic topos. In 1 Thessalonians 5:4–5 we see this pattern most clearly:

> But you, beloved, are not in darkness, for that day to surprise you like a thief; for you are all children of light and children of the day; we are not of the night or of darkness.

Paul's call links moral exhortation to apocalyptic expectation, but it adds the dimension of identity: those who are in Christ as children of the light as opposed to their neighbors who dwell in darkness. This recalls the identical division from Qumran and other apocalyptic texts. Thus, instances in which Paul's moral exhortation employs light/darkness discourse may also reflect apocalyptic antinomies (cf. Rom. 13:11–14; 2 Cor. 6:14; 11:14–15).

The light/darkness distinction may hold two connotations with respect to community identity. First, as we have seen in 1 Thessalonians 5:4–5, people may be classified as children of light or of darkness. Here, we have a matter of the *nature* or the *origins* of human beings, what we might call anthropological dualism that is common within apocalyptic discourse. Are some simply *created* as people of the darkness, or do they *become* such through their life choices and behaviors? We may not be able to determine whether Paul implies either connotation or both. Yet the larger implication remains clear: People simply are what they are. They possess an essence that remains stable over time, and one may eventually discriminate one group from the other.

A second light/darkness discourse can also relate to *knowledge,* for the children of light have been *enlightened.*

> And even if our gospel is veiled, it is veiled [only] to those who are perishing. In their case the god of this world has blinded the minds of the unbelievers, to keep them from seeing the light of the gospel of the glory of Christ, who is the image of God...For it is the God who said, "Let light shine out of darkness," who has shone in our hearts to give the light of the knowledge of the glory of God in the face of Jesus Christ. (2 Cor. 4:3–4, 6)

For Paul, is it conceivable that persons might move from one realm to another, from darkness to light, by being enlightened? This is a difficult question with many dimensions. Yet with respect to community identity, apocalyptic distinctions between the realms and persons of light and darkness serve as an important rhetorical resource for Paul.

6. We have seen earlier that in his most intense struggles over *authority* Paul appeals to his apocalyptic or mystical experiences. As Meeks has noted,

Paul can invoke his authority in opposite ways. In 1 Corinthians (and 2 Corinthians, as well), Paul's apocalyptic knowledge aims to *restrain* innovation, whereas in Galatians he uses it to *promote* change (that is, Gentile inclusion in the church without circumcision).[22] Throughout the epistles Paul grounds his primary claims to authority in his experience of the risen Jesus and his faithful ministry. It is remarkable, then, that his most heated claims–the ones involving "other" gospels–depend upon his personal revelations (apocalypses). As noted above, Paul only evokes the language of "other" gospels in 2 Corinthians 11–12 and Galatians 1. In both contexts he appeals to his revelatory experiences: his "visions and revelations of the Lord" (2 Cor. 12:1; Gal. 1:12). In both cases the translation could be his "apocalypse," for that is the Greek term used.

Paul, Celibacy, and the Parousia

Paul's views on sex and gender stand among the most disputed aspects of his letters. For one thing, these topics remain controversial today, especially because many religious groups regard Paul as an authority on such matters. Moreover, it remains unclear what exactly Paul has to say about these topics. Beyond the meaning of Paul's words, how do we discern his larger assumptions and motivations? In other words, we may fairly ask not just *what* Paul said, but *why he said it* and *what his words may have meant* for his ancient audiences.

Apparently, Paul was both unmarried and celibate. In 1 Corinthians 9:5 he notes that he and his colleagues travel without wives, and nowhere does he indicate that he is or has been married. In 1 Corinthians 7 he recommends celibacy, though he also recognizes marriage as a legitimate option. Even so, he offers himself as a model: "I wish that every person were as I am" (7:7, author's trans.).

Here we receive a window into Paul's way of thinking. He regards his celibacy as a sort of gift (*charisma*), and he recognizes that not everyone can sustain a celibate lifestyle. But why does Paul recommend celibacy and adopt it for himself? What values does it serve?[23]

First, asceticism was widely practiced in the ancient world—by Gentiles as well as Jews—as a means of self-control. As Calvin Roetzel writes, "Asceticism enabled one to transcend the physical limits so irrevocably imposed upon all humanity and provided a means of escape from a sinister world and a bodily prison."[24] Thus, asceticism was a sort of spiritual or psychic discipline, a means of cultivating the self. For example, though he was one of the wealthiest men in Rome, the philosopher and public figure Seneca would literally practice homelessness, just in case he came upon hard times. By disciplining desire, one could liberate oneself from attachment to things one could not control, whether sexual gratification, material luxury, or public status. One could also focus one's energies upon the pursuit of virtue or of mystical experience.

Second, asceticism may also have held a sociopolitical dimension. Many scholars have begun to point out that asceticism can literally embody a countercultural act, a form of personal liberation. In this respect Gail Corrington Streete has observed a link between apocalyptic discourses and ascetic practices:

> One type of apocalypticism, like one type of asceticism, represents an attempt by those disaffected with, or feeling themselves robbed of power by, the present situation.[25]

According to Streete, ascetic practices create space for personal freedom, an attempt to gain control over one's environment. She maintains that as social movements, both apocalypticism and asceticism

a. make radically dualistic distinctions between the ordinary and the ideal worlds
b. represent the present situation as the realm of Satan or the demonic
c. refuse to conform the self to the present situation or world
d. look beyond the present situation to another, ideal reality[26]

For example, some feminist scholars have noted that celibacy could free some women from the sexually determined conventions that bound them to particular men. The early Christian *Acts of Paul and Thecla* reveals how destabilizing celibacy could have been in the ancient world. A young woman named Thecla hears Paul proclaiming the gospel of celibacy, embraces it, and breaks off her engagement. Because it destabilizes society by bringing shame upon a prominent young man, her choice leads to persecution and, almost, to death. Likewise, celibate men could live free of attachment to place, status, or family origins. Whether or not this is what Paul believed or taught, that is in fact what he did. He traveled from one place to another, building alternative social networks.

Finally, celibate practices could be—and have been—inspired by eschatological hope. Distinctly apocalyptic communities such as the one at Qumran (CD 12:1–2) and the audiences in the book of Revelation (14:1–5) attest to this. People could ground eschatological celibacy in two assumptions. On the one hand, they could believe that the end of this age lies at hand and that sexual activity poses an unnecessary diversion in a time of crisis. On the other hand, they could look ahead to the new age, in which people could live like the angels who, Jesus said, "neither marry nor are given in marriage" (Mk. 12:25 par. Mt. 22:30; Lk. 20:35).

First Corinthians 7 reveals that all of these factors may have been at work in Paul's mind. He counsels that those who are married "will experience fleshly distress" (7:28, author's trans.), which may reflect either celibacy's philosophical or its countercultural dimensions—or, very possibly, both. Paul has already identified self-control (*akrasia* and *engkrateia*) among his concerns (7:5, 9), but he also emphasizes mutuality rather than male domination (e.g., 7:4–5, 12–16). At the same time, he adds an eschatological clarification: "I am saying this…the time is drawing near" (7:29, author's trans.). "For," he adds, "the present form of this world is passing away" (7:31).

Paul's Earliest Interpreters

In introductions to Ephesians, Colossians, 2 Thessalonians, 1 and 2 Timothy, and Titus, the question of authorship almost always comes first. Many considerations come into play in these discussions. First is the matter of *content*. Do the letters say things that are consistent with what Paul himself writes elsewhere? Next is the matter of *expression*. Are the words and stylistic features consistent with Paul's usage?

In my opinion, it is unlikely that Paul wrote any of these disputed epistles. Whoever wrote these epistles, one aspect of their content deserves particular attention when the authorship question is discussed: *How do these epistles employ or relate to apocalyptic discourse and apocalyptic eschatology?* For in each of the disputed epistles, the eschatology differs in significant ways from Paul's own.

Beyond authorship alone comes the more important issue of interpretation. Debates about authorship often get confused with the value or status of these epistles. If Paul didn't write them, then their importance is diminished in the eyes of some. Thus, the authorship question often plays into a thumbs-up/thumbs-down assessment. I would rather press beyond authorship to meaning. *How does apocalyptic discourse contribute to the larger meaning of these epistles?* What eschatologies are represented here, and what implications do they have?

Ephesians and Colossians

Ephesians and Colossians develop a markedly positive apocalyptic eschatology. Paul's understanding of the resurrection offers a grand vision, as he ties the redemption of human beings with that of the entire cosmos.

> We know that the whole creation has been groaning in labor pains until now; and not only the creation, but we ourselves, who have the first fruits of the Spirit, groan inwardly while we wait for adoption, the redemption of our bodies. (Rom. 8:22–23)

Ephesians and Colossians reflect a full appreciation of the apocalyptic dimensions of Paul's gospel, but they develop them even more. In Ephesians, for example, God's plan for "the fullness of time" is "to gather up all things in [Christ], things in heaven and things on earth" (1:10). Through the resurrection, Christ has become "head over all things for the church...the fullness of [Christ] who fills all in all" (1:22–23). Likewise, in Colossians, not only is Christ "the image of the invisible God, the firstborn of all creation" (1:15), but also he is the "firstborn from the dead" (1:18).

> For in [Christ] all the fullness of God was pleased to dwell, and through him God was pleased to reconcile to himself all things, whether on earth or in heaven, by making peace through the blood of his cross. (1:19–20)

This is a grand vision, one that I believe is consistent with Paul's gospel and yet one that seems to extend the horizons of what Paul himself claimed. Moreover, Ephesians and Colossians both draw implications from the resurrection that Paul himself rejects. Most notably, both Ephesians and Colossians reflect a somewhat *realized eschatology*. That is, whereas Paul expressly regards the resurrection of believers–and the transformation of their status that goes along with it–as a future event, Ephesians and Colossians both depict the resurrection as having been already accomplished. Consider the following examples:

For if we believe that Jesus died and arose, even so, through Jesus, God *will bring* those who have fallen asleep along with him. (1 Thess. 4:14, author's trans.)

Behold, I am telling you a mystery: We shall not all sleep, but *we shall all be transformed* in a moment, in the twinkling of an eye, at the last trumpet. For the trumpet will sound, and the dead will be raised incorruptible, and so shall we be transformed. (1 Cor. 15:51–52, author's trans.)

For if we have been united with him in a death like his, *we will certainly be* united with him in a resurrection like his. (Rom 6:5)

But God, who is rich in mercy, out of the great love with which he loved us even when we were dead through our trespasses, *made us alive together with Christ*–by grace you have been saved–*and raised us up with him* and *seated us with him* in the heavenly places in Christ Jesus... (Eph. 2:4–6)

In [Christ] also you were circumcised with a spiritual circumcision, by putting off the body of the flesh in the circumcision of Christ; when you were buried with him in baptism, *you were also raised* with him through faith in the power of God, who raised him from the dead. And when you were dead in trespasses and the uncircumcision of your flesh, God *made you alive together with him*...(Col. 2:11–13)

For Paul, Christ's resurrection guarantees the resurrection of his followers, which remains a future event; in Ephesians and Colossians the resurrection, with the transformation that accompanies it, is already accomplished.

Despite their similar takes on apocalyptic eschatology, Ephesians and Colossians apply that eschatology to differing rhetorical ends. For Ephesians, the critical issue is unity, for the epistle seems primarily concerned with the *unity* of Jewish and Gentile persons in the church. Thus, God's accomplishment of cosmic reconciliation in Christ serves as the warrant for unity within the church. In Colossians, the issue involves the requirements for salvation: Does one need to acquire special knowledge or to adopt particular practices to reside among the elect? There, the key issue is the *completeness* of salvation in Christ. Because Christ has already accomplished reconciliation and transformation, nothing more than faith (2:12) is needed. Remarkably, though Ephesians and Colossians address quite different concerns, they appropriate very similar eschatological convictions to address those concerns.

Second Thessalonians

Second Thessalonians also elaborates Paul's eschatology, but in a different direction. In his undisputed letters Paul outlines a fairly simple eschatological scenario: Christ will return from heaven, bringing with him all of his followers whether living or dead. A final judgment follows, but its nature and implications are unclear. Second Thessalonians is much more specific and detailed in its eschatological speculation. For one thing, it proclaims judgment and vengeance against those who neither know God nor obey the gospel. Especially significant is the element of revenge: God will "repay with affliction those who afflict you" (1:6). Moreover, although the day of Jesus' coming remains hidden, we do have signs. A general apostasy or falling away accompanies the emergence of "the lawless one," an antichrist-like figure who seeks to be worshiped and declares his own divinity (2:3–4).

It is difficult to discern *for what purpose* 2 Thessalonians develops these eschatological scenarios. The epistle as a whole does not address any clear rhetorical situation, though it does reflect a concern for perseverance during affliction (1:4; 2:15; 3:3–5). Perhaps the detailed eschatological system promises a sense of certainty during trying times. The sense that one's experience is part of a history with a larger cosmic design has often inspired individuals and communities. If that is so, then the apocalyptic discourse in 2 Thessalonians serves a sort of epideictic purpose, reinforcing the audience's current practices by validating its sense of place and purpose.

The Pastoral Epistles

The Pastoral Epistles—1 and 2 Timothy and Titus—are also difficult to locate in any particular social or historical context. Their literary addressees are close associates of Paul's, though few scholars believe that the epistles were actually written for those individuals. The Pastoral Epistles reflect a desire for order in the churches, marked by adherence to a set content of teaching and the orderly transfer of office and authority.

Although they do not reject apocalyptic eschatology, neither do they emphasize it. For example, 1 Timothy 6:13–15 exhorts Timothy to continue in his faithful observance until Jesus' return. Likewise, 2 Timothy 2:11–13 recites a bit of early Christian poetry in exhorting the audience to persevere as they progress toward their eschatological rewards. Like 2 Thessalonians, however, 2 Timothy adds a detailed eschatological program: One should know that "in the last days distressing times will come" (3:1). These motifs—endurance and end-time apostasy—come together in 2 Timothy 4:1–5, which calls Timothy to faithful endurance in the awareness of Jesus' future judgment and of the coming apostasy. The epistle to Titus is little different, as it recalls the great hope of Jesus' manifestation in calling for sensibility, justice, and godliness in the present (2:11–14).

In sum, the Pastorals reflect a time in which apocalyptic eschatology has become familiar and conventional. One may assume that Jesus will return to judge humankind, applying this belief to the need for ongoing faithfulness. But in the Pastorals, apocalyptic eschatology is hardly a matter for invention or creative interpretation; it is not even a point of emphasis.

Reading the Apocalyptic Paul

In this chapter we have encountered Paul as a visionary, Paul as an apostle of the risen Jesus, and Paul as an apocalyptic thinker. Paul's visionary experiences included his foundational revelation of the risen Jesus and at least one mystical ascent to the third heaven. His proclamation of the risen Messiah announced a turning of the ages and anticipated Jesus' return and the resurrection of his followers. And his several letters apply this core apocalyptic message for a range of persuasive ends. We have also grappled with the appropriations of apocalyptic discourse by those who chose to write in Paul's name by appropriating his style and his message.

Paul's ministry testifies to two things. First, apocalyptic eschatology and apocalyptic discourse pigment all of our earliest strata of Christian literature. As the earliest extant Christian writer, Paul never roams far from his core proclamation that not only has Israel's messiah come and died, he is risen and coming again. And second, apocalyptic discourse proved a remarkably flexible resource for early Christian imagination. The message of Jesus' resurrection and return could warn people as easily as it could comfort them; it could restrain innovation just as surely as it could promote change. Ever present and ever useful, apocalyptic discourse gave shape to early Christian communities and their hopes.

FOR FURTHER READING

Beker, J. Christiaan. *Paul the Apostle.* Philadelphia: Fortress Press, 1980, 2d ed., 1984.

Boyarin, Daniel. *A Radical Jew: Paul and the Politics of Identity.* Berkeley: University of California Press, 1994.

de Boer, M. C. "Paul and Apocalyptic Eschatology." Pages 345–83 in *The Encyclopedia of Apocalypticism: Volume 1: The Origins of Apocalypticism in Judaism and Christianity.* Edited by John J. Collins. New York: Continuum, 1998.

Dunn, James D. G. *The Theology of Paul the Apostle.* Grand Rapids, Mich.: Eerdmans, 1998.

Horsley, Richard A., ed. *Paul and Empire: Religion and Power in Roman Imperial Society.* Philadelphia: Trinity Press International, 1996.

Roetzel, Calvin. *Paul: The Man and the Myth.* Studies on the Personalities of the New Testament. Minneapolis: Fortress Press, 1999.

Wright, N. T. *What Saint Paul Really Said: Was Paul of Tarsus the Real Founder of Christianity?* Grand Rapids, Mich.: Eerdmans, 1997.

CHAPTER 6

Responses to Tragedy

Jewish Apocalypses after 70 C.E.

The First Jewish Revolt against Rome (66–73/74 C.E.) ended in disaster. When Roman troops captured Jerusalem in 70 C.E., they destroyed the city and the temple, marking a critical moment in the development–some would say the emergence–of both Judaism and Christianity. The destruction of the temple in 70 C.E. forced many Jews to redefine their self-understanding. No longer could the temple provide a central symbol of ethnic and religious identity, nor could religious imagination focus on Jerusalem in precisely the same way. Finally, a Second Jewish Revolt (132–135 C.E.) led Jews once again to examine their identity as a people.

Four significant Jewish apocalypses–4 Ezra, 2 Baruch, 3 Baruch, and the Apocalypse of Abraham–emerged during the interim between the two revolts. They reflect explicitly upon the significance of Jerusalem's fall. In my view, these apocalypses are remarkable for their religious and theological sophistication. Each of these works deals with how to understand Jewish identity in the absence of the temple, though 3 Baruch and the Apocalypse of Abraham tend to emphasize the individual more than the collective people. And each grapples mightily with questions concerning God's role in history:

1. If God elected Israel, why would God allow the symbols of its spatial, political, and religious identity to be destroyed?
2. Is God unjust? Why would God allow God's people to be destroyed by pagans?
3. Does God have larger purposes for God's people? What might they be?

At no point do these apocalypses question God's existence, which is for them a given. The problems run deeper than that. They challenge God's righteousness, whether God acts in ways that are just, purposeful, and consistent. How does one justify God in an unjust world? It's hard to imagine a tougher question than that.

4 Ezra

Languages and Texts

Our primary witnesses to 4 Ezra are in Latin though it was likely composed in Hebrew or Aramaic. Fourth Ezra has been combined with two Christian apocalypses to form what is known as 2 Esdras in the Christian Apocrypha. It may be found in 2 Esdras 3—14.

Likely Date

Fourth Ezra apparently comes from the period between the Jewish revolts, around 100 C.E.

Written within a generation of Jerusalem's fall, 4 Ezra evokes both pathos and suspense. Even from a historical and cultural distance, many readers can identify with protests such as 4 Ezra 4:12: "It would be better for us not to be here than to come here and live in ungodliness, and to suffer and not understand why." The logical and emotional force of this complaint creates suspense. How can the apocalypse can resolve such serious challenges?

Like other apocalypses, 4 Ezra has a double setting. The *narrative setting* places Ezra in Babylon thirty years after Jerusalem's destruction, suggesting a date of 556 or 557 B.C.E. We must face the question of how this narrative setting might relate to the apocalypse's *historical setting*, its actual time of composition. For the biblical story of Ezra is set much later than is 4 Ezra, in 458 or 398 B.C.E.–far too late for Ezra to have been in Babylon only thirty years after Jerusalem's desolation. This discrepancy suggests that the book's narrative setting serves as a fictional device.

In later Jewish and Christian literature, "Babylon" functions as a cipher for Rome. The common link is that Babylon and Rome are notorious as the two empires that destroyed Jerusalem and its temple. Thus, 4 Ezra was almost certainly composed after Jerusalem's *second* great fall. The "thirtieth year" would be around the year 100 C.E., or an indeterminate time after Roman forces decimated the city. Indeed, it is Zion's "desolation"–compared to the prosperity of Babylon/Rome–that incites Ezra's anxiety and provides the context for his vision.

Ezra the Visionary

One could hardly ask for a more qualified visionary authority than Ezra, for Ezra deserves notoriety both for his importance and for his elusiveness in Jewish tradition. According to the biblical book of Ezra, Ezra was a priest, scribe, and scholar of Jewish law, or Torah (Ezra 7:11). King Artaxerxes of Persia sends Ezra to Jerusalem with explicit instructions. Among other things, he receives the resources to revitalize the temple cult, along with authorization to study and establish the law of Israel's God in the land. As a result, Ezra is sometimes credited as a sort of second author of the Torah, because his work involves its rediscovery and restoration. Thus, Ezra is intimately associated with the city of Jerusalem and the foundations of Judaism. His grief over Jerusalem's demise, therefore, seems credible, as does his concern that the people observe the Torah.

Ezra's association with Moses is more than coincidental. In 4 Ezra's closing vision, several strategies link the two figures. Just as YHWH addresses Moses from a bush in Exodus 3, so does God speak to Ezra from a bush (14:1–3). Just as Moses responds, "Here I am," after hearing his name called twice ("Moses, Moses"), so Ezra's experience follows the same pattern. Just as Moses resides on the mountain with God for forty days, so Ezra fasts for a total of forty days throughout the apocalypse, and in this final vision Ezra is alone for forty days (14:23).[1] Obviously, just as Moses delivers the law, Ezra delivers the entire corpus of Jewish Scripture (twenty-four books; 14:45), not to mention seventy books of secret knowledge that are available only to the wise (14:46). This link between Ezra and Moses continues beyond 4 Ezra, even into rabbinic tradition. The Talmud claims that had Moses not come first, Ezra would certainly have been worthy of receiving the Torah (*b. Sanh.* 21b; cf. *t. Sanh.* 4:7; Tertullian, *De cultu feminarum* 1:3).[2]

Yet Ezra remains an elusive figure. We don't know for sure when he lived or how his career related to that of Nehemiah? Was Ezra's work earlier than, contemporaneous with, or later than that of Nehemiah? Scholars offer conflicting proposals to this day. And what ultimately happened to Ezra? How did he die, and where? This we also do not know. Thus, Ezra's importance stands in tension with the lack of details concerning his career and his fate.

Among the apocalypses, Ezra plays a remarkable role as a protagonist. Far more than a recipient of revelation, he also is its catalyst. The visions respond to Ezra's prayers on behalf of Israel. Three times Ezra voices his complaints and petitions regarding Jerusalem's devastation, and each time he has an encounter with the angel Uriel. As we shall see, Ezra advocates eloquently for his people. His role as Israel's intercessor recalls Abraham's intercession for Sodom in Genesis 18 and Moses' advocacy for Israel in Exodus 33. These associations evidence his access to God and his compassion for his people, marking Ezra's exceptional status as a person of holiness and virtue. Indeed, four times God and the angel praise Ezra's exceptional righteousness (6:32–33; 7:76–77; 8:48–49; 10:38–39).[3]

A ritual dimension also marks the visions. As Uriel instructs him at the end of his first vision, Ezra repeatedly prepares for his visions through a pattern of prayer, mourning, and fasting (4:13; cf. 5:13; 6:31; with an exception in 9:22–25). Though we may interpret these passages in other ways, it also seems that part of Ezra's preparation may have involved ingesting flowers and beverages that may have "assisted" his visionary receptivity (9:22–26; 14:38–40)! At any rate, the visions affect Ezra in both spiritual and physiological ways. At the end of his first vision,

> Then I woke up, and my body shuddered violently, and my soul was so troubled that it fainted. But the angel who had come and talked with me held me and strengthened me and set me on my feet. (2 Esd. 5:14–15)

Ezra emerges as a person of character, spiritual giftedness, and compassion. His subjective mystical experiences complement his passion for his people to convey his goodwill. His prayers characterize him as Israel's intercessor. Together with Ezra's credentials as a second author of the Torah and a contributor to Jerusalem's restoration, these traits establish Ezra's visionary authority. His cachet is only enhanced by his elusiveness, for no one knows what ultimately became of him.

Process and Mode of Revelation

The apocalypse moves through a series of seven units. The first three units pair dialogues and visions, whereas the final three involve visions followed by interpretations. This difference reflects an important transformation that occurs in the fourth unit. In the first three units, Ezra plays the role of one who challenges God and receives heavenly replies that do not satisfy him. (Nor are many readers satisfied with these replies!) But in units five through seven, Ezra comes across as a much more assenting figure. Something has transformed him from an aggressive questioner to a compliant learner. Thus, whereas a question-and-reply format suits the first three units, the vision and interpretation structure is more appropriate for the final three. The fourth unit, then, represents the centerpiece of the apocalypse.

The fourth unit, unique in format, is the fulcrum. The first three units (3:1–5:20; 5:21–6:34; 6:35–9:26) voice Ezra's complaints. How could God create humanity with an evil heart, then punish people for their wickedness? How could God turn over Zion to people more wicked than its inhabitants, and why do the wicked appear to prosper? Why would God turn over God's elect people to be punished by others? And why, if God intended the world as Israel's inheritance, is Israel subjected to foreign powers?

> "I implore you, my lord, why have I been endowed with the power of understanding? For I did not wish to inquire about the ways above, but about those things that we daily experience: why Israel has been given over to the Gentiles in disgrace; why the people

whom you loved has been given over to godless tribes, and the law of our ancestors has been brought to destruction and the written covenants no longer exist. We pass from the world like locusts, and our life is like a mist, and we are not worthy to obtain mercy. But what will God do for his name that is invoked over us? It is about these things that I have asked." (2 Esd. 4:22–25)

Ezra voices each of these challenges in the form of a prayer, and in each case his conversation partner is an angel. (Careful readers will notice however that this "angel" occasionally represents the divine voice [5:40–41; 6:6].) The angel's replies are twofold. First, as a mere mortal Ezra cannot possibly comprehend the divine mysteries. He is incompetent to judge such weighty matters, nor can his concern for Israel match that of God:

"Are you greatly disturbed in mind over Israel? Or do you love him more than his Maker does?" (5:33)

Ezra cannot count the earth's future inhabitants, nor can he gather the scattered raindrops, cause withered flowers to bloom, bring forth the constrained winds, or show the picture of a voice (5:36–37). Thus, how can he comprehend the divine mysteries?

"Just as you cannot do one of the things that were mentioned, so you cannot discover my judgment, or the goal of the love that I have promised to my people." (5:40)

Remarkably, Ezra is apparently unfazed by this rebuttal. He continues to stand his moral ground, insisting that God's ways apparently do not make sense:

"If the world has been created for [Israel], why do we not possess our world as an inheritance? How long will this be so?" (6:59)

The second reply involves the matter of *future eschatology*, God's purposes for Israel and the world. If things may not appear just in the present, Ezra is assured, God's purposes remain righteous and will eventually be manifest. The third vision presents the apocalypse's most detailed eschatological scenario.[4] Ezra is informed that his revelation is a mystery, accessible only to the righteous few (7:25). Then he learns the following:

1. Appointed signs will precede the end.
2. A new city, evidently a new Jerusalem, will appear.
3. The Messiah (the word rendered "Messiah" literally means Anointed One) and his company will be revealed to judge the world for four hundred years.
4. After the Messiah's death, there will be a period of "primeval silence" (7:30), followed by a final judgment in which some find "delight and rest" while others are consigned to "fire and torments."

WRESTLING WITH GOD IN APOCALYPTIC LITERATURE

The Hebrew Scriptures include several accounts of individuals who voice complaints against God. The most famous case is Job, who defends his own righteousness despite his friends' insistence that his suffering is a punishment for his own sin. The Psalms also feature cries to a God who is apparently unresponsive. In some notable cases God actually relents. Abraham convinces Yahweh to withhold the destruction of Sodom if even ten righteous persons may be found there (unfortunately, even ten cannot be found). And Moses intervenes when Yahweh is about to destroy the people of Israel. Indeed, the very name *Israel* means "one who wrestles with God."

Accounts of apocalyptic visions provide a particularly rich context in which to set such encounters, as they present visionaries in direct conversation with heavenly beings. Ordinarily, confusion, fear, and awe represent the visionaries' primary responses. Baffled by the bizarre content of the revelations and overwhelmed by the presence of heavenly beings, the visionaries usually do three things:

a. ask questions ("What does this mean?")
b. demonstrate their fear by bowing or trembling
c. offer worship

But the conversations also allow for the opportunity to ask pointed questions, of the sort advanced by Job. Why are things the way they are? How can God defend God's actions—or God's apparent inaction? May one hope that all things will come to an appropriate resolution?

Thus, apocalyptic discourse provides especially promising literary resources in which to pursue the most challenging issues. It offers a space in which authors may develop creative theological and philosophical reasoning in an indirect manner.

Here are a few of the questions advanced in various apocalypses and apocalyptic texts:

1. Seeing the seven stars of heaven bound in some sort of judgment, Enoch asks, "For which sin are they bound, and for what reason were they cast in here?" (1 Enoch 21:4, *OTP*).
2. At the end of his vision Daniel asks, "My lord, what shall be the outcome of these things?" (Dan. 12:8).
3. In the early Christian apocalypse The Shepherd of Hermas, a vision is apparently provoked by questions Hermas ponders within himself: "If this sin is recorded against me, how can I be saved? Or how will I propitiate God for my conscious sins? Or with what words will I ask the Lord to be gracious to me?" (Vis. 1.2.1 Holmes).

The questions posed in 2 and 3 Baruch and 4 Ezra are especially pointed, as they are grounded in Jerusalem's tragedy. They amount to charges against the character of God, to which God must answer.

1. If you destroy your city and deliver up your country to those who hate us, how will the name of Israel be remembered again? Or how shall we speak about your glorious deeds?...And where is all that which you said to Moses about us? (2 Baruch 3:5–6, 9, *OTP*)
2. Lord, why have you set fire to your vineyard and laid it waste? Why have you done this? And why, Lord, did you not requite us with another punishment, but rather handed us over to such heathen so that they reproach us saying, "Where is their God?" (3 Baruch 1:2, *OTP*)
3. And now, O Lord, why have you handed the one [Israel] over to the many, and dishonored the one root beyond the others, and scattered your only one among the many? And those who opposed your promises have trodden down on those who believed your covenants. If you really hate your people, they should be punished at your own hands. (2 Esdras 5:28–30)

The fourth and central vision (9:26–10:59) clearly poses a turning point for Ezra. Again Ezra begins with a prayer of lament, but this time he encounters not an angel but a woman mourning the death of her son. Barren for thirty years, she had prayed for children. When she finally had a son, he died while entering the bridal chamber. Ezra responds with a stinging rebuke of the woman: Her loss is much smaller in scale than that of Zion, for though she has lost one son, Zion's catastrophe involves thousands.

> "You are sorrowing for one son, but we, the whole world, for our mother. Now ask the earth, and she will tell you that it is she who ought to mourn over so many who have come into being upon her." (10:8–9)

Perhaps one might not find such advice in a textbook on grief counseling, but Ezra insists that the woman should stop grieving altogether:

> "Shake off your great sadness and lay aside your many sorrows, so that the Mighty One may be merciful to you again, and the Most High may give you rest, a respite from your troubles." (10:24)

At this moment the woman's appearance is transformed, and Ezra sees the building of a glorious new Jerusalem. In fear he cries out for the angel, who returns and explains the vision to Ezra. The woman he saw was Zion, who had indeed suffered calamity but whose glory could return. Zion's catastrophe has indeed been great, but hope remains.

The tone of the book changes dramatically in visions five, six, and seven. Challenges to God are not the starting place anymore. No longer do the visions begin with Ezra fasting and praying, but immediately they narrate the content of Ezra's dreams. The fifth and sixth visions offer detailed eschatological scenarios, and the seventh involves a legend about Ezra and his relationship to sacred literature. The fifth vision (11:1–12:51) introduces the Eagle, symbol of Roman imperial oppression. This vision interprets the course of history, leading up to God's intervention through the Messiah, who will judge the wicked rulers and deliver God's people from oppression. The sixth vision (13:1–58) depicts the Man from the Sea, who conquers the nations from Mount Zion, judges the wicked, gathers Israel's dispersed tribes, and inaugurates a miraculous new age for Israel. These two messianic images do not confirm each other point by point, but that is not the point. Rather, as poetic and visionary literature, they reinforce each other by means of image and common aspiration. God's Messiah will judge Israel's oppressors and bring a restored Israel into a blessed age.

The seventh vision (14:1–48)–and its relationship to the larger body of the apocalypse–inspires curiosity. To some this vision seems disconnected from the rest of the apocalypse. It stands apart from the others, as it begins with the divine voice calling Ezra from a bush: "Ezra, Ezra!" The link to Moses is unmistakable: The voice explicitly reminds Ezra that Moses, too, was called from a bush, and like Moses, Ezra is commissioned to write books. Yet in a larger sense the vision provides an appropriate culmination of the book, for it concludes as Ezra calls the people together to admonish them to be faithful to the Torah. The speech recalls Moses' great speech in Deuteronomy, as it begins, "Hear [these words], O Israel" (Deut. 6:4), and pronounces blessing for the obedient and woe for the disobedient.

> "If you, then, will rule over your minds and discipline your hearts,
> you shall be kept alive, and after death you shall obtain mercy.
> For after death the judgment will come, when we shall live again;
> and then the names of the righteous shall become manifest, and
> the deeds of the ungodly shall be disclosed." (14:34–35)

The seventh vision is also noteworthy in that it involves the revelation of the ninety-four books to Ezra. The first twenty-four represent the traditional Hebrew canon, but the other seventy are reserved only for "the wise among [the] people" (14:46). On the basis of 14:47 ("For in them is the spring of understanding, the fountain of wisdom, and the river of knowledge") one leading scholar has written that these seventy books–more than the twenty-four canonical ones–contain saving knowledge.[5] In my view, they are presented as supplemental knowledge; that is, the Law remains the "Law of life" (14:30), but even more wisdom is available through this esoteric literature.

Because so much of 4 Ezra is devoted to Ezra's debates with the angel, some readers believe that the classic problem it addresses is theodicy, the justification of God in the face of apparent evil or injustice. Certainly the protests and challenges voiced by Ezra impeach God with the significance of Jerusalem's destruction. Yet 4 Ezra is an apocalypse, not a formal piece of philosophical or theological argumentation. Although there is a sense in which 4 Ezra offers "answers" to the questions of God's righteousness and

God's purposes for history, these answers are embedded in a moving piece of religious literature. Ezra is not so much *convinced* as he is *moved*. His initial protests against God receive no compelling answer, and yet Ezra eventually becomes God's defender rather than God's accuser. How this happens may be the most interesting feature of the book.[6]

Reading 4 Ezra

These weighty theological and religious matters naturally draw the attention of scholars, most of whom delight in discussing such things. (I know I do.) Indeed, they take up a significant portion of 4 Ezra. *But was this apocalypse designed primarily to address these questions, or might it serve another, larger purpose?* This is a question of literary design and rhetorical function. Modern readers may find questions concerning providence and theodicy compelling—and 4 Ezra certainly engages them—but many scholars find its primary emphasis elsewhere. One might speak of how 4 Ezra provides a sense of meaning in the face of chaos, "a coherence that has been lost or profoundly threatened by the [temple's] destruction."[7] The resolution of the problem posed by God's role in Zion's fall lies not in abstract theodicy, however, nor does it reside in the religious experience of the fictional Ezra or the apocalypse's author. *Instead, 4 Ezra moves its audience from disillusionment to obedience.* As Ezra finds meaning in the revelation of the Torah, so does the Torah establish a new frame of meaning for his potential audience.[8]

This is why the seventh vision and dialogue provide a fitting conclusion to the apocalypse. Fourth Ezra is written in response to a catastrophe. The fundamental symbol of cosmic order, the temple, has been destroyed. In the realm of contemporary events no available evidence clarifies God's purposes. In fact, Ezra points out that Zion's inhabitants had been more righteous than its conquerors (3:35–36). No signs of providence appear; we have no apparent reason to believe that God is trustworthy.

Here is a fundamental challenge to order. If God has not protected the people who have kept God's Law best, how does one find meaning in the world? Through the visions and dialogues, 4 Ezra offers two primary answers: Mortals are unable to perceive God's purposes, and in the future God will bring a blessed new age. These are new hopes, promising new possibilities and a new order. But in the meantime, how are God's people to respond? The seventh vision and dialogue provides the answer: *By remaining faithful to Torah, the righteous can expect salvation.* The structure of 4 Ezra leads to this one place: Order is possible only through faithfulness to the Torah.

By subordinating the Torah to the seventy esoteric books, Fourth Ezra locates itself toward the margins of ancient Judaism. But by emphasizing that life and order are possible only through faithful observance of the Torah, Fourth Ezra participates in a much larger movement within Judaism. For in the wake of the temple's destruction, the Torah becomes an even more central marker of Jewish identity.[9] The holiness embodied by the temple could be instantiated in the lives of Jewish individuals, households, and communities. Such holiness could be imagined through careful sifting of the Torah. With an emphasis on personal piety and works of compassion, observance and interpretation of the Torah would become the hallmark of rabbinic Judaism. Fourth Ezra not only diagnosed the need for a new symbolic center, it also prescribed the same remedy.

2 Baruch

Languages and Texts

According to George W. E. Nickelsburg, "*Second Baruch* is extant in one Syriac manuscript, which is translated from the Greek, which itself may be a translation of a Semitic original."[10]

Likely Date

In its present form 2 Baruch was composed after Jerusalem's fall in 70 c.e., though parts of the book may have been composed decades before that.

Some passages reflect a *historical setting* after the devastation of 70 c.e.. For example, 2 Baruch 32:2–4 alludes to two destructions of Zion. Second Baruch also has close affinities—as well as some significant differences—with 4 Ezra, which suggest that the two apocalypses may have addressed a common context. Finally, 2 Baruch 61:7 is quoted by the early Christian Epistle of Barnabas, which was certainly composed after 70 c.e. and was probably written before 132 c.e. Thus, 2 Baruch attained its final form not long after 70 c.e., perhaps around 100 c.e.[11]

Relationship to 4 Ezra

Much of the content of 2 Baruch parallels content in 4 Ezra, but there are many points at which the two books conflict. While some scholars have suggested that 2 Baruch was composed in response to and in conversation with 4 Ezra, others are not persuaded.

Second Baruch begins with the same exigency 4 Ezra faced. Like 4 Ezra, 2 Baruch presents a powerful sense of challenge and pathos–challenge to God's justice in allowing Jerusalem's destruction, pathos in Baruch's grief for Zion. Again like 4 Ezra, 2 Baruch offers a series of eschatological promises that in part justify God's ways. Unlike 4 Ezra, however, these promises apparently satisfy the visionary's sense of justice. The book moves more directly from grief to consolation.[12] Moreover, 2 Baruch's eschatology is much richer in detail than is that of 4 Ezra. Still, at a fundamental level, 2 Baruch and 4 Ezra offer the same essential message: In the aftermath of Zion's fall, Israel's hope lies in its faithfulness to Torah.

Setting

Though 2 Baruch is inconsistent in its description of historical events, the apocalypse clearly presents a *narrative setting* that begins in the sixth century B.C.E. just before Jerusalem's fall to Babylon and continues after the catastrophe. This narrative setting functions as a potent literary-rhetorical device, for Baruch actually watches Zion's destruction in chapters 6–7. As we shall see, his experience of watching this event provides a means for interpreting its significance. Some passages reflect a *historical setting* after the devastation of 70 C.E.

Second Baruch's narrative and historical settings converge with one concern: a response to Rome's destruction of the Jerusalem Temple.

Baruch the Visionary

Biblical tradition ties Baruch more intimately to Jerusalem's fall in 587/ 586 B.C.E. than it does Ezra, but his association with the Torah is more vague. In the book of Jeremiah, Baruch appears as the prophet's scribe. When Jeremiah purchases a plot of land during Jerusalem's siege (Jer. 32), he hands over the deed to Baruch so that Baruch can secure its safety. This prophetic act points to hope, for even with the Babylonians at the gates Jeremiah expects a return to the land in the future. Baruch's role is to secure the record of this prophetic action.

In Jeremiah 36, Baruch records Jeremiah's oracles and delivers them on the prophet's behalf. Then, when these subversive oracles reach the king's attention, Baruch and Jeremiah go into hiding. When the king's officials seek the two fugitives, something mysterious happens–"The LORD hid them" (36:26)–and Jeremiah dictates a second scroll to Baruch. Baruch's reputation increases later in the story, as Jeremiah's opponents blame the scribe for the prophet's oracles and send the pair into exile in Egypt along with many others (43:1–7). Finally, Jeremiah blesses Baruch and promises the scribe that God will deliver his life from war "in every place to which you may go" (45:1–5). The rest of Baruch's story remains untold.

Thus, the book of Jeremiah depicts Baruch as the recorder of Jeremiah's collected oracles–and possibly as the book's author or primary source. Moreover, Baruch participates in the hope that Jerusalem's devastation will not be permanent, but that God will restore the people into the city in the future. Baruch's own identity is marked by the unusual sign of God's protection, both in his flight from King Jehoiakim and in his ultimate fate.

Baruch's story continues in the apocryphal book of Baruch. The book conflicts with Jeremiah by locating Baruch in Babylon (1:1) rather than Egypt (Jer. 43:1–7), a tradition that continues in later rabbinic literature.[13] The book of Baruch attributes Jerusalem's fall to its own sin, seeks God's mercy, promotes the Torah as the path of salvation, and offers hope for a restored but chastened Jerusalem–all themes that occur in 2 Baruch.

These factors qualify Baruch for the status he receives in 2 Baruch. Not only is he a faithful scribe who eventually attains prophet-like status, but also he is specially marked for divine protection. Several features also mark Baruch's authority in 2 Baruch. Immediately he is associated with Jeremiah and other righteous persons who receive divine protection:

> This, then, I have said to you that you may say to Jeremiah and all those who are like you that you may retire from this city. For your works are for this city like a firm pillar and your prayers like a strong wall. (2:1, *OTP*)

Indeed, Baruch eventually surpasses Jeremiah's status, as Jeremiah goes off with the exiles to Babylon while Baruch remains in the city and receives a divine revelation. Now Jeremiah receives God's word from Baruch rather than the other way around (10:1–5). Baruch's virtue is complemented by his love for the city, for when he learns of Jerusalem's forthcoming devastation he voices his despair:

> No, my Lord. If I have found grace in your eyes, take away my spirit first that I may go to my fathers and I may not see the destruction of my mother [Zion]. (3:2, *OTP*)

Is Baruch Immortal?

Perhaps the most notorious question concerning Baruch involves his mortality. Two biblical figures, Enoch and Elijah, are said to have escaped death by being transported to the heavenly realms (Gen. 5:24; 2 Kings 2:11), and Moses' own death is somewhat mysterious (Deut. 34:5–7). Jeremiah's enigmatic oracle promised that YHWH would preserve Baruch's life (Jer. 45:5). In 2 Baruch the matter first surfaces when a heavenly voice promises, "you will surely be preserved until the end of times" (13:2, *OTP*). We might interpret this promise in a variety of ways:

1. It may indicate that Baruch will dwell in a heavenly realm until the resurrection
2. It may hint to some sort of immortality like that of Enoch or Elijah
3. It may simply promise Baruch a fate identical to that of all of the righteous, death followed by a resurrection life.

Second Baruch, however, follows this claim with several possibly contradictory pronouncements concerning Baruch's fate. Second Baruch echoes the promise that Baruch will be "preserved" until the end times (25:1; 76:2–3); repeats the expectation that Baruch will leave the world and become immortal (43:2; 46:7; 48:30); and shares the expectation that Baruch actually will die (44:2; 78:5; 84:1).

The first two options, preservation and immortality, are easily reconciled: Perhaps Baruch will dwell in a heavenly realm until the end times. But it is extremely difficult to combine that view with the expectation that Baruch will actually experience death.

Baruch's virtue includes repeated attention to spiritual practices such as fasting and prayer. Four cycles (chaps. 9, 12, 20–21, and 43–44) report that the visionary fasts for seven days before receiving his revelations. (In the first two cases, Baruch fasts on his own; in the latter two, he does so in response to divine instruction.)

Even more impressive is the intense attention devoted to prayers (chaps. 3, 10–12, 14, 16, 18, 21, 26, 28, 38, 41, 48, and 54), occasionally so intense as to promote physical symptoms such as weakness (21:26; 48:25) or fatigue (55:1). Some of these prayers simply seek understanding following particular revelations, while others are quite elaborate. Baruch's prayers often involve intercessions on Zion's behalf. In contrast to Ezra, who for nearly the first half of 4 Ezra continues to pray in a mode of protest, Baruch is much more submissive. He seeks understanding and explanation, but his prayers are not accusatory. Baruch further demonstrates his goodwill through a series of direct addresses to the people, in which he offers them consolation and exhortation.

As an advocate for the people, Baruch clearly plays a more compliant role than does Ezra in 4 Ezra. He tends to ask for clarification or explanation rather than challenge God's righteousness directly. For example, his first address to God includes questions such as, "Now, what will happen after these things?" (3:4, *OTP*); "If you destroy your city and deliver up your country to those who hate us, how will the name of Israel be remembered again?" (3:5, *OTP*); and "Where is all that which you said to Moses about us?" (3:9, *OTP*).

Later, Baruch asks more challenging questions such as what benefit do the righteous receive (14:3–6), why would God not forgive Zion on account of the righteous (as God did Israel for Moses' sake in Ex. 33; 14:7), and how long must the righteous endure corruption (21:19). All of these questions implicitly challenge God's justice, yet they do so indirectly by opening the way for a divine response. Indeed, once God answers the questions, Baruch moves on to other topics, as if one set of concerns has been satisfactorily addressed and it is time to seek further clarification. (Compare this to Ezra's resistance to the divine answers in his first three visions.) It is a remarkable strategy: Baruch comes across as one who voices Israel's concerns faithfully, though in such a way as to enhance the authority of God's replies.

In summary, Baruch's character builds upon his legendary status as a faithful scribe who merits special divine care. While a divine voice testifies to Baruch's virtue, his character is enhanced by the love he demonstrates for Zion through his laments, fasts, and prayers. Baruch further expresses his continuing compassion by directing the people through a series of speeches and an epistle. In addition to his virtue, Baruch is also exceptionally privileged, as he receives auditions and visions directly from God, and as God promises that he will somehow be preserved for the last days.

Finally, Baruch's overall tone is the perfect vehicle through which the apocalypse can address its historical setting. Through Baruch, the apocalypse voices Israel's objections concerning its current devastation, clearing the path for the apocalypse to address those objections one at a time and even to offer a resolution.

Process and Mode of Revelation

Second Baruch does not reflect a symmetrical or repetitive structure, though two features define its overall movement. First, the larger movement progresses from Baruch's grief concerning Zion's fate to his role as a comforter and encourager of the people. Thus, the larger flow of 2 Baruch moves from chaos to clarity. Chapter 31 may represent a major turning point in the narrative, as there for the first time Baruch addresses the people, a motif that recurs throughout the rest of the book.

Second, four types of material recur throughout the apocalypse:

a. Baruch's dialogues with heavenly figures, usually God
b. cycles of prayer or lamentation, sometimes in conversation with God (as part of the dialogues) concerning matters of revelation and sometimes preceded by periods of fasting
c. major visions, accompanied by interpretations
d. addresses to the people, including an epistle to fellow Jews in Babylon

Thus, 2 Baruch features two major vehicles of revelation: dialogue with heavenly figures and visions that require interpretation. At the same time, the interaction of these dialogues and visions with Baruch's prayers, lamentations, and addresses enables 2 Baruch to interpret history and to provide a point of view from which to shape communal identity and action. As a result, we will engage 2 Baruch not through a section-by-section survey but by taking a look at each of these four types of material.

DIALOGUES

Second Baruch begins when the "word of the Lord" comes to the scribe concerning "this people's" evil and God's plan to chasten them through destruction and scattering. Importantly, this address includes an interpretation of the crisis: "The time will come that they will look for that which can make their times prosperous" (1:5, *OTP*). Unlike 4 Ezra, Baruch begins with the foreshadowing of future good by insisting that Zion's calamity is a necessary means to a blessed end.

Some readers have identified theodicy as 2 Baruch's primary issue. The question, of course, is how can a just God allow injustice? In particular, how would God allow Zion, even a corrupt Zion, to be destroyed by an even more corrupt empire? In such disasters, why does not God discriminate between the righteous and the wicked among the people? Has God turned the divine posterior to God's promises to Israel? Indeed, 2 Baruch touches on these challenges repeatedly, though I would suggest that 2 Baruch is not primarily an attempt to defend

God's righteousness. Nevertheless, it is through dialogue that the apocalypse answers many of the challenges to God's goodness. Here are a few examples of this process:

Questions:	Replies:
What lies in the future? How will God's name be glorified? (3:1–9)	Zion's devastation is only temporary, and a future Zion will be revealed. (4:1–7)
Will not Zion's devastation be a scandal against God's reputation? (5:1)	God's name and glory are eternal, but God's judgment must be executed in time and history. (5:2–4)
How can it be that wicked Babylon fares better than Zion? (11:1–3)	God is impartial: The nations also must undergo judgment, while God judges Israel in order to forgive it. (13:5–12)
What reward is there for the righteous? (14:4–7)	The world to come is the reward of the righteous. (15:1–8)
How long will the apparent injustice remain? (21:19)	History is divinely ordained, and things will happen in their time. (chaps. 23–30)
Will the final tribulations last a long time? (26:1)	The tribulations have a set—but unspecified—order and duration. (chaps. 27–28)

The final question in the table above involves the duration of the end-time tribulations. It prepares the way for the revelation (not a vision) of the twelve tribulations in chapter 27, which along with the visions of the forest, vine, fountain, and cedar (chaps. 36–37) and the cloud (chap. 53) are the most significant vehicles through which 2 Baruch presents its detailed eschatological teachings. Chapter 25 invokes the common topic of an end-time tribulation, and in response to Baruch's query he receives the teaching concerning the twelve tribulations (chap. 27).

God's reply is remarkable in that it insists that these end-time calamities have order and purpose, but it also leaves significant room for ambiguity. People will not recognize that these tribulations mark the end times, because the twelve tribulations overlap and intermingle with one another. Moreover, 2 Baruch reveals that these calamities prepare the way for the messianic age, a time of fruitfulness and plenty. At the end of the messianic age, the righteous will be raised while the wicked will waste away while they see these things (chap. 30).

The revelation concerning the twelve calamities and the coming of the Anointed One ends after chapter 30. This marks a significant point in the movement of 2 Baruch. Dialogues are the most prominent feature in 2 Baruch 1–30, but in chapter 31 Baruch addresses "the people" for the first time. From this point the book's movement becomes largely (but not exclusively) one of revelation, prayer, and address. The dialogues have established the apocalypse's ideological framework by responding to questions concerning God's righteousness and role in history. Now, the apocalypse will move on to sketch a more elaborate scenario for the last days, with clear implications for Israel's continuing life. Baruch will continue to dialogue with God, particularly in response to his visions and their interpretation. But it will now be the visions that provoke Baruch's questions, and the answers he receives will interpret and explain those visions.

PRAYERS AND LAMENTATIONS

In one sense, Baruch prays whenever he addresses God. Thus, most of his prayers relate to the larger context of dialogue, voicing questions to which Baruch receives a divine reply. Yet 2 Baruch features some formal and lengthy prayers and lamentations. These invite reflection in their own right.

Lamentation is a remarkable vehicle. Not only does it express grief concerning Jerusalem's fate, it can also give voice to critical questions without addressing them as direct challenges to God. Second Baruch 10–12 offers the most extensive example of this form. When Baruch confesses, "Blessed is he who was not born, / or he who was born and died. / But we, the living, woe to us, / because we have seen those afflictions of Zion, / and that which has befallen Jerusalem," (10:6–7, *OTP*), he implicitly questions the goodness of the life for which God is responsible. Likewise, in 2 Baruch 11:1–2 the visionary rhetorically asks *Babylon* how it can be that Babylon can prosper while Zion suffers, again indicting God without addressing God directly.

At other points Baruch's speech sounds more like prayer than challenge. The prayer in 2 Baruch 48 is more a cry for mercy on account of human frailty ("Be, therefore, not angry at [humankind] because [we are] nothing"; 48:14, *OTP*) than a challenge or plea for understanding, yet God voices a reply to this prayer. Despite human weakness, God must execute judgment against the wicked (48:26–29).

Second Baruch 54 provides another interesting case of prayer that serves an auxiliary purpose. The prayer begins—as do others (cf. 21:4–11; 48:1–24)—with the expression of wonder at the works of creation. Yet more than halfway into the prayer, Baruch turns to confess the righteousness of God's judgment against the wicked (54:13–16). Then Baruch gets right to the point by shifting from speaking directly to God to a fictive address to the wicked (54:17–19). The wicked deserve their judgment, for "Adam is…not the cause, except only for himself, but each of us has become our own Adam" (54:19, *OTP*). Thus, the larger prayer functions to reinforce the justice of God's judgment against the wicked. The prayer then turns to address God directly by seeking an interpretation of the vision of the cloud (54:20–22; cf. chap. 53).

Thus, in 2 Baruch prayer and lamentation usually foster Baruch's dialogue with God, but they can also perform other functions. They can voice grief for Zion, present indirect challenges to God's justice, seek divine mercy, or simply reinforce the apocalypse's larger message. In any case, the prayers and lamentations work together with dialogue and visionary experience to move along the process of revelation.

MAJOR VISIONS

Second Baruch features three major visions, the visions of Zion's devastation (chaps. 6–8), the forest, vine, fountain, and cedar (chaps. 36–37), and the cloud (chap. 53). Although the vision of Zion's devastation sets the stage for the rest of the apocalypse, the latter two visions and their interpretations reveal its eschatological teachings most prominently. (Detailed eschatological teachings also occur in the dialogue concerning the twelve tribulations [chap. 27].) The latter two visions follow Baruch's first address to the people in chapter 31, as they participate in the continuing pattern of revelation and address to the people. They also are explicitly allegorical and receive elaborate interpretation (chaps. 38–40; 55–74).

Baruch's vision of Zion's devastation is far more than a simple setting for the apocalypse; it provides a stunning interpretation of the event itself. Carried away by a strong spirit (or wind; 6:3), Baruch is lifted up above the city. There, he sees four angels preparing to destroy the city. (This scene also reveals 2 Baruch's interest in priestly things, including holy items and priestly dress [6:7].) Having seen this preparation, Baruch is returned to his original place. Then the angels destroy one of the walls and invite Zion's enemies into the city. Thus, 2 Baruch leaves no room for doubt: Zion's destruction is primarily an act of divine judgment, not a tragedy of history.

With its interpretation, Baruch's vision of the forest, vine, fountain, and cedar (chaps. 36–40) draws upon the traditional theme of the four kingdoms. However, the sequence necessarily has a new twist, given 2 Baruch's historical setting after Jerusalem's *second* destruction. It remains unclear how the four kingdoms relate to one another,[14] except that the reign of the "last ruler" will end with the Messiah's arrival. When the Messiah comes, he will convict and then kill the last ruler, creating a dominion that will last until the final things (40:1–3).

Baruch's vision of the cloud is brief (chap. 53), but its interpretation represents the most extended single section of 2 Baruch (chaps. 55–74). It not only embodies a review of history, it also presents a sort of theory of human history. Baruch sees a cloud that initially pours down black water upon the earth. That black water becomes bright, but with less bright water than the black that had preceded it. This sequence repeats twelve times, finally culminating in "devastation and destruction" (53:7, *OTP*). Finally, lightning breaks through, bringing healing to the world and bringing forth twelve rivers that flow in submission to the lightning.

The interpretation of the vision articulates its historical review, beginning with Adam and moving on until the eleventh cycle, Zion's "current" disaster at the hands of the Babylonians. The twelfth cycle involves Zion's restoration, though with less glory than that preceding the Babylonian conquest. But that is not all, for 2 Baruch is interested primarily in the events of the first century C.E., not those nearly seven hundred years before. And so the final cycle of black waters—after the twelfth—represents the end-time tribulation, the end of which marks the Messiah's arrival. The Messiah brings good to Israel and to its friends as well as to those who have not known Israel. However, the Messiah brings destruction to the nations who have ruled and oppressed Israel. Peace and prosperity accompany the messianic age. These last bright waters mark the end of the temporal and the beginning of the eternal (74:2).

Though Second Baruch's eschatological scenario is interesting in its own right, it probably serves a larger and more immediate purpose: to interpret history from the point of view of a very present crisis. By describing history as a cycle of good and bad—mostly bad—times, then skipping into a future tribulation, 2 Baruch presents a peculiar worldview:

a. History is orderly and predictable. Thus, it remains under divine control, as reflected in the lightning, which is present from the very beginning of the vision (53:1). (By setting the vision in the sixth century C.E., during the eleventh cycle, and "predicting" the events of 70 C.E. within the twelfth cycle, the vision proves its own reliability.)

b. Human existence is more negative than positive. In the long haul, suffering and unrighteousness outweigh peace, prosperity, and goodness.

c. The present time is the ultimate crisis. All of history has pointed to this moment, so how people behave in this crisis is of ultimate importance.

These points, of course, leave open the question of the future, which Second Baruch promises will be blessed for some but destructive for others. How people may live in order to receive their blessings is the subject matter when Baruch addresses the people.

ADDRESSES TO THE PEOPLE

From one perspective, the dialogues and visions are the most interesting things about 2 Baruch because they articulate the apocalypse's eschatology in the most systematic way. In these dialogues and visions—along with their interpretations—we learn about the course of history, the reasons for Zion's calamity, the tribulation before the end times, the coming of the Anointed One, the final judgment, and Israel's restoration. But from a rhetorical point of view, these teachings serve as the argument for a particular way of living in the world. For 2 Baruch indeed responds to the events of 70 C.E., but it does not so much look back as it looks ahead. How should God's people live in their particular time of crisis? The answer is 2 Baruch's reason for being, and it emerges most clearly when Baruch addresses the people. These addresses offer consolation, but they also present direction. We find three such set addresses in chapters 31–34, 44–46, and 77–87 (an epistle).

The address in 2 Baruch 31–34 follows the dialogue concerning the twelve tribulations. On his own initiative Baruch calls the people together.[15] He warns them of the coming tribulation, even more intense than Jerusalem's two calamities (32:6), but he also promises their deliverance on certain conditions. In particular, Baruch calls the people to turn to the Law.

> If you prepare your minds to sow into them the fruits of the law, [God] shall protect you in the time in which the Mighty One shall shake the entire creation. (32:1, *OTP*)

Though brief, this address fully expresses 2 Baruch's basic challenge. Whatever the present calamity, the Law is the present path for salvation. Baruch's advocacy for the Law continues in his second address.

> Behold, I go to my fathers in accordance with the way of the whole earth. You, however, do not withdraw from the way of the Law, but guard and admonish the people who are left lest they withdraw from the commandments of the Mighty One. (44:2–3, *OTP*)

Indeed, Baruch interprets Jerusalem's fall as God's judgment, but he promises that if the people turn again to the Law, a better time is coming (44:6–7; cf. 46:5–6). In part, this argument contrasts the present distress, which is "nothing" (44:8), and the grand future that awaits the righteous. It warns that although those who keep the Law are headed for blessing, the unrighteous are destined for fire (44:15) and torment (46:6). Thus, 2 Baruch combines admonishment concerning the fate of the wicked with exhortation to keep the Law.

Baruch's final address is both his longest and his most indirect. Though it begins with a short speech to the people in Jerusalem, Baruch writes on their behalf to the exiles in Babylon. His brief Jerusalem address is instructive, however, for it combines the same themes we have already encountered: a reminder of the Torah and exhortation to its observance. It begins:

> Hear, O children of Israel, behold how many are left from the twelve tribes of Israel. To you and to your [ancestors] the Lord gave the Law above all nations. (77:2–3, *OTP*)

Having reminded the people that Jerusalem's devastation had resulted from its disobedience, he then exhorts them by offering perhaps the most captivating promise in the entire book:

> If, therefore, you will make straight your ways, you will not go away as your brothers [and sisters] went away, but they will come to you. (77:6)

Thus, obedience to the Torah is more than a path of individual salvation. It embodies the very means by which the people may be reconstituted. It is Israel's only hope.

Inspired by this speech, the people commission Baruch to write to their comrades in Babylon. Their request again emphasizes Torah and exhortation, as the letter will present "a letter of doctrine and a roll of hope" (77:12, *OTP*). The interchange may also open a window as to how the actual author of this passage viewed the effects of Jerusalem's devastation. Apparently, it is a time of social disorder, with no authoritative public voices to guide the people or to provide models for their self-definition.

> For the shepherds of Israel have perished, and the lamps which gave light are extinguished, and the fountains from which we used to drink have withheld their streams. Now we have been left in the darkness and in the thick forest and in the aridness of the desert. (77:13–14, *OTP*)

Baruch's answer is brilliant. He insists that shepherds, lamps, and fountains all derive from the Law in the first place, whereas the Law is eternal. Israel's proper source of guidance, then, will always reside in the Law (77:15–16).

Remarkably, Baruch does not exactly follow his commission in precise detail. The people request a letter to Babylon. Baruch agrees *in principle,* but he adds that he will also write to the nine-and-a-half tribes that were destroyed in the Assyrian conquest of the eighth century. Presumably assimilated into various surrounding cultures, those tribes effectively no longer existed. Their reconstitution would constitute a grand miracle in Baruch's own day, much more so in the first century C.E. Baruch's method of delivery confirms the impossibility of this exercise: He ties the letter to an eagle and sends it off. Just as remarkably, the apocalypse does not include his letter to Babylon, nor does it relate its sending.

So why end the apocalypse with a letter that never reaches its "audience"? And why does Baruch fail (as far as we can tell) to write to Babylon? For one thing, this final epistle appears "attached" to the larger apocalypse, suggesting that it may represent an independent composition.[16] Yet the epistle also expresses the major emphases of 2 Baruch as a whole, thus inviting us to ask about its purpose and its contribution to the apocalypse. Perhaps the epistle reflects the eschatological hope–familiar from other Jewish sources such as Baruch, Ben Sira, 2 Maccabees, the Psalms of Solomon, the Assumption (or Testament) of Moses, the Qumran War Scroll, and perhaps 1 Enoch[17] –that in the end times God would miraculously reconstitute Israel's twelve tribes.

Such an explanation surely merits consideration. However, we may also recall that 2 Baruch addresses an entirely different context. Its first actual readers would have *overheard* this epistle as part of the larger apocalypse. In other words, the epistle provides a vehicle through which the apocalypse addresses its actual audience indirectly. The letter, then, offers a sort of conclusion for 2 Baruch, in which its main emphases come into focus. Why 2 Baruch includes the letter to the nine-and-a-half tribes but not to Babylon may remain a mystery.

The letter itself begins by establishing Baruch's common bond with the tribes, then moves immediately to familiar territory: Their mutual suffering can lead to eternal salvation if they will simply turn from their errors (78:6). (The Messiah or Anointed One does not appear in the epistle.) Baruch promises God's retaliation against Israel's oppressors, and he indicates the movement of history, period by period, to the final judgment. Naturally, the emphasis turns to the Law, recalling Moses' warning that Israel would be driven off the land for its disobedience (84:1–11; 85:3–4, 14).

To a large degree Baruch's addresses to the people bear the rhetorical weight of the entire apocalypse. They express the view that Jerusalem's devastation has resulted from its sin, that God is preparing to act in history to redeem the righteous, and–particularly–that one's eternal salvation depends upon one's adherence to the Law. They do not explicitly articulate the messianic hope embodied in Baruch's visions. In the confusion created by the absence of the temple and the holy city, 2 Baruch–along with 4 Ezra and other Jewish voices of the period–identifies the Torah as the preeminent symbol of Jewish identity and faithfulness.

Reading 2 Baruch with 4 Ezra

Second Baruch and Fourth Ezra differ in important ways. Ezra is far less compliant than is Baruch in his challenges to God, though he is eventually won over. On the other hand, 2 Baruch attributes Jerusalem's fall more directly to heavenly agents than does 4 Ezra. This is possible because 2 Baruch begins its story before the catastrophe itself. From the very beginning, Baruch not only sees Jerusalem's fate, he also sees its brighter future. Things never seem as bleak in 2 Baruch as they are in the first half of 4 Ezra.

Yet 2 Baruch and 4 Ezra share a common historical setting and some common concerns. In the wake of Jerusalem's devastation, they seek to articulate God's role in history; and they imagine a better future for God's people. Through a process that involves questions and challenges concerning God's justice, they interpret Jerusalem's fall as a punishment for its sin. Yet they also insist upon God's faithfulness: After eschatological tribulation, God will deliver the people from their oppressors; the Messiah will establish an age of peace and prosperity; and judgment will set things right. Perhaps most importantly, these apocalypses share the conviction that the Torah must be the foremost symbol of Jewish faithfulness in the years to come.[18]

Some scholars believe that 2 Baruch addresses an audience that sees itself as the faithful minority within a largely apostate Judaism. Thus, its blessings come with a reservation: Only the faithful few among Judaism will enjoy these blessings.[19] Indeed, chapters 41–42 make a clear distinction between the faithful and those "who have cast away from them the yoke of [the] Law" (41:3, *OTP*). Yet it seems to me that the larger emphasis of 2 Baruch intends not to strengthen the convictions of a minority but to shape the consciousness of a people. Though the addresses to the people require the response of individuals, 2 Baruch's eschatology emphasizes Israel as a people, primarily opposing Zion to its oppressors rather than the faithful to the unfaithful. In my view, 2 Baruch proposes societal redefinition.

In conclusion, Second Baruch attempts to fill a particular social void. In the absence of the temple, Israel's primary symbol of identity and sacred presence, how may the people constitute themselves? Like many others, most notably the rabbis, 2 Baruch replies that adherence to Torah is the means by which the people may find their salvation. But in contrast to the rabbis, the apocalypse also may see its own time as the end time, so that a final judgment may transcend even corporate identity in importance.

3 Baruch

Languages and Texts

Third Baruch is extant in both Greek and Slavonic. While the Slavonic texts represent translations from Greek, they differ from the two extant Greek texts to such a degree that H.E. Gaylord translates both traditions rather than trying to create an edition that represents an "original" text.[20] Because the Slavonic texts include fewer Christian elements than do the Greek manuscripts, some scholars believe the Slavonic versions reflect an earlier Jewish stage of the apocalypse.[21]

Likely Date

This apocalypse was apparently written after Jerusalem's destruction in 70 C.E., perhaps as late as 150 C.E.

Like 4 Ezra and 2 Baruch, 3 Baruch begins with sorrow and disillusionment in the wake of Jerusalem's fall. And yet 3 Baruch differs from those other two apocalypses in several important ways. First, the figure of Baruch is much less developed—and much less active—than are Ezra in 4 Ezra and Baruch in 2 Baruch. Second, though Jerusalem's fall provides the starting point for 3 Baruch, it plays little, if any, role in how the apocalypse actually develops. Third, 3 Baruch does not articulate a particular social vision or a response to a specific circumstance; it is difficult to identify what its authors were trying to accomplish. Fourth, 3 Baruch includes some clearly Christian material that expresses far less interest in Jerusalem's fall. Fifth, whereas 4 Ezra and 2 Baruch reveal both a divine design for history and the centrality of Torah, 3 Baruch transfers salvation from the future (emphasizing time) to the heavenly realms (emphasizing space). Indeed, 3 Baruch resides among what Martha Himmelfarb has named the "ascent to heaven" apocalypses.[22] The body of the apocalypse records Baruch's journeys to five heavens, and it may originally have included seven.

Third Baruch begins with the scribe weeping over "the captivity of Jerusalem" (Preface). This *narrative setting* is in the sixth century B.C.E., though we have every reason to locate the *historical setting,* or actual time of composition, in the aftermath of 70 C.E. Indeed, Jerusalem's destruction functions as a mere pretext for the apocalypse, and scholars suspect that 3 Baruch depends upon 2 Baruch and the Paraleipomena ("things which have been left out") of Jeremiah, which may date from around 136 C.E.[23]

In its present forms, Baruch's vision emerges from his grief concerning Jerusalem. Thus, the revelation of heavenly things serves as a satisfactory response to questions concerning God's faithfulness and God's role in history.

Baruch the Visionary

Like 2 Baruch, 3 Baruch draws upon Baruch's identity as Jeremiah's scribe who receives divine protection. As in 4 Ezra and 2 Baruch, here Baruch also questions God's justice. In the Greek tradition, he asks,

> "Lord, why have you set fire to your vineyard and laid it waste? Why have you done this? And why, Lord, did you not requite us with another punishment, but rather handed us over to such heathen so that they reproach us, saying, 'Where is their God?'" (1:2 Greek, *OTP*).

In the Slavonic version, his challenge is even more succinct, and it ends with the same concern: "Why have you acted so, Lord?" (1:2 Slav., *OTP*).

But from this point on, Baruch plays a fairly passive role. In response to his tour of the heavens, his questions seek clarification at particular points; and they receive reasonably direct answers. Thus, his defining characteristic is his *curiosity.* This proves to benefit all of humanity through the contents of his revelation. He is also *compliant,* in that his initial reservations appear to be satisfied. Indeed, the introduction to 3 Baruch foreshadows this development: Baruch promises that if the angel reveals something to him, he will listen. He even pronounces a curse on himself if he is not obedient to the revelation (1:7).

In the Greek tradition, Baruch's response to his vision involves two steps: He praises God, and he encourages his readers to do so as well (17:3–4 Greek). The Slavonic texts end with a doxology pronounced by a heavenly voice: "Glory be to our God forever" (17:1 Slav., *OTP*). Finally, whereas the visionaries in most ascent apocalypses experience a transformation to angelic status, Baruch does not.[24] Yet in 3 Baruch 11:7 (Greek), the chief angel Michael identifies Baruch as "our brother, interpreter of revelations to those who pass through life rightly"(*OTP*). Thus, Baruch is more a vehicle for the revelation than he is an agent in the story.

Mode of Revelation

Third Baruch presents a heavenly ascent, in which the visionary travels through five heavens. Modern readers should beware, however, for in the ancient apocalypses not every "heaven" is heavenly. In 3 Baruch, the first, second, and third heavens include places of judgment. The righteous dwell in the fourth heaven. While the fifth heaven is reserved for God and the angels, the deeds of mortals are remembered there.

How Many Heavens?

In 3 Baruch the scribe apparently ascends through five heavens, though a textual problem confuses the issue. The appearance in the third heaven is not explicitly indicated, though it almost certainly occurs at 3 Baruch 4:1. When Baruch arrives at the fourth heaven (10:1), the Greek manuscripts indicate that this is the third heaven, while the Slavonic texts again do not indicate a transition from one heaven to another. Then, in both the Greek and the Slavonic texts Baruch explicitly arrives at the fifth heaven at 11:1.

To compound the curiosity, Jewish and Christian apocalyptic literature offer varying accounts of just how many heavens they believe to exist. The Christian apostle Paul mentions transport to the *third* heaven, a tradition that is naturally duplicated in the Apocalypse of Paul. Third Baruch is the only apocalypse to relate *five* heavens, though we have reasons to believe that it may have included *seven* at some stage.[25] The early Christian writer Origen alludes to a book of "Baruch the prophet" that offers explicit information concerning the seven heavens" (*De principiis* 2.3.6), and 3 Baruch lacks the usual vision of God's throne in the highest heaven. Likewise, other important texts feature *seven* heavens. These include the Testament of Levi, 2 Enoch, the Ascension of Isaiah, the Apocalypse of Abraham, and many rabbinic texts. Finally, 2 Enoch 20:3b alludes to *ten* heavens.[26] Apparently, seven heavens was the most common view.[27]

But why did apocalyptic literature begin to theorize concerning the multiple heavens? One answer seems obvious: by describing various heavens, the apocalyptic writers could depict the various fates human beings might encounter. Thus, the multiple levels of heaven could discourage behaviors that would lead to torment in the lower regions, while encouraging those that would lead to bliss.

A second function may be more directly theological. The tours of heaven reveal a sophisticated organization, a place for everything and everything in its place. The apocalypses are building an argument about God's relationship to the world: Beyond the chaos that apparently defines human existence lies a larger and more significant order.

Third Baruch also reveals another function, one that may be more difficult for modern persons to grasp. In chapters 6–9, for example, Baruch investigates the movements of the sun, moon, and stars. As we have seen with 1 Enoch, these tours of the heavens may represent a form of ancient science, a means of imagining the fundamental workings of the cosmos.[28] Moreover, they offer an alternative voice to competing cosmologies from the ancient world.

As in most apocalypses, Baruch has an angelic escort who interprets and explains the vision to him. Baruch often voices questions. The angel either answers them directly, or new dimensions of the vision address them. At one point the angel requires Baruch to read a mysterious writing on his own (6:7–8).

Both the Greek and Slavonic versions of 3 Baruch conclude in a doxolgy, but the materials immediately preceding the doxology are quite different. Both versions feature an emphasis on God's justice in punishing the wicked. We find no direct exhortation to Baruch's audience, as we do in 4 Ezra and 2 Baruch, apart from the Greek version's command that they should glorify God. Thus, 3 Baruch moves from crisis and questioning to vindication and praise.

A JEWISH OR A CHRISTIAN APOCALYPSE?

Almost all scholars acknowledge that 3 Baruch includes Christian passages, but they disagree as to "how Christian" the apocalypse is. Some see it as a Jewish apocalypse, with Christian insertions (*interpolations*), while others regard it as a Christian composition altogether. Exacerbating this problem are the differences between the extant Greek and Slavonic texts, because the clearest Christian passages reside in the Greek and not in the Slavonic.

Some evidence is inconclusive. The translation one uses can make a difference in the impression one receives. In particular, the appearance of the word *ekklesia* in 3 Baruch 13:4 and 16:4 *may* refer to the Christian institution of the church, but *ekklesia* may also simply indicate Jewish assemblies. Although lists of vices from 3 Baruch 4:17; 8:5; and 13:4 have parallels in the New Testament (Mt. 15:19 par. Mk. 7:21–22; Gal. 5:19–21), other such lists occur elsewhere in the New Testament and also in Jewish and Greco-Roman sources.[29]

Yet several passages in 3 Baruch do reflect Christian convictions or appear to depend upon other early Christian literature. Chapter 4 is the most obvious case. In the Greek, Baruch asks for a complete revelation "for the Lord's sake" (4:1, *OTP*). Later, verse 15 (again, only in Greek) reveals that "through Jesus Christ Emmanuel" mortals may enter Paradise. Elsewhere, the saying "You have been faithful over a little, he will set you over much; enter into the delight of our Lord" (15:4 Greek, *OTP*) sounds eerily like Matthew 25:23. And H. F. D. Sparks has argued that the Greek word *dichotomesate* ("cut in two") that appears at 3 Baruch 16:3 (Greek) also appears "in an almost identical context" in Matthew 24:51 paralleling Luke 12:46,[30] though the evidence seems much less clear to me.

Thus, at a minimum the Greek version of 3 Baruch has received some Christian reworking. Unlike 4 Ezra and 2 Baruch, 3 Baruch encourages good deeds in general rather than Torah observance in particular, though there is a reference to God's commands (16:4 Greek; 16:6 Slavonic). Because the vast majority of early Christian communities did not expect Torah observance, this difference lends itself to the conclusion that 3 Baruch might be an altogether Christian apocalypse.

Although it begins with Jerusalem's fall, that issue seems more of a pretext than a pressing crisis–again potentially distancing 3 Baruch from Jewish concerns. Yet the differences between the Slavonic and the Greek texts suggest that the solution is likely to be more complicated, including the possibility that Christian scribes radically reworked an originally Jewish text. After all, most of the noncanonical Jewish texts that survive are in our hands because Christians–not Jews–preserved them.

WHAT BARUCH LEARNS

Baruch receives most of his education through his journey to the five heavens. The first two heavens are devoted to those who attempted to build the tower of Babel (Gen. 11), with the builders in the first heaven and the planners and those who oppressed the labor in the second. Their appearance includes features of various wild beasts, presumably indicating that their status has been both confused and debased in the other world. The third heaven receives the most attention, and it combines the revelation of Hades–a "gloomy and unclean" place where a dragon devours the bodies of the wicked!–the vision of the vine involved in Adam's fall, and the revelation concerning the sun, moon, and stars. (In the Greek version, Hades is the dragon's belly [5:3].)

The fourth heaven apparently depicts the souls of the righteous as grand birds whose songs voice praise to God. When Baruch arrives at the fifth heaven, he finds the gate closed until the chief angel Michael commands that it be opened. Michael takes a great bowl filled with the deeds of the righteous and presents it before God. Baruch also encounters those angels assigned to evil persons–guardian angels, as it were–who complain about their tasks. Then Baruch sees that people's rewards reflect the degree of their good deeds. He learns that for those who lack good deeds, mourning is inappropriate, as God's judgment is just. The apocalypse ends when the gate to the fifth heaven is shut and Baruch is returned to earth.

Reading 3 Baruch

Like 4 Ezra and 2 Baruch, 3 Baruch begins with the question of theodicy—in the face of evil, how does one imagine God's agency in the world?—but moves to a very different place. Unlike 4 Ezra and 2 Baruch, 3 Baruch's interest is not temporal. It voices no expectation of a messianic age or a redemption of Israel. Unlike 4 Ezra and 2 Baruch, 3 Baruch does not call for Torah observance as the path of salvation.

Instead, 3 Baruch locates salvation not so much in the future as in the heavenly realms. It presents alternative human destinies: one devoted to suffering and another defined by the blessed praise of God. The difference between one fate and another lies simply in whether one pursues evil or good. Indeed, 3 Baruch even provides for an intermediate state: a realm of blessedness, which apportions the rewards according to one's relative virtue.

For these reasons, it appears that 3 Baruch is devoted to admonition and exhortation: warning concerning evil and encouragement to pursue righteousness. Unlike 4 Ezra and 2 Baruch, it apparently does not intervene at a social level. It does not envision a future for Israel as Israel or establish any sort of corporate identity.

Moreover, 3 Baruch's interest in the sun, moon, and stars seems somewhat out of place in a vision that primarily emphasizes the fates of the righteous and the wicked. But we find this sort of "scientific" curiosity among several of the heavenly journey apocalypses, and to some degree it does represent a theological response to the question of theodicy. Confronted by the chaos of Jerusalem's fall, 3 Baruch affirms a larger cosmic order that determines everything. If one could truly understand the efficiency of the heavenly realms, one might not worry about the apparent disorder of the world.

Apocalypse of Abraham

Languages and Texts

The Apocalypse of Abraham now exists only in Church Slavonic, which has been translated from Greek. It may derive from a Hebrew or Aramaic original.

Likely Date

In its present form the Apocalypse of Abraham postdates 70 c.e., to which it refers in chapter 27.

Unlike the three apocalypses we have previously reviewed in this chapter, the Apocalypse of Abraham does not begin with lamentation concerning Jerusalem's destruction. Instead, like Daniel, it begins with legends that reveal its hero's virtue and insight. The Apocalypse–or parts of it–does offer a response to the events of 70 C.E., one somewhat more similar to 3 Baruch than to 4 Ezra or 2 Baruch, but with its own distinctiveness as well.

Abraham the Visionary

Given Abraham's status as Israel's exalted ancestor, it is no surprise that quite a lot of Abraham literature survives from the ancient world. In the Bible, Abraham is a sort of proto-Israelite, the first mortal to respond to God's election with faith. God's promises to Abraham, particularly in Genesis 12 and 15, indicate that from him would derive a great people, that God would bless those people with a particular land, and that through this people God would bless the entire world.

Having presumably lived as a pagan, Abraham is the first man to enter into covenant with God through circumcision; and his grandson Jacob, who would be renamed Israel, is the father of Israel's twelve tribes. Thus, Abraham is Israel's foremost patriarch. As Christian readers will recognize, in John's gospel to claim Abraham as one's father is to name oneself as a Jew (8:33). For Paul, to receive the inheritance of Abraham is to participate in God's blessings for the world, regardless of whether one is a Jew or a Gentile (note especially the argument in Gal. 3:15–4:7). The Apocalypse of Abraham reflects intense concern with the contrast between Jews and pagan Gentiles, and Abraham's legacy makes him the ideal visionary for this apocalypse.

Abraham also represents a somewhat mystical figure who repeatedly receives visitations from God or God's messengers, such as the vision in Genesis 15 and the visitations in chapters 17 and 18. For drama, these visitations go beyond God's routine addresses to Abraham. The Apocalypse of Abraham locates its major revelation in the context of Genesis 15, though it adds an important detail: Abraham fasts for forty days and nights.

The Apocalypse introduces Abraham as an obedient son. Young Abraham is a well-intentioned pagan, whose religious questions make him a kind of seeker. Legends concerning Abraham's conversion from a pagan background had become fairly common in Judaism, as attested in Jubilees 11–12, Josephus (*Ant.* 1.7.1), Philo (*De Abrahamo* 15), and in some examples of rabbinic biblical interpretation.[31] In fact, the Apocalypse portrays Abraham as singularly insightful in posing the obvious questions concerning how people confuse material artifacts for gods when they have created the artifacts and have seen they are vulnerable to destruction.

Once God calls Abraham to leave his father's house (chap. 8), the path clears for his revelation. When the revelation begins, it so overwhelms Abraham that he loses all strength (10:2; cf. 16:1), thus revealing his innate responsiveness to holy things. The angel commands Abraham to stand up and addresses him as "friend of God" (10:5, *OTP*), indicating his intimacy with the Divine One.

Abraham is an obedient visionary. In preparation for the vision, he walks and fasts for forty days and nights (12:1). In response to a command, he sings praise to God and prays just as he is taught. His questions to God usually involve simple matters of clarification. (Martha Himmelfarb suggests that his participation in the heavenly liturgy indicates that he has achieved angelic status.[32]) Accordingly, Abraham comes across as faithful, sensitive, insightful, and obedient.

Plot and Mode of Revelation

Like the book of Daniel, the Apocalypse of Abraham begins with a series of legends concerning Abraham, then moves to the visionary content of Abraham's revelation. Like Daniel, the legends relate to the apocalypse's primary concerns. In the case of the Apocalypse of Abraham, the issue in question is idolatry.

The story begins with Abraham guarding and selling the gods his father Terah manufactures. Depending upon one's perspective, the stories can be quite funny. For example, an accident breaks some of the gods he is to sell on his father's behalf, so Abraham throws their fragments into a river—adding for emphasis that they sank and "were no more" (chap. 2). When he asks his father how these breakable gods can do humans any good at all, his father breaks into a rage (chap. 4).

When a god gets consumed in a cooking fire, Terah praises the god for its contribution to his meal and then promises to make another god who will prepare his food (chap. 5). Clearly, these episodes ridicule paganism through parody. No pagans were so naive as to actually believe that the stone images were divine in themselves, but such parodies were commonplace in Jewish—and Christian—rhetoric.[33]

Abraham receives two promises concerning his revelation that spell out the contents of the apocalypse (9:9–10; 12:10). The first case offers the fullest description: God promises to reveal both the mysteries of creation and the fates of mortals (9:9–10). Hence, the Apocalypse of Abraham addresses historical concerns as well as heavenly mysteries, the future as well as the other world.

The apocalypse devotes significant time to narrating Abraham's preparation for his visionary ascent. Drawing upon Abraham's sacrifice in Genesis 15, the story promises that, "in this sacrifice I will place the ages" (9:5, *OTP*). Abraham overhears the divine voice as it orders an angel to accompany him. His encounter with that angel so overwhelms him that he requires divine strengthening. The Apocalypse appears to recall Genesis 22, when God provided the sacrifice in place of Abraham's son Isaac. The Apocalypse also relates how the sacrifice itself immediately appears, how the devil (named Azazel) in the form of a bird attempts to divert Abraham from the sacrifice, and, finally, how a pigeon carries Abraham up into the heavenly realms.

On his arrival, Abraham sees a fiery place of torment, inhabited by a great crowd (15:6–7). But the vision does not dwell there, as other apocalypses will. Instead, it turns to Abraham's preparation to see the Eternal One by reciting the heavenly song he has learned. Then Abraham sees a fiery throne, surrounded by mysterious heavenly beings reminiscent of Ezekiel 1:6–12. His ascent stands out among the apocalypses because Abraham immediately enters the seventh heaven, rather than working his way up from the first. From this vantage point he surveys only the sixth (where angels dwell), the fifth (where the astral powers reside), and what is perhaps the third (which includes the earth, along with its plants and animals, and a division among human beings).[34]

This heavenly-yet-earthly realm is especially significant, for in it Abraham discerns that humankind has been divided into two groups: those on the left and those on the right. As in Matthew 25:31–46, being on the right is far better than finding oneself on the left. Yet knowing who gets to be on the right side is difficult at best. According to 21:7, the populations of both groups are equal, and yet 22:4–5 creates the impression that only Abraham's righteous descendants are on the right side.

Abraham's vision then moves into a condensed review of history, explaining how humankind has reached its present divisions. He sees Adam and Eve with the serpent, and he sees the effects of sin when Cain slays Abel. His vision shifts immediately to an idealized temple, at once glorious and corrupt. At that point the Apocalypse of Abraham addresses Jerusalem's fall. Abraham sees it and grieves, but the divine voice explains that the calamity is due to how Abraham's descendants have provoked God. He also learns that an indeterminate "twelve periods" will mark the "impious age" (29:2, *OTP*) before the end time. Ten plagues will occur during this horrific period. People will worship a person who comes from humanity's "left" half, but God will protect and sustain a small remnant of the righteous.

One wonders whether the apocalypse may have ended at this point, between what are now chapters 29 and 30. Chapter 30 explicitly names the ten plagues, and then chapter 31 introduces a messianic figure, the "Chosen One," who will gather God's people and deliver their enemies to judgment. (The story locates this punishment in the devil's belly 31:5, reminding us of 3 Bar. 5:3.) This material may have been added by a Christian editor, though such a conclusion may not be necessary. The apocalypse ends with Abraham taking the contents of his revelation into his heart.

Reading the Apocalypse of Abraham

From a literary perspective, the Apocalypse of Abraham is not nearly so artfully designed as are 4 Ezra and 2 and 3 Baruch. It joins legendary and visionary material but lacks explicit reflection as to how the two relate. It offers a review of history, but it skips from humanity's second major scene, Cain and Abel, to the temple and its fall. It informs us of seven heavens but reveals only heavens seven, six, five, and perhaps three. It divides humankind into two halves, yet it ties one of those halves to a specific people. Aesthetically speaking, the Apocalypse of Abraham is a mess.

But it is not a complete mess, for it contains lines of continuity and concern. As Martha Himmelfarb observes, the Apocalypse of Abraham moves from concerns regarding idolatry to Jerusalem's demise. This development suggests that the apocalypse locates Israel's struggles within a much larger framework of human history.[35] Yet the Apocalypse of Abraham also presents a distinctly Jewish response to the human crisis in general and to Zion's fall in particular. The tension between idolatry and temple may explain why the Apocalypse—like 3 Baruch but unlike 4 Ezra and 2 Baruch—emphasizes cult rather than Torah. Proper worship of God is the issue. Jerusalem's calamity was due to its improper—or idolatrous—worship practices. This complaint against the temple was not unique in first-century Judaism, as the Dead Sea Scrolls attest, though it is remarkable that Jews after 70 C.E. would focus upon cult rather than the ethical or corporate identity that Torah could promise.

The Apocalypse of Abraham further insists that God is just. Like the other post-70 apocalypses, it attributes Zion's demise to God's judgment. It further identifies the righteous among the few rather than the majority, even within Judaism. Because it promises blessing to those few, it serves at once to warn against idolatry and to encourage faithfulness. The Apocalypse further affirms God's justice by promising that God's activity continues in the world, preserving the righteous until the coming of the Elect One to make things right.

For Further Reading

Burkes, Shannon. "'Life' Redefined: Wisdom and Law in Fourth Ezra and *Second Baruch.*" *CBQ* 63 (2001): 55–71.

deSilva, David A. "Fourth Ezra: Reaffirming Jewish Cultural Values through Apocalyptic Rhetoric." Pages 123–39 in *Vision and Persuasion: Rhetorical Dimensions of Apocalyptic Discourse.* Edited by Greg Carey and L. Gregory Bloomquist. St. Louis: Chalice Press, 1999.

Esler, Philip F. "The Social Function of Fourth Ezra." Pages 110–30 in *The First Christians in Their Social Worlds: Social-Scientific Approaches to New Testament Interpretation.* New York: Routledge, 1994.

Harlow, Daniel. *The Greek Apocalypse of Baruch (3 Baruch) in Hellenistic Judaism and Early Christianity.* SVTP 12. Leiden: Brill, 1996.

Longenecker, Bruce W. *2 Esdras.* Guides to Apocrypha and Pseudepigrapha. Sheffield: Sheffield Academic Press, 1995.

Sayler, Gwendolyn. *Have the Promises Failed? A Literary Analysis of 2 Baruch.* SBLDS 72. Chico, Calif.: Scholars Press, 1984.

Stone, Michael Edward. *Fourth Ezra.* Hermeneia. Minneapolis: Fortress Press, 1990.

CHAPTER 7

Christian Historical Apocalypses

When apocalyptic literature comes to mind, people immediately think of the book of Revelation. But the decades around 100 C.E. produced other historically-oriented apocalypses, such as 4 Ezra, 2 and 3 Baruch, and the Apocalypse of Abraham. A Christian apocalypse, the Shepherd of Hermas, emerged from the same period and rivaled Revelation for both popularity and acceptance well into the fourth century. Indeed, Revelation and Hermas share important common concerns, as they address the plight of early Christians in the Roman imperial context. They grapple with issues such as community boundaries, social justice, persecution, and powerlessness; and they depict alternative realities in which faithfulness to Christ will meet its reward. They are also distinctive in that they appear not to be pseudonymous. Neither John nor Hermas presents himself as a hero from the remote past, but rather, both apocalypses address their immediate contexts. Moreover, both Revelation and Hermas insist on standards of faithfulness so high that they may have alienated some of their first readers.

Despite these common features and concerns, Revelation and Hermas are very different books. Nothing indicates that either author was aware of the other book. They have different literary structures and devices, different outlooks regarding the most important signs of faithful living, and different views of society as a whole. We can learn a great deal about these two early Christian apocalypses by reading them in conversation with each other.

Revelation

Setting

Revelation was composed in the late first century C.E., almost certainly between 68 and 96. It is addressed to seven churches in Asia Minor, which we know today as the western region of Turkey.

179

Texts and Languages

Revelation was composed in Greek, and its text is fairly well established due to the many ancient manuscripts available.

Is the book of Revelation an apocalypse? It presents itself as a prophecy (1:3; 10:9-11; 22:7, 10, 18–19; cf. 19:10), claiming that it authoritatively addresses its own times. It also displays the form of a letter (1:4; chaps. 2–3) with specific addresses for seven churches in Asia Minor, indicating its concern with the development of those churches. Most notoriously, of course, Revelation is the first book to introduce itself as an apocalypse: The Greek word *apocalypsis* appears as Revelation's first word and possibly its title (1:1). Revelation claims to unveil heavenly truth that addresses the circumstances of its first-century addressees.

While Revelation claims to predict future events, it also insists that its predictions will take effect "soon." The book's beginning and its ending emphasize this sense of urgency (1:1; 22:6, 7, 12, 20), so that this point was likely a matter of emphasis. Yet because Revelation concludes the biblical canon and because its visions of Christ's one-thousand-year reign and the New Jerusalem's descent have not seen its fulfillment, many readers continue to see Revelation as a roadmap for humanity's future. Ironically, then, these very readers who seek contemporary meaning from Revelation ignore how Revelation's first audiences may have understood it.

Setting

Because the book of Revelation is not pseudonymous, its literary and historical settings coincide. The book itself does not reveal a particular date of composition, leaving scholars to guess based on early Christian traditions and indirect evidence from within Revelation itself. Most scholars have concluded that Revelation was composed toward the end of the reign of the emperor Domitian, probably in 95 or 96 C.E., but a strong argument has suggested a date around the fall of Jerusalem in 70 C.E.[1] Revelation provides lots of information concerning its general cultural context. It addresses seven specific churches in a region of Asia Minor. It seems preoccupied with Roman imperial pretensions and practices and claims that some of Jesus' followers have met their deaths as a result of their confessions. It reflects tensions within the churches and between the churches and local synagogues. John himself claims to have received his vision on the island of Patmos "because of the word of God and the testimony of Jesus" (1:9). This may reflect his own identity as a victim of persecution.

Most modern scholars have argued that Revelation was written in response to persecution by Roman authorities, but today that topic is hotly debated. The few sources that might document such persecution are somewhat dubious, and Revelation isn't explicit as to the nature or origin of the struggles it depicts. In my view, Revelation does respond to instances of persecution, perhaps only isolated ones, but it imagines that things will get much worse before they improve. John mentions one Antipas, who met his death as a "faithful witness" (2:13; for those who suffer because of their witness to Jesus, John uses the Greek word *martys,* from which derives our word *martyr).* In chapter 6 he envisions a heavenly realm in which those who have died for their faith seek vengeance.

John the Visionary

In comparison with other apocalyptic visionaries, John plays an extremely active role in his own story. For one thing, he writes entirely in the first person, emphasizing "I saw" and "I heard" literally dozens of times. He travels, marvels, asks questions, and receives instructions. Sometimes he records the very words he hears. He claims to relate "all that he saw" (1:2), yet on one occasion he is commanded not to share what he hears (10:4). In short, John is a most important character in his own apocalypse.

Yet we do not know much about John. Very few scholars link him directly with John the follower of Jesus, or with the author of the gospel according to John, or with the author of the Johannine Epistles. John does not assign himself any particular title, yet he seems to assume that his intended audiences will recognize his name and his circumstances.

Some scholars have made much of the fact that Revelation and Hermas stand alone among the apocalypses by not being pseudonymous. It is an important point in some ways, but one can readily imagine the reasons for this phenomenon. The Christian movement was new, and these two apocalypses were addressing the concerns of specific communities in Asia Minor and in Rome to persuade those audiences to adopt particular perspectives and practices. Presumably, these authors were known to their audiences.

Meanwhile, other Christian apocalypses such as the Ascension of Isaiah and the Greek Apocalypse of Peter were composed not much later and yet employ pseudonymity. Those texts reflect a markedly less direct relationship with their audiences. For Revelation and Hermas, the authors' identity likely reflects more intimacy—and perhaps direct conflict—with members of their audiences.

John's self-presentation plays on a tension between identifying with his audience members and standing above them.[2] He introduces himself as a fellow-slave of Christ, an identity he and his audience hold in common, and he avers—as we have seen—that he shares his entire vision with them (1:1–2; cf. 19:5; 22:3, 6). At once he claims that they share status as rulers and priests (1:6), along with the experiences of "the persecution and the kingdom and the patient endurance" that are in Jesus (1:9). Furthermore, he includes them in the very blessings to which he himself aspires. Thus, many contemporary interpreters remark upon the "egalitarian" or "democratic" nature of John's address to his audience.[3]

Yet John also distances himself from his audience. He presents himself as the privileged visionary on whom the audience depends for the disclosure of heavenly truth. Indeed, his vision promises blessings and curses, depending on one's obedience to it. This is a remarkable feature of Revelation for two reasons. First, the alternatives concerning blessing and cursing literally frame the apocalypse: It begins with such an admonition (1:3) and concludes by essentially repeating it (22:18–19). Second, with Hermas, Revelation stands alone among the apocalypses in relating people's eschatological future so directly to its own contents. While obviously many apocalypses introduce their audiences to the two alternative paths, only Revelation explicitly ties those paths to its own textualized message. Thus,

> Blessed is the one who reads aloud the words of the prophecy, and blessed are those who hear and who keep what is written in it; for the time is near. (1:3)

And,

> I warn everyone who hears the words of the prophecy of this book: if anyone adds to them, God will add to that person the plagues described in this book; if anyone takes away from the words of the book of this prophecy, God will take away that person's share in the tree of life and in the holy city, which are described in this book. (22:18–19; cf. Hermas, Visions 5.1.5–7)

Hence, Revelation does not employ pseudepigraphy by attributing its contents to an exalted figure of the past. And yet, perhaps because his relationship to the seven churches is so direct, John himself plays a prominent role in the revelatory experience, establishing close ties to his audience even as he claims absolute authority for his message.

Cast of Characters

Revelation develops a remarkable cast of characters. Within the churches, it includes mysterious figures John names Nicolaitans, Balaam, and Jezebel; beyond or within the churches resides the "synagogue of Satan." Appearances also introduce the Lamb, the Woman Clothed with the Sun, the Dragon, the Beast, the Other Beast, Babylon the Whore, and the New Jerusalem, among others. These characters personify John's most immediate concerns, and because John explicitly identifies only one of these figures (the Dragon is Satan; 12:9), any discussion of Revelation's setting requires that we engage these characters directly.

Positive Characters

The Lamb, the New Jerusalem, and the Woman Clothed with the Sun convey positive symbolic values. The Lamb's identity is fairly clear, indicating Jesus as one whose death has brought life to his followers. John employs the intriguing phrase, "standing as if it had been slaughtered" (5:6), to indicate the tension between Jesus' death and his risen life. The Lamb alone opens the scrolls that reveal humanity's fate, and his power and glory are acknowledged by the heavenly chorus.

The New Jerusalem appears at 21:2 as a holy city coming down from heaven to earth. Metaphors mix because the New Jerusalem is also the Lamb's bride. The New Jerusalem functions as the dwelling place of the saints. It embodies both a relational identity and a future hope.

The Woman Clothed with the Sun figures prominently in chapter 12. Persecuted by the Dragon (Satan; 12:9) but divinely protected, she represents God's covenant people. She gives birth to a son (the Messiah?), and "the rest of her children" are Jesus' followers (12:17).

The contrast between the Woman Clothed with the Sun and the New Jerusalem is critical. Both female characters represent the corporate people of God, the Woman Clothed with the Sun through her children and the New Jerusalem through her inhabitants. Yet while the Woman Clothed with the Sun apparently gives birth to the Messiah, the New Jerusalem marries the Lamb. Moreover, the Woman Clothed with the Sun flees persecution, whereas the New Jerusalem descends in glory. Hence, these two images relate to different periods in time. The Woman Clothed with the Sun represents God's vulnerable yet faithful people past and present, and the New Jerusalem relates to the ultimate future.

NEGATIVE CHARACTERS

As we have seen, the Dragon represents Satan, God's ultimate demonic adversary. This offers a starting point for understanding other important negative symbols, the Beast, the Other Beast, and Babylon the Whore, for John has a way of bringing all of his symbols into conversation with one another. The Dragon gives its authority to the Beast (13:2, 4), whereas the Other Beast inspires worship of the First Beast (13:12) even as it speaks *like* a dragon (13:11). Finally, John depicts Babylon the Whore as riding the Beast (17:3), thus completing the chain of relationships: The Dragon inspires the Beast, who supports the Whore and is served by the Other Beast. So John is creating a network of associations, all of which he ultimately labels as demonic.

For many reasons, scholars agree that the two beasts and the Whore have something to do with Roman imperial authority and commerce. The Other Beast compels the earth's inhabitants to worship the First Beast, and we know that worship of the emperor or the imperial gods figured prominently in the civic culture in Asia Minor. Cities actually competed for the privilege of hosting an imperial shrine or observance. It was a measure of civic status, much as cities today vie for athletic, entertainment, or political events.[4] But many followers of Jesus believed that participation in the imperial cults amounted to apostasy. Thus, Revelation depicts conflict on precisely this point: The Other Beast commands that those who refuse to participate in the cult must be put to death or excluded from access to commerce (13:15–17). Given the greatness of Roman imperial power, John paints a bleak picture, for "Who is like the beast, and who can fight against it?" (13:4). Thus, in John's eyes faithfulness and martyrdom go hand in hand:

> I also saw the souls of those who had been beheaded for their testimony to Jesus and for the word of God. They had not worshiped the beast or its image and had not received its mark on their foreheads or their hands. They came to life and reigned with Christ a thousand years. (20:4)

Faithfulness to Jesus implies refusal to worship the imperial deities, but such resistance brings its own dangers.

---

666 AND THE MARK OF THE BEAST

Perhaps no technical detail in the Bible has provoked more speculation—with more bizarre implications!—than the cryptic number in Revelation 13:18:

> This calls for wisdom: let anyone with understanding calculate the number of the beast, for it is the number of a person. Its number is six hundred sixty-six.

Several items make this verse simply irresistible to certain curious minds. First, the verse invites calculation. How does one make sense out of a number? Second, John implicitly congratulates those who can solve his riddle. Only the wise and understanding are up to the task. Third, John offers a hint. It is the number of a mortal, probably indicating a single individual.

One can only wonder at the energy devoted to pinning the number on the Beast. A long tradition tags the papacy, or specific popes, with the number. Martin Luther linked the Pope with the Beast, and the Westminster Confession of 1646, a foundational document for Presbyterianism, identifies the Pope as the antichrist. But other candidates have emerged. In Tolstoy's *War and Peace,* a character assigns the number to Napoleon. And Ronald Wilson Reagan's names all have *six* letters; in 1988 Reagan requested that his street address be changed from 666 to 668![5]

It is entirely possible that 666 is an ideal number. Just as the numerals three and seven reflect completeness or perfection in biblical symbolism, three sixes might indicate perfect imperfection, or absolute evil. Assigning the number 666 to the Beast may simply indicate its complete opposition to God and to the Lamb.

However, it seems to me that John is inviting his audience to identify an individual with the Beast. Many scholars have named the Roman emperor Nero (d. 68 c.e.) as that person. Nero was the first great persecutor of Christians.

Seeking to exonerate himself, he blamed them for the great fire that devastated Rome in 64 c.e., executing literally thousands of them in gruesome fashion. This identification is somewhat complicated, but it explains a great deal.

First, Revelation insists that one of the Beast's heads has a mortal wound that has been healed (13:3, 12, 14; 17:11). This detail almost certainly reflects the early tradition that Nero would return from his apparent death to persecute the saints.[6] (See the discussion on pp.97–98)

Second, in Hebrew numerology the name *NRON QSR* (= Neron Caesar) holds a numerical value of 666.

Third, this theory accounts for the significant number of ancient manuscripts in which the number is 616; the Hebrew letter *N* in *NRON* is optional, and its value is fifty: 666 - 50 = 616![7]

So what does John mean by associating the Beast with Nero? One qualification is essential. Nero represents only one of the Beast's seven heads. Thus, Nero himself is not the Beast. Moreover, though it is entirely possible that John literally expects Nero's return to power, the grisly reminder of Nero may serve another purpose. Perhaps John intimates that if Nero's reign produced terror for Christians, the future promises similar yet even greater horror.

Another reason scholars identify the Beasts and the Whore with Rome involves the imagery associated with the Whore. As we have seen, the Whore rides the Beast, signifying their interdependence. We find other clues as well. The very name Babylon echoes the use of Babylon in contemporary apocalypses that discuss Roman imperialism by recalling the first empire to overrun Jerusalem. Moreover, the Beast upon which she rides has seven heads, which the angel indicates as the seven mountains upon which the Whore sits. Rome, then as now, was known as the city on seven hills.

Perhaps most significantly, we notice those who mourn when Babylon meets its destruction: kings (18:9–10), merchants (18:11–17a), and "all whose trade is on the sea" (18:17b–19). They grieve the loss of wealth brought about through her commerce: luxury items such as "gold, silver, jewels and pearls"; military necessities such as "horses and chariots"; and even the human cost of these exchanges, "slaves–and human lives" (18:12–13). If the image of the Beast charges the empire with authoritarianism and blasphemy, the Whore indicts the oppressive nature of imperial commerce. By linking these figures–Dragon, Beasts, and Whore–John seeks to *reveal* that behind Roman imperial pretensions are blasphemy, corruption, and death.[8]

Several devices contrast the Beast and the Whore, on the one hand, against the Lamb and the Woman Clothed with the Sun and the New Jerusalem, on the other.

1. The Lamb conquers evil through its death, but the Beast conquers by killing.

2. The Lamb has died and yet lives, as the Beast's head has survived a mortal wound.
3. The Lamb's followers are sealed (7:3; 14:1), while those of the Beast receive a mark.
4. The Lamb has a revealed name (19:12–13), yet the Beast's name is blasphemous.
5. The Lamb receives worship with God (5:13–14), but the Beast accepts worship with the Dragon.[9]
6. Likewise, the New Jerusalem is the heavenly city, but earthly Babylon meets its destruction.
7. The Dragon chases the Woman clothed with the Sun, and the Lamb marries the New Jerusalem; but the Whore rides upon the Beast.
8. The Woman of Revelation 12 wears the Sun as a garment, and the New Jerusalem is adorned as if for her wedding (21:2); but the Whore is gaudy in appearance and decadent in manner.
9. The earth's rulers come to honor the New Jerusalem, but they have intercourse with the Whore and mourn her fate.

These contrasts demonstrate the absolute divide that alienates John and his audience from the empire and its values.

This context frames Revelation's other players: Balaam, the Nicolaitans, Jezebel, and Satan's Synagogue. All of these characters appear only in chapters 2 and 3, the letters to the churches. Clearly, Balaam, the Nicolaitans, and Jezebel represent voices from within the churches, but just as clearly they are John's enemies. So what are they doing, and what issues are at stake?

The names Balaam and Jezebel derive from scripture. The book of Numbers blames Balaam for leading Israel into idolatry (31:16), and in 1 and 2 Kings Jezebel promotes idolatry in Israel. The term *Nicolaitans* derives from roots meaning "one who conquers the people," and *Balaam* is remarkably similar ("lord of the people"). Finally, John accuses the entire set of opponents with the same two offenses: eating food that has been offered to idols and *porneia,* a catch-all term for sexual immorality. Because some Hebrew prophets, notably Hosea, employ sexual sin as a metaphor for idolatry, most scholars believe that John really means only one thing: his opponents participate in the larger pagan society, including eating meat that had passed through pagan ceremonies.

Meat eating evidently presented a divisive topic among early Christians, one Paul addressed in both 1 Corinthians (chaps. 8 and 10) and Romans (chap. 14). It involved several related issues. Most meat derived from the various temple sacrifices in the ancient cities, implying the taint of idolatry from the beginning. Meals, public or private, typically included thanksgivings to the gods, so participation in civic life–trade guilds, social functions, public festivals–also linked one to idolatry. Because participation in many civil functions presupposed a measure of status and because meat was relatively expensive, most people could rarely afford it. Thus, the "eating meat" argument could also divide along status lines.[10]

Apparently, John is accusing his opponents of compromising with the idolatrous pagan world—the realm of the Beast—by participating in certain common practices. Ironically, one can imagine that John's opponents would sound somewhat like Paul, arguing that it doesn't matter where food comes from and that incidental association with pagan deities posed no real threat to Christian faithfulness.

John's enemies also include a group he labels "the synagogue of Satan," who "say they are Jews and are not" (2:9; 3:9). For a variety of reasons most scholars believe that Revelation's author was himself a Jew. Because Rome exempted Jews from the imperial cults and from military service, John would have appreciated that Jewish status carried practical value. Yet how may we identify this group that he opposes? Are they actually Jews, who live beyond John's churches and somehow pose problems for John and his audience? Or do they belong within the churches, perhaps as Gentile followers of Jesus who also seek identification as Jews? Alternatively, what if John identifies himself as a Jew and accuses other Jews (who may themselves participate in the churches) of faithlessness? While I hold the first view, that Revelation testifies to tensions between churches and synagogues, all three explanations share an essential assumption: John names Jewish identity as a fundamental problem for the churches.[11]

Thus, John addresses internal opponents (Balaam, the Nicolaitans, and Jezebel), enemies on the boundaries of his audience (Satan's synagogue), and the imperial world in general (the Beasts and the Whore). One may wonder, and some readers have, if perhaps John simply hates everybody. After all, "the inhabitants of the earth" also meet their doom in Revelation. (See Rev. 3:10; 6:10; 8:13; 11:10; 13:8–14; 17:2, 8.) We cannot know John's personality, but his motivations run deeper than that. *John is writing counter-imperial resistance literature.*

For John, the Beast-ly Empire presents the major concern: Thus, he devotes most of his negative attention to the Beasts and the Whore. But his confession of Jesus so places him at odds with Rome's domination and its imperial festivals that he defines faithfulness to Jesus in terms of how one resists the Beast. Imperial pressure thus defines his relationships to other followers of Jesus and possibly even to the synagogue.

Plot and Mode of Revelation

Among the apocalypses, Revelation's distinctiveness may lie primarily in what literary critics call direct address. Revelation begins and ends as a letter so that the vision itself, which constitutes the body of the apocalypse, speaks to a particular audience. Having introduced his vision, John adapts the Pauline letter form to his own context:

John to the seven churches that are in Asia: Grace to you and peace from him who is and who was and who is to come, and from the seven spirits who are before his throne, and from Jesus Christ, the faithful witness, the firstborn of the dead, and the ruler of the kings of the earth. To him who loves us and freed us from our sins by his blood, and made us to be a kingdom, priests serving his God and Father, to him be glory and dominion forever and ever. Amen. (1:4–6)

And he closes on the same note:

The grace of the Lord Jesus be with all the saints. Amen. (22:21)

In reflecting upon Revelation's epistolary form, we should also note the *letters* to the seven churches. Each letter speaks to a church individually, naming its strengths and/or its weaknesses and promising blessing to those who "conquer." While each letter directs its specific audience to pay close attention, it also invites others to overhear these messages. Each letter includes the refrain, "Let any one who has an ear listen to what the Spirit is saying to the churches."

Direct address to his audience extends beyond Revelation's epistolary framework. Not only does John remind the audience to pay attention (13:10, 18), but the audience also hears directly from Jesus and other heavenly voices. These instances include the many songs and exclamations by heavenly beings, as well as the occasional piece of exhortation (14:2; 18:4).

Though proposed outlines for Revelation outnumber the sands on the seashore, John's vision basically has two major parts. First, there is his encounter with the risen Jesus, in which Jesus dictates letters to each of the seven churches (1:9–3:22). The seven letters share many common elements; most notably, Jesus praises and/or censures the churches, promising salvation to those who "conquer." The major transition occurs at 4:1, when John notices an open door in the heavens, then hears a voice calling him to "come up." From this point until the end of the apocalypse, John views the heavenly realms; observes the spiraling catastrophes of the seven seals, trumpets, and bowls; and previews the devil's defeat and the New Jerusalem's descent.

This major visionary block employs several common apocalyptic devices. Most obvious are the many bizarre images and symbolic numbers. John frequently interacts with an angel, who alternatively pronounces commands and interprets his vision. But perhaps most importantly, Revelation combines features of the heavenly ascent and the historical apocalypse. During his vision, John tours the heavenly realms, where he sees the throne and encounters the Lamb. That heavenly realm never disappears, as heavenly choruses repeatedly comment on the things John sees. John also sees the pit (or abyss; 20:3), in which the Dragon is bound for a thousand years, and the lake of fire, the future dwelling of the Dragon and the damned (20:10–15).

While John's tours are fairly complete, Revelation demonstrates just as much concern with time as with space, with the future as with the heavenly realms. Scholars debate whether the visions concerning Jerusalem in chapter 11 narrate the past or the future. The vision of the Woman Clothed with the Sun at once alludes to Israel's past and the churches' future. John's vision also imagines how God will act in the future, destroying the Beast and the Whore and creating a New Jerusalem for the Lamb's followers.

John's Program

Like the letters to the churches in chapters 2–3, Revelation as a whole features a mixture of exhortation and admonition. The letters all include praise, censure, or both; and they all culminate with a final pronouncement: to "everyone who conquers" Jesus will give the ultimate blessing (2:7, 11, 17, 26–28; 3:5; 12, 21). "Let anyone who has an ear listen to what the Spirit is saying to the churches" (3:22). Likewise, we have seen that John blesses those who obey his vision and curses those who don't (1:3; 22:18–19). In addition to these very direct addresses to the audience, John throws in some meaningful asides. Having warned that whoever worships the Beast would be excluded from the Lamb's book of life, John adds:

> Let anyone who has an ear listen: If you are to be taken captive, into captivity you go; if you kill with the sword, with the sword you must be killed. *Here is a call for the endurance and faith of the saints.* (13:9–10)

There may be no escape from the Beast, but even more important, there is no escape from God's judgment. Likewise, John warns of the eternal torment that faces those who worship the Beast–among other things,

> they will be tormented with fire and sulfur in the presence of the holy angels and in the presence of the Lamb. And the smoke of their torment goes up forever and ever. (14:10–11)

And again,

> Here is a call for the endurance of the saints... (14:12a)

Linking the saints' endurance to their resistance to the imperial cults, John also invokes the language of purity. Not only does John wish his audience to avoid direct participation in pagan practices, he exhorts them to a totally separatist stance. For example, the risen Jesus commends the "few" in Sardis "who have not soiled their clothes" (3:4). In a later context Jesus (almost parenthetically) blesses those who have kept their clothes unsoiled (16:15). At the same time, in the heavenly realms the martyrs wear white robes (6:11), a promise that applies to other believers as well (3:18), and those who survive the end-time judgments also wear white robes, which they have washed in the Lamb's blood (7:9, 13–14). This call to purity–white characterizes John's initial vision of Jesus (1:14)–extends into how one relates to the imperial culture. At Babylon's fall, a heavenly voice cries out:

> "Come out of her, my people,
>   so that you do not take part in her sins,
> and so that you do not share in her plagues;
> for her sins are heaped high as heaven,
>   and God has remembered her iniquities." (18:4–5)

Thus, John calls upon the churches to abstain from any accommodation to pagan culture, whether religious, economic, or social. Along the spectrum of religious responses to society, his is among the most radical.

Yet Revelation advocates not simply *avoiding* a beastly society, but also *resisting* it. We see this most clearly in the rhetoric of conquest. John names Roman might, but he also argues that it is directed against God's people. When the earth's inhabitants marvel, "Who is like the Beast, and who can fight against it?" (13:4), they testify to the Beast's lust for conquest. Indeed, the Beast fights against the saints and conquers them (11:7; 13:7). In reply to the Beast's power, the risen Jesus insists that it is the saints themselves who must conquer. This expectation appears in each of the letters to the churches and also near the book's end (21:7). The remarkable thing is *how* the saints conquer. They do not employ violence, as the Lamb does, but they conquer through their faithful endurance and testimony.

> "But they have conquered him by
>   the blood of the Lamb
> and by the word of their
>   testimony,
> for they did not cling to life even
>   in the face of death." (12:11; cf. 15:2)

Separation and conquest, withdrawal and confrontation–how do such apparently conflicting values relate to one another? This tension marks Revelation, even as it lives on among Revelation's contemporary readers. Many sociologists distinguish between introversionist and revolutionary religious movements. The introversionist model typically understands the world as hopelessly evil and calls for complete or partial withdrawal, whereas the revolutionary awaits the world's divine transformation.[12] Both models express essentially negative views of the world and its immediate future, but they call for different ways of relating to the world. Introversionists abandon the world altogether, whereas revolutionaries wait for God to turn things around. John's apocalypse affirms elements of both programs, calling the churches to *remove themselves from a corrupt society, precisely as a means of subverting it.*

Who Likes Revelation (and Who Doesn't)?

Because the book of Revelation has always had its advocates and detractors, it may be helpful to sketch the issues that so divide its readers. Many people know Revelation primarily through a group we may call the "prophecy teachers." The prophecy teachers use mass Christian media such as television, film, and Christian bookstores, and now of course the Internet, as a means of disseminating their views. Whatever their disagreements, they share one trait in common: They argue that Revelation and other biblical books predict the sequence of earth's final days, and those days, they argue, are upon us. While many ignore or ridicule them, and no serious biblical scholar shares their interpretations, their influence upon certain segments of the public is enormous. Hal Lindsey's *The Late Great Planet Earth* (1970) was the nonfiction bestseller of the 1970s and has sold 35 million copies according to the author's Web site.[13] The twelve-volume series of *Left Behind* novels by Tim LaHaye and Jerry Jenkins has enjoyed sales of 60 million, with a forty-volume "Kids' Series" to accompany it.[14]

Those who reject Revelation most often object to its depiction of violence and its desire for vengeance. In Revelation, most of the earth's inhabitants come to destruction, and heavenly voices congratulate God for carrying out such grisly judgment. "It is what they deserve!" sings an angel (16:6). So the philosopher Friedrich Nietzsche esteemed Revelation "the most rabid outburst of vindictiveness in all recorded history."[15] So prominent a psychologist as C. J. Jung diagnosed such sentiment as the overflow of perfectionism run amok.[16] Some, such as the novelist D. H. Lawrence, simply find Revelation distasteful. Lawrence rated it "the product of a second-rate mind," which has appealed to other second-rate minds throughout history.[17]

More recently, some feminist readers have noted that female characters in Revelation are all defined in terms of their sexual roles. Jezebel and the Whore are prostitutes; the Woman Clothed with the Sun is a mother; and the New Jerusalem is a bride. Revelation, which also praises the 144,000 "who have not defiled themselves with women" (14:4), apparently cannot imagine women in terms of independent value or autonomy.[18]

Yet Revelation has also inspired communities in their resistance to injustice and tyranny. Allan Boesak composed a commentary on Revelation during the most intense years of South Africa's anti-Apartheid struggle; solitary confinement provided the context for some of his reflections.[19] Some Latin American readers have emphasized Revelation's critique of imperial commercial exploitation.[20] Likewise, Brian K. Blount finds "a correspondence between John's counsel to witness and Martin Luther King Jr.'s call to march."[21] Elisabeth Schüssler Fiorenza, perhaps the Bible's most influential feminist interpreter, contends that readers do best to approach Revelation's representation of women within the larger framework of its concern with "the politics of power."[22]

Many readers insist that one should reevaluate Revelation's violent imagery before judging the book's overall merit. Revelation indeed features horrific violence, they observe, but such violence is primarily of two kinds.

First, the Beast and the Whore commit great violence, both against the earth's inhabitants and particularly against the saints. In depicting such violence, some argue, Revelation is merely realistic, "revealing" the nature of violent oppression in its own context and for the world in general, for that matter.

Second, the empire's violence creates its own backlash, whether as a natural consequence or as the Lamb's judgment. In any event, Revelation's most remarkable violence is that which is absent: At no point does John call for or depict violence on the part of his audience. Indeed, David Barr has argued that in Revelation even God relies not on might but on the faithful witness—and death—of the Lamb and his followers.[23]

Readers and their communities will draw their own conclusions with respect to Revelation. However, one personal anecdote may demonstrate its continuing and global appeal. When Archbishop Desmond Tutu was visiting my campus not long ago, I could not resist asking him whether the book of Revelation had been important to him in the anti-Apartheid struggle. His first reaction was to say that no, it had not, but then he reflected upon Revelation 6:9–11. In that scene the martyrs cry out for vengeance, to learn that they must wait until their number would be fulfilled. Archbishop Tutu shared that that image had often come to mind, as one day after another he participated in the funerals of the Apartheid government's victims. As funerals evolved into protests and then government forces suppressed the protests, he said, the processions themselves led to more funerals. "How long," one would ask, "will good people die?" But the passage not only evoked lament; in its realism it also inspired hope. Indeed, many faithful witnesses would die before Apartheid would end. Yet it would end.

The Shepherd of Hermas

Languages and Texts

Composed in Greek, Hermas was known only in Latin until the nineteenth century. Four Greek manuscripts exist, two of which are relatively complete. For the ending of Hermas, *Similitudes* 9.30.3—10.4.5, scholars rely on Latin traditions.[24] Apparently, separate parts of Hermas may have circulated independently for some time.

Likely Date

Most scholars locate Hermas in the first half of the second century; a later date is hardly possible, as a handful of late-second-century authors discuss Hermas.

Note on Identifying Passages

Scholars use two competing methods to designate passages in Hermas. The older, which we shall use here, divides Hermas into three sections: the Visions (= Vis.), the Mandates (= Man.), and the Similitudes (= Sim.). Unlike most early Jewish and Christian texts, these sections are further divided into numbers, chapters, and verses: for example, "Vis. 2.2.3." More recently, some scholars have developed a consecutive numbering system of chapters and verses, so that Vision 2.2.3 and Hermas 6.3 refer to the same passage.

Carolyn Osiek, the foremost authority on Hermas, describes it as "a long and rather complicated work."[25] Despite that forbidding introduction, Hermas is in some ways a most engaging and personal book, and it reveals a great deal about the development of early Christianity in Rome.

Hermas the Visiouary

The Shepherd of Hermas raises no suspicions of pseudonymity. Hermas is not an exalted figure from the past, nor did he attain particular prominence in his own day.

We can reconstruct very little about Hermas from the text itself. Apparently a former slave, he lives in Rome (Vis. 1.1.1–3). Toward the end of the book we learn that he functions as some sort of a minister within the churches (Sim. 10.4.1). He apparently once possessed a fortune (Vis. 3.6.7). From time to time, Hermas also receives criticism for allowing his family to fall into sin (Vis. 1.3.1; 2.3.1).

On several occasions his story claims that he is under command to share his revelations with other Christians. These commands to relate what he learns occur in all three major sections (e.g., Vis. 2.4.2; 2.6.6; 3.8.11; 5.1.5–7; Man. 12.3.3; Sim. 8.11.1; 10.1.3). On one occasion he claims that he lacked the strength to remember the words he hears in a vision (Vis. 1.3.3), but more typical is this command:

> "First of all, write down my commandments and parables, but write down the other matters as I show them to you. This is why," he said, "I am commanding you to write down first the commandments and parables, in order that you may be able to read them at once and be able to keep them." So I wrote down the commandments and parables, just as he commanded me. If, then, when you hear them you keep them and walk in them and carry them out with a clean heart, you will receive from the Lord whatever he promised you. But if after hearing them you do not repent, but continue to add to your sins, you will receive from the Lord the opposite. All these things the shepherd, the angel of repentance, commanded me to write as follows. (Vis. 5.1.5–7; Holmes)[26]

This key passage, which provides the transition from the Visions to the Mandates and looks ahead to the Similitudes, reveals several things about Hermas and his work. *Hermas is the human intermediary through whom other believers receive this angelic message.* The purpose of his work involves exhorting the audience to faithfulness and calling them to repentance. Like John in Revelation, Hermas calls the audience to obey the contents of the revelation, assuming repentance as a prerequisite for such obedience.

Within the narrative, Hermas comes across as an appealing character. Vision 1, in which Hermas is indicted for harboring desire for a woman, establishes him as a petty sinner. Such characterization likely enhances the audience's appreciation for Hermas. After all, if his worst sin involves mere desire, he can't be all bad. Yet anxiety for his own salvation hounds the visionary, so that he does not regard himself as superior to his audience (cf. Man. 3.1.3).

If Hermas has a dominant trait, it is his curiosity, which repeatedly provokes wonder and some consternation from his heavenly intermediaries. Hermas often takes the initiative to seek explanation or clarification concerning his revelation. Like most apocalyptic visionaries, Hermas's understanding is limited. His extreme privilege as one who receives heavenly truth does not preclude bouts of cluelessness that occur in each section of the book, though Hermas occasionally stands up for himself when he is chastised (e.g., Vis. 3.10.10). Moreover, Hermas does not alienate his audience by claiming superior piety. Instead, he learns that

> It is not because you are more worthy than all others to have it revealed to you, for others are before you and better than you, to whom these visions ought to have been revealed. (Vis. 3.4.3)

If anything, one might argue that Hermas actually demonstrates some growth during the process of his revelation.[27] Throughout the book he fasts and expresses his concern for his fellow human beings, yet he also develops over time. For example, a woman guides Hermas through his first visions. Hermas learns that she is the Church, yet her appearance gradually becomes more youthful as the visions progress. Eventually, the angelic mediator of the Revelation, the Shepherd, reveals the reason for this transformation: Her youthfulness reflects the growing vitality of Hermas's own Spirit (Vis. 3.10–13). Likewise, the revelations grow more elaborate as Hermas's spiritual strength matures (Sim. 9.1.1–2). Hermas's growth apparently culminates in Similitude 9, as he assists in constructing a tower, another figure for the church. Here, Hermas actually participates in his own vision.

Despite such high moments, Hermas comes across as a relatively passive visionary. His primary contribution is to press for explanation and clarification. Virtuous, but not exceptionally so, Hermas faithfully records his vision so that his audience will listen, learn, and repent.

Setting

Unlike the book of Revelation, Hermas tends to emphasize dynamics internal to Christian communities rather than external forces. Apart from the expectation of "distress" (*thlipsis* in Greek), it has little to say about the Roman Empire or about the world in general.

The word *thlipsis*, often translated "persecution," poses an interesting question. (*Thlipsis* occurs several times in Revelation as well [1:9; 2:9–10, 22; 7:14].) Ordinarily, it simply means "distress," though in early Christianity it sometimes served to indicate persecution. One could take *thlipsis* to point to the end-time "tribulation." Yet Hermas, like Revelation, not only looks ahead to *thlipsis*, it also describes believers who suffer on account of their faith, even to the point of death. Moreover, because Hermas identifies himself as a Roman, he and his audience would recall memories of Nero's great persecution as well as other pressures against Christians and Jews. Hence, it seems that the Shepherd anticipates a time of persecution, even as it recalls instances of persecution from the past.

Hermas does reflect some measure of institutional development within the churches. The first four Visions, which set the tone for the larger work, all feature revelations from the Church, appearing in the form of a woman (2.4.1). That the Church could figure so prominently as a vehicle of revelation demonstrates its emergence as a source of institutional authority. Moreover, Vision 3 depicts the Church as a building in progress (3.3.3). The first and best stones, "square and white and fit at the joints," are the apostles, bishops, teachers, and deacons (3.5.1), those who fulfill the church's institutionalized offices.

Hermas idealizes their relationships through the Woman's insistence that these officials always agree and cooperate with one another in peace (3.5.1). The tower rises from the sea, symbolizing how the church's members find life through the waters of baptism (3.3.5). Likewise, the tower appears again in Similitude 9, with the prophets, deacons, apostles, and teachers at its foundation, along with some pre-Christian righteous persons.[28] Here, the Shepherd declares that these figures had been carried along by the virtuous spirits, again idealizing the church's authority figures (9.15.4–6).

Finally, Hermas demonstrates a remarkable level of theological systematization, which we do not find in Revelation. This is not the theological refinement of the classical creeds or the sophisticated interpretation of Origen or Augustine. Rather, it involves the classification of sinners and their sins.

Similitude 8 provides the most comprehensive example of this tendency, in which those bearing different kinds of sticks to plant in the ground reflect different categories of persons. The worst are those who have abandoned or betrayed the church: They have no hope of salvation (8.6.4). Hypocrites and false teachers, however, do much better (8.6.5–6), as do those who are double-minded, preoccupied with commerce, and so forth. There is even a category for those whose sins involve "small desires and petty matters" (8.10.1). Classificatory schemes such as these emerged after Christians had responded to persecution in diverse ways and after they had had opportunities to reflect upon the various manifestations of faithfulness.

Structure and Mode of Revelation

Scholars have often debated whether the Shepherd is an apocalypse at all. Though it begins with a series of visions, it also features independent sections of ethical and mystical material. Indeed, Hermas divides into three identifiable units: five Visions, twelve Mandates (or sets of commandments), and ten Similitudes (or parables). As distinct as these sections may appear, they also reveal strategic relationships to one another. Moreover, their literary forms sometimes overlap.

The Shepherd of Hermas employs two basic modes of revelation: visions, accompanied by interpretations from the Woman Church and the Shepherd, and commands from the Shepherd. Although the Woman Church is the initial revealer figure, in Vision 5 the focus turns toward the Shepherd, who is the angel of repentance (Vis. 5.1.7; Sim. 9.33.1).

The Visions

The Visions constitute the most clearly "apocalyptic" section of Hermas. These visions create a powerful rhetorical effect, as they

a. indicate many of the apocalypse's pressing concerns
b. provide the imaginative framework within which Hermas's ethical instruction makes sense

Thus, the Shepherd's apocalyptic material presents the arguments for its ethical teachings.

In the first vision Hermas encounters his former owner Rhoda. His desire for her amounts to no more than the desire for such a beautiful and virtuous wife, yet Hermas learns that even this desire constitutes a sin. The vision demonstrates that sin is a deadly serious matter, and it clears the way for later discussions of sin and repentance.

In Vision 2 Hermas receives a book from an elderly woman, revealing what is at stake in the drama of salvation. The book reveals that there is one chance for repentance after baptism, but that for those who have been baptized, that opportunity is drawing to a close. Those who repent will take their place with the angels; presumably, those who do not will face judgment.

Repentance after Baptism?

Augustine of Hippo (354–430), who became the most influential of early Christian writers, recalls his mother's struggle concerning whether to baptize her young son when he was gravely ill. She decided not to baptize him in the belief that inevitable post-baptismal sin would do even more harm than sin before baptism. He also describes how casually people regarded the sins of those who had yet to be baptized, again relying on the hope that baptism itself would bring their forgiveness (*Confessions* 1.11). Augustine's story provokes the question, What did early Christians believe about sin and its relationship to repentance and baptism?

The Shepherd of Hermas represents one voice in the development of this conversation. Already, the New Testament book of Hebrews had argued that for those who had received the Holy Spirit, but had later "fallen away," repentance was impossible (Heb. 6:4–6; 10:26–31), though there is no direct evidence that Hebrews influenced Hermas in any way. In comparison with Hebrews, Hermas's position is somewhat liberal, offering one opportunity for repentance after baptism (Vis. 2.2.4–8; Man. 4.3.1–7). However, according to Hermas, some sinners—particularly those who have denied their faith under persecution—remain without hope. When the tower is complete—that is, when the divinely determined number of persons has entered the church—history will end, and the opportunity for repentance will be closed (Vis. 3.8.9; 3.9.5; Sim. 9.32.1; 10.4.4).[29]

Vision 3 presents the tower built on the sea. The tower, Hermas learns, is the Woman Church; and Hermas's pressing concern involves which stones—or persons—are suitable for it. This vision is particularly important. For one thing, it demonstrates the boundaries of salvation—which persons are included and which are excluded. Even among those who may repent, their sin will hold them in an "inferior place" between blessing and torment (3.7.5–6). In its closing sections the book refers back to this tower. Similitudes 8, 9, and 10 all refer to the Tower, indicating that in a fundamental sense the book's subject is how one may find salvation.

Vision 4 constitutes Hermas's most dramatic vision. It expresses the book's characteristic concerns with persecution and single-minded endurance. While Hermas is praying for additional revelations, a voice calls out, "Do not be double-minded, Hermas" (4.1.4). Hermas then encounters a "huge beast" that resembles a sea monster and breathes fire. In Hermas's apparent panic he hears the voice again, "Do not be double-minded, Hermas," so he determines to face the monster in faith. As Hermas and the beast draw near to each other, the beast simply lies down on the ground and allows Hermas to pass. (Hermas later learns that he had received angelic assistance on account of his faith.) The lesson, of course, is that single-minded faith is sufficient to withstand the eschatological tribulation or persecution (4.2.4).

Vision 5 is transitional, preparing the way for the Mandates and Similitudes. Whereas Visions 1–4 are titled "visions" (*oraseis*), Vision 5 is a "revelation" (*apokalypsis*). In it Hermas meets an angel, who instructs him to be strong in the commandments and to write down the commandments and parables. The angel's identity is unclear, as Hermas describes him as a guardian angel (5.1.3–4), but then names him as the "angel of repentance" (5.1.7).

Taken together, the Visions amount to an argument that merits analysis in its own right. By combining images of the church, final judgment, and a great tribulation with the exhortations to single-minded faith and moral virtue, the Visions sketch the path to salvation. They also clear the way for more specific instruction through the Mandates and Similitudes.

THE MANDATES

Compared to the Visions and Similitudes, the Mandates appear relatively pedestrian. Yet they are no less important for revealing the specific program to which the Shepherd calls its audience. Each of the Mandates emphasizes a particular dimension of faithful practice, though Mandates 11 and 12 differ from the rest in both form and complexity. The Mandates promote

1. faith in God (Man. 1)
2. sincerity and innocence (Man. 2)
3. commitment to truthfulness (Man. 3)
4. purity, especially sexual purity (Man. 4)
5. patience and good sense (Man. 5)
6. the combination of faith, fear, and self-control (Man. 6–8)
7. single-mindedness (actually, a command to avoid double-mindedness; Man. 9)
8. freedom from attachment, which brings grief (Man. 10)
9. avoiding false prophets and fortune tellers (Man. 11)
10. removing evil desire, primarily sexual and material covetousness (Man. p12)

THE SIMILITUDES

The ten Similitudes are largely revelatory allegories through which the Shepherd offers pointed instruction. They represent apocalypses within the apocalypse. The first four similitudes pair parables to construct combined arguments. Similitudes 1 and 2 picture the temptations of possessions, then address the relationship between the rich and the poor. Similitudes 3 and 4 demonstrate that though one cannot distinguish sinners from the righteous in this world, clarity will arrive with the judgment. Similitude 5 shows that although meritorious works such as fasting are no substitute for obeying the Mandates, one who keeps the commandments may accrue additional merit through such additional practices. Similitudes 6 and 7 are another paired set, emphasizing the roles of angels. In Similitude 6, Hermas encounters the angels of luxury and of punishment. The angel of punishment, he learns in both Similitudes 6 and 7, is an agent of grace who inspires repentance. Similitudes 8 and 9 also form a pair, with a common emphasis on judgment and repentance. Though they maintain the allegorical form common to the Similitudes, these are the most complex among the group. Similitude 8 develops the possibilities of judgment for diverse categories of people; the point is to point out the need for repentance (8.11.1). Similitude 9 is even longer, as the Shepherd returns to the topic of the tower and elaborates how various classes of persons can be included in it or excluded from it. The point? "Mend your ways while the Tower is still being built" (9.32.1). Finally, Similitude 10 is not actually a "similitude" at all, but a concluding exhortation. When Hermas has completed his book, the Shepherd calls him to continuing virtue and "manful" ministry.

Hermas as Sacred Scripture?

The earliest surviving manuscript containing all twenty-seven books of the New Testament is Codex Sinaiticus, which dates from the early fourth century. In addition to those twenty-seven books, it also includes copies of the Shepherd of Hermas and the Epistle of Barnabas.[30]

That such an ancient collection could include Hermas along with the books we now know as the New Testament is not surprising. Several influential early Christian authors cite Hermas as scripture, including Irenaeus, Tertullian (early in his career), Clement of Alexandria, and Origen. The ancient Muratorian Canon, for which unfortunately scholars have not agreed on a date, includes Hermas among those books that are not to be read in church but are beneficial for private reading. The Canon argues that Hermas is not scripture because it was composed after the time of the prophets and the apostles (78–80). Writing in the first half of the fourth century (before 350 C.E.), Eusebius lists Hermas and Revelation among the "disputed" books with respect to the canon, though he adds that Revelation has its advocates (*Ecclesiastical History* 3.25.1–7).

The book of Revelation itself struggled to find widespread acceptance, and perhaps competed with Hermas for inclusion in some locations. Whereas Hermas was apparently popular in Egypt, Revelation fared better in the Western churches than in the Eastern ones. Apparently, Revelation did not enter Syriac canons until after the fifth century, nor Armenian canons until the twelfth century.[31]

Distinctive Concerns

Hermas is indeed a wide-ranging book, yet several of its interests merit our attention. None of these are unique to Hermas, yet each of these receives sustained and repeated attention in the book.

TRIBULATION OR PERSECUTION

The beast in Vision 4 locates the book's moral commands within the context of crisis. It is indeed possible to understand *thlipsis* as indicating end-times distress, but it also applies to generic trouble (Vis. 2.3.1). In Hermas it also refers to those who have already suffered and died on account of their faith. Vision 3 discriminates between Hermas, who is relatively faithful, and those who "have suffered for the sake of the name" (3.1.9).

"What," I asked, "have they endured?" "Listen," she [the Woman Church] said. "Scourgings, imprisonments, severe persecutions (*thlipseis*), crosses, wild beasts, for the sake of the Name." (3.2.1) Likewise, in Similitude 9 Hermas wants to know about those trees that have especially beautiful fruit. He learns that these are those who persisted in their testimony, even under torture (9.28.1–8). (The angel also mentions those "cowards" who merely *pondered* whether to deny or to confess!) These passages indicate the highly exalted status of martyrs, and Hermas inquires concerning the nature of their suffering.

SIN, PUNISHMENT, AND THE AFTERLIFE

Given Hermas's charge to promote repentance among his family and his audience, we expect an emphasis on sin, punishment, and the afterlife. The apocalypse's distinctive presentation of these issues, however, justifies our continuing attention in several respects.

First, the Shepherd's expectations are remarkably exacting. We see this immediately in Vision 1, where Hermas accepts censure for simply contemplating a woman's beauty without harboring prurient thoughts. Likewise, Hermas's vision of the tower mentions those stones that are too short. These represent people who are thrown away from the tower–but not far. They "are those who have believed and live for the most part in righteousness, but they have a certain amount of lawlessness; that is why they are too short and not perfect" (Vis. 3.6.4). These short stones lie among several classes of partially flawed stones. They may find inclusion in the tower, but only if they repent.

Likewise, in Similitude 8 Hermas sees those whose sticks were green, indicating life, but with withered and cracked tips, reflecting "small desires and petty matters" (8.10.1). These also are in need of repentance. Similar warnings, such as the admonitions that an angry temper or sadness drive away the Holy Spirit (Man. 5.1.3; 10.2.5), reinforce Hermas's perfectionist trajectories. When Hermas asks if these expectations are too difficult, the Shepherd merely invokes an angry tone of voice and says they are not very hard (Man. 12.3.4–12.4.7). Even though the Shepherd softens his tone and promises spiritual help, we cannot avoid the tension between Hermas's anxiety and the Shepherd's casual reply. Purity remains the standard (Man. 4.3.2).

Second, though we shall also note Hermas's concern with relationships between the rich and the poor, the sins that concern Hermas deal primarily with individual behavior. For example, when Hermas investigates the works of the "angel of wickedness," he learns about anger, drunkenness, luxury, lust, and pride (Man. 6.1.4–5).

This individualistic focus also expresses itself in ascetic sensibilities, particularly with respect to sexuality. Not only does the first Vision feature the censure against Hermas's modest desire, but also the first Mandate calls for *enkrateia,* or self-control (1.1.2). Mandate 4, which concerns purity, quickly intensifies its focus on matters of sex and marriage. In fact, it is Hermas's own self-control, along with his faithfulness and sincerity, that commend him (Vis. 2.3.2). Among the seven women who surround the tower, each representing an essential virtue, Self-control is second only to Faith not only in order but also in importance (Vis. 3.8). That self-control is most notably tested when Hermas spends the night among ten young women—a circumstance that clearly provokes his anxiety—and claims to outperform them in prayer (Sim. 9.11).

Mandate 8, however, qualifies Hermas's promotion of self-control by distinguishing between self-serving desires and wicked practices on one hand, and virtuous works on the other. Self-control is essential for the former, but no restraint is necessary for the latter.

Third, we have the related issues of repentance and forgiveness. As we have seen, the entire book promotes repentance. Hermas's own commission is to record his revelation so that people can repent (e.g., Vis. 5.1.5–7). The book's message, summarized perhaps in its conclusion, is that the tower is almost complete, and the time of repentance is quickly drawing to a close (Sim. 10.4.4).

The Shepherd allows for the forgiveness of post-baptismal sin, but only once and for a limited time (Vis. 2.2.4–8; Man. 4.3.1–7). Moreover, the Shepherd notes that for some sinners repentance comes harder than for others, whereas for some repentance is altogether impossible. This system finds its expression in Vision 3 and Similitudes 8 and 9. Vision 3.5–7 articulates which sinners have hope for repentance; in Similitude 8 we learn that God grants repentance to some sinners but not to others (8.6.2).

Likewise, when Similitude 9 returns to the image of the tower, some stones require repentance for inclusion (e.g., 9.14.1–2). Those who have fallen away, blasphemed, or betrayed fellow believers have no hope (9.19.1), while precious little hope is extended to hypocrites and false teachers (9.19.2). Thus, Hermas articulates detailed scenarios concerning particular classes of sinners and their eschatological prospects. Some other Jewish and Christian apocalypses match specific punishments to particular categories of sin, but Hermas's interest lies elsewhere, in the possibility for repentance for certain kinds of sinners and in the relative merits of the righteous.

Fourth, Hermas offers constructive proposals regarding judgment and the afterlife. In Vision 3.7.5–6 Hermas conceives of an intermediate state between blessedness and hellish torment. Hermas learns that some who have been excluded from the tower have hope of repentance, but they cannot enter "this tower." Instead, they avoid *final* torment by being transferred to "another much inferior place," where *temporary* torment purifies them of their sins. Even there, however, their salvation is not secure. Alternatively, Similitude 9.16 considers those who died before the gospel's proclamation. To them the apostles delivered the gospel, and through a postmortem process they received both baptism and salvation.

DOUBLE-MINDEDNESS

Hermas owes his success in Vision 4 to the instruction he hears both before and after he spies the beast, "Do not be double-minded, Hermas." In this case, being double-minded, *dipsychos,* amounts to being divided between faith and doubt, as it also does in James 1:8, though *dipsychos* in other contexts describes persons torn between two values or mindsets. Mandate 9 underscores this admonition, opposing double-mindedness to faith, insisting that double-mindedness hinders prayer, and linking double-mindedness to the attachment to worldly goods. Mandate 10, which instructs believers to avoid grief, suggests that double-mindedness strengthens the attachment to worldly goods that makes grief possible. Mandate 11 likewise argues that the double-minded are especially susceptible to false teaching. Thus, for Hermas double-mindedness not only makes one vulnerable during persecution, it also strengthens a variety of spiritual threats.

WEALTH AND POVERTY

As Osiek has shown, Hermas discusses wealth, poverty, and commerce in a wide variety of literary forms and contexts.[32] Hermas maintains that within the Christian community (Hermas does not employ the term *Christian*) the rich are obliged to help the poor. It grounds this argument in several considerations. For one thing, attachment to riches tempts one to deny one's faith under persecution (Vis. 3.6.5–7; Sim. 8.8.1–3). For another, overabundance is bad for the self, both for one's body now and in the coming judgment (Vis. 3.9.3–5). But most importantly, clinging to wealth divides the community, creating divisions between the rich and the poor (Vis. 3.9.4–9; Sim. 8.8.1).

Because wealth poses such a threat, the Shepherd devotes the first Similitude to it, arguing that Christians should store wealth in the heavenly realms rather than on earth. Instead of fields, persons should buy souls; instead of pursuing additional wealth, they should visit widows and orphans (Sim. 1.1.8). The upshot is that wealth and devotion to God are incompatible; wealth nourishes double-mindedness (Man. 10.1.1–6). The pursuit of luxury is even a symptom that the spirit of false prophecy is present (Man. 11.1.11–12). The angel of luxury dulls one's receptivity to the truth and leads people to pursue the very things that will bring their destruction (Sim. 6.2.1–3).

Particularly fascinating is Hermas's discussion concerning the interdependence of the rich and the poor in the parable of the elm and the vine (Similitude 2). Just as the elm and the vine depend on each other to enable their fruitfulness–the elm produces no fruit on its own, and the vine's fruit would simply rot if it were left on the ground–so do the rich and poor alike contribute to one another's usefulness. Osiek notes that Hermas does describe the poor as "objects of oppression by church officials" (Sim. 9.26.2). Vision 3.9.6 claims that God hears the cries of the poor against their oppressors, but it is in Similitude 2 that the poor receive attention in their own right.[33] At the same time, Similitude 2 sketches a somewhat romanticized image of the poor. It maintains that the rich are wealthy in material things but poor in faith. Their counterparts, however, are rich in faith and in virtue–and particularly in prayer–as a result of their poverty. Thus, while the rich bring material benefit to the poor, the prayers of the poor bring salvation to the rich. Advocating compassion and charity, Hermas does not challenge the fundamental structures of society.

THE CHURCH

As we have seen before, the Church figures prominently in the book, both as an object of theological reflection and as an agent of revelation. The image of the tower, around which revolve Hermas's most prominent vision and his two most detailed similitudes (the willow tree and the mountains), reflects a multidimensional ecclesiology. On the one hand, the tower is glorious. The requirements for its stones are rigorous, with perfection as the standard. Yet the tower also accommodates imperfection, as those who are in sin are invited to repent.[34] As Edith McEwan Humphrey has suggested, Hermas's church defies static idealism; its transformations through Visions 1–3 parallel responses within Hermas himself. As Hermas–and his audience–mature, by an organic process they invigorate the church.[35] In the apt words of Lage Pernveden, "God...is realizing [the] Church in a human context."[36]

Institutionally, Hermas alludes to various church offices, including the authority of the first-generation apostles (Vis. 3.5.1; Sim. 9.13.4; 9.16.5–7; 9:17.1; 9.25.2). Perhaps Hermas himself is some sort of minister (Sim. 10.4.1). But Hermas also expresses concern that the church's leaders might be ineffective (Sim. 9.31.5–6) or, worse, that they might oppress the poor (Sim. 9.26.2).

ANGELS, SPIRITS, AND CHRISTOLOGY

Many commentators note a lack of precision in the Shepherd of Hermas's references to supernatural beings. The Shepherd himself is the angel of repentance. As part of a larger angelic hierarchy, he is commissioned by the greatest angel to present the revelation to Hermas (Vis. 5.1.2). Apparently, angels perform a variety of assigned roles, not all of which are positive. Mandate 6.2 warns that two angels accompany mortals, an angel of righteousness and one of wickedness. Apparently, the book suggests that individuals are assigned guardian angels (Vis. 5.1.3–4).

Moreover, the "women" who represent virtues and vices in Similitude 9 may represent angels, spirits, or personified virtues. It is perhaps best not to discriminate among these possibilities.[37] Likewise, Similitudes 6 and 7 introduce the angels of grace and punishment. Surprisingly, the angel of punishment is a kind angel who leads one to repentance.

Though it presents the ability to distinguish good spirits from evil ones as essential, Hermas fails to distinguish spirits from one another–and from the Holy Spirit–with absolute clarity. Hermas's first and second visions begin when "a spirit" carries him away (Vis. 1.1.3; 2.1.1). In Mandate 5 Hermas learns that the Holy Spirit dwells within persons, but that it cannot abide evil, particularly anger and grief, due to its own sensitivity (cf. Man. 3.1.4; 10.1.2; 10.2.1–10.3.4). Evil spirits also lurk, promoting such evils as double-mindedness (Man. 9.1.10) and grief (Man. 10.1.2). Mandate 11 traces the roots of false prophecy to the presence of true and false spirits, who come either from God or from the devil. Indeed, the ultimate sources of true prophecy are the Holy Spirit and God (Man. 11.1.8).

Readers may find traces of trinitarian thought in Hermas. Similitude 5.6.5–7 contains some particularly noteworthy claims.

> The preexistent Holy Spirit, which created the whole creation, God caused to live in the flesh that he wished...So he [probably God] took the Son and the glorious angels as counselors, in order that this flesh also, having served the Spirit blamelessly, might have some place to live, and not appear to have lost the reward of its service.

The Holy Spirit, thus, is an agent of creation that existed before the world's foundation yet dwells within mortals. Some contemporary readers are likely to encounter confusion in Hermas's mention of the Son however (Hermas never employs the terms *Jesus* or *Christ*). Is the Son greater than the angels, or is the Son among them as either their superior or as a sort of first among equals?

Indeed, the *Son* is a slippery term in Hermas.[38] Interpreters still debate whether or not "Christ" is the "most holy angel" who sends the Shepherd (Vis. 5.1.2). After all, this most holy angel justifies (a technical word having to do with salvation) those who repent (Man. 5.1.7). However, Similitude 8.3.2–3 distinguishes between "the great and glorious angel," who is Michael, and the Son: The Son *is* the Law of God, while Michael *puts* that law into people's hearts. The text does, however, identify the Son with the Spirit as the ultimate source of Hermas's revelation (Sim 9.1.1); and Vision 2.2.8 clearly links salvation with confessing God's Son (Sim. 8.3.2; 8.11.1; 9.12.4–5). At the same time, Similitude 5.5.2 establishes a priority of God over both the Holy Spirit (ironically characterized as the "Son" in the parable) and the Son (who in the parable is a "slave"). The Son creates the church and appoints angels to care for it. Similitude 9 advances this train of thought by identifying the Son as the rock upon which the tower rests. Like the Spirit, the Son existed before creation and assisted (literally, advised) in the process of creation (9.12.1–2).

What may one conclude concerning the Son and the Spirit in Hermas? Both figures precede creation, and both figures perform divine functions. At the same time, Hermas seems to subordinate them to the figure of God. The Son at once reveals God's purposes for the world and is the source of salvation, while the Spirit dwells within mortals and is the source of righteousness and true prophecy.

Reading the Shepherd of Hermas and the Book of Revelation

The Shepherd of Hermas outlines detailed moral and religious exhortation, and it expresses some distinctive theological interests as well. Yet Hermas primarily aims not to provide exhortation or information, but to voice admonition that inspires faithfulness. The time is short, the tower is almost complete, and those who would find themselves within the tower had better repent.

The Shepherd of Hermas and Revelation share some notable features. Each invokes a beast, reflecting the threat of persecution. Each employs the figure of a woman-city, complemented by architectural details, to represent the church.[39] Blessedness lies within the city; damnation beyond. With an emphasis on faithful testimony in the face of martyrdom, each apocalypse employs the language of purity to uphold exacting standards. Revelation promotes withdrawal from a corrupt culture, and Hermas exalts moral purity.

Yet Revelation and Hermas are significantly different works: Anti-imperial and countercultural energies charge Revelation, while individual faithfulness and repentance animate Hermas. Although both books address churches, Revelation reflects a more fluid ecclesial situation over a wider area with prophets contending against one another for authority. Hermas also reflects conflict over authoritative prophecy—but it also grounds its program in the church's institutional life.

FOR FURTHER READING

Bauckham, Richard. *The Theology of the Book of Revelation.* New Testament Theology. Cambridge: Cambridge University Press, 1993.

Ehrman, Bart. "The Shepherd of Hermas." Pages 161–473 in *The Apostolic Fathers: Volume 2.* LCL 25. Cambridge, Mass.: Harvard University Press, 2003.

Osiek, Carolyn. *Shepherd of Hermas: A Commentary.* Minneapolis: Fortress Press, 1999.

Pernveden, Lage. *The Concept of the Church in the Shepherd of Hermas.* Studia theologica Ludensia 27. Lund: Gleerup, 1966.

Schüssler Fiorenza, Elisabeth. *Revelation: Vision of a Just World.* Proclamation Commentaries. Minneapolis: Fortress Press, 1991.

Snyder, Graydon F. *The Shepherd of Hermas.* The Apostolic Fathers 6. Camden, N. J.: Nelson, 1968.

Wainwright, Arthur W. *Mysterious Apocalypse: Interpreting the Book of Revelation.* Nashville: Abingdon Press, 1993.

CHAPTER 8

Christian Ascents

What Are They Good For?

Christians continued writing apocalypses after the book of Revelation. This movement emerges from widespread roots, as the Shepherd of Hermas, the Ascension of Isaiah, and the Apocalypse of Peter show no dependence upon Revelation. Nor do they interact directly with one another. Instead, each of these apocalypses develops its own literary techniques and addresses distinctive social and religious concerns. A later apocalypse, the Apocalypse of Paul, employs the Apocalypse of Peter as a foundation, though it also adds its own creative literary devices and pursues its own interests. Hence, the emergence of the early Christian apocalypses surely required impressively broad and diverse literary and religious resources.

We have seen that while Revelation and Hermas demonstrate an interest in the heavenly realms, their primary emphases lie in addressing imminent crises from a historical perspective. Both works anticipate intense persecution. To some degree persecution motivates the Ascension of Isaiah and the Apocalypse of Peter as well, but historical interests give way to speculation concerning the otherworldly realms. These two apocalypses foreground otherworldly tours, as does the Apocalypse of Paul. Their interests lie not so much in the world's future as in the *other* world's compelling reality. David Frankfurter locates these interests in an emphasis on "revelatory texts and wisdom" rather than in a "search for eschatological details."[1] Blending contemporary and historical concerns with speculation concerning the heavenly realms, the Ascension of Isaiah retains an interest in the imminent future.

The Ascension of Isaiah

Languages and Texts

The most extensive manuscripts are in Ethiopic, but the Ascension was probably written in Greek.

Likely Date

This apocalypse was probably written shortly after 100 C.E.

The Ascension of Isaiah incorporates an old Jewish legend called the "Martyrdom of Isaiah," framing it with new Christian material to completely transform its meaning. In its present form, the Ascension portrays Isaiah as a Christian martyr who dies for his testimony to the Beloved One, Jesus, centuries ahead of Jesus' arrival.

The Jewish Legend

The Ascension of Isaiah paints a gruesome scene. Manasseh, successor to the righteous King Hezekiah, executes Isaiah by sawing him in half. During the preparations, a crowd of false prophets stands by to taunt Isaiah. Their chief advises the prophet to recant his prophecies, especially his accusations against Manasseh and the circle of wicked prophets. If Isaiah recants, Belkira promises, the torture will cease and all the people, even the king, will worship him. But Isaiah remains impervious both to his fate and to this temptation. After all, even with his eyes surveying the mocking crowd, Isaiah experiences a "vision of the LORD" that empowers his resolve as he condemns the king and his prophets.[2] During his ordeal Isaiah instructs his prophetic circle to escape. The prophet suffers without crying out or weeping but rather continues to speak by the Holy Spirit. And so Isaiah dies (5:1–16).

Although the canonical book of Isaiah does not reveal how the prophet's career unfolded, these traditions concerning Isaiah's martyrdom made their way into popular legend before the emergence of Christianity. The little known book Lives of the Prophets probably dates to Jewish traditions current by the first century C.E. It claims that Isaiah "died under [King] Manasseh by being sawn in two."[3] Reflecting what must have been a pre-Christian tradition, the New Testament epistle to the Hebrews recalls one or more prophets who were "sawn in two" (11:37).

But why did Isaiah meet a martyr's end? According to 2 Chronicles 24:20–22 (cf. Heb 11:37), the prophet Zechariah (not the Zechariah for whom the book is named) was stoned to death at the king's orders. His offense: The prophet condemned the king and the public for their idolatry, warning, "Because you have forsaken the LORD, he has forsaken you" (24:20). Even as he is dying, Zechariah calls out, "May the LORD see and avenge!" (24:22). Apparently, the Jewish legend attributes Isaiah's end to analogous circumstances. Consider Belkira's original accusation against Isaiah:

> Isaiah and the prophets who (are) with him prophesy against Jerusalem and against the cities of Judah that they will be laid waste, and also (against) Benjamin that it will go into captivity, and also against you, O lord king, that you will go (bound) with hooks and chains of iron. But they prophesy lies against Israel and Judah. And Isaiah himself has said, "I see more than Moses the prophet"...And he has called Jerusalem Sodom, and the princes of Judah and Jerusalem he has declared (to be) the people of Gomorrah. (Asc. Isa. 3:6–10, *OTP*)

In this vein Belkira's advice to Isaiah involves simply Isaiah's words against the king and the prophets, but not his testimony to Christ, the Beloved One:

> Say, "I have lied in everything I have spoken; the ways of Manasseh are good and right, and also the ways of Belkira and those who are with him are good." (Asc. Isa. 5:4–5, *OTP*)

Two basic matters stand out in Belkira's indictment. For one thing, Isaiah claims that his revelations are superior to those of the competing prophets, especially that he has seen God. This charge apparently refers to Isaiah 6, in which the prophet sees God seated upon the throne on the heavenly temple. Isaiah's experience even transcends that of Moses. Whereas Moses requested a vision of God's glory ("I see more than Moses the prophet" [Asc. Isa. 3:8]), his experience "revealed" only God's glorious backside—an encounter sufficient to alter Moses' appearance so that people could not bear to look at his face (Ex. 33:12–34:35). But a second charge receives far more emphasis: Isaiah has condemned Jerusalem and its leaders. This accusation essentially duplicates the motivations for Zechariah's execution and resonates with parts of the canonical book of Isaiah (cf. Isa. 1:10). This second charge seems sufficient to motivate a legend such as Isaiah's martyrdom.

How Isaiah Became a Christian Martyr

The person or people who composed the Ascension of Isaiah did not leave this tradition untouched, however. Instead, they did a lot of work to transform the motivations for Isaiah's martyrdom. For example, in its present form the book begins with Isaiah's audience before the righteous king Hezekiah and his heir Manasseh. (The setting is around 700 B.C.E.) Apparently, Hezekiah intends to instruct Manasseh in the ways of righteousness—a plan that fails miserably. Remarkably, the session features not *Isaiah's* revelations but *Hezekiah's*:

the words of righteousness which the king himself had seen, and (the words concerning) the eternal judgments, and the torments of Gehenna, and the prince of this world, and his angels, and his authorities, and his powers, and the words concerning faith in the Beloved which he himself had seen in the fifteenth year of his reign during his sickness. (1:2–4, *OTP*)

Only then does the scene report the contents of Isaiah's prophecies

concerning the judgment of the angels, and concerning the destruction of this world, and concerning the robes of the saints and their going out, and concerning their transformation and the persecution and ascension of the Beloved. (1:5, *OTP*)

Thus, not only Isaiah but also the king testify to revelations concerning Jesus, "the Beloved." According to the story, revelations concerning Jesus were available—and recorded in writing—more than seven hundred years before Jesus' birth. But also according to the story, these revelations never had a chance. Isaiah proclaims that Manasseh, inspired by the devil—named Sammael, Malkira, Beliar, Matanbukus, and Mekembukus in the book—would torment the prophet and suppress his revelations. Tragically, the revelations concerning Jesus shared by Isaiah and Hezekiah would remain hidden until after the Beloved's career. Centuries ahead of his time, Isaiah would die as the first Christian martyr.

Naming the Devil

Contemporary readers are used to the figure called "Satan" or "the devil" in scripture. But one curiosity of apocalyptic literature is the variety of names assigned to God's primary supernatural adversary. Sometimes, as in the Ascension of Isaiah, this occurs even within one text. In the Book of the Watchers, for example, the leader of the rebellious angels is alternatively called Semihazah and Azazel, and Jubilees speaks of Mastema, Satan, and Belial. Indeed, even the New Testament gospels include the epithet Beelzebul (Mt. 10:25; 12:24, 27; Mk. 3:22; Lk. 11:15, 18–19).

And so he dies. Supplementing the charges that he placed himself above Moses and spoke against the king and the holy city, the Ascension's Christian composers insert additional explanations for Isaiah's death. They do so in part by attributing two vision reports to Isaiah (3:13–4:22 and 7:1–11:43) and by explaining that Beliar had "dwelt in the heart of Manasseh" and his followers (3:11, *OTP*). Ultimately, Manasseh executes Isaiah not on the basis of his official charges, but because the prophet has angered the devil:

For Beliar was very angry with Isaiah because of the vision, and because of the exposure with which he had exposed Sammael, and that *through him there had been revealed the coming of the Beloved* from the seventh heaven... (3:13, *OTP*, author's emphasis)

At the conclusion of this first report, Isaiah meets his doom. Once again, the Ascension's editors ensure that we know the "real" reason for these events: They occur because Beliar is angry about Isaiah's visions (5:1). Again at the end of the execution scene the narrator insists that Beliar/Sammael/Satan did these things to Isaiah because of his vision of the Beloved and because he had spoken against Jerusalem (5:15–16).

These explanations, then, provide the framework within which the Ascension narrates the first vision report (3:13–4:22). (A second and more expansive visionary report occurs in chapters 6–11 after the narration of Isaiah's execution.) The first vision report presents a review of history, including the career of the Beloved—his advent, transformation, descent, ministry, crucifixion, and resurrection—as well as the corruption that plagues the church after the resurrection. This first report culminates in God's eschatological intervention to redeem the righteous and to judge God's adversaries. From a literary point of view we may conclude that in the larger flow of the narrative, the first vision report enhances the Ascension's ultimate explanation for Isaiah's execution. Having testified to his vision of the Beloved, Isaiah died as a Christian martyr.

If Isaiah's death results from his testimony to the Beloved, his fate parallels that of Jesus in two other respects. Both executions invoke tree imagery: Isaiah is sawed in two with a wood saw (5:1, 11), whereas Jesus is crucified on a tree (3:13; 9:14; 11:20).[4] Moreover, with respect to both Isaiah and Jesus, Beliar instigates the people's violence (3:13; 5:12; 9:14; 11:19). Hence, the Ascension of Isaiah characterizes the prophet as a model Christian martyr, who emulates the sufferings of Jesus.

Isaiah's fate prompts a theological question: Who is to blame for these things? From the outset (1:7–13), Isaiah explains to Hezekiah that Manasseh is the evil villain, yet Manasseh himself receives inspiration from a higher source, the devil. As is often the case in apocalyptic cosmology, the chain of causation runs deeper. Isaiah admonishes Hezekiah give up hope for his son:

The Beloved has made your plan ineffective, and the thought of your heart will not come about; for with this calling have I been called, and the inheritance of the Beloved will I inherit. (1:13, *OTP*)

Ultimately, God is to account for Isaiah's martyrdom. The prophet's calling includes this vocation.

God's responsibility for Isaiah's death opens the path to an even more troubling issue: God's role in the concealment of Isaiah's revelation. The Ascension holds the people of Jerusalem accountable for both Isaiah's death and for the crucifixion of the Beloved. Note these accounts of the Beloved's career. His miraculous birth elicits wonder from the people, but "they were all blinded concerning him; they all knew about him, but they did not know from where he was" (11:14, *OTP*). Indeed, the infant Jesus nursed only so "that he might not be recognized" (11:17, *OTP*). And finally,

> the adversary [Beliar] envied him and roused the children of Israel, who did not know who he was, against him. And they handed him to the ruler, and crucified him. (11:19, *OTP*)

At the end of the day, Isaiah's witness *to* the Beloved also functions as an indictment *against* the Jewish people. They participate in the executions of both Isaiah and the Beloved. The people's elimination of Isaiah also prevents their descendants from receiving his revelation. For that reason, the people also fail to recognize the Beloved, handing him over to be crucified. And–according to the Ascension of Isaiah–all of this is God's plan.

Thus, in the Ascension of Isaiah we are witnessing a key stage in the development of anti-Jewish polemic in early Christianity. The first Christian generations proclaimed Jesus to be the Jewish messiah, and their message apparently enjoyed remarkable success in some Jewish circles. But how could they explain that most Jews–like most people in general–remained unpersuaded? To answer this question, many early Christians turned precisely to Isaiah 6, which provides the impetus for a good deal of the Ascension of Isaiah. Indeed, many parts of Isaiah resonated within early Christian imaginations, so that Isaiah eventually came to be called "the fifth gospel."[5] For in Isaiah 6, not only does the prophet experience a vision of the divine throne, the very focal point of Isaiah's heavenly tour in the Ascension, but he also receives hard news:

> And [God] said, "Go and say to this people:
> 'Keep listening, but do not comprehend;
> keep looking, but do not understand.'
> Make the mind of this people dull,
>   and stop their ears,
>   and shut their eyes,
> so that they may not look with their eyes,
>   and listen with their ears,
>   and comprehend with their minds,
>   and turn and be healed."
> Then I said, "How long, O Lord?" And he said:
> "Until cities lie waste
>   without inhabitant,

and houses without people,
> and the land is utterly desolate;
until the LORD sends everyone far away,
> and vast is the emptiness in the midst of the land." (Isa. 6:9–12)

This passage warns Isaiah that his message will fail and that Jerusalem will face judgment. Apparently, early Christians applied this passage to account for their gospel's mixed reception among Jews, even tracing Jerusalem's fall to the Romans to this one cause. All four of the canonical gospels quote this passage to explain negative responses to Jesus (Mk. 4:10–12; Mt. 13:13–17; Lk. 8:9–10; Jn. 12:39–40). Even more ominously, the book of Acts concludes its narrative by quoting the passage to explain why the gospel moves from Jewish to Gentile audiences (28:25–28). Thus, the Ascension of Isaiah draws upon Isaiah 6 to attack non-Christian Jews: They would have received the revelation of the Beloved had not God judged them centuries earlier. At this point, their rejection of Jesus results from at least three causes: their own wickedness, Beliar's deception, and God's judgment.

Two Vision Reports

Two vision reports appear in the Ascension. The first (3:13–4:22) is framed by the accusations against the prophet and by his execution, whereas the second (7:1–11:43) represents the body of the book's second "half." Manuscript evidence suggests that the second report, along with its introduction (chaps. 6–11), once surfaced independently from chapters 1–5.[6] As we shall see, apart from the Ascension's anti-Jewish polemic, these two reports convey the book's distinctive interests.

While the Ascension presents *two* reports with different content, the first report presents itself as a summary of Isaiah's journey to the seven heavens, which is narrated in the second report. From a literary perspective, this first report has some rough edges. From 3:13–20, the vision is related through the voice not of Isaiah himself but of a narrator. But at 4:1, Isaiah clearly speaks in his own person, addressing King Hezekiah and his son Josab. In between (3:21–31), it is difficult to identify whether the speaking voice is Isaiah's or the narrator's. These verses present the content of the revelation more directly, but they do not specify their addressee. Although such details may seem arcane, they reveal the tension between the two vision reports: Whereas the second report directly relates Isaiah's journey through the seven heavens, it is unclear whether this vision includes the contents of the first report. To oversimplify, the tension between the two reports amounts to this: The first report *mentions* Isaiah's heavenly journey, but it *emphasizes* a review of history, whereas the second report *contains* historical review, but it *presents itself* as a heavenly journey.

The first report begins by explaining that Beliar's anger results from Isaiah's vision. The report relates so many details of the vision that we may identify only some of the high points:

1. the coming of the Beloved from the seventh heaven, with an emphasis on his incarnation in "the form of a man" (3:13, *OTP*)
2. the Beloved's career
3. the emergence of the early church, which accompanies the Beloved's return to the seventh heaven
4. apostasy and corruption in the church in the last days, especially among its leaders
5. an eschatological persecution of the church that features the returned Nero
6. God's final triumph over Beliar and his allies
7. a resurrection and judgment, bringing about the glorification of God's faithful ones

In short, the first vision report sketches a complete last-days scenario that begins with Jesus' career and apparently culminates in the age of its readers.

The heading that introduces chapters 6–11–"The Vision Which Isaiah the Son of Amoz Saw"–probably represents a title for this once-independent work. According to the introduction that precedes the second vision report, Isaiah receives his vision during an audience with King Hezekiah. The vision is a mystical experience: the prophet's "eyes indeed were open, but his mouth was silent, and the mind in his body was taken up from him" (6:11, *OTP*). The vision report (7:1–11:35) narrates Isaiah's journey through the seven heavens, with particular attention to the transformation of the Beloved as he descends to earth and then ascends to his place in the seventh heaven.

Taken up by an angel, Isaiah observes each of the seven heavens. In the firmament–that dividing wall between the earthly and heavenly realms– dwell Satan and his hosts, who live in strife. Things improve as one goes up. As he ascends, the prophet notices how the glory of his own face increases. Each of the seven heavens contains a throne. The first five heavens all contain two classes of angels who praise God continually, though their glory increases from one heaven to the next.

Things change radically at the sixth heaven, however, as even in the "air" of the sixth heaven (apparently an intermediate place between the fifth and sixth heavens) Isaiah senses a new order of holiness. No longer are the angels divided into two orders, but now all turn their attention to the seventh heaven, where the Holy One and the Chosen One dwell. Isaiah himself experiences transformation in the sixth heaven, as he learns that he will eventually achieve equality with the angels of the seventh heaven (8:14–15). In the sixth heaven the prophet himself sings along with the angels. In comparison to this glory, the light of all the other heavens amounts only to darkness (8:21).

As Isaiah enters the air of the seventh heaven, the LORD personally authorizes him to enter. There in the seventh heaven dwell all the righteous from Adam onward. The prophet also encounters the book containing the deeds of the "children of Israel," along with the robes, thrones, and crowns reserved for the saints. He sees the Beloved, the "angel of the Holy Spirit," and also the LORD—all of whom receive worship. He also hears the praise to God from the six heavens below.

The real focus of Isaiah's journey seems to lie not in the heavenly details, important though they are, but in his revelation concerning the journey and transformation of the Beloved. After all, that revelation unites the plotline for the entire book. In short, for the Beloved to descend through the heavens to earth, his glory must diminish from one level to the next.[7] Thus, Isaiah witnesses the Beloved's miraculous birth, his infancy (a sham, designed to hide his true identity, 11:17–18), his crucifixion and resurrection, and his ascent through the seven heavens.

One might assume that this transformation derives from the necessity of the incarnation, the mystery of how the divine Beloved One lives a human life. To some degree that is true, but the Ascension of Isaiah ties the Beloved's transformation to another mystery: Jesus will conquer the powers of evil by deceiving them. Perceiving him as a mere mortal, the devil and his minions will "hang him upon a tree, not knowing who he is" (9:14, *OTP*, cf. 11:19). This disguise enables the Beloved to plunder the angel of death (9:16), so that when the Most High calls him to ascend and return to the seventh heaven, even Satan and the wicked angels must acknowledge their defeat (11:23–24). This pattern corresponds to an ancient theory of the atonement (the mystery of how Christ brings salvation), according to which Christ's death and resurrection bring salvation by means of deceiving and defeating the powers of evil.

One might characterize the interests of this second report as cosmological and christological. That is, whereas the first vision report investigates the eschatological currents of history, the second report dwells on the nature of the heavenly realms and the mystery of how the heavenly Beloved One could manifest himself as the human Jesus.

The Ascension of Isaiah: Contexts and Motivations

Why did its editors go to such great lengths to unite diverse material concerning Isaiah's martyrdom and his heavenly journey in composing the Ascension of Isaiah? Scholars have proposed a variety of motivations, all of which have some grounding in the story's details.[8] At a minimum, we may suggest that the Ascension addresses several particular concerns.

While the majority of the Ascension narrates the cosmological and christological details of Isaiah's vision, *historical eschatology* also plays a role in the story. When the Ascension narrates the rise of apostasy and false prophets in the early church, it describes those events as "afterwards" (3:21, *OTP*), "in those days" (3:23, 25, *OTP*), and "in the last days" (3:30, *OTP*), with "the approach of the LORD" (3:26, *OTP*) in view. The Ascension also presents an end-time scenario in which Beliar will descend to the world in the form of Nero, the infamous Roman emperor who executed thousands of Christians in Rome and whom many believed would return to persecute the faithful in the last days.[9] (See discussion on pp. 97–98) Nero's return sends the saints "from desert to desert" searching for a safe haven (4:13, *OTP*). Thus, according to the Ascension's historical eschatology, Jesus' appearance is quickly followed by the church's decline and the pressures of persecution. In the last days only the few remaining saints await Jesus' return. Ultimately, then, it is the Beloved's own career that inaugurates the last days (cf. 9:13).

Keyed to this eschatological scenario, the Ascension also projects concerns regarding *the state of the church.* "Elders and shepherds" corrupt the apostles' teaching and harm their followers, all the while seeking money and glory (3:21–26). Because of this apostasy, the Holy Spirit withdraws and prophecy declines. Eschatological persecution necessarily follows closely. These concerns lead some interpreters to locate the Ascension between the church conflicts and the final crisis, at a period during which the churches had achieved some degree of institutional development but had also attracted the sort of public attention that might provoke persecution. Furthermore, one might combine three threads—the tradition of Isaiah and his circle of prophets who hide in the mountains and the desert (2:7–16), the conflict over the decline of prophecy (3:26–31), and the faithful remnant who hide in the desert (4:13)—to construct a more specific context for the Ascension. Perhaps the Ascension of Isaiah derives from early Christian prophetic groups who live on the margins of the developing churches.[10] While evidence of early Christian prophetic groups survives from the late first and early second centuries, we cannot verify such detailed proposals.

Surely the Ascension demonstrates an interest in speculative *christology.* Jonathan Knight has argued for an "angelomorphic Christology," according to which the Beloved's pre-incarnational state corresponded to that of the angels: Either the Beloved was superior *among* the angels, or he was superior *to* the angels. (Knight points out that angelic models for understanding the being of Christ appear in a variety of early Christian materials.) The Beloved receives worship from the angels prior to his descent, and during his descent he so resembles the angels in the various heavens that his true identity remains hidden.[11]

Whatever the claims regarding the *ontology* (or essential being) of the pre-incarnational Christ, the Ascension also presents a *docetic* view of Jesus' career. That is, it emphasizes that Jesus only *seemed* to be human. Unlike some christologies, according to which Christ actually took on the fullness of human experience, including the need to grow in knowledge and vulnerability to human frailty and limitation, the christology of the Ascension presents Jesus' infancy and his mortality as a guise for fooling his enemies. As an infant he even nurses "as was customary, that he might not be recognized" (11:17, *OTP*)! But when God calls the Beloved back to his former dwelling place, his glory returns not gradually but immediately (11:22–33), so that all the beings recognize him as he ascends.

How does one assess the relative priority of the Ascension's various emphases? Is anti-Jewish polemic more or less important than historical eschatology, church conflict, prophecy, anticipated persecution, cosmology, or christology? One might note that we encounter some of these issues—church conflict, prophecy, and anticipated persecution—only in isolated sections of the Ascension. On the other hand, while historical eschatology receives detailed attention only with respect to those same passages, it also appears to function as a presupposition for the Ascension as a whole. Whereas the Ascension's entire second "half" combines cosmology and christology, it appears that the cosmological details largely function as a vehicle for delivering christological images. That leaves us with two prominent emphases: anti-Jewish polemic and christology. While the anti-Jewish arguments are largely confined to the book's first "half," they also result from detailed redactional activity: Isaiah's martyrdom results from his vision of the Beloved. Historically speaking, the linkage between anti-Jewish claims and christology may have been just that intimate, for in the second century, Christian claims that Jesus was the Messiah accompanied denunciations of Jews for refusing to acknowledge him as such.

The Apocalypse of Peter

Texts and Languages

The Apocalypse of Peter is extant in three Greek fragments and an Ethiopic version, though most scholars believe the Ethiopic version most closely relates the original Greek text.[12]

Date

The Apocalypse of Peter apparently found written form shortly after 100 C.E., perhaps during the Second Jewish Revolt of 132–135.[13]

Not to be confused with the Gnostic Apocalypse of Peter,[14] the Apocalypse of Peter was recognized as scripture in late–second-century sources such as the Muratorian Fragment and by Clement of Alexandria (*Eclogae Propheticae* 41, 48–49; cf. Eusebius, *Ecclesiastical History* 6.14.1).[15] Reflecting its wide influence, the Apocalypse of Peter also serves as the model for the later Apocalypse of Paul. Set in the contexts of Jesus' apocalyptic discourse (Matthew 24) and the transfiguration (Mt. 17:1–9a), it relates the parable of the fig tree (Mt. 24:32 par. Mk. 13:28; Lk. 21:29–30): "As soon as its shoots have gone forth and its boughs have sprouted, the end of the world will come" (Apoc. Pet. 2). When Peter requests an explanation of the parable, Jesus reveals the eschatological scenario on the palm of his right hand (Apoc. Pet. 3). While chapters 3–6 sketch those ultimate events, the Apocalypse of Peter is best known for the detailed portrayal of heaven and hell in chapters 7–17. This passage represents the earliest Christian description of hell.[16]

Settings

The Apocalypse of Peter builds upon material from Matthew's gospel to explore the fate of mortals after their deaths. The longest section (chaps. 1–14) builds from the eschatological discourse of Matthew 24, while chapters 15–17 draw upon Matthew's transfiguration scene (17:1–9a). As Richard Bauckham indicates, the story does not simply retell Matthew's version; rather, by presenting the revelation as a response to the disciples' questions, it conveys deeper eschatological details.[17]

Peter the Visionary

The Jewish apocalypses apparently employ specific visionaries for strategic reasons.[18] Enoch, who "walked with God [and] was no more, because God took him" (Gen. 5:24), provides the perfect guide for a tour of the heavens. Fourth Ezra does well to draw upon the famous scribe who collected Israel's laws. Although the book of Revelation and the Shepherd of Hermas do not draw upon such exalted figures, other Christian apocalypses do. The Ascension of Isaiah makes much of the prophet's vision of the heavenly throne, and the apocalypses of Peter and Paul appeal to two of the early church's most prominent leaders. In fact, Peter possesses a variety of qualifications for his role as an apocalyptic visionary. Not only was Peter one of Jesus' apostles, tradition also places him within an inner circle of Jesus' most intimate companions. Peter, named first along with James and John, is present for Jesus' transfiguration as well as for his agony in Gethsemane. All four of the canonical gospels find ways to acknowledge Peter's authority, though some apparently seek to rein it in. In Luke and John, Peter is among the first to witness the empty tomb; in Mark, the angel commands the women who visit the tomb to "tell his disciples and Peter" where they will encounter the risen Jesus (16:7). Peter emerges as the leader among the Jerusalem disciples, a tradition reflected in Matthew 16:18 ("You are Peter, and on this rock I will build my church") and in Peter's bold preaching on the day of Pentecost (Acts 2:14–36). In addition to his authority, Peter also carries mystical associations: His advocacy for the church's inclusion of Gentiles begins with a dramatic vision, in which "the heaven opened" (Acts 10:11) and a heavenly voice interprets the significance of Peter's revelation (10:9–16). In Acts, Peter's vision, along with Paul's encounter with the risen Jesus, legitimates the book's essential plot device: the spread of the gospel among Gentiles.

The Apocalypse of Peter draws upon these associations by locating Peter's revelations within the contexts of Jesus' apocalyptic discourse on the Mount of Olives and of Jesus' transfiguration. Within the narrative itself, Peter plays a modest but active role. Narrating in the first person, Peter recounts his response to the fig tree parable: "And I, Peter, answered and said to him, 'Interpret the fig-tree to me: how can we understand it?'" (2).[19] Jesus' reply conveys an implied rebuke–"Do you not understand that the fig-tree is the house of Israel?"–but this sort of reply is common among the apocalypses. Likewise, when Peter sees the fates of mortals revealed in Jesus' right hand, he intervenes on behalf of the sinners, "Lord, allow me to speak your word concerning the sinners: 'It were better for them if they had not been created.'" Again, he receives a mild correction: "Peter, why do you say that not to have been created were better for them? You resist God." Yet even this rebuke does not cut off the conversation; rather, Peter's intervention leads to the more detailed revelation of how future punishments correspond to present sins.

Peter's encounter with the transfigured Jesus depends more closely upon the Matthean text that inspires it, but it demonstrates similar characteristics. His question about the identities of Moses and Elijah leads to a larger concern: "Where then are Abraham and Isaac and Jacob and the rest of the righteous fathers?" (16). Jesus' account of their blessed state inspires Peter to rejoice and believe, but again Peter reveals his need for correction by offering to build three tabernacles. However, Jesus' stern rebuke–"Satan makes war against you, and has veiled your understanding…"–elicits not shame but gladness on Peter's part. Likewise, the fear Peter experiences when he hears the heavenly voice yields promptly to gladness that his name has been recorded in the book of life (17).

In one respect it is difficult to assess Peter's role in the apocalypse. The issue involves Peter's relative privilege: To what degree does Peter receive revelation from which the other disciples are excluded? On several occasions the apocalypse vacillates from the first person singular "I" to the plural "we." This occurs with respect to the vision in Jesus' palm (3), as well as at the end of the book, when "I trembled and was afraid" but immediately "we looked up" (17). Likewise, Jesus invites "me" to go to the holy mountain, but "his disciples went with him, praying" (15). Thus, while Peter receives particular focus, it remains unclear whether this implies his unique access to revelation. In any case, at the conclusion of the tour of hell Jesus addresses Peter directly: "I have spoke this to you, Peter, and declared it to you" (14). This address leads to Peter's commission to spread the gospel.

One might say that the apocalypse does not emphasize Peter's role. One might even add that Peter's characterization fits the typical apocalyptic pattern: He asks questions, receives clarifications and instructions, and sometimes he even suffers rebuke. But Peter's role transcends these fairly generic observations, for his questions and comments—even the ones that earn him rebuke—provide the motivation for the book's major revelations concerning the nature of hell and the fate of the righteous dead.

Mode of Revelation

While it employs the framework of familiar gospel narrative, the Apocalypse of Peter conveys its revelatory contents through less conventional means. Its tour of hell combines a vision presented on the palm of Jesus' right hand with Jesus' straightforward description, and its teaching regarding the righteous dead combines a vision of the blessed garden with further explanation by Jesus. Martha Himmelfarb has called attention to the pattern of straightforward "demonstrative explanations" ("this is"), which are so prominent in Peter's tour of hell.[20] This blending of dramatic vision and pedestrian discourse distinguishes the Apocalypse of Peter.

One might ask—and many have—where the notion of a tour of hell originated. We may simply remark that the resources for such traditions were rich and varied, ranging from Egyptian and Greco-Roman mythology, including the *Odyssey* and the *Aeneid,* to ancient Near Eastern epics of visits to the realm of the dead, such as we find in the *Epic of Gilgamesh.* At the same time, Jewish and Christian apocalyptic literature demonstrate an emerging tradition regarding the various levels of heaven, with some apocalypses locating the places of punishment in the heavenly realms.[21]

Punishments That Fit the Crime

To the extent that the Apocalypse of Peter has exerted an influence on culture, its signal contribution has involved its application of the *lex talionis,* or the measure-for-measure punishment.[22] In Peter's hell, blasphemers hang by their tongues; murderers and their conspirators are tormented by venomous beasts; and those who commit slander and yield to doubt are tortured with red-hot irons. Women who adorn themselves to attract men's sexual attention hang by their hair, while the male adulterers hang by their—well, you get the picture.

Remarkably, the Apocalypse of Peter devotes its largest block of material—chapters 7 through 12—to these individual punishments. In comparison, the description of the blessed state of the righteous receives only cursory attention. Though the righteous occupy part of chapters 13–17, these chapters do not sustain a focus upon their rewards. Nor do the rewards follow a measure-for-measure pattern. Even more noteworthy is the link between the suffering of the wicked and the realm of the righteous. The Apocalypse of Peter portrays the righteous as watching—and enjoying!—the torments of their counterparts.

Apparently, the suffering of the elect has resulted from the activities of the wicked:

> They [the elect] shall see their desire on those who hated them, when he punishes them and the torment of every one shall be forever according to his works. (13)

Despite its apparent vindictiveness, however, the Apocalypse of Peter teases us with the hope that all persons, even the wicked, may "enter the everlasting kingdom," though it does not spell out how this process might work (14). At the end of the day, most readers have emphasized the book's lust for vengeance over its hope for restoration, a judgment that reflects the relative amount of attention these topics receive throughout Peter's revelation.

Reading the Apocalypse of Peter

The Apocalypse of Peter's greatest influence, then, resides in its vivid portrayals of diverse punishments for various classes of sinners. This legacy, though grounded in the apocalypse's own literary emphasis, can occlude the motivations for its vindictiveness. More importantly, focusing solely on the punishments would lead us to overlook the multilayered rhetoric of the Apocalypse of Peter.

The Apocalypse of Peter emerged from a strong sensitivity to the dangers of persecution. For example, "the persecutors and betrayers of my righteous ones" receive special attention in chapter 9, as do those "who caused martyrs to die" through their false accusations. We might see a second response to persecution in chapter 5, where judgment befalls "those who have fallen away from faith." In anticipation of persecution, some early Christian groups warn against such apostasy. The Shepherd of Hermas expresses this concern in its condemnation of double-mindedness and in its insistence that Christians receive only one chance to repent after their baptism (cf. Jn. 15; Heb. 6:1–12; 10:19–39; Rev. 2:9–10; 3:8–12). We might also interpret the apocalypse's general concern with sinful behavior along these lines. Deviance from a group's norms threatens its identity, especially when the group experiences external pressure. The most familiar response to persecution, however, is the promise of heavenly life for the faithful, and the Apocalypse of Peter concludes on that note: "such also is the honour and the glory of those who are persecuted for my righteousness' sake" (chap. 16).

The Apocalypse of Peter does not project hate for hate's sake. Rather, its hatred emerges, as perhaps all hatred does, from fear—fear that outsiders might harm the righteous community, fear that insiders might succumb to the pressure and abandon the faithful, and fear that behaviors among the faithful might undermine group solidarity. Peter's otherworldly tour provides the means by which the apocalypse articulates at least three responses:

1. the righteous victims will see vengeance exacted on their behalf
2. those who consider abandoning the community or who threaten its values through their behavior should weigh the cost of judgment
3. those who persevere may expect a glorious reward

The Apocalypse of Paul

Texts and Languages

Though probably composed in Greek, the Apocalypse of Paul exists in several languages. Most scholars rely especially upon a fifth- or sixth-century Latin manuscript.[23]

Date

The preface in the Latin manuscript traditions indicates a date of 388 C.E., but some believe that Origen, who died in 253 C.E., was aware of the book.[24]

Although the Apocalypse of Paul likely depends—either directly or indirectly—upon the Apocalypse of Peter,[25] the Apocalypse of Paul proved far more influential throughout the centuries. The lone exception was in the Greek churches, among which thrived a later apocalypse attributed to the Virgin Mary, but the Apocalypse of Paul flourished in Latin, Coptic, Syriac, and Armenian. While the Apocalypse of Paul includes tours of both heavenly and hellish regions, in the Latin West it often traveled in abbreviated forms that emphasized only the punishments. In Richard Bauckham's words, "Medieval Christian conceptions of the other world, the fate of the dead, paradise and hell, come from the Apocalypse of Paul probably more than from any other source."[26]

Settings

Like the Apocalypse of Peter, the Apocalypse of Paul draws upon biblical antecedents to present two settings. In the most ancient manuscript traditions the apocalypse begins by quoting 2 Corinthians 12:1–5, Paul's account of his journey to the third heaven. Thus, the literary setting sets forth the revelation as Paul's first-person recollection of his mystical experience, one that occurred in a body other than his ordinary one (Apoc. Paul 3). But, again only in some manuscripts, the literary setting also features a remarkable time shift. Apparently, Paul hid his record of the revelation in a marble box under the foundation of a house in Tarsus. Its discovery requires a second revelation—actually *three* appearances by an angel—to the noble owner of the house "during the consulship of Theodosius Augustus the Younger and Cynegius" (Introduction), that is, in 388 C.E.[27] Afraid of what the box might contain, the owner of the house turns it over to the local judge, who then forwards it to the Emperor Theodosius. Theodosius sends a copy of the revelation to Jerusalem while keeping the original for himself (2).

The contents of the apocalypse feature tours of both heavenly and hellish regions. In part, this expresses an interest like that of the Apocalypse of Peter: speculation concerning the fate of the dead, with a strong motivation to inspire repentance.

Like the Apocalypse of Peter, Paul's apocalypse features the notorious measure-for-measure punishments. Indeed, later copyists often left out the visions concerning the fate of the blessed, preferring to extend the stick of torment rather than the carrot of blessedness. The Apocalypse of Paul also serves a speculative interest. Beyond the questions of punishments that fit the crime, the apocalypse also portrays the most prominent saints who populate paradise, particularly those who precede Jesus. Ignoring chronology, the apocalypse sketches the Virgin, Abraham, Isaac, Jacob, the twelve patriarchs, the martyred prophets (with particular attention to Isaiah, Jeremiah, and Ezekiel), Lot, Job, Noah, Elijah, and Elisha.

This double setting performs several functions. For one thing, unlike persons in contemporary Western societies, ancient Mediterranean people generally regarded new things with suspicion. The Apocalypse counters objections that it might convey new innovations by setting the revelation within a specific episode known from the apostle's own career. At the same time, the legends concerning the finding of the apocalypse doubly attest to its status as revealed literature: Not only do the contents derive from Paul's revelation, but they also required the revelatory discovery of Paul's text.

Paul the Visionary and Mode of Revelation

Paul, like Peter, represents a classic vehicle for the delivery of a mystical revelation. As with Peter's vision of the unclean foods, Paul's encounter with the risen Jesus plays a critical role in the unfolding of the book of Acts. Indeed, the book narrates Peter's revelation twice, but Paul's three times (9:1–19; 22:1–21; 26:2–23). This vision marks Paul as an apostle to the Gentiles (9:15), and his missionary work comprises the most substantial body of material in Acts. Paul himself attributes his call as a missionary to the Gentiles to his "apocalypse of Jesus Christ" (Gal. 1:12–16), and he introduces his journey to the third heaven as one of the "visions and revelations *(apokalypseis)* of the Lord" (2 Cor. 12:1) that legitimate his authority over against the claims of other early Christian preachers. Thus, Paul represents not only a figure of the highest authority in the emergence of Christianity but also a person with unmistakable mystical associations.

In this apocalypse Paul plays a remarkably complex role. Obviously, his status as a visionary endows him with extraordinary privilege, the access to heavenly secrets. His commission involves warning the children of God who are "doing the works of the devil in the faith of Christ" (3)—a mission to inspire repentance within the churches. As in the Apocalypse of Peter and other apocalypses, Paul pushes along the drama by asking questions and receiving explanations, but this merely functional role does not exhaust his contribution. Throughout the vision Paul demonstrates his compassion for sinners, especially by sighing, weeping, and groaning when he encounters their suffering. His weeping may elicit sympathy for sinners, but in the long run it actually confirms the justice of their fate.[28] Moreover, it contributes to the emotional appeal directed toward the audience, dramatizing the severity of their own potential fate:

> I wept and groaned over the human race. The angel answered and said to me, "Why do you weep? Are you more merciful than God? For though God is good, [God] knows that there are punishments, and [God] patiently bears with the human race, allowing each one to do [their] own will in the time in which [they] dwell on the earth." (33; cf. 40, 42, 43)

Indeed, Paul becomes an intercessor for sinners, as he joins the archangel Michael and other heavenly beings in praying for them.[29] Their prayers for the sinners are effective, moving the Son of God to grant one day's "refreshment on the Lord's Day for the sake of Paul the well-beloved of God who descended to you" (43–44).

Finally, we should note the ways in which the Apocalypse of Paul dramatically enhances the apostle's stature. As Paul tours the heavenly realms, the Virgin extends this greeting:

> "Hail, Paul, well-beloved of God and angels and [mortals]! For all the saints prayed to my Son Jesus who is my Lord that you might come here in the body that they might see you before you go out of the world." (46)

According to the Virgin, Paul's prominence results from his effectiveness as an evangelist, an impression confirmed by the twelve martyred prophets, who acclaim Paul as "the one who is glorified in heaven and on earth" on account of the people who have believed through his work (49).

Packaged as a revelation within a revelation, because Paul's original vision required a revelation concerning its hiding place, the body of the Apocalypse of Paul follows the standard cosmic tour format. "Snatched up into the third heaven" (3), Paul encounters celestial bodies, heavenly beings, and the dwelling places of the just and the sinners. His angelic guide often says, "Follow me, and I will show you," or "Look," as a means of indicating and interpreting the subjects of his vision, along with demonstrative explanations such as "this is" or "these are." Paul's questions also lead the angel to provide necessary interpretations. In short, the Apocalypse of Paul employs the standard conventions of apocalyptic tours.

Topics

Commentators routinely characterize the Apocalypse of Paul in terms of its rambling nature and incoherent structure, but those qualities—combined with its substantial length—provide the means by which the apocalypse addresses varied and wide-ranging concerns.

SPECULATIVE THEOLOGICAL QUESTIONS

The apocalypse perhaps answers several speculative theological questions. As for *what happens to people between their individual deaths and the final judgment,* we learn how people experience immediate blessedness or punishment upon their deaths (14–15). These states, however, are not permanent, but merely consistent with persons' final disposition. The righteous, for example, live in a blessed place until the return of Jesus (21). We also encounter *the relationship between the resurrection and the body,* for though the soul leaves the body at death, it returns to the same body at the general resurrection (15). Two other speculative theological concerns involve *the activities of angels* and the fates of those saints who preceded Jesus and thus could not have believed in him. Angels are assigned to individuals (7–10, 14, 16), not only assisting them and guiding them toward repentance but also reporting on their conduct. Clearly, those righteous persons who preceded Jesus enjoy the reward of the righteous (46–51).

ECCLESIASTICAL CONCERNS

Ecclesiastical concerns also figure prominently in the Apocalypse of Paul. The vision exalts ascetic practices (9, 22), though the precise practices it addresses are lost to us. At the same time, it condemns church persons who incite division (31), abuse church offices (34–36), and teach certain doctrines concerning the nature of Christ and of the eucharist (41–42). Apparently, the Apocalypse of Paul is particularly concerned with docetic christologies that valued the spiritual Christ but not the fleshly Jesus.

DIVINE JUSTICE AND MERCY

Finally, we have seen that in the Apocalypse Paul voices concern for divine justice and mercy. While the vision repeatedly insists upon the righteousness of God's judgment, it also promotes a remarkable idea: the one day of rest for condemned sinners. Also noteworthy is the effectiveness of Paul's intercession—along with intercession by heavenly beings—on their behalf. The text could be more clear on this point, but most scholars believe that the Sunday rest implies not a single day of refreshment throughout time but refreshment on every Lord's Day.[30]

Reading the Apocalypse of Paul

The Apocalypse of Paul portrays the desperate plight of sinners as a means to promote repentance. The apocalypse evokes the emotional values of fear and hope through a variety of means. These include reports from the angels that mourn the sinners' fate, visions of people's souls upon their deaths, Paul's intercession on their behalf, and the commentaries of heavenly beings. The apocalypse evokes the emotional values of fear and hope. By portraying the punishments that fit particular sins, the apocalypse especially identifies the most pressing concerns of some, if not all, early Christians. Though it devotes significant attention to the realms of the blessed, its particular portrayal of the rewards the just inherit is far less graphic than its depiction of the torment faced by sinners.

Yet the Apocalypse of Paul's most noteworthy literary weakness—its rambling style and shifting focus—also empowers it to address an impressive list of other concerns. Thus, it demonstrates the flexibility of the cosmological journey genre to embody and promote particular sets of values at the expense of others. We also observe how times have changed between the apocalypses of Peter and Paul. Whereas Peter's apocalypse reflects some degree of preoccupation with the *external* pressures of persecution, Paul's identifies *internal* stresses such as ecclesiastical strife, corrupt leadership, and doctrinal controversy.

Concluding Reflections

The Ascension of Isaiah, the Apocalypse of Peter, and the Apocalypse of Paul all share an interest in the otherworldly realms. They also share significant literary conventions that identify them among the cosmological journeys. Yet these three apocalypses also reveal that genre's flexibility, for they employ it to address a variety of concerns. For the Ascension of Isaiah, the heavenly journey primarily dramatizes a christology—a docetic one at that, of the sort that the much later Apocalypse of Paul refutes. In the Apocalypse of Peter the tour offers hope for the righteous, who may look ahead to their own blessedness while imagining the suffering of their persecutors and their accomplices. The Apocalypse of Paul guides its audience through heavenly and hellish regions to inspire their repentance. Although the Apocalypse of Peter shares this interest in cataloguing the sins one must avoid, its "us versus them" perspective differs markedly from the Apocalypse of Paul's more ominous tone.

At the same time, these comparisons reflect a perhaps necessary oversimplification. For none of these three apocalypses should be reduced to a single message or function. Instead, legends concerning the nature and method of the revelation unite with stock motifs from the cosmological journey genre to build a strong platform. From this platform these apocalypses can address a vast array of concerns, from early relationships between Christians and their Jewish neighbors, to ecclesiastical conflict, to speculative matters concerning the otherworldly regions. Despite the strong measure of vindictiveness that pervades these texts, the apocalypses of Peter and Paul also hold out some measure of hope or comfort for their adversaries.

FOR FURTHER READING

Bauckham, Richard. *The Fate of the Dead: Studies on the Jewish and Christian Apocalypses.* NovTSup 93. Leiden: Brill, 1998.

Buchholz, Dennis D. *Your Eyes Will Be Opened: A Study of the Greek (Ethiopic) Apocalypse of Peter.* SBLDS 97. Atlanta: Scholars Press, 1988.

Carey, Greg. "The *Ascension of Isaiah*: Characterization and Conflict." Pages 161–79 in *Vision and Persuasion: Rhetorical Dimensions of Apocalyptic Discourse.* Edited by Greg Carey and L. Gregory Bloomquist. St. Louis: Chalice Press, 1999.

Himmelfarb, Martha. *Ascent to Heaven in Jewish and Christian Apocalypses.* New York: Oxford University Press, 1993.

_____. *Tours of Hell: An Apocalyptic Form in Jewish and Christian Literature.* Philadelphia: Fortress Press, 1983.

Knight, Jonathan. *The Ascension of Isaiah.* Guides to Apocrypha and Pseudepigrapha. Sheffield: Sheffield Academic Press, 1995.

CHAPTER 9

Epilogue

Legacies and Prospects

What does *apocalyptic* mean? In popular culture, apocalyptic portends final threats to humanity—cataclysmic eruptions, nuclear holocausts, environmental disaster, even (we're in the twenty-first century now) viral terrorism. Among many Christians, apocalyptic sets forth the last days before Jesus' return, and contemporary observers can mark off their calendars as the signs pass by one by one. For those who stop short of naming humanity's end, apocalyptic evokes the reign of chaos, which renders meaningless concepts such as justice and goodness. The classic film *Apocalypse Now* plays out this sort of apocalypse in the Vietnam jungle.

For those ancient Jews and Christians who cultivated and adapted it, apocalyptic discourse certainly involved images of the end and depictions of chaos. But apocalyptic discourse emerged neither as an entertaining sideshow nor as a catchall category for things bizarre. At its core, the term *apocalyptic* refers to revelation, or unveiling. Apocalyptic discourse claims to render sacred mysteries accessible. It discloses things people would not perceive otherwise. So the ancient apocalyptic writers of Judaism and Christianity revealed not only the future course of history, or the final disposition of mortals, they also unveiled—that is, interpreted—present reality. Monsters characterize imperial brutality; cosmic portents reflect social injustice; heavenly glories display the rule of the transcendent over the ordinary.

Those ancient Jews and Christians developed apocalyptic discourse as a theological resource for engaging the world. They adapted the topics of apocalyptic discourse to address unavoidable religious issues and to shape the attitudes and behaviors of individuals and communities. In the face of pressing religious questions such as, *Is God faithful? How do the physical and moral elements of the cosmos operate? Will present injustices find resolution?* and *How should God's people define themselves in rapidly changing circumstances?* they channeled their theological imagination, poetic creativity, and rhetorical power through apocalyptic discourse. In a multiplicity of contexts and for diverse ends, apocalyptic discourse intervened in the ongoing lives of early Jewish and Christian communities.

Contributions of Apocalyptic Discourse

Imagine an intelligent person who decides to read the Bible from cover to cover even though she knows almost nothing about it and very little about theology. After she finishes the "Old Testament" (she's reading a Christian Bible), she turns to the New. How many surprising concepts will she find in the New Testament, for which the Old Testament did not adequately prepare her? How is she to make sense of Satan and other angels and demons, the resurrection, the final judgment, or the eschatological tribulation? And when Jesus, Paul, and John (in the book of Revelation) describe the things they have seen in heaven, how is she to imagine those realms?

Perhaps the apocalyptic writers did not *invent* these ideas. Surely many of them reveal connections with the ancient sacred traditions of Persia, Egypt, and Greece. Yet within the development of ancient Judaism and the emergence of earliest Christianity, these topics first take their definitive form within apocalyptic discourse. For example, messianic expectations apparently flourished among Palestinian Jews in the decades before and after Jesus. Many Jews probably did not cherish messianic hopes, but for those who did messianic expectation figured as part of the larger vision of the end of days.[1] Although the roots of messianic ideology precede the emergence of apocalyptic literature, explicit messianic expectation first surfaces among apocalyptic texts and apocalyptic communities. So also for critical doctrines such as the resurrection, the judgment, and the world to come. To move from the Jewish Scriptures to the New Testament, our imaginary reader would benefit a great deal by reading ancient apocalyptic literature.

Distaste for Apocalyptic Eschatology in Judaism and Christianity

Throughout this book we have carefully distinguished between apocalyptic eschatology (ideas about ultimate things), apocalypticism (social movements with apocalyptic ideas), and apocalyptic discourse (the cultural productions that employ apocalyptic topics). In the cultural expressions of Judaism and Christianity, however, all things apocalyptic have fed into two major streams: personal and historical eschatology. Apocalyptic discourse's influence on personal eschatology has shaped cultural expressions regarding heaven, hell, purgatory, and the last judgment, while its manifestation in historical eschatology has most often been associated with millenarianism. Even people with little to no involvement in religion share common imagery concerning heaven, hell, and Jesus' return. When both Bugs Bunny and Bart Simpson encounter similar versions of Satan and hell, we have met the long arm of apocalyptic imagination.

Yet formidable forces within Jewish and Christian history have opposed apocalyptic eschatology, especially in its millenarian forms. One might even conclude that mainstream Judaism and Christianity have marginalized apocalyptic discourse.

Millenarianism, or millennialism, refers to the expectation that God's reign will interrupt history in a dramatic way. More specifically, we identify millenarianism among those who anticipate the end of the present age and the advent of the age to come in the imminent future. North American millenarians would include the popular prophecy teachers of Christian broadcasting and evangelical bookstores and those who share their message, many of whom conduct relatively mainstream lifestyles. But millenarianism would also include more radical Christian sects such as the Branch Davidians and the marginally Christian Heaven's Gate movement. Millenarian beliefs have comforted those people in their experience of oppression and inspired mass revolts. On the whole, however, mainstream Jewish and Christian traditions have discouraged millenarian enthusiasm for a variety of reasons.

As for Jewish thought, we distinguish between messianism and apocalypticism. Though we encounter it in ancient apocalyptic literature, Jewish messianic expectation is somewhat more specific and often lacks some of the most characteristic topics of apocalyptic discourse. For example, messianism may evolve apart from appeals to the resurrection of the dead or eternal life.[2] Jewish messianism implies the hope that through a human agent God will initiate "a fundamental change in the current situation of Jewish life," including the liberation of Jews from oppression from around the world, their ingathering to the land of Israel, reestablishment of classic Jewish institutions, and the reformation of Jewish society—and perhaps the entire world—toward the ends of justice and peace.[3] According to Moshe Idel, such messianism has fared better in Jewish history than has apocalypticism:

> The concept of messianism was promoted from a secondary status in biblical literature to one of much greater importance in subsequent Jewish literature, even sometimes reaching the status of an essential article of faith...This was never the case with apocalypticism. Calculations of the end were often attacked explicitly in rabbinic literature, and attempts to determine the date of the coming of the Messiah by invoking angels or demons have been discounted by medieval authors. Hence, we may distinguish some forms of messianism from apocalyptic speculations, though the two modes of thought are often closely related.[4]

If messianism flourished within Jewish tradition, while apocalypticism has lingered among the fringes of Jewish culture, Idel adds, then we will rarely encounter apocalyptic discourse apart from messianic discourse, while we occasionally encounter messianic hopes apart from apocalyptic scenarios.[5]

Rabbinic literature manifests ambivalence toward apocalyptic eschatology. The rabbis frequently engage apocalyptic topics, but they also discourage both eschatological speculation and the sort of mystical experience characteristic of the classical apocalypses.[6] Both systems of esoteric knowledge possessed many dangers. For one thing, they challenged the traditions of communal reasoning that made rabbinic discourse possible. Like Christian Gnostics, Jewish mystics possessed independent access to revelation that posed a threat to more conventional modes of religious discernment.

But the rabbis also warned that eschatological and mystical speculation held a more personal danger. Like the Sirens of Greek mythology, whose songs so enchanted sailors as to cause shipwrecks, heavenly visions could captivate those who beheld them. They could lead individuals into heresy and even destroy their souls. Such was the case, according to one rabbinic legend, for three of four mystics who entered a mystical paradise: One died, one went insane, and one became a heretic (*y. Hag.* 2:1; cf. *t. Hag.* 2.3–4; *b. Hag.* 2.1). According to this example, one is better off avoiding mystical revelations altogether.[7] Indeed, some said, it's safer just to leave alone the heavenly realms and the eschatological future altogether:

> Whoever speculates about four things, it would have been better for him if he had not come into the world: what is above, what is below, what was before, and what will be afterwards. (*m. Hag.* 2:1)[8]

Why avoid speculation about the end times and God's heavenly dwelling? Because it's bad for you.

Perhaps ordinary this-worldly developments influenced Jewish and Christian attitudes toward apocalyptic eschatology. Jews had good reason to link messianism and apocalypticism with danger. Both Jewish revolts against Rome, one from 66–73 C.E. and another from 132–35 C.E., apparently featured some degree of messianic and eschatological speculation—and both revolts ended with devastation. In his account of the first war, the Jewish historian Josephus alludes to an ambiguous oracle that one of their own people would come to rule the world (*War* 6.12). The Roman historians Tacitus (*Histories* 5.13.1–2) and Suetonius (*Vespasian* 4.5) likewise associate the first revolt with Jewish eschatology. As for the second revolt, its leader Simeon Bar Kosiba (or Bar Kokhba) apparently assumed messianic pretensions. In any case, that is how later rabbinic tradition recalled the revolt (cf. *y. Taʿan.* 4:6; *Lam. Rab.* 2:2).

Christians may have turned away from apocalyptic eschatology for very different reasons. Subversive associations can only hinder a movement in search of respectability. Whereas Jewish fortunes fell after the revolts, Christian influence expanded in the movement's first four centuries. Jews sought to protect a small community, but eventually Christians aimed their movement at the center of Roman imperial culture. Although Christianity emerged as a tiny and vulnerable sect, by the fourth century it had evolved into a major social force. Whatever their motivations, both mainstream rabbinic Judaism and orthodox Christianity eventually judged apocalyptic hopes as more dangerous than beneficial.

Perhaps ambivalence toward the empire accounts for why Revelation competed with the Shepherd of Hermas and the Apocalypse of Peter for inclusion in the canon. All three apocalypses reflect concern with persecution. But Hermas and Peter, with their emphases on individual faithfulness and survival, look tame in comparison with Revelation's fierce anti-imperial polemics.

If Christian intellectuals eventually disapproved of apocalyptic eschatology, things had once been different. In the second and third centuries most of Revelation's interpreters were millennialists, expecting the literal fulfillment of Christ's reign on earth. Their numbers included Papias of Hierapolis (c. 80–140), Justin Martyr (d. c. 165), Melito of Sardis (late second century), Irenaeus of Lyons (c. 115–c. 202), Tertullian (160–c. 225), Hippolytus of Rome (c. 170–c. 230), Julius Africanus (c.160–c. 240), and Victorinus of Pettau (d. 303). The Christian historian Eusebius, who also accused Papias of stupidity, blamed him for inciting millennialism in the church, including a negative influence on Irenaeus. For their part, Justin and Irenaeus awaited the rebuilding of Jerusalem, whereas Victorinus anticipated the return of Elijah, who would convert the 144,000 of Revelation 7:4 and 14:1.[9] Tertullian and Hippolytus respectively identified Rome with Revelation's Whore and Beast.[10] Hence, despite different emphases and interpretations of particular details, for these early interpreters apocalyptic eschatology implied the end of the present global order, including the empire, and the future inauguration of Christ's rule.

But things changed. As Christianity assumed power, eventually linking its own identity and welfare with the empire's, counter-imperial visions made less sense. Many historians identify two particular interpreters of Revelation who defined the transition from a subversive appropriation of apocalyptic discourse to one that celebrated the church's temporal power. Whereas some interpreters had expressed their discomfort with Revelation by either rejecting it outright or by allegorizing its historical particulars, millenarianism flourished in North Africa. Because some influential interpreters had proclaimed Christ's advent around the year 500, millenarian pressure continued to build in the fourth and fifth centuries. But Tyconius, and Augustine after him, both leaders within North African

Christianity, articulated an interpretation of Revelation that rejected insurgent millenarianism, on the one hand, and ahistorical allegorization, on the other. Asserting that no one can know the time of the end, Tyconius and Augustine found Revelation's historical fulfillment in the ongoing development of the church. The millennium itself, according to Tyconius, included the time from Christ's passion until his second coming, an indeterminate amount of time. Together, Tyconius and Augustine discouraged millenarian subversion by identifying God's eschatological intervention among institutions of the present, and they set the tone for mainstream interpretation of Revelation for a thousand years.[11]

This broader distrust of apocalyptic eschatology continues into the present. Within Judaism we find the awareness that apocalyptic imagination—defined by Arthur P. Mendel as "the total and violent destruction of the present world and creation of a radically new order under the leadership of a saviour and his disciples in the name of a higher power and Providence"—unites all sorts of evil forces through the ages: Crusaders, Inquisitors, the Munster rebellion, Leninists, Stalinists, and especially Nazis.[12] Any claim that a group knows God's absolute will for the future implies the possibility of annihilating those who differ. Moreover, Jewish thinkers such as Gershom Scholem have warned that popular messianism has usually involved not only an optimistic utopianism but also "uninhibited fantasies about the catastrophic aspects of redemption."[13]

Many Christian theologians, notably feminists, have also developed a sensitivity to these implications. Turning away from visions of a radically different future "concerned with immortality" toward commitment to "ecological and cosmic sustainability," some call for a "renewal of *this* creation—not the deadly expectation of the end of this one."[14] Such a drive toward history's absolute end leads us to ignore the suffering of real people and the destruction of the ecosystem in the present.[15] For example, the United States once had a Secretary of the Interior who was a millenarian. This political leader testified before Congress that in light of Christ's imminent return, destruction of the earth's natural resources was not a priority: "I do not know how many future generations we can count on before the Lord returns."[16] Fixation upon end-time events can, some say, either derive from or promote social and psychological disorder.[17]

Diverse Settings and Functions

We have reflected on apocalyptic discourse's distinctive contributions to Jewish and Christian thought. We have seen apocalyptic eschatology's mixed reception in both traditions. To appreciate the multivalent potential of ancient apocalyptic discourse, we may also review the diverse contexts in which it flourished and several of the functions it performed.

A second visit to the book of Revelation provides a helpful starting place, particularly the letters to the churches in chapters 2 and 3. On first glance, the letters look tediously similar. The risen Jesus speaks to each of seven churches in Asia Minor, promising eschatological rewards and punishments in response to their obedience or disobedience. But on closer inspection we find that not only does John perceive marked diversity among these churches, the letters also address them in different ways.

The church in Smyrna (Rev. 2:8–11) apparently is struggling. Jesus notes its "affliction" and its "poverty," yet the tone of the letter also reflects affirmation. Though slander surrounds them, and prison awaits some, the Smyrneans are actually rich. The letter has nothing negative to say about them; it simply pushes them on: "Do not fear," Jesus says, and, "Be faithful unto death, and I will give you the crown of life." Hardly a comforting outlook, but on the whole this letter aims at *exhortation,* encouraging the Smyrneans to press on.

How different things appear in Laodicea (Rev. 3:14–22)! Here, we meet a church in much more comfortable circumstances. According to Jesus, the Laodicean Christians congratulate themselves. "I am rich, I have prospered, and I need nothing." Yet on the whole their situation is the obverse of that in Smyrna. Thinking themselves rich, they are in fact "wretched, pitiable, poor, blind, and naked." Neither hot nor cold, their works reflect a lukewarm discipleship, so Jesus threatens to spit the Laodiceans out from his mouth. This letter voices *admonition,* for "I reprove and discipline those whom I love."

Two of the seven letters congratulate the churches and exhort them, two censure and admonish them, but three offer mixed reports. The churches in Pergamum (2:12–17) and Thyatira (2:18–28) receive congratulations for their steadfastness and continuing service, yet Jesus warns against their tolerance of competing prophets. Jesus commands the entire church at Pergamum to repent, though in Thyatira he requires contrition from only some members of the audience.

We can easily imagine how apocalyptic discourse could sponsor both exhortation and admonition. Exhortation might look like this: "The time is near; keep at it!" Admonition simply adjusts the direction: "The time is near; stop that!" Another obvious function is *consolation.* When Paul addresses the Thessalonians' concern for those who have died before Jesus' return, he concludes, "Comfort one another with these words" (1 Thess. 4:18, author's trans.). For those who live in distress, apocalyptic comfort implies a final resolution to suffering.

So exhortation, admonition, and consolation provide obvious uses for apocalyptic eschatology. We might even press beyond these functions to greater levels of specificity. For example, we have seen apocalyptic discourse function as a sort of laboratory for *cosmological and theological reasoning.* For example, cosmic tours such as those we find in 1 Enoch reflect not only a doctrinal interest but also a genuine concern to understand the movements of heavenly bodies, the reasons for the weather, and the like. Without a fully developed scientific method, people sought orderly ways to account for their observations.

In this way some sections of 1 Enoch sound as much like the Greek pre-Socratic philosophers as they resemble, say, Daniel or Revelation. Because ancient people typically associated heavenly bodies with sacred beings, we readily understand why 1 Enoch's discussions of the stars and planets so smoothly blend with its speculations concerning the righteous and wicked angels.

Apocalyptic discourse also provides the space for 4 Ezra to pursue *theodicy,* the defense of God's justice. Although we have argued that theodicy represents a secondary concern for the book, Ezra's dialogues with the heavenly being express both poignant challenges to God's administration and the eschatological scenario according to which all things work out in the end. The most remarkable thing about 4 Ezra's engagement with theodicy is not that the angel resolves Ezra's questions; he doesn't. Instead, Ezra's satisfaction is experiential rather than abstractly theological. Only his own religious experience moves Ezra from one who distrusts the angel's answers to one prepared to voice them for himself. Instead of argument, 4 Ezra prefers mysticism.

Of course, people can turn apocalyptic discourse against others, aiming *polemic* attacks against particular ideas, people, or movements. Jubilees and the Ascension of Isaiah certainly engage theological speculation. Jubilees explores the roles and identities of heavenly beings, and the Ascension considers how the Beloved One could descend from his glorious heavenly state and live among humankind undetected. Both texts also target particular enemies. Jubilees expresses discontent with the Jerusalem priesthood, who follow a faulty calendar and improperly administer the sacrifices. The Ascension employs the Jewish legend of Isaiah's martyrdom as a vehicle for blaming Jews for failing to acknowledge Jesus. After all, Isaiah and even King Hezekiah had received revelations of the Beloved, but the people chose to reject them. Isaiah's vision of Jesus, then, lends itself to Christian arguments against their non-Christian Jewish neighbors.

Apocalyptic discourse can also build *authority.*[18] Only when confronted by challenges so serious that he refers to them as "other gospels" does Paul appeal to his own personal revelations (2 Cor. 11–12; Gal. 1). Facing down the "superapostles" who have won over some of the Corinthians, Paul recalls his tour of the third heaven, or Paradise. Over against those who had persuaded the Galatians that participation in Christianity also implies conversion to Judaism, Paul stands his ground: He received his gospel directly from God by an *apocalypse.*

One of apocalyptic discourse's most powerful uses involves its application to *regulate community identity and behavior.* The book of Revelation warns against soiling one's garments (3:4; cf. 7:14), expressing an aversion to contamination by a pagan culture. The Apocalypses of Peter and Paul both dramatize what is at stake for Christians who veer from the paths of righteousness. Apocalyptic discourse provides many such resources for strengthening communal identity and solidifying social boundaries. Take the metaphor of "light" and "darkness," for example. Paul uses it to mark off his audience's distinctive identity. "You are all children of light," Paul argues, so you should live in a distinctive way (1 Thess. 5:4–11). Though Paul does not advocate violence, apocalyptic discourse encourages a baseline enmity between the in-group and the out-group. Among the Dead Sea Scrolls, the enigmatic War Scroll (1QM) envisions an eschatological battle between the "sons of light" and the "sons of darkness." Despite its apparent subject matter, however, the War Rule does not sketch out an actual plan. Rather, it instills a distinctive sense of identity. Standing among the sons of light locates one among the righteous remnant on whose side the angels fight. Even if the group seems small, their positive identification as God's holy army empowers them to hold together.

How flexible is apocalyptic discourse? As Wayne A. Meeks has observed, it can even serve opposite ends, whether to *sustain cultural values* or to *argue for innovation*.[19] In the wake of Jerusalem's devastation by the Romans, 4 Ezra and 2 Baruch return to traditional values. Obedience to the Torah represents the path to individual and corporate salvation. But the Acts of the Apostles and the Shepherd of Hermas argue for new practices and concepts. Acts employs visions to justify the inclusion of Gentiles among the churches without requiring their full conversion to Judaism. Two key revelations legitimate this practice—Paul's encounter with the risen Jesus on the way to Damascus accompanied by the vision to the disciple Ananias, and Peter's vision of the unclean food prior to his encounter with Cornelius. Among other things, the audience learns of Paul's commission to the Gentiles, and Peter learns that "What God has made clean, you must not call profane" (10:15). To make the point even more strongly, Acts repeats these stories, narrating Paul's vision three times (9:1–29; 22:3–21; 26:9–20) and Peter's twice (10:9–48; 11:1–17). Likewise, the Shepherd of Hermas addresses what must have posed a controversial problem in the early church: whether people whose faithfulness had failed them, especially in the face of persecution, could return to good standing before the church and before God. Hermas's revelation expresses the answer: The Shepherd allows for the forgiveness of post-baptismal sin, but only once and for a limited time (Vis. 2.2.4–8; Man. 4.3.1–7). This doctrinal innovation derives its authority solely from its association with a heavenly revelation.

Many texts employ apocalyptic discourse to *sustain struggling communities*. When we reflect upon the Shepherd of Hermas, we observe this phenomenon at several levels. For example, its innovation concerning repentance–one opportunity for repentance of post-baptismal sin–works in a couple of directions, extending both a carrot and a switch. In a context of anticipated persecution, Hermas offers a chance for failed Christians to return to the community–that's the carrot–but the switch reminds the audience of apostasy's serious consequences. Together, the invitation to return and the warning concerning sin encourage people to take their participation in the community seriously. In the face of persecution, Hermas's warnings against double-mindedness likewise bolster community solidarity, promising success to those who persevere but warning of judgment for those who waver.

Apocalyptic discourse can also *voice political critique and resistance.* Some interpreters, for whom Daniel and Revelation effectively define apocalyptic literature, have oversimplified matters by claiming apocalyptic discourse as the exclusive language of the oppressed. Acknowledging that overstatement, we must recognize that apocalyptic discourse does present powerful tools for political engagement. Daniel, after all, contrasts the "beastly" imperial powers with the "human" rule ordained by God, specifically characterizing Antiochus Epiphanes as a "contemptible person" who has gained power by intrigue (11:21). According to Revelation, Rome's power and glory, seen through the Beast and the Whore, merely conceal its dependence on corruption and death. Almost like the power of contemporary animation, apocalyptic discourse enables this kind of critique through its ability to depict an alternative reality and its claim to reach into the future. Consider how Sibylline Oracle Five (5:137–54) indicts the notorious Nero's past, even as it speculates concerning his fate. A "great king of Rome," a "godlike man," purported offspring of Zeus and Hera, Nero has murdered his own mother and his pregnant wife. Yet the Oracle also imagines Nero coming to shame, fleeing to Babylon for refuge under public scorn. Other forms of literature could convey these characterizations, even as I have done so here, but with apocalyptic discourse the oracle seamlessly combines the rumors concerning Nero's past with frightening possibilities concerning his unknown fate.

This discussion merely synthesizes what we have already seen. Throughout this book we have explored apocalyptic discourse's flexibility and imaginative potential. Yet in a popular culture that reduces apocalyptic literature to a fascination with catastrophe or to its supposed ability to analyze the news or predict the future events, no wonder many people simply dismiss these ancient texts as bizarre relics. Either alternative–holding on to the hope the we can map God's plan for the final days or sending off apocalyptic literature into benign neglect–loses sight of the rich and varied power demonstrated by ancient apocalyptic discourse. Surely we can find more creative ways to engage it.

Apocalyptic Discourse and Contemporary Christian Communities

Some people reject apocalyptic discourse due to its political subversiveness or its visionary violence. Others cling to it as the only way to interpret a chaotic present and predict an orderly future. Perhaps many, many more people simply push it aside, an odd and perhaps unfortunate deposit from a primitive past.

The past few decades have witnessed revived engagement with apocalyptic discourse on the part of Christian theologians. In the mid twentieth century we observed the conflict between Ernst Käsemann, who named apocalyptic eschatology "the mother of all Christian theology," and Rudolf Bultmann, who asserted that the "mythological" character of ancient eschatology must be reinterpreted for modern persons who cannot share its world view.[20] Both thinkers acknowledged the pervasive status of apocalyptic eschatology throughout the New Testament. Every level of the New Testament, these scholars acknowledged, from traces of the historical Jesus, to Q and the Synoptic Tradition, to John's gospel and Paul's epistles and beyond, reflects and develops apocalyptic topics. The question was—and is—whether and how contemporary readers can make sense of eschatology in general, and of apocalyptic eschatology in particular.

Some Christians hold a view of scripture that implies that all biblical "predictions" must somehow come to pass. Even in these circles we find an expanding awareness of the poetic dimension of apocalyptic discourse. For example, some acknowledge the tension between imminent expectation of Jesus' return and awareness of its delay within the New Testament, and some recognize that biblical authors themselves reinterpreted scripture to address later circumstances. Such readers might pass over literal details for a more general application: Even though Revelation identifies the eschatological Beast with Rome, contemporary Christians ought not await a last-days revival of the Roman Empire. Yet the expectation of some literal and future manifestation of the Beast remains.[21] Others turn to literary theory and linguistic philosophy to appreciate the poetic nature of apocalyptic discourse. Thus, D. Brent Sandy emphasizes the poetic nature of end-time language, yet he also cannot resist enumerating certain things we *know* about the future; for example,

> Jesus will return in the most dramatic divine visitation of earth ever to occur. Precisely what circumstances will accompany his return are not clear, but we will certainly recognize it when it happens.[22]

Sustaining the elusive balance between recognizing apocalyptic symbolism and adhering to a doctrinally determined understanding of biblical inspiration forces this choice: Eventually one must distill the authentic predictions from among the vivid images.

Most critical readers find these solutions dissatisfying. Apocalyptic literature does not require that we develop interpretive shoehorns with which we may squeeze every biblical text into a snug fit, but rather it evokes an active and creative engagement of the sort that the ancient authors themselves employed.

Among recent Christian theologies that have indeed appropriated apocalyptic discourse, two particular movements stand out. Liberation theologians, who emphasize the gospel's implications for economic and social justice, have found an affinity for the "hunger and thirst for righteousness" expressed in apocalyptic literature. A more diffuse trend has sought to reclaim an apocalyptic vision through serious engagement with–but not literal acceptance of–biblical images such as Jesus' return on clouds, pearly gates, and golden streets.

One way to engage apocalyptic discourse is to fuse the experiences of one's own time and place with the circumstances of the ancient texts. This interpretive model marks liberationist readers in particular. Locating biblical apocalyptic discourse among oppressed communities in ancient Judaism and Christianity, liberationists find instructive points of correspondence between their own experiences and those of their biblical forebears. This model transcends culture and location. In Costa Rica, Pablo Richard recognizes the mythical (i.e., non-literal) nature of Revelation's symbols, arguing that their purpose "is to enable us to discern when an authority is beast and when it is not."[23] In the United States, African American scholar Brian K. Blount rejects the notion that Revelation simply helps oppressed people sleep off their suffering. Instead, drawing upon a host of African American activists, Blount finds in their testimony–and that of the Apocalypse–a call to witness against injustice, to take on practices that lead toward freedom.[24] Writing from Apartheid South Africa, Allen A. Boesak adopted the scholarly opinion that apocalyptic literature always surfaces among the persecuted. Somehow looking beyond the horror in which he lived, Boesak proclaimed that Revelation forces the choice between God and Caesar, while offering hope for God's suffering people.[25] And in India, C. I. David Joy appropriates Revelation to articulate a "human based value system and eco-friendly trade and development" over against the postcolonial global economy.[26]

Feminist liberationists have found it more difficult to appropriate apocalyptic discourse so directly, particularly the book of Revelation. It comes as no coincidence that two influential students of apocalyptic literature and of Revelation–Elisabeth Schüssler Fiorenza and Adela Yarbro Collins–have contributed mightily to the development of feminist biblical interpretation in general.[27] Revelation features extremely troublesome female images, among other problems. This has led some feminist commentators to conclude that Revelation's desire for the destruction of this world intertwines with "the desire for and death of the female."[28] Indeed, in her essay "A Good Apocalypse Is Hard to Find" Tina Pippin maintains that *all* apocalyptic end-talk implies bad news for most people.[29]

Yet while Yarbro Collins and Schüssler Fiorenza acknowledge Revelation's dangers, they also call attention to its liberative dimensions. Yarbro Collins stresses Revelation's ambiguity: Revelation may be "a partial and imperfect vision,"[30] but it also "expresses the anguish of those who live on the margins," offering hope for them and a challenge for the comfortable.[31] Schüssler Fiorenza inclines toward more direct advocacy. Revelation packs dangerous potential, both in its characterization of the feminine and in its visions of destruction, but interpreters may emphasize its passion for justice. Schüssler Fiorenza calls attention to Revelation's resistance against Roman hegemony, but she also calls for "critical assessment and theo-ethical evaluation" by contemporary readers.[32] One *chooses* how to read Revelation:

> Such a liberationist reading of Revelation's rhetoric subordinates the book's depiction of cosmic destruction and holy war to its desire for justice, which is repeated throughout the book. It puts in the foreground those rhetorical features of the text that aim at moving the audience to practical engagement in this struggle for God's qualitatively new world of salvation.[33]

If liberationist readers construct a serious dialogue with apocalyptic discourse, so do contemporary theologians who emphasize the poetic and imaginative dimensions of apocalyptic language. Eschatology's most prominent spokesperson over the past thirty years has been the German theologian Jürgen Moltmann.[34] Moltmann considers how apocalyptic images of chaos speak to people's misery in the present age. He appreciates how apocalyptic eschatology fundamentally emerges from convictions concerning God's faithfulness. For Christians, this means that apocalyptic hope springs from the resurrection of Jesus as a sign of God's intention for all of creation.[35] To take apocalyptic eschatology seriously, then, means to stand in a paradoxical relationship between past and future. One grounds one's hopes for the future in the demonstrations of God's faithfulness to Israel and the church, but one also recognizes a "qualitative differentiation between past and future."[36] Thus, theological description cannot hope to capture the future, but must imagine it by analogy to past and present experience.[37]

Like many modern critics, Moltmann expresses reservations concerning the violent imagination of contemporary millenarianism. The temptation, according to Moltmann, is the fascination with the eschatological chaos. Such fascination overlooks eschatology's proper setting within the larger trajectory of God's purposes: the salvation of the world. Grounded in conviction concerning God's faithfulness, he argues, eschatological hope does not immobilize people; rather, it leads them into active engagement with the world.

> [It] causes not rest but unrest, not patience but impatience...Those who hope in Christ can no longer put up with reality as it is, but begin to suffer under it, to contradict it...This hope makes the Christian church a constant disturbance in human society...[and] the source of new impulses towards the realization of righteousness, freedom and humanity here in the light of the promised future that is to come.[38]

Without expressing direct dependence on Moltmann, Richard Bauckham and Trevor Hart also appeal to the poetic dimension of eschatological discourse. Apocalyptic literature's ancient readers would not have understood their texts as charting the course of history, they reason, so neither should we.[39] Instead, the ancients developed imaginative–as opposed to imaginary–ways of drawing upon common experiences and symbols to depict the radical otherness of God's future.[40] Like literary fantasy, eschatological discourse disturbs conventional ways of perceiving the world by introducing elements that stretch our conceptions of ordinary reality.[41] The point is not to spell out details about the future, but to dramatize the dramatic otherness of God's intentions for the world over against present conditions. Like Moltmann, Bauckham and Hart ground eschatological discourse in the faithfulness of God. And like Moltmann, they argue that imagining a radically different future sets people free for action in the present, particularly for resistance against oppression.[42]

Bauckham and Hart develop what is basically a pragmatic argument: People *need* eschatological imagination that empowers them to resist hurtful and oppressive practices. To Moltmann's eschatological vision, they add literary and philosophical sophistication concerning *how* apocalyptic discourse functions. They take one more vital step by dealing with specific apocalyptic topics directly. Drawing upon Bauckham's expertise in ancient Jewish and Christian apocalyptic literature, they identify ten "images of hope" from biblical eschatology. For example, when modern readers consider Jesus' return, the parousia, they can scarcely force themselves to imagine an event experienced by every person around the globe ("every eye will see him"; Rev. 1:7). As we have seen, some people *try* to convince themselves so, but that's quite a reach for most of us. So Bauckham and Hart take this distinctively apocalyptic image "seriously, not literally." What's really at stake in the parousia, they argue, is "the achievement by Jesus Christ of the full and final sovereignty of God over the world," something hidden from our present vision.[43]

This sensitivity to the poetic and evocative nature of apocalyptic discourse forces choices upon contemporary Christian thinkers. How much can we say–in ordinary language–about ultimate things? From biblical apocalyptic discourse one might distill a core affirmation something like the one formulated by Richard B. Hays:

> the ultimate glorification of Jesus Christ as Lord over all creation, the resurrection of the body, God's final judgment of all humanity, and the "life of the world to come" in true justice and peace.[44]

Or one may tend toward agnosticism about the specifics, embracing an eschatology that hints toward something more nebulous, as in Valarie A. Karras's evocation of "creation's uniting itself ever more organically to God."[45] In the face of such diverse possibilities, these various contemporary appropriations of eschatology share a fundamental assessment: Because humankind and the cosmos have not demonstrated the potential to save themselves, their ultimate salvation resides in the newness of God's future.[46]

What we see in contemporary theological discourse is a movement *back* toward serious engagement with eschatology in general and apocalyptic discourse in particular. Whereas many have marginalized apocalyptic discourse as irrelevant to the modern imagination, new voices find it an essential dimension of Christian expression. Liberationists valorize its potential to reveal present injustices and to inspire resistance, while others point to its power to imagine an alternative future that transforms how people live in the present.

A *Final* Thought: Really

Is there a logic to apocalyptic discourse? If we expect apocalyptic discourse to submit to a single rubric of analysis, we'll likely disappoint ourselves. Yet we may have found a hint within our survey of contemporary theological reflection. Apocalyptic discourse starts with convictions concerning the character of God and what God is about in the world, then it projects those convictions upon unfamiliar or unknown circumstances. Conviction fuels eschatological imagination.

Let us consider one example, Paul's teaching regarding the resurrection and the parousia in 1 Thessalonians 4:13–5:11. How does Paul arrive at his conviction that the righteous dead will rise to meet Christ even before those who are alive? What is the source of his graphic imagery, in which the saints meet Jesus in the air?

One might suggest two sources for this conception. Perhaps Paul has received this teaching from early Christian tradition, which he is just passing along. Or maybe Paul has received this information through an independent revelation. We know of other such cases in Paul's writings.

Both suggestions make sense, but what if we approached this passage as a creative theological response to the needs of his audience? Paul has proclaimed a gospel that includes the resurrection and the parousia. But his audience consists of converted pagans (1 Thess. 1:9–10) who are new to such hopes. When some of their beloved companions in the faith die before Jesus' return, these new believers experience severe disorientation. Did our friends believe in vain? If *we* die, might we also fail to receive these eschatological blessings? Faced with this crisis, how does Paul respond?

I would suggest that Paul answers with both conviction and imagination. We modern people tend to assume that these two values tug against each other, but not so in apocalyptic discourse. Paul considers his gospel: Jesus has been raised, and he is returning to gather his people. Even if some have died, God remains faithful. This is Paul's conviction: No one will be left out. "For since we believe that Jesus died and rose again, even so, through Jesus, God will bring with him those who have died" (4:14). And now for the imagination: How does Paul communicate this radical expectation? He turns to the conventional language of Christian apocalyptic expectation. Jesus will return on the clouds with the sound of a trumpet. When he does, God's people will be there to meet him! Conviction expresses itself in imagination, so that Paul can console his audience: "Therefore encourage one another with these words" (4:18).

Religious expression necessarily involves this blend of conviction and imagination. One can scarcely find richer resources for that process than we find in apocalyptic discourse.

FOR FURTHER READING

Bauckham, Richard, and Trevor Hart. *Hope against Hope: Christian Eschatology at the Turn of the Millennium.* Grand Rapids, Mich.: Eerdmans, 1999.

Boesak, Allan A. *Comfort and Protest: The Apocalypse from a South African Perspective.* Philadelphia: Westminster Press, 1987.

Boyer, Paul. *When Time Shall Be No More: Prophecy Belief in Modern American Culture.* Cambridge, Mass.: Harvard University Press, 1992.

Hill, Craig C. *In God's Time: The Bible and the Future.* Grand Rapids, Mich.: Eerdmans, 2002.

Idel, Moshe. "Jewish Apocalypticism: 670–1670." Pages 204–37 in *The Encyclopedia of Apocalypticism: Volume 2: Apocalypticism in Western History and Culture.* Edited by Bernard McGinn. New York: Continuum, 2000.

Karras, Valerie A. "Eschatology." Pages 243–60 in *The Cambridge Companion to Feminist Theology.* Edited by Susan Frank Parsons. New York: Cambridge University Press, 2002.

Keller, Catherine. *Apocalypse Now and Then: A Feminist Guide to the End of the World.* Boston: Beacon, 1996.

Moltmann, Jürgen. *The Coming of God: Christian Eschatology.* Translated by Margaret Kohl. Minneapolis: Fortress Press, 1996.

O'Leary, Stephen D. *Arguing the Apocalypse: A Theory of Millennial Rhetoric.* New York: Oxford University Press, 1994.

Pippin, Tina. "A Good Apocalypse Is Hard to Find: Crossing the Apocalyptic Borders of Mark 13." *Semeia* 72 (1995): 153–71.

Schüssler Fiorenza, Elisabeth. *The Book of Revelation: Justice and Judgment.* 2d ed. Minneapolis: Fortress Press, 1998.

Wainwright, Arthur W. *Mysterious Apocalypse: Interpreting the Book of Revelation.* Nashville: Abingdon Press, 1993.

Notes

Introduction

[1]Umberto Eco, *Baudolino* (New York: Harcourt, 2002), 99.

[2]Notable exceptions apply.

[3]Stephen D. O'Leary, *Arguing the Apocalypse: A Theory of Millennial Rhetoric* (New York: Oxford University Press, 1994); Greg Carey, *Elusive Apocalypse: Reading Authority in the Revelation to John* (StABH 15; Macon, Ga.: Mercer University Press, 1999).

[4]O'Leary, *Arguing the Apocalypse*, 77.

[5]John J. Collins, "Introduction: Towards the Morphology of a Genre," *Semeia* 14 (1979): 9.

[6]James C. VanderKam, *An Introduction to Early Judaism* (Grand Rapids, Mich.: Eerdmans, 2001), 102.

[7]Paul D. Hanson, "Apocalypses and Apocalypticism," *ABD*, 1.281.

[8]For *apocalypse, apocalyptic eschatology,* and *apocalypticism,* see Paul D. Hanson, "Apocalypse, Genre" and "Apocalypticism," *IDBSup* 27–34; and "Apocalypses and Apocalypticism," *ABD,* 1.279–81.

[9]For the addition, Adela Yarbro Collins, "Introduction: Early Christian Apocalypticism," *Semeia* 36 (1986): 7; John J. Collins, "Genre, Ideology, and Social Movements in Jewish Apocalypticism," in *Mysteries and Revelations: Apocalyptic Studies since the Uppsala Colloquium* (ed. John J. Collins and James H. Charlesworth; JSPSup 9; Sheffield: Sheffield Academic Press, 1991), 24. John J. Collins has omitted this functional amendment in his revised *The Apocalyptic Imagination: An Introduction to Jewish Apocalyptic Literature* (2d ed.; The Biblical Resource Series; Grand Rapids, Mich.: Eerdmans, 1998), 5. Cf. Greg Carey, "Introduction: Apocalyptic Discourse, Apocalyptic Rhetoric," in *Vision and Persuasion: Rhetorical Dimensions of Apocalyptic Discourse* (ed. Greg Carey and L. Gregory Bloomquist; St. Louis: Chalice Press, 1999), 9; and L. Gregory Bloomquist, "Methodological Criteria for Apocalyptic Rhetoric: A Suggestion for the Expanded Use of Sociorhetorical Analysis," in *Vision and Persuasion,* 183.

[10]Linda Hutcheon, *The Politics of Postmodernism* (New Accents; New York: Routledge, 1989), 7; Chris Weedon, *Feminist Practice and Poststructuralist Theory* (Cambridge, Mass.: Blackwell, 1987), 35.

[11]Cf. Edward W. Said, *Orientalism* (New York: Vintage, 1979), 94.

[12]By way of analogy, consider Michel Foucault's distinction between the "scientific" discourse concerning sexuality that is so prominent in Europe and North America with more "artistic" discourses in other societies (*Religion and Culture* [ed. Jeremy R. Carrette; New York: Routledge, 1999], 120–22). Foucault's work on discourses of mental health, rehabilitation, and sexuality is formative for this approach to discourse. Cf. Foucault, *Madness and Civilization* (New York: Random House, 1965); *The Order of Things: An Archaeology of the Human Sciences* (New York: Random House, 1970); *Discipline and Punish: The Birth of the Prison* (New York: Pantheon, 1977); *The History of Sexuality, Volume 1: An Introduction* (New York: Random House, 1978).

[13]Stephen D. O'Leary, *Arguing the Apocalypse,* 22; cf. O'Leary's broader discussion in pp. 20–60. Whereas the term *topos* derives from the Greek rhetorical tradition, studies in comparative rhetoric reveal the self-conscious elaboration of *topoi* in a variety of cultural contexts (George A. Kennedy, *Comparative Rhetoric: An Historical and Cross-Cultural Introduction* [New York: Oxford University Press, 1998]).

[14]Cf. Vernon K. Robbins, "The Intertexture of Apocalyptic Discourse in the Gospel of Mark," in *The Intertexture of Apocalyptic Discourse in the New Testament* (ed. Duane F. Watson; SBLSymS 14; Atlanta: Society of Biblical Literature, 2002), 11–18; Robbins, *The Tapestry of Early Christian Discourse: Rhetoric, Society, and Ideology* (New York: Routledge, 1996), 147–91.

[15]Carey, "Introduction," 10. Cf. the application of this framework by several scholars in Duane F. Watson, ed., *The Intertexture of Apocalyptic Discourse in the New Testament* (SBLSymS 14; Atlanta: Society of Biblical Literature, 2002), 1, 11, 60, 138.

[16]This discussion both relies on and modifies my earlier discussion in "Introduction," 4–5.

[17]Stephen D. O'Leary identifies time, evil, and authority as the fundamental *topoi* of apocalyptic rhetoric (*Arguing the Apocalypse, 20–60.* However, O'Leary's primary interests

245

were in building a rhetorical framework that could account for both the book of Revelation and contemporary millenarian discourse. O'Leary did not consider the broad range of ancient apocalyptic literature, which in some cases reflects more interest in space than in time. The work of the Society of Biblical Literature Apocalypse Group first called attention to the prominence of otherworldly speculation in apocalyptic literature (John J. Collins, ed., *Apocalypse: The Morphology of a Genre, Semeia* 14 [1979]).

[18]Greg Carey, "Apocalyptic *Ethos*," *SBLSP* 37/2 (1998): 731–61.

[19]Eco, *Baudolino*, 125.

[20]Wayne A. Meeks, "Social Functions of Apocalyptic Language in Pauline Christianity," *AMWNE*, 687–705.

[21]Contemporary prophecy teachers appeal to this principle. If some biblical prophecies (as they interpret them) have come to pass, then the fulfillment of others must lie in the future. The classic instance of this argument appears in Hal Lindsey, *The Late Great Planet Earth* (Grand Rapids, Mich.: Zondervan, 1970), 9–31.

[22]Collins, "Genre, Ideology," 24.

[23]Martin Dibelius, "The Shepherd of Hermas," *NTA*, 2.642, cited in Tarif Khalidi, *The Muslim Jesus: Sayings and Stories in Islamic Literature* (Cambridge, Mass.: Harvard University Press, 2001), 17.

[24]Though they offer diverse perspectives, I have found the following sources especially helpful on the relationship among apocalyptic, wisdom, and prophetic discourses: Jonathan Z. Smith, "Wisdom and Apocalyptic," in *Map Is Not Territory: Studies in the History of Religions* (SJLA 23; Leiden: Brill, 1978), 67–87; John J. Collins, "Wisdom, Apocalypticism, and Generic Compatibility," in *In Search of Wisdom: Essays in Memory of John G. Gammie* (ed. Leo G. Perdue, Bernard Brandon Scott, and William Johnston Wiseman; Louisville: Westminster John Knox Press, 1993), 165–85; Collins, *Apocalyptic Imagination*, 23–42; Collins, "From Prophecy to Apocalypticism: The Expectation of the End," in *The Encyclopedia of Apocalypticism: Volume 1: The Origins of Apocalypticism in Judaism and Early Christianity* (ed. John J. Collins; New York: Continuum, 1998), 129–61; Frederick J. Murphy, "Introduction to Apocalyptic Literature," *NIB*, 7.4–7; Michael E. Stone, "Apocalyptic Literature," in *Jewish Writings of the Second Temple Period* (ed. Michael E. Stone; CRINT 2/2; Philadelphia: Fortress Press, 1984), 383–92; and N. T. Wright, *Jesus and the Victory of God* (Minneapolis: Fortress Press, 1996), 311–16.

[25]Cf. Markus Bockmuehl, *Revelation and Mystery in Ancient Judaism and Pauline Christianity* (Grand Rapids, Mich.: Eerdmans, 1997), esp. 24–41.

[26]Collins, *Apocalyptic Imagination.*

[27]Eco, *Baudolino*, 122.

[28]Ibid., 123.

[29]See Collins, *Apocalyptic Imagination*, 108–9.

[30]Paul D. Hanson, *The Dawn of Apocalyptic: The Historical and Sociological Roots of Jewish Apocalyptic Eschatology* (rev. ed.; Philadelphia: Fortress Press, 1979), esp. 408–9, 435. Hanson applies this principle so rigorously as to exclude Zechariah as a primary source for apocalyptic eschatology on the grounds that Zechariah represents a group that possesses power (251).

[31]For a case-by-case rebuttal of Hanson's position, see Stephen L. Cook, *Prophecy and Apocalypticism: The Postexilic Social Setting* (Minneapolis: Fortress Press, 1995).

[32]O'Leary, *Arguing the Apocalypse.*

[33]Richard A. Horsley, "The Kingdom of God and the Renewal of Israel: Synoptic Gospels, Jesus Movements, and Apocalypticism," in *The Encyclopedia of Apocalypticism: Volume 1: The Origins of Apocalypticism in Judaism and Christianity* (ed. John J. Collins; New York: Continuum, 1998), 308–9.

[34]David A. deSilva, "Fourth Ezra: Reaffirming Jewish Cultural Values through Apocalyptic Rhetoric," in *Vision and Persuasion: Rhetorical Dimensions of Apocalyptic Discourse* (ed. Greg Carey and L. Gregory Bloomquist; St. Louis: Chalice Press, 1999), 126–27.

[35]Horsley, "Kingdom of God," 309.

[36]See Wayne A. Meeks's seminal essay on apocalyptic discourse in Paul's writings, "Social Functions of Apocalyptic Language in Pauline Christianity," in *AMWNE*, 700.

Chapter 1: The Earliest Apocalypses

[1]See J. T. Milik, *The Books of Enoch: Aramaic Fragments from Qumran Cave 4* (Oxford: Clarendon, 1976).

²For discussion of the available manuscript tradition, see George W. E. Nickelsburg, *1 Enoch 1: A Commentary on the Book of 1 Enoch, Chapters 1–36; 81–108* (Hermeneia; Minneapolis: Fortress Press, 2001), 9–20. Nickelsburg's commentary is by far the most definitive source on 1 Enoch available in English.

³Again, for a concise assessment of 1 Enoch's continuing influence and authority, see Nickelsburg, *1 Enoch 1*, 71–108. Cf. James C. VanderKam, *Enoch: A Man for All Generations* (Studies on Personalities of the Old Testament; Columbia: University of South Carolina Press, 1995); VanderKam, *Enoch and the Growth of an Apocalyptic Tradition* (CBQMS 16; Washington, D.C.: Catholic Biblical Association, 1984); and Philip S. Alexander, "From Son of Man to Second God: Transformations of the Biblical Enoch," in *Biblical Figures Outside the Bible* (ed. Michael E. Stone and Theodore A. Bergen; Harrisburg, Pa.: Trinity Press International, 1998), 87–122.

⁴VanderKam, *Enoch: A Man for All Generations*, 174–75.

⁵Alexander, "From Son of Man to Second God," 107–10, is fascinating on this point.

⁶Matthew Black, in consultation with James C. VanderKam, *The Book of Enoch or 1 Enoch: A New English Edition with Commentary and Textual Notes* (Leiden: Brill, 1985), 106.

⁷Alexander, "From Son of Adam to Second God," 87. Scholars have speculated that Enoch may have developed from an appropriation of Mesopotamian traditions such as the diviner king Enmeduranki, but one wonders whether ancient Jewish audiences would have recognized this association (VanderKam, *Enoch and the Growth of an Apocalyptic Tradition*, 33–51, 91–104).

⁸For discussion, see VanderKam, *Enoch: A Man for All Generations*, 110–21.

⁹In the Qran the name occurs as "Idris."

¹⁰Greg Carey, "Apocalyptic *Ethos*," *SBLSP* 37/2 (1998): 731–61.

¹¹Matthew Black, "The Messianism of the Parables of Enoch: Their Date and Contributions to Christian Origins," in *The Messiah: Developments in Earliest Judaism and Christianity* (ed. James H. Charlesworth; Minneapolis: Fortress Press, 1992), 166.

¹²The syntax is ambiguous. Isaac, *OTP*, renders the key phrase, "You, son of man," while the other major English translations read something like, "You are the Son of Man" (Black, *Book of Enoch*; R. H. Charles, *The Book of Enoch* [Oxford: Clarendon, 1893]; M. A. Knibb, "Martyrdom and Ascension of Isaiah," in *OTP* vol. 2, 143–76.

¹³VanderKam, *Enoch: A Man for All Generations*, 141–42; VanderKam, "Righteous One, Messiah, Chosen One, and Son of Man in 1 Enoch 37–71," in *The Messiah: Developments in Earliest Judaism and Christianity* (ed. James H. Charlesworth; Minneapolis: Fortress Press, 1992), 177–85.

¹⁴VanderKam opposes this view ("Righteous One," 179–80).

¹⁵Gabriele Boccaccini, "Jewish Apocalyptic Tradition: The Contribution of Italian Scholarship," in *Mysteries and Revelations: Apocalyptic Studies since the Uppsala Colloquium* (ed. John J. Collins and James H. Charlesworth; JSPSup 9; Sheffield: JSPT Press, 1991), 34.

¹⁶George W. E. Nickelsburg, "The Apocalyptic Construction of Reality in *1 Enoch*," in *Mysteries and Revelations: Apocalyptic Studies since the Uppsala Colloquium* (ed. John J. Collins and James H. Charlesworth; JSPSup 9; Sheffield: JSPT Press, 1991), 53–57.

¹⁷For the classic formulation of this axiom, see John J. Collins, "Introduction: Towards the Morphology of a Genre," *Semeia* 14 (1979): 1–20.

¹⁸ For discussion of this difficult problem, see Nickelsburg, *1 Enoch*, 306–9.

¹⁹Richard Bauckham, *The Fate of the Dead: Studies on the Jewish and Christian Apocalypses* (NovTSup 93; Leiden: Brill, 1998), 55.

²⁰VanderKam, "Righteous One," 169–70.

²¹For reservations concerning the Bull's messianic status, see George W. E. Nickelsburg, "Salvation without and with a Messiah: Developing Beliefs in Writings Ascribed to Enoch," in *Judaisms and Their Messiahs at the Turn of the Christian Era* (ed. Jacob Neusner, William S. Green, and Ernest Frerichs; Cambridge: Cambridge University Press, 1987), 55–56.

²²Black's translation, *Book of Enoch*, 51.

²³Bauckham, *Fate of the Dead*, 255.

²⁴John Kaltner has identified a similar strategy in Daniel ("Is Daniel Also among the Prophets? The Rhetoric of Daniel 10–12," in *Vision and Persuasion: Rhetorical Dimensions of Apocalyptic Discourse* [ed. Greg Carey and L. Gregory Bloomquist; St. Louis: Chalice Press, 1999], 41–59).

[25]Christopher Rowland, *The Open Heaven: A Study of Apocalyptic in Judaism and Early Christianity* (New York: Crossroad, 1982), 222.

[26]For discussion of Enoch's throne vision, see Martha Himmelfarb, *Ascent to Heaven in Jewish and Christian Apocalypses* (Oxford: Oxford University Press, 1993), 9–28.

[27]Nickelsburg, *1 Enoch 1*, 287–88.

[28]Rowland, *Open Heaven*, 232.

[29]Himmelfarb, *Ascent*, 21.

[30]Martin Luther King, Jr., "Where Do We Go from Here?" in *A Testament of Hope: The Essential Writings of Martin Luther King, Jr.* (ed. James Melvin Washington; San Francisco: Harper & Row, 1986), 252. King frequently adapted Theodore Parker's maxim, "The moral arc of the universe is long, but it bends toward justice."

[31]*Where's God When I'm S-scared?* VeggieTales video (Chicago: Big Idea Productions, 1994); *Rack, Shack, and Benny,* VeggieTales video (Chicago: Big Idea Productions, 1995).

[32]While some passages in scripture, notably Psalm 49:15; Isaiah 26:19; Ezekiel 37; and Job 19:25–27, apparently express hope for life after death, Daniel offers the first clear expression of resurrection hope.

[33]Adela Yarbro Collins, "The Influence of Daniel on the New Testament," in John J. Collins, *Daniel: A Commentary on the Book of Daniel* (ed. Frank Moore Cross; Hermeneia; Minneapolis: Fortress Press, 1993), 90–123.

[34]For discussions of Daniel's influence, see Gregory K. Beale, *The Use of Daniel in Jewish Apocalyptic Literature and in the Revelation of St. John* (Lanham, Md.: University Press of America, 1984); Klaus Koch, "Stages in the Canonization of the Book of Daniel," in *The Book of Daniel: Composition and Reception* (vol. 2; ed. John J. Collins and Peter W. Flint; Leiden: Brill, 2001), 421–46; and from the same volume, Craig Evans, "Daniel in the New Testament: Visions of God's Kingdom," 490–527; and James D. G. Dunn, "The Danielic Son of Man in the New Testament," 528–49.

[35]Translations of these scrolls (4Q242, 4Q243–44, 4Q245) may be found in Florentino García Martínez, *The Dead Sea Scrolls Translated: The Qumran Texts in English* (Leiden: Brill, 1994), 288–89.

[36]Karel van der Toorn, "Scholars at the Oriental Court: The Figure of Daniel against Its Mesopotamian Background," in *The Book of Daniel: Composition and Reception* (vol. 1; ed. John J. Collins and Peter W. Flint; Leiden: Brill, 2001), 37–54.

[37]For the tale of Aqhat, see James B. Pritchard, ed., *The Ancient Near East: Volume 1: An Anthology of Texts and Pictures* (Princeton, N.J.: Princeton University Press, 1958), 118–32.

[38]Kaltner, "Is Daniel Also among the Prophets?"

[39]Collins, *Daniel*, 29–33.

[40]For a survey of the period, see John H. Hayes and Sara R. Mandell, *The Jewish People in Classical Antiquity: From Alexander to Bar Kochba* (Louisville: Westminster John Knox Press, 1998), 49–74. Or, more briefly and with a slightly different assessment, James C. VanderKam, *An Introduction to Early Judaism* (Grand Rapids, Mich.: Eerdmans, 2001), 18–24.

[41]Cf. Richard A. Horsley, "The Kingdom of God and the Renewal of Israel: Synoptic Gospels, Jesus Movements, and Apocalypticism," in *The Encyclopedia of Apocalypticism: Volume 1: The Origins of Apocalypticism in Judaism and Early Christianity* (ed. John J. Collins; New York: Crossroad, 1998), 303–44.

[42]See the excursus in Collins, *Daniel*, 304–10, which is both detailed and helpful.

[43]Daniel offers four proposals related to the duration of the Little Horn's persecution: three-and-a-half years ("a time, two times, and half a time": 7:25; 12:11); 1,150 days (8:14); 1,190 days (12:11); and 1,335 days (12:12).

[44]Cf. Paul L. Redditt, "Daniel 11 and the Sociohistorical Setting of the Book of Daniel," *CBQ* 60 (1998): 463–74.

Chapter 2: Emerging Apocalyptic Discourse in the Hebrew Scriptures

[1]Paul D. Hanson, *The Dawn of Apocalyptic: The Historical and Sociological Roots of Jewish Apocalyptic Eschatology* (rev. ed.; Philadelphia: Fortress Press, 1979).

[2]Paul D. Hanson, "Old Testament Apocalyptic Reexamined," in *Visionaries and Their Apocalypses* (ed. Paul D. Hanson; Issues in Religion and Theology 2; Philadelphia: Fortress Press, 1983), 42.

[3]Hanson, *Dawn of Apocalyptic,* esp. 210–12.

[4]Philip R. Davies, "The Social World of Apocalyptic Writings," in *The World of Ancient Israel: Sociological, Anthropological and Political Perspectives* (ed. R. E. Clements; Cambridge: Cambridge University Press, 1989), 258.

[5]Stephen L. Cook, *Prophecy and Apocalypticism: The Postexilic Social Setting* (Minneapolis: Fortress Press, 1995).

[6]Jon L. Berquist, *In Persia's Shadow: A Social and Historical Approach* (Minneapolis: Fortress Press, 1995), 184–85.

[7]John J. Collins, *The Apocalyptic Imagination: An Introduction to Apocalyptic Literature* (2d ed.; The Biblical Resource Series; Grand Rapids, Mich.: Eerdmans, 1998), 15.

[8]Joseph Blenkinsopp, *A History of Prophecy in Israel* (rev. ed.; Louisville: Westminster John Knox Press, 1996), 168.

[9]Claiming to derive from the high priest Zadok, who served during the time of David and Solomon, Zadokites controlled the high priestly office until just before the Maccabean Revolt. In Ezekiel's depiction of the renewed temple, for example, the Zadokites figure prominently (40:46; 43:19; 44:15; 48:11).

[10]Cook, *Prophecy and Apocalypticism,* 97–98.

[11]Katheryn Pfisterer Darr, "The Book of Ezekiel," *NIB,* 6.1082–85.

[12]Christopher Rowland, *The Open Heaven: A Study of Apocalyptic in Judaism and Early Christianity* (New York: Crossroad, 1982), esp. 218–40, 282–348.

[13]Darr, "Ezekiel," 1121. For more on the Son of Man, see Delbert Burkett, *The Son of Man Debate: A History and Evaluation* (SNTMS 107; Cambridge: Cambridge University Press, 2000).

[14]The "hand of the LORD" also introduces major visionary sections at Ezekiel 1:3; 8:1; and 40:1; cf. 3:14, 22 (Darr, 1499).

[15]See the discussion in Joseph Blenkinsopp, *Ezekiel* (Interpretation; Louisville: John Knox, 1990), 170–73.

[16]See Blenkinsopp, *History of Prophecy,* 178.

[17]Cook, *Prophecy and Apocalypticism,* 85–105.

[18]See the brief discussion in Darr, "Ezekiel," 1534–55; or Kalinda Rose Stevenson, *The Vision of Transformation: The Territorial Rhetoric of Ezekiel 40–48* (SBLDS 154; Atlanta: Scholars, 1996).]

[19]Blenkinsopp, *History of Prophecy,* 179.

[20]Eibert J. C. Tigchelaar, *Prophets of Old and the Day of the End: Zechariah, the Book of the Watchers, and Apocalyptic* (*OtSt* 35; Leiden: Brill, 1996), 13, citing Hanson, *Dawn of Apocalyptic,* esp. 240–62, 280–401.

[21]See the discussions in James D. Nogalski and Marvin A. Sweeney, ed., *Reading and Hearing the Book of the Twelve* (SBLSymS 15; Atlanta: Society of Biblical Literature, 2000), and the literature cited therein.

[22]Julia O'Brien, "Zechariah," *Nahum-Malachi* (Abingdon Old Testament Commentaries; Nashville: Abingdon Press, 2004), 167.

[23]As Tigchelaar notes, "The allegory itself has been interpreted in many different ways" (*Prophets of Old,* 112).

[24]David L. Petersen, *Zechariah 9–14 and Malachi* (OTL; Louisville: Westminster John Knox Press, 1995), 90.

[25]Ben Witherington III, *The Gospel of Mark: A Socio-Rhetorical Commentary* (Grand Rapids, Mich.: Eerdmans, 2001), 347.

[26]Ronald K. Simkins, "Joel, Book of," *EDB,* 720.

[27]See the detailed and technical arguments in Cook, *Prophecy and Apocalypticism,* 167–209.

[28]Blenkinsopp, *History of Prophecy,* 224.

[29]Some commentators, of course, argue that the "day of the LORD" passages are later interpolations or redactions. However, that argument depends on the assumption that such apocalyptic concerns could not have developed by the time when those first oracles were written (Blenkinsopp, *History of Prophecy,* 224, provides an example of such argumentation). For those of us with an interest in the emergence of apocalyptic motifs, that argument simply begs the question.

[30]John F. A. Sawyer, *The Fifth Gospel: Isaiah in the History of Christianity* (Cambridge: Cambridge University Press, 1996).

[31]Paul D. Hanson, "Apocalyptic Literature," in *The Hebrew Bible and Its Modern Interpreters* (ed. Douglas A. Knight and Gene M. Tucker; Chico, Calif.: Scholars Press, 1985), 480, though Hanson also labels Second Isaiah as "proto-apocalyptic." See Hanson, *Dawn of Apocalyptic.*

[32]Donald C. Polaski, "Destruction, Construction, Argumentation: A Rhetorical Reading of Isaiah 24–27," in *Vision and Persuasion: Rhetorical Dimensions of Apocalyptic Discourse* (ed. Greg Carey and L. Gregory Bloomquist; St. Louis: Chalice Press, 1999), 19–20.

[33]John J. Collins, "Introduction: Towards the Morphology of a Genre," *Semeia* 14 (1979): 9.

[34]Blenkinsopp, *History of Prophecy,* 237.

[35]See ibid., 99–100.

[36]See the discussion in Polaski, "Deconstruction, Construction, Argumentation," 19–21.

[37]Ibid., 38–39.

[38]Timothy K. Beal, "Intertextuality," in *Handbook of Postmodern Biblical Interpretation* (ed. A. K. M. Adam; St. Louis: Chalice Press, 2000), 128.

Chapter 3: Interpreting the Times

[1]J. T. A. G. M. van Ruiten, *Primaeval History Interpreted: The Rewriting of Genesis 1–11 in the Book of Jubilees* JSJSup 66 (Leiden: Brill, 2000), 1–2.

[2]Although it is unclear what functions the "angel of the presence" fulfills beyond the dictation of this book, his role as a mediator of revelation is significant for Jubilees (cf. James C. VanderKam, *The Book of Jubilees* [Guides to Apocrypha and Pseudepigrapha; Sheffield: Sheffield Academic Press, 2001], 125–27).

[3]George W. E. Nickelsburg, "The Bible Rewritten and Expanded," in *Jewish Writings of the Second Temple Period,* ed. Michael E. Stone, CRINT 2.2 (Philadelphia: Fortress Press, 1984), 101.

[4]VanderKam, *Book of Jubilees,* 143–48; O. S. Wintermute, "Jubilees," *OTP,* 2.48–50.

[5]Nickelsburg, "The Bible Rewritten and Expanded," 97–98.

[6]Lester L. Grabbe, *Judaism from Cyrus to Hadrian: Volume 1: The Persian and Greek Periods* (Minneapolis: Fortress Press, 1991), 309.

[7]James C. VanderKam, *Textual and Historical Studies in the Book of Jubilees* (HSM 14; Missoula, Mont.: Scholars Press, 1977), 270–77.

[8]VanderKam, *Book of Jubilees,* 59.

[9]For a discussion of "Abraham the monotheist" and legends of his pagan background, see James L. Kugel, *The Bible as It Was* (Cambridge, Mass.: Harvard University Press, 1997), 131–48.

[10]Calvin Roetzel provides a helpful survey of this topic in "The Model Ascetic," in *Paul: The Man and the Myth* (Studies on the Personalities of the New Testament; Minneapolis: Fortress Press, 1999 [1997]), 135–51.

[11]Betsy Halpern-Amaru, *Rewriting the Bible: Land and Covenant in Postbiblical Jewish Literature* (Valley Forge, Pa.: Trinity Press International, 1994), 48–54.

[12]Cf. John J. Collins, *The Apocalyptic Imagination: An Introduction to Jewish Apocalyptic Literature* (2d ed.; The Biblical Resource Series; Grand Rapids, Mich.: Eerdmans, 1998), 133–36; H. C. Kee, "Testaments of the Twelve Patriarchs," *OTP,* 1.777–78.

[13]Robert A. Kugler, *The Testaments of the Twelve Patriarchs* (Guides to Apocrypha and Pseudepigrapha; Sheffield: Sheffield Academic Press, 2001), 26–28; Kee, "Testaments," 1.775–77; John J. Collins, "Testaments," in *Jewish Writings of the Second Temple Period* (ed. Michael E. Stone; CRINT 2.2; Philadelphia: Fortress Press, 1984), 331.

[14]George W. E. Nickelsburg, *Jewish Literature Between the Bible and the Mishnah,* (Philadelphia: Fortress Press, 1981), 232; Kugler, *Testaments of the Twelve Patriarchs,* 12–15.

[15]Kugler, *Testaments of the Twelve Patriarchs,* 24.

[16]Luke Timothy Johnson, *The Letter of James* (AB 37A; New York: Doubleday, 1995), 43–46.

[17]For the former position, see Kee, "Testaments," esp. 776–78; for the latter, see M. de Jonge, "The Interpretation of the Testaments of the Twelve Patriarchs in Recent Years," and "Christian Influence in the Testaments of the Twelve Patriarchs," in *Studies on the Testaments of the Twelve Patriarchs* (ed. M. de Jonge; SVTP 3; Leiden: Brill, 1975), 183–246.

[18]Cf. Martha Himmelfarb, *Ascent to Heaven in Jewish and Christian Apocalypses* (New York: Oxford University Press, 1993), 31, 126–27 n. 7 (seven heavens); Kee, "Testaments," *OTP,*

1.779; M. de Jonge, "Notes on Testament of Levi II-VII," in *Studies on the Testaments of the Twelve Patriarchs* (ed. M. de Jonge; SVTP 3; Leiden: Brill, 1975), 259–60.

[19]H. W. Hollander and M. de Jonge, *The Testaments of the Twelve Patriarchs: A Commentary* (SVTP 8; Leiden: Brill, 1985), 137.

[20]Kugler, *Testaments of the Twelve Patriarchs,* 55–56.

[21]VanderKam, *Book of Jubilees,* 146.

[22]According to some reconstructions, the Testaments reflect two diverse and somewhat contradictory eschatological scenarios; see Hollander and de Jonge, *Testaments,* 53–61.

[23]Compare the discussions of John J. Collins, "The Date and Provenance of the Testament of Moses," in *Studies on the Testament of Moses* (ed. George W. E. Nickelsburg; Septuagint and Cognate Studies 4; Cambridge, Mass.: Society of Biblical Literature, 1973), 15–32, though Collins's position has changed (*Apocalyptic Imagination,* 129); George W. E. Nickelsburg, *Jewish Literature,* 80–82, 212–15; and James C. VanderKam, *An Introduction to Early Judaism* (Grand Rapids, Mich.: Eerdmans, 2001), 114–15.

[24]J. Priest, "Testament of Moses," *OTP,* 1.919–20. Translations from the Testament are taken from this source.

[25]Johannes Tromp, *The Assumption of Moses: A Critical Edition with Commentary* (SVTP 10; Leiden: Brill, 1993), 200.

[26]See the transcription in Tromp, *Assumption of Moses,* 16.

[27]Collins, "Date and Provenance," 30–32.

[28]For a brief account, see James C. VanderKam, *The Dead Sea Scrolls Today* (Grand Rapids, Mich.: Eerdmans, 1994), 1–27; but for a sensational (i.e., entertaining but sometimes misleading) book-length account, refer to Neil Asher Silberman, *The Hidden Scrolls: Christianity, Judaism, and the War for the Dead Sea Scrolls* (New York: Riverhead, 1994).

[29]VanderKam, *Dead Sea Scrolls,* 30–32.

[30]Ibid., 29–70. For the most complete English translation of the Qumran documents, see Florentino García Martínez, *The Dead Sea Scrolls Translated: The Qumran Texts in English* (Leiden: Brill, 1994).

[31]A handy but incomplete collection of these sources may be found in Lawrence H. Schiffman, *Texts and Traditions: A Source Reader for the Study of Second Temple and Rabbinic Judaism* (Hoboken, N.J.: KTAV, 1998), 275–84.

[32]VanderKam, *Dead Sea Scrolls,* 74.

[33]See James C. VanderKam, "Apocalyptic Tradition in the Dead Sea Scrolls and the Religion of Qumran," in *Religion in the Dead Sea Scrolls* (ed. John J. Collins and Robert A. Kugler; Studies in the Dead Sea Scrolls and Related Literature; Grand Rapids, Mich.: Eerdmans, 2000), 113–34.

[34]Translations of the Qumran texts derive from Martínez, *Dead Sea Scrolls Translated.*

[35]John J. Collins and Florentino García Martínez agree: The instructions vaguely resemble Hellenistic and Roman military tactics, but they also feature strong ritual elements (Collins, *Apocalypticism in the Dead Sea Scrolls* [Literature of the Dead Sea Scrolls; New York: Routledge, 1997], 95–99; García Martínez, "Apocalypticism in the Dead Sea Scrolls," in *The Encyclopedia of Apocalypticism: Volume 1: The Origins of Apocalypticism in Judaism and Christianity* [New York: Crossroad, 1998], 189).

[36]García Martínez, "Apocalypticism," 190.

[37]VanderKam, *Dead Sea Scrolls,* 59.

[38]Ibid., 68–69.

[39]Collins, *Apocalypticism in the Dead Sea Scrolls,* provides a thorough introduction to these topics.

[40]Cf. 4Q267 17:1:9; 1QS 11:7–9; 1QH 11:20–22 (García Martínez, "Apocalypticism," 180–81).

[41]García Martínez, "Apocalypticism," 48–49.

[42]John J. Collins, "The Expectation of the End in the Dead Sea Scrolls," in *Eschatology, Messianism, and the Dead Sea Scrolls* (ed. Craig A. Evans and Peter W. Flint; Studies in the Dead Sea Scrolls and Related Literature; Grand Rapids, Mich.: Eerdmans, 1997), 80–81.

[43]Collins, *Apocalypticism in the Dead Sea Scrolls,* 116–17.

[44]John J. Collins, "The Sibylline Oracles," *OTP,* 1.320–21.

[45]John J. Collins, *Seers, Sibyls and Sages in Hellenistic-Roman Judaism* (JSJSup 54; Leiden: Brill, 1997), 181.

⁴⁶Quoted from the LCL edition in John J. Collins, *The Sibylline Oracles of Egyptian Judaism* (SBLDS 13; Missoula, Mont.: Scholars Press, 1974), 1.

⁴⁷H. W. Parke, *Sibyls and Sibylline Prophecy in Classical Antiquity* (ed. B. C. McGing; New York: Routledge, 1988), 51.

⁴⁸Collins, *Seers, Sibyls, and Sages*, 184; Mary Beard, John North, and Simon Price, *Religions of Rome: Volume 1: A History* (Cambridge: Cambridge University Press, 1998), 18, 27, 62–63.

⁴⁹These examples derive from Mary Beard, John North, and Simon Price, *Religions of Rome: Volume 2: A Sourcebook* (Cambridge: Cambridge University Press, 1998), 43, 130.

⁵⁰Parke, *Sibyls*, 137.

⁵¹Collins, *Apocalyptic Imagination*, 126–27.

⁵²Ibid., 119–22; Collins, *Between Athens and Jerusalem: Jewish Identity in the Hellenistic Diaspora* (2d ed.; The Biblical Resource Series; Grand Rapids, Mich.: Eerdmans, 2000), 88–95; Nickelsburg, *Jewish Literature*, 164.

⁵³John J. Collins argues that verses 46–50 must have been composed before the Second Jewish Revolt of 132–135 C.E., with verse 51 a later interpolation. His argument relies on two assumptions: (a) Jews could not have composed such favorable references to Hadrian after he had snuffed out the revolt so violently; and (b) therefore, the history narrated in v. 51, which names Hadrian's successors, must be inauthentic (*Sibylline Oracles*, 73). In my view, these conclusions are less than obvious, but neither is this matter essential for engaging the book's basic political outlook.

⁵⁴Collins, *Apocalyptic Imagination*, 235; cf. David Aune, *Revelation 6–16* (WBC 52B; Nashville: Thomas Nelson, 1998), 737–40.

⁵⁵See the summary of Nero's career in Helmut Koester, *History, Culture and Religion of the Hellenistic Age: Volume 1: Introduction to the New Testament* (New York: Walter de Gruyter, 1982), 311–14.

⁵⁶Collins, *Between Athens and Jerusalem*, 264.

Chapter 4: The Gospels and Jesus

¹For example, see Charles Marsh, *The Last Days: A Son's Story of Sin and Segregation at the Dawn of a New South* (New York: Basic, 2001).

²One valuable and affordable edition is Kurt Aland, ed., *Synopsis of the Four Gospels* (rev. ed.; New York: United Bible Societies, 1985).

³James C. VanderKam, *The Dead Sea Scrolls Today* (Grand Rapids, Mich.: Eerdmans, 1994), 105.

⁴John Dominic Crossan, *The Historical Jesus: The Life of a Mediterranean Jewish Peasant* (San Francisco: HarperCollins, 1991), 235.

⁵Cf. Ex. 32:32–33; Ps. 69:28; 139:16 [LXX]. Luke Timothy Johnson, *The Gospel of Luke* (SP 3; Collegeville, Min..: Michael Glazier, 1991), 169.

⁶W. D. Davies and Dale C. Allison, Jr., *The Gospel according to Saint Matthew* (3 vols.; ICC; Edinburgh: T. & T. Clark, 1991), 2.337–38.

⁷Stephen J. Patterson, *The Gospel of Thomas and Jesus* (Foundations & Facets; Sonoma, Calif.: Polebridge, 1993), 225.

⁸Dale C. Allison, *Jesus of Nazareth: Millenarian Prophet* (Minneapolis: Fortress Press, 1998), 34.

⁹Bart D. Ehrman, *Jesus: Apocalyptic Prophet of the New Millennium* (New York: Oxford University Press, 1999), 142–43.

¹⁰The juxtaposition of the Lord's Prayer, the Last Supper, and the banquet image is from John P. Meier, *A Marginal Jew: Rethinking the Historical Jesus. Volume 2: Mentor, Message, and Miracles* (ABRL; New York: Doubleday, 1991), 291–317.

¹¹A much fuller discussion is available in E. P. Sanders, *The Historical Figure of Jesus* (New York: Penguin, 1993), 169–88.

¹²Some have argued that the Similitudes of Enoch postdate Jesus and the gospels. If so, the Similitudes are irrelevant to the meaning of "Son of Man" in the Jesus traditions.

¹³Donald P. Senior, "Son of Man," *EDB*, 1242.

¹⁴Davies and Allison, *Matthew*, 3.76.

¹⁵Sanders, *The Historical Figure of Jesus*, 120.

¹⁶E. P. Sanders, *Judaism: Practice and Belief 63 B.C.E.–66 C.E.* (Valley Forge, Pa.: Trinity Press International, 1992), 290–91.

[17]Cf. VanderKam, *The Dead Sea Scrolls Today,* 84–86.

[18]"Asceticism," in *The HarperCollins Dictionary of Religion* (ed. Jonathan Z. Smith; San Francisco: HarperSanFrancisco, 1995), 77.

[19]Richard Valantasis, "Constructions of Power in Asceticism," *JAAR* 36 (1995): 815; cf. Gail Corrington Streete, "Outrageous (Speech) Acts and Everyday (Performative) Rebellions: A Response to Rhetorics of Resistance," *Semeia* 79 (1997): 97–105.

[20]Many of the points in this paragraph are adapted from Allison, *Jesus of Nazareth,* 172–216.

[21]For the reference to 4Q521, I am indebted to David Ralph Seely, "Resurrection," *EDB,* 1121.

[22]The precise identity of the veil as Mark presents it remains open to speculation: Is this the veil that sets off the Holy of Holies, the temple's most sacred space, or is it one that could have been seen by the public? For discussion, see Ben Witherington III, *The Gospel of Mark: A Socio-Rhetorical Commentary* (Grand Rapids, Mich.: Eerdmans, 2001), 399–400.

[23]See Pheme Perkins, "The Gospel of Mark," (*NIB* 8; Nashville: Abingdon Press, 1995), 630.

[24]At the time of this writing, Elaine Pagels's fascinating new book, *Beyond Belief: The Secret Gospel of Thomas* (New York: Random House, 2003), has just appeared. As far as John and Thomas are concerned, Pagels's primary thesis–that John's gospel intentionally refutes some of the content that we find in Thomas's (whether John's author knew Thomas's gospel or not)–will remain controversial. But her acute analysis of these two gospels–and their responses to early Christian apocalypticism–has stimulated me to reconsider my approach to this problem.

[25]The standard English translation of the Nag Hammadi texts is James M. Robinson, ed., *The Nag Hammadi Library in English* (3d ed.; San Francisco: HarperCollins, 1988). In the present volume translations from Thomas derive from Bentley Layton, *The Gnostic Scriptures* (ABRL; New York: Doubleday, 1987), 376–99.

[26]"Hidden sayings" derives from the most frequent translation of Thomas's prologue, and "comprehend" represents a plausible translation of John 1:5.

[27]Richard Valantasis, *The Gospel of Thomas* (New Testament Readings; New York: Routledge, 1997), 31, cf. 20. Cf. Stephen J. Patterson, "Understanding the Gospel of Thomas Today," in *The Fifth Gospel: The Gospel of Thomas Comes of Age* (by Stephen J. Patterson, James M. Robinson, and Hans-Gebhard Bethge; Harrisburg, Pa.: Trinity Press International, 1998), 58–65.

[28]As cited in Eusebius, *Hist. Eccl.* 6.14.7.

[29]Origen, *Commentary on John* 10.4–6; 1.6, cited in Pagels, *Beyond Belief,* 37.

[30]Rod Cameron, ed., *The Other Gospels* (Philadelphia: The Westminster Press, 1982), 27.

[31]Ibid., 31.

[32]D. Moody Smith, *The Theology of the Gospel of John* (New Testament Theology; New York: Cambridge University Press, 1995), 149–51.

[33]On the matter of Thomas's relevance for reconstructing the historical Jesus and his teaching, Thomas advocates include Stephen J. Patterson, *The Gospel of Thomas and Jesus* (Foundations and Facets; Sonoma, Calif.: Polebridge, 1993); and John Dominic Crossan, *The Birth of Christianity* (San Francisco: HarperSanFrancisco, 1998), esp. 239–56; while its detractors include Dale C. Allison, *Jesus of Nazareth: Millenarian Prophet* (Minneapolis: Fortress Press, 1998), 95–171; and John P. Meier, *A Marginal Jew: Rethinking the Historical Jesus: Volume 1: The Roots of the Problem and the Person* (ABRL; New York: Doubleday, 1991), esp. 112–66.

[34]Among those who believe Q's earlier layers lacked apocalyptic discourse, see John S. Kloppenborg, *The Formation of Q: Trajectories in Ancient Christian Wisdom Collections* (Traditions in Antiquity and Christianity; Philadelphia: Fortress Press, 1987); and Burton L. Mack, *The Lost Gospel: The Book of Q and Christian Origins* (San Francisco: HarperCollins, 1993). Others disagree: Dale C. Allison, Jr., *The Jesus Tradition in Q* (Harrisburg, Pa.: Trinity Press International, 1997), esp. 1–103; and Christopher M. Tuckett, *Q and the History of Early Christianity: Studies on Q* (Edinburgh: T. & T. Clark, 1996), 41–82.

[35]Cameron, *Other Gospels,* 35.

[36]Patterson, *Gospel of Thomas and Jesus,* 18–19.

[37]The two most popular–and compelling–accounts of the nonapocalyptic Jesus are those of Marcus J. Borg and John Dominic Crossan, both of whom have developed more technical

and more popular presentations of their case. Borg's full presentation is *Jesus: A New Vision* (San Francisco: Harper & Row, 1987); he addresses a wider audience in *Meeting Jesus Again for the First Time: The Historical Jesus and the Heart of Contemporary Faith* (San Francisco: HarperSanFrancisco, 1995). Crossan presents his full case in *The Historical Jesus: The Life of a Mediterranean Jewish Peasant* (San Francisco: HarperSanFrancisco, 1991); condensed and updated in *Jesus: A Revolutionary Biography* (San Francisco: HarperSanFrancisco, 1994).

[38]Albert Schweitzer, *The Quest of the Historical Jesus* (trans. James M. Robinson; New York: Macmillan, 1968). The original title in German was *Von Reimarus zu Wrede (From Reimarus to Wrede)*.

[39]Ibid., 399, 398.

[40]On this question, see the collection of essays, many by evangelical scholars, in Carey C. Newman, ed., *Jesus and the Restoration of Israel: A Critical Assessment of N. T. Wright's* Jesus and the Victory of God (Downers Grove, Ill.: InterVarsity, 1999).

[41]Ehrman, *Jesus,* 127.

[42]For a brief but fuller account of these arguments, see Dale C. Allison, "The Eschatology of Jesus," in *The Encyclopedia of Apocalypticism: Volume 1: The Origins of Apocalypticism in Judaism and Christianity* (ed. John J. Collins; New York: Crossroad, 1998), 269–80.

[43]Kloppenborg, *Formation of Q;* Allison, *Jesus Tradition in Q.*

[44]This case has been argued most forcefully by Meier, *A Marginal Jew,* 19–233; and Sanders, *Historical Figure of Jesus,* 78–97.

[45]Cf. Ehrman, *Jesus,* 145–48.

[46]Allison, "Eschatology of Jesus," 271.

[47]For portraits of the apocalyptic Jesus, see Allison, *Jesus of Nazareth;* Ehrman, *Jesus;* Paula Fredriksen, *Jesus of Nazareth, King of the Jews: A Jewish Life and the Emergence of Christianity* (2d ed.; New Haven, Conn: Yale University Press, 2000); Meier, *Marginal Jew;* Sanders, *Historical Figure of Jesus;* and N. T. Wright, *Jesus and the Victory of God* (Minneapolis: Fortress Press, 1996).

[48]On this score, see Crossan's *Jesus: A Revolutionary Biography.*

[49]As in William R. Herzog II, *Jesus, Justice, and the Reign of God* (Louisville: Westminster John Knox Press, 2000), esp. 111–216.

[50]One scholar who has wrestled with this question is Craig C. Hill, *In God's Time: The Bible and the Future* (Grand Rapids, Mich.: Eerdmans, 2002), 130–69.

[51]Martin Luther King, Jr., "Where Do We Go From Here?" in *A Testament of Hope: The Essential Writings of Martin Luther King, Jr.* (ed. James Melvin Washington; San Francisco: Harper & Row, 1986), 252.

Chapter 5: The Pauline Epistles

[1]Calvin Roetzel, *Paul: The Man and the Myth* (Studies on the Personalities of the New Testament; Philadelphia: Fortress Press, 1999 [1997]), 128.

[2]For an engaging review of this question, see Dale B. Martin, "Paul and the Judaism/ Hellenism Dichotomy: Toward a Social History of the Question," in *Paul Beyond the Judaism/ Hellenism Divide* (ed. Troels Engberg-Pedersen; Louisville: Westminster John Knox Press, 2001), 29–61.

[3]Abraham J. Malherbe, *Paul and the Popular Philosophers* (Minneapolis: Fortress Press, 1989), 67.

[4]Daniel Boyarin, *A Radical Jew: Paul and the Politics of Identity* (Berkeley: University of California Press, 1994), 63–64.

[5]Alan F. Segal, *Paul the Convert: The Apostolate and Apostasy of Saul the Pharisee* (New Haven, Conn.: Yale University Press, 1990), 37.

[6]Ibid., 35.

[7]Markus Bockmuehl, *Revelation and Mystery in Ancient Judaism and Pauline Christianity* (Grand Rapids, Mich.: Eerdmans, 1997 [1990]), 136.

[8]For a more detailed discussion of this point, see N. T. Wright, *The New Testament and the People of God* (Minneapolis: Fortress Press, 1992), 321–32.

[9]N. T. Wright, *The Resurrection of the Son of God* (Minneapolis: Fortress Press, 2003), 361. See also the discussion on pp. 312–61.

[10]M. C. de Boer, "Paul and Apocalyptic Eschatology," in *The Encyclopedia of Apocalypticism: Volume 1: The Origins of Apocalypticism in Judaism and Christianity* (ed. John J. Collins; New York: Continuum, 1998), 357.

[11]N. T. Wright, *What Saint Paul Really Said: Was Paul of Tarsus the Real Founder of Christianity?* (Grand Rapids, Mich.: Eerdmans, 1997), 90.

[12]J. Christiaan Beker, *Paul the Apostle: The Triumph of God in Life and Thought* (Philadelphia: Fortress Press, 1980), 144.

[13]J. Louis Martyn, "The Apocalyptic Gospel in Galatians," *Int* 54 (2000): 253–56.

[14]The definitive study of this matter is Richard Bauckham, *The Fate of the Dead: Studies on the Jewish and Christian Apocalypses* (NovTSup 93; Leiden: Brill, 1998), esp. 86–96.

[15]Gordon D. Fee, *Paul's Letter to the Philippians* (NICNT; Grand Rapids, Mich.: Eerdmans, 1995), 149.

[16]Ibid., 149; Cf. Markus Bockmuehl, *The Epistle to the Philippians* (BNTC; London: A & C Black, 1997), 92. Nor am I satisfied by the account of N. T. Wright, who sees only an apparent tension between the Philippians passage and Paul's teaching in 1 Thessalonians and 1 Corinthians (*Resurrection*, 226–27).

[17]Peter T. O'Brien, *The Epistle to the Philippians: A Commentary on the Greek Text* (NIGTC; Grand Rapids, Mich.: Eerdmans, 1991), 136.

[18]Wayne Meeks, "Social Functions of Apocalyptic Language in Pauline Christianity," in *Apocalypticism in the Mediterranean World and the Near East: Proceedings of the International Colloquium on Apocalypticism, Uppsala, August 12–17, 1979* (ed. David Hellholm; Tübingen: Mohr-Siebeck, 1982), 700.

[19]Duane F. Watson, "Paul's Appropriation of Apocalyptic Discourse: The Rhetorical Strategy of 1 Thessalonians," in *Vision and Persuasion: Rhetorical Dimensions of Apocalyptic Discourse* (ed. Greg Carey and L. Gregory Bloomquist; St. Louis: Chalice Press, 1999), 68.

[20]For an insightful and concise discussion of this question, with its own distinctive contribution, see Dale B. Martin, *The Corinthian Body* (New Haven, Conn.: Yale University Press, 1995), 105–6.

[21]Pseudo-Libanius, *Epistolary Styles*, 5, cited in both Stanley K. Stowers, *Letter Writing in Greco-Roman Antiquity* (LEC 7; Philadelphia: Westminster Press, 1986), 94; and Jeffrey T. Reed, "The Epistle," in *Handbook of Classical Rhetoric in the Hellenistic Period, 330 B.C.–A.D. 400* (ed. Stanley E. Porter; Boston: Brill, 2001), 175.

[22]Meeks, "Social Functions," 699–700.

[23]Outstanding introductions to sexual asceticism in the ancient world are available in Martin, *The Corinthian Body*, 198–208; and Roetzel, *Paul*, 135–45.

[24]Roetzel, *Paul*, 139.

[25]Gail Corrington Streete, "Discipline and Disclosure: Paul's Apocalyptic Asceticism in 1 Corinthians," in *Vision and Persuasion: Rhetorical Dimensions of Apocalyptic Discourse* (ed. Greg Carey and L. Gregory Bloomquist; St. Louis: Chalice Press, 1999), 82.

[26]Ibid., 82.

Chapter 6: Responses to Tragedy

[1]Bruce N. Longenecker, *2 Esdras* (Guides to Apocrypha and Pseudepigrapha; Sheffield: Sheffield Academic Press, 1995), 86–87.

[2]Michael Edward Stone, *4 Ezra* (Hermeneia; Minneapolis: Fortress Press, 1990), 411.

[3]David A. deSilva, "Fourth Ezra: Reaffirming Jewish Cultural Values through Apocalyptic Rhetoric," in *Vision and Persuasion: Rhetorical Dimensions of Apocalyptic Discourse* (ed. Greg Carey and L. Gregory Bloomquist; St. Louis: Chalice Press, 1999), 128.

[4]John J. Collins, *The Apocalyptic Imagination: An Introduction to Jewish Apocalyptic Literature* (2d ed.; The Biblical Resource Series; Grand Rapids, Mich.: Eerdmans, 1998), 203.

[5]Stone, *4 Ezra*, 439; idem, "Apocalyptic Literature," in *Jewish Writings of the Second Temple Period* (ed. Michael E. Stone; CRINT 2/2; Philadelphia: Fortress, 1984), 428.

[6]My reading of 4 Ezra is heavily influenced by the work of Michael E. Stone (*4 Ezra*; and "On Reading an Apocalypse," in *Mysteries and Revelations: Apocalyptic Studies Since the Uppsala Colloquium* [ed. John J. Collins and James H. Charlesworth; JSPS 9; Sheffield: JSOT Press, 1991], 65–78). Stone argues that Ezra's transformation is due to a religious experience undergone or intimately known by the author of the apocalypse. I would suggest that this transformation may just as well indicate a sophisticated literary device. Nevertheless, Stone's larger point—that Ezra is moved through experience more than through abstract reflection—has the critical advantage of explaining how Ezra can move from the disillusionment he shows in 9:14–16 to his advocacy on God's behalf that we see at 10:16.

[7]Stone, *4 Ezra,* 36.

[8]See Philip F. Esler, "The Social Function of Fourth Ezra," in *The First Christians in Their Social Worlds: Social-Scientific Approaches to New Testament Interpretation* (New York: Routledge, 1994), 110–30; deSilva, "Fourth Ezra."

[9]See Alan F. Segal, *Rebecca's Children: Judaism and Christianity in the Roman World* (Cambridge, Mass.: Harvard University Press, 1986), 128–41.

[10]George W. E. Nickelsburg, *Jewish Literature between the Bible and the Mishnah* (Philadelphia: Fortress Press, 1981), 287.

[11]A. F. J. Klijn, "2 (Syriac Apocalypse of) Baruch," in *The Old Testament Pseudepigrapha: Volume 1: Apocalyptic Literature and Testaments* (ed. James H. Charlesworth; New York: Doubleday, 1983), 616–17.

[12]Gwendolyn B. Sayler, *Have the Promises Failed? A Literary Analysis of 2 Baruch* (SBLDS 72; Chico, Calif.: Scholars Press, 1984), 8–9.

[13]Carol A. Newsom, "Baruch: Introduction," in *The HarperCollins Study Bible* (ed. Wayne A. Meeks; San Francisco: HarperCollins, 1993), 1617.

[14]So judges Collins (*Apocalyptic Imagination,* 219), and I agree.

[15]It is unclear whether Baruch is addressing the people directly or only their elders.

[16]I am grateful to Mark Whitters, who first pointed this out to me. See his *The Epistle of Second Baruch: A Study in Form and Message* (JSPS 42; Sheffield: Sheffield Academic Press, 2003).

[17]For specific references, see E. P. Sanders, *Jesus and Judaism* (Philadelphia: Fortress Press, 1985), 95–98. The reference to 1 Enoch is to 90:33, and is supplied in *OTP* 1.648 n. n.

[18]Shannon Burkes, "'Life' Redefined: Wisdom and Law in Fourth Ezra and *Second Baruch,*" *CBQ* 63 (2001): 55–71.

[19]Sayler, *Have the Promises Failed?* 115.

[20]H. E. Gaylord, Jr., "3 (Greek Apocalypse of) Baruch," *OTP,* 1.653–54.

[21]Cf. Richard Bauckham, *The Fate of the Dead: Studies on the Jewish and Christian Apocalypses* (NovTSup 93; Leiden: Brill, 1998), 66; Martha Himmelfarb, *Ascent to Heaven in Jewish and Christian Apocalypses* (New York: Oxford University Press, 1993), 87.

[22]Himmelfarb, *Ascent to Heaven.*

[23]Gaylord, "3 Baruch," 656; H. F. D. Sparks, *The Apocryphal Old Testament* (New York: Oxford University Press, 1984), 818.

[24]Himmelfarb, *Ascent to Heaven.*

[25]For a fairly extensive argument, see Bauckham, *The Fate of the Dead,* 66–69. Daniel Harlow has argued that 3 Baruch presupposes seven heavens but only narrates five (*The Greek Apocalypse of Baruch (3 Baruch) in Hellenistic Judaism and Early Christianity* [SVTP 12; Leiden: Brill, 1996], 34–76).

[26]The texts cited here are gleaned in part from Ralph P. Martin, *2 Corinthians* (WBC 40; Waco, Tex.: Word, 1986), 402.

[27]Gerhard von Rad and Helmut Traub, "*ouranos,*" *TDNT* 5.511.

[28]One of my students, Stock Weinstock-Collins, shares this opinion. A former college professor in chemistry, Stock has read a fair amount in ancient scientific and philosophical writing.

[29]Sparks, *Apocryphal Old Testament,* 899.

[30]Ibid.

[31]Collins, *Apocalyptic Imagination,* 226.

[32]Himmelfarb, *Ascent to Heaven,* 61.

[33]See George M. Soares-Prabhu, "Laughing at Idols: The Dark Side of Biblical Monotheism (an Indian Reading of Isaiah 44:9–20," in *Reading from This Place: Volume 2: Social Location and Biblical Interpretation in Global Perspective* (ed. Fernando F. Segovia and Mary Ann Tolbert; Minneapolis: Fortress Press, 1995), 109–31.

[34]The extant manuscripts differ at Apoc. Abr. 21:2, with some indicating a third heaven while others do not indicate a specific heaven (Sparks, ed., *Apocryphal Old Testament,* 383 n. 1).

[35]Himmelfarb, *Ascent to Heaven,* 66.

Chapter 7: Christian Historical Apocalypses

[1]Many readers have proposed that Revelation may incorporate sources from before 70 C.E., then reached its final form late in the century. David Aune has developed a particularly

influential version of this view (*Revelation* [WBC 52A; Dallas, Tex.: Word, 1997], 1.lvi-lxx, cv-cxxxiv). For the argument that Revelation in its entirety predates 70, see J. Christian Wilson, "The Problem of the Domitianic Date of Revelation," *NTS* 39 (1993): 587–605; and John W. Marshall, *Parables of War: Reading John's Jewish Apocalypse* (ESCJ 10; Waterloo, Ontario: Wilfrid Laurier University Press, 2001), esp. 88–97.

²Greg Carey, *Elusive Apocalypse: Reading Authority in the Revelation to John* (StABH 15; Macon, Ga.: Mercer University Press, 1999), 93–133.

³For example, David Aune, "The Social Matrix of the Apocalypse of John," *BR* 26 (1981): 19.

⁴The imperial cults have received a great deal of scholarly attention. The most recent major assessment of Revelation and the imperial cults is Steven J. Friesen, *Imperial Cults and the Apocalypse of John: Reading Revelation in the Ruins* (New York: Oxford University Press, 2001).

⁵Paul Boyer, *When Time Shall Be No More: Prophecy Belief in Modern American Culture* (Cambridge, Mass.: Harvard University Press, 1992), 274–76.

⁶Cf. Seutonius, *Nero* 57; Tacitus, *History* 2.8; Sib. Or. 3:53–74; 4:119–22; 5.94–110, 137–54, 214–27, 231, 361–85; 8:68–72, 139–69; 12:78–94. For discussion, see R. H. Charles, *A Critical and Exegetical Commentary on the Revelation of St. John* (2 vols.; ICC; Edinburgh: Charles Scribner's Sons, 1920), 2.80–81; and Aune, *Revelation*, 2.737–40, with bibliography.

⁷The origins of this interpretation are unclear, but one may find a full argument in Charles's classic commentary, *Revelation*, 1.364–68.

⁸For a contemporary political assessment, see Néstor Míguez, "Apocalyptic and the Economy: A Reading of Revelation 18 from the Experience of Economic Exclusion," in *Reading from This Place: Volume 2: Social Location and Biblical Interpretation in Global Perspective* (ed. Fernando F. Segovia and Mary Ann Tolbert; Minneapolis: Fortress Press, 1995), 250–62; cf. Richard Bauckham, "The Economic Critique of Rome in Revelation 18," in *The Climax of Prophecy: Studies on the Book of Revelation* (Edinburgh: T. & T. Clark, 1993), 338–83.

⁹Sophie Laws, *In the Light of the Lamb: Imagery, Parody, and Theology in the Apocalypse of John* (GNS 31; Wilmington, Del.: Michael Glazer, 1988), 41–42.

¹⁰See the excellent discussion in Philip A. Harland, *Associations, Synagogues, and Congregations: Claiming a Place in Ancient Mediterranean Society* (Minneapolis: Fortress Press, 2003), 259–63.

¹¹For various perspectives on these difficult issues, see David Frankfurter, "Jews or Not? Reconstructing the 'Other' in Rev 2:9 and 3:9," *HTR* 94 (2001): 403–25; Marshall, *Parables of War*, 12–16, 122–48; Stephen G. Wilson, *Related Strangers: Jews and Christians, 70–170 C.E.* (Minneapolis: Fortress Press, 1995), 162–65; Carey, *Elusive Apocalypse*, 18–21; and Aune, *Revelation*, 1.162–72.

¹²The classic case for this model is Bryan R. Wilson, *Magic and the Millennium: A Sociological Study of Religious Movements of Protest Among Tribal and Third-World Peoples* (New York: Harper & Row, 1973). One may observe Wilson's influence in contemporary introductions to religion such as Ronald L. Johnstone, *Religion in Society: A Sociology of Religion* (5th ed.; Upper Saddle River, N.J.: Prentice Hall, 1997); and James C. Livingston, *Anatomy of the Sacred: An Introduction to Religion* (3d ed.; Upper Saddle River, N.J.: Prentice Hall, 1998).

¹³Hal Lindsey, *Late Great Planet Earth* (Grand Rapids, Mich.: Zondervan, 1970).

¹⁴The first novel in the series is *Left Behind: A Novel of the Earth's Last Days* (Wheaton, Ill.: Tyndale House, 1995). The series has even spawned a *Left Behind* movie.

¹⁵Friedrich Nietzsche, *The Birth of Tragedy and the Genealogy of Morals* (New York: Anchor/Doubleday, 1956), 185, cited in Catherine Keller, *Apocalypse Now and Then: A Feminist Guide to the End of the World* (Boston: Beacon, 1996), 50.

¹⁶C. J. Jung, *Answer to Job* (trans. R. F. C. Hull; London: Routledge & Keegan Paul, 1954), 125, cited in William Klassen, "Vengeance in the Apocalypse of John," *CBQ* 28 (1966): 301.

¹⁷D. H. Lawrence, *Apocalypse* (Harmondsworth, Eng.: Penguin, 1960), 14, cited in Arthur W. Wainwright, *Mysterious Apocalypse: Interpreting the Book of Revelation* (Nashville: Abingdon Press, 1993), 199.

¹⁸Tina Pippin, *Death and Desire: The Rhetoric of Gender in the Apocalypse of John* (Literary Currents in Biblical Interpretation; Louisville: Westminster/John Knox Press, 1992); Keller, *Apocalypse Now and Then*.

[19]Allan Boesak, *Comfort and Protest: The Apocalypse from a South African Perspective* (Philadelphia: Westminster Press, 1987).

[20]For example, Pablo Richard, *Apocalypse: A People's Commentary on the Book of Revelation* (Maryknoll, N.Y.: Orbis, 1995).

[21]Brian K. Blount, "Reading Revelation Today: Witness as Active Resistance," *Int* 54 (2000): 398. Blount is currently completing a commentary on Revelation for the Westminster John Knox Press New Testament Library series.

[22]Elisabeth Schüssler Fiorenza, "Epilogue: The Rhetoricality of Apocalypse and the Politics of Interpretation," in *The Book of Revelation: Justice and Judgment* (2d ed.; Minneapolis: Fortress Press, 1998), 205–36.

[23]David Barr, "Towards an Ethical Reading of the Apocalypse: Reflections on John's Use of Power, Violence, and Misogyny," *SBLSP* 36 (1997): 358–74; cf. Barr's *Tales of the End: A Narrative Commentary on the Book of Revelation* (The Storytellers Bible 1; Santa Rosa, Calif.: Polebridge, 1998).

[24]Carolyn Osiek, *Shepherd of Hermas: A Commentary* (Hermeneia; Minneapolis: Fortress Press, 1999), 1–2.

[25]Carolyn Osiek, "Hermas, Shepherd of," *EDB,* 577.

[26]The translation I am using is from Michael W. Holmes, *The Apostolic Fathers: Greek Texts and English Translations of Their Writings* (2d ed.; Grand Rapids, Mich.: Baker, 1992). For decades, the standard edition of the Apostolic Fathers, including Hermas, has been the Loeb Classical Library edition by J. B. Lightfoot. Lightfoot's work is, however, dated, and has just been be replaced in the series by a new critical edition and text by Bart D. Ehrman ("The Shepherd of Hermas," in *The Apostolic Fathers: Volume 2* [LCL 25; Cambridge, Mass.: Harvard University Press, 2003], 161–473). Unfortunately, I have not had time to incorporate Ehrman's text, translation, or comments into this chapter adequately.

[27]Character development is relatively rare in ancient narrative.

[28]For more explication of this passage, see Osiek, *Shepherd of Hermas,* 237.

[29]Ibid., 55.

[30]The discussion that follows is heavily dependent on Osiek, *Shepherd of Hermas,* 4–7; and Bruce M. Metzger, *The Canon of the New Testament: Its Origin, Development, and Significance* (New York: Oxford University Press, 1987), passim.

[31]Wainwright, *Mysterious Apocalypse,* 33–34.

[32]Carolyn Osiek, *Rich and Poor in the* Shepherd of Hermas*: An Exegetical-Social Investigation* (CBQMS 15; Washington, D.C.: Catholic Biblical Association of America, 1983), 41–45.

[33]Ibid., 46–47.

[34]Osiek, *Shepherd of Hermas,* 36.

[35]Edith McEwan Humphrey, *The Ladies and the Cities: Transformation and Apocalyptic Identity in Joseph and Aseneth, 4 Ezra, the Apocalypse and The Shepherd of Hermas* (JSPSup 17; Sheffield: Sheffield Academic Press, 1995), 142–44.

[36]Lage Pernveden, *The Concept of the Church in the Shepherd of Hermas* (Studia theologica Ludensia 27 Lund: Gleerup, 1966), 60.

[37]Osiek, *Shepherd of Hermas,* 33–34.

[38]See the discussions in Osiek, *Shepherd of Hermas,* 34–36; and Clayton N. Jefford, *Reading the Apostolic Fathers: An Introduction* (Peabody, Mass.: Hendrickson, 1996), 144–45.

[39]See Humphrey, *The Ladies and the Cities,* for a detailed analysis of this trope.

Chapter 8: Christian Ascents

[1]David Frankfurter, "Early Christian Apocalypticism: Literature and Social World," in *The Encyclopedia of Apocalypticism: Volume 1: The Origins of Apocalypticism in Judaism and Christianity* (ed. John J. Collins; New York: Continuum, 1998), 416.

[2]Translation, with introduction, by M. A. Knibb, "Martyrdom and Ascension of Isaiah," in *The Old Testament Pseudepigrapha: Volume 2: Expansions of the "Old Testament" and Legends, Wisdom and Philosophical Literature, Prayers, Psalms and Odes, Fragments of Lost Judeo-Hellenistic Works* (ed. James H. Charlesworth; New York: Doubleday, 1985), 143–76.

[3]Translation, with introduction, by D. R. A. Hare, "The Lives of the Prophets," in *The Old Testament Pseudepigrapha: Volume 2: Expansions of the "Old Testament" and Legends, Wisdom and Philosophical Literature, Prayers, Psalms and Odes, Fragments of Lost Judeo-Hellenistic Works* (ed. James H. Charlesworth; New York: Doubleday, 1985), 379–99.

⁴A textual problem at Asc. Isa. 8:12, in which the Ethiopic manuscripts suggest that Isaiah will share in "the lot of the tree," confirms that ancient readers appreciated this association.

⁵John F. A. Sawyer, *The Fifth Gospel: Isaiah in the History of Christianity* (Cambridge: Cambridge University Press, 1996); cf. Craig A. Evans, *To See and Not Perceive: Isaiah 6:9–10 in Early Jewish and Christian Interpretation* (JSOTSup 64; Sheffield: Sheffield Academic Press, 1989). For the Ascension of Isaiah's use of the canonical Isaiah, see Greg Carey, "The *Ascension of Isaiah*: Characterization and Conflict," in *Vision and Persuasion: Rhetorical Dimensions of Apocalyptic Discourse* (ed. Greg Carey and L. Gregory Bloomquist; St. Louis: Chalice Press, 1999), 161–79.

⁶Jonathan Knight, *The Ascension of Isaiah* (Guides to Apocrypha and Pseudepigrapha; Sheffield: Sheffield Academic Press, 1995), 14.

⁷Precisely, this process begins between the sixth and fifth heavens, as the sixth heaven "is in full harmony with the seventh" (Adela Yarbro Collins, "The Seven Heavens in Jewish and Christian Apocalypses," in *Cosmology and Eschatology in Jewish and Christian Apocalypticism* [JSJSup 50; Leiden: Brill, 1996], 41).

⁸See the discussion in Jonathan Knight, *Disciples of the Beloved One: The Christology, Social Setting and Theological Context of the Ascension of Isaiah* (JSPSup 18; Sheffield: Sheffield Academic Press, 1996), 186–273. Cf. Richard Bauckham, "The Ascension of Isaiah: Genre, Unity and Date," in *The Fate of the Dead: Studies on the Jewish and Christian Apocalypses* (NovTSup 93; Leiden: Brill, 1998), 363–90.

⁹Cf. Sib. Or. 3:53–74; 4:119–22; 5:94–110, 137–54, 214–27, 231, 361–85; 8:68–72, 139–69; 12:78–94; Rev. 13:3, 12, 14; 17:11.

¹⁰Mauro Pesce, "Presupposti per l'utilizzazione storica dell'*Ascensione di Isaiah*: Formazione e tradizione del testo; genere letterario; cosmologia angelica," in *Isaiah: il Diletto e la Chiesa: Visione ed esegesi profetica cristiano-primitiva nell'*Ascensione di Isaiah (ed. Mauro Pesce; Testi e recherche di scienze religiose 20; Brescia: Paideia Editrice, 1983), 13–76; Pesce, *L'Ascensione di Isaiah: Cristologia e profetismo in Siria nei primi decenni del II secolo* (Studia Patristica Mediolanensia 17; Milan: Vita e Pensiero, 1989); Robert G. Hall, "The *Ascension of Isaiah*: Community Situation, Date, and Place in Early Christianity," *JBL* 109 (1990): 289–306; Hall, *Revealed Histories: Techniques for Ancient Jewish and Christian Historiography* (JSPSup 6; Sheffield: Sheffield Academic Press, 1991), esp. 137–47.

¹¹Knight, *Disciples of the Beloved One*, 71–185, esp. 139–43.

¹²Dennis D. Buchholz, *Your Eyes Will Be Opened: A Study of the Greek (Ethiopic) Apocalypse of Peter* (SBLDS 97; Atlanta: Scholars Press, 1987), 119–56; Richard Bauckham, "The Apocalypse of Peter: A Jewish Christian Apocalypse from the Time of Bar Kokhba," in *The Fate of the Dead: Studies on the Jewish and Christian Apocalypses* (NovTSup 93; Leiden: Brill, 1998), 162–65.

¹³Bauckham, "The Apocalypse of Peter," 168–94.

¹⁴J. Brashler and R. A. Bullard, "Apocalypse of Peter (VII, 3)," in *The Nag Hammadi Library* (ed. James M. Robinson; rev. ed.; San Francisco: HarperSanFrancisco, 1990), 372–78.

¹⁵Buchholz, *Your Eyes Will Be Opened*, 20–25.

¹⁶Patrick Gray, "Abortion, Infanticide, and the Social Rhetoric of the *Apocalypse of Peter*," *JECS* 9 (2001): 315.

¹⁷Bauckham, "The Apocalypse of Peter," 174–76.

¹⁸Greg Carey, "Apocalyptic *Ethos*," *SBLSP* 37/2 (1998): 731–61.

¹⁹Quotations from the Apocalypse of Peter follow the translation by J. K. Elliott, *The Apocryphal New Testament* (Oxford: Clarendon, 1993), 593–612.

²⁰Martha Himmelfarb, *Tours of Hell: An Apocalyptic Form in Jewish and Christian Literature* (Philadelphia: Fortress Press, 1983), 41–50.

²¹Bauckham, "Descents to the Underworld," 9–48.

²²David Fiensy, "*Lex Talionis* in the *Apocalypse of Peter*," *HTR* 76 (1983): 255–58; Himmelfarb, *Tours of Hell*, 68–126.

²³Elliott, *Apocryphal New Testament*, 616.

²⁴Himmelfarb, *Tours of Hell*, 16–19; cf. Hugo Duensing and Aurelio de Santos Otero, "Apocalypse of Paul," in *New Testament Apocrypha: Volume 2: Writings Related to the Apostles; Apocalypses and Related Subjects* (ed. Wilhelm Schneemelcher; trans. R. McL. Wilson; rev. ed.; Louisville: Westminster / John Knox Press, 1992), 712–13. The Origen tradition derives from

the medieval Syrian bishop Bar Hebraeus (*Noncanon* 7.9) and from Origen's description of the fate of a soul after death (*Homily 5 on Psalms*).

[25]For conflicting judgments, see Himmelfarb, *Tours of Hell,* 142–44; and Duensing and de Santos Otero, "Apocalypse of Paul," 2.714.

[26]Bauckham, *Fate of the Dead,* 93.

[27]Translations derive from Elliott, *Apocryphal New Testament,* 616–44.

[28]The justice of judgment is a common motif in the apocalypses (Bauckham, *Fate of the Dead,* 132–48).

[29]Ibid., 137.

[30]Bauckham, *Fate of the Dead,* 141; Duensing and de Santos Otero, "Apocalypse of Paul," 2.714.

Chapter 9: Epilogue

[1]Claudia J. Setzer, "The Parousia of Jesus and Jewish Messianic Hopes," in John T. Carroll, Alexandra R. Brown, Claudia J. Setzer, and Jeffrey S. Siker, *The Return of Jesus in Early Christianity* (Peabody, Mass.: Hendrickson, 2000), 179–80; cf. Richard A. Horsley, "Popular Messianic Movements around the Time of Jesus," *CBQ* 46 (1984): 471–95.

[2]R. J. Zvi Werblowsky, "Messianism in Jewish History," in *Essential Papers on Messianic Movements and Personalities in Jewish History* (ed. Marc Saperstein; Essential Papers on Jewish Studies; New York: New York University Press, 1992), 40; Eliezer Schweid, "Jewish Messianism: Metamorphoses of an Idea," in *Essential Papers on Messianic Movements and Personalities in Jewish History* (ed. Marc Saperstein; Essential Papers on Jewish Studies; New York: New York University Press, 1992), 60–61.

[3]Marc Saperstein, "Introduction," in *Essential Papers on Messianic Movements and Personalities in Jewish History* (ed. Marc Saperstein; Essential Papers on Jewish Studies; New York: New York University Press, 1992), 2–4.

[4]Moshe Idel, "Jewish Apocalypticism: 670–1670," in *The Encyclopedia of Apocalypticism: Volume 2: Apocalypticism in Western History and Culture* (ed. Bernard McGinn; New York: Continuum, 2000), 205.

[5]Ibid., 208.

[6]Joshua Bloch, *On the Apocalyptic in Judaism* (JQRMS 2; Philadelphia: Dropsie College Press, 1952), 57–153; Christopher Rowland, *The Open Heaven: A Study of Apocalyptic in Judaism and Early Christianity* (New York: Crossroad, 1982), 271–348.

[7]Rowland argues that the point concerns how prospective students should prepare themselves for the contemplation of scripture (*Open Heaven,* 317–19).

[8]Translation by Shani Berrin, in *Texts and Traditions: A Source Reader for the Study of Second Temple and Rabbinic Judaism* (ed. Lawrence H. Schiffman; Hoboken, N.J.: KTAV, 1998), 735.

[9]Gerhard A. Krodel, *Revelation* (ACNT; Minneapolis: Augsburg, 1989), 28–32; Arthur W. Wainwright, *Mysterious Apocalypse: Interpreting the Book of Revelation* (Nashville: Abingdon Press, 1993), 21–30. I have taken some of the dates from Everett Ferguson, ed., *Encyclopedia of Early Christianity* (2d ed.; New York: Garland, 1998).

[10]Wainwright, *Mysterious Apocalypse,* 25.

[11]Paula Fredriksen, "Tyconius and Augustine on the Apocalypse," in *The Apocalypse in the Middle Ages* (ed. Richard K. Emmerson and Bernard McGinn; Ithaca, N.Y.: Cornell University Press, 1992), 20–37; Brian E. Daley, "Apocalypticism in Early Christian Theology," in *The Encyclopedia of Apocalypticism: Volume 2: Apocalypticism in Western History and Culture* (ed. Bernard McGinn; New York: Continuum, 2000), 3–47; Krodel, *Revelation,* 30; Wainwright, *Mysterious Apocalypse,* 33–44.

[12]Arthur P. Mendel, *Vision and Violence* (Ann Arbor: University of Michigan Press, 1992), 218.

[13]Gershom Scholem, "Sabbatai Sevi: The Mystical Messiah," in *Essential Papers on Messianic Movements and Personalities in Jewish History* (ed. Marc Saperstein; Essential Papers on Jewish Studies; New York: New York University Press, 1992), 295–96. Cf. Scholem, *Judaica: Volume 1* (Frankfurt: Suhrkamp, 1963), 266, cited in Jürgen Moltmann, *The Coming of God: Christian Eschatology* (trans. Margaret Kohl; Minneapolis: Fortress Press, 1996), 36.

[14]Noting this development, but qualifying it, Valerie A. Karras, "Eschatology," in *The Cambridge Companion to Feminist Theology* (ed. Susan Frank Parsons; New York: Cambridge University Press, 2002), 243–60; cf. Catherine Keller, "Pneumatic Nudges: The Theology of

Moltmann, Feminism, and the Future," in *The Future of Theology: Essays in Honor of Jürgen Moltmann* (ed. Miroslav Volf, Carmen Krieg, and Thomas Kucharz; Grand Rapids, Mich.: Eerdmans, 1996), 153.

[15]Cf. Catherine Keller, *Apocalypse Now and Then: A Feminist Guide to the End of the World* (Boston: Beacon, 1996).

[16]Grace Halsell, *Prophecy and Politics: The Secret Alliance between Israel and the U.S. Christian Right* (Chicago: Lawrence Hill, 1986), 10.

[17]Charles B. Strozier, *Apocalypse: On the Psychology of Fundamentalism in America* (Boston: Beacon, 1994).

[18]The first major study of this topic is Stephen D. O'Leary, *Arguing the Apocalypse: A Theory of Millennial Rhetoric* (New York: Oxford University Press, 1994). Developing this emphasis, Greg Carey, "Apocalyptic *Ethos*," *SBLSP* 37/2 (1998): 731–61; and idem, *Elusive Apocalypse: Reading Authority in the Revelation to John* (StABH 15; Macon, Ga.: Mercer University Press, 1999).

[19]Wayne A. Meeks, "Social Functions of Apocalyptic Language in Pauline Christianity," in *Apocalypticism in the Mediterranean World and the Near East: Proceedings of the International Colloquium on Apocalypticism, Uppsala, August 12–17, 1979* (ed. David Hellholm; Tübingen: Mohr-Siebeck, 1982), 687–705.

[20]Ernst Käsemann, "The Beginnings of Christian Theology," in *New Testament Questions of Today* (Philadelphia: Fortress Press, 1969 [originally published in 1960]), 102; Rudolf Bultmann, *Jesus Christ and Mythology* (New York: Scribners, 1958).

[21]Charles L. Holman, *Till Jesus Comes: Origins of Christian Apocalyptic Expectation* (Peabody, Mass.: Hendrickson, 1996), 154–63.

[22]D. Brent Sandy, *Plowshares & Pruning Hooks: Rethinking the Language of Biblical Prophecy and Apocalyptic* (Downers Grove, Ill.: InterVarsity, 2002), 188.

[23]Pablo Richard, *Apocalypse: A People's Commentary on the Book of Revelation* (Maryknoll, N.Y.: Orbis, 1995), 31–32.

[24]Brian K. Blount, *Then the Whisper Put on Flesh: New Testament Ethics in an African American Context* (Nashville: Abingdon Press, 2001), 158–84.

[25]Allen A. Boesak, *Comfort and Protest: The Apocalypse from a South African Perspective* (Philadelphia: Westminster Press, 1987), 15, 38–39.

[26]C. I. David Joy, *Revelation: A Post-Colonial View Point* (Delhi: ISPCK, 2001), 97–98.

[27]Note especially Elisabeth Schüssler Fiorenza, *Revelation: Vision of a Just World* (Proclamation Commentaries; Minneapolis: Fortress Press, 1991); idem, *The Book of Revelation: Justice and Judgment* (2d ed.; Minneapolis: Fortress Press, 1998); idem, "The Words of Prophecy: Reading the Apocalypse Theologically," in *Studies in the Book of Revelation* (ed. Steve Moyise; New York: T&T Clark, 2001), 1–19; Adela Yarbro Collins, *Crisis and Catharsis: The Power of the Apocalypse* (Louisville: Westminster Press, 1984); idem, "Feminine Symbolism in the Book of Revelation," *BibInt* 1 (1993): 20–33; and idem, "The Political Perspective of the Revelation to John," *JBL* 96 (1977): 241–56.

[28]Tina Pippin, *Death and Desire: The Rhetoric of Gender in the Apocalypse of John* (Literary Currents in Biblical Interpretation; Louisville: Westminster/John Knox Press, 1992), 16.

[29]Tina Pippin, "A Good Apocalypse Is Hard to Find: Crossing the Apocalyptic Borders of Mark 13," *Semeia* 72 (1995): 153.

[30]Yarbro Collins, *Crisis and Catharsis,* 172.

[31]Adela Yarbro Collins, "The Book of Revelation," in *The Encyclopedia of Apocalypticism: Volume 1: The Origins of Apocalypticism in Judaism and Christianity* (ed. John J. Collins; New York: Crossroad, 1998), 412.

[32]Schüssler Fiorenza, "The Words of Prophecy," 11.

[33]Schüssler Fiorenza, *Revelation: Vision of a Just World,* 122.

[34]Moltmann's recent book, *In the End–the Beginning: The Life of Hope* (Minneapolis: Fortress Press, 2004), articulates his eschatological thought in a manner that is at once thorough, concise, pastoral, and accessible.

[35]Moltmann, *The Coming of God,* 229–34. Cf. his earlier *Theology of Hope: On the Ground and Implications of a Christian Eschatology* (New York: Harper & Row, 1967).

[36]Moltmann, *The Coming of God,* 138–39.

[37]Ibid., 141.

[38]Moltmann, *Theology of Hope,* 21–22.

[39]Richard Bauckham and Trevor Hart, *Hope against Hope: Christian Eschatology at the Turn of the Millennium* (Grand Rapids, Mich.: Eerdmans, 1999), 74–76.

[40]Ibid., 84.

[41]Ibid., 89–108.

[42]Ibid., 193, 206.

[43]Ibid., 119.

[44]Richard B. Hays, "'Why Do You Stand Looking Up toward Heaven?' New Testament Eschatology at the Turn of the Millennium," *Modern Theology* 16 (2000): 133.

[45]Karras, "Eschatology," 257.

[46]See James Fodor and Stanley Hauerwas, "Performing Faith: The Peaceable Rhetoric of God's Church," in *Rhetorical Invention and Religious Inquiry: New Perspectives* (ed. Walter Jost and Wendy Olmsted; New Haven: Yale University Press, 2000), 394.

Bibliography

Note on Translations

Unless indicated otherwise, translations of passages from the Bible, including the Apocrypha, derive from the *New Revised Standard Version* (Division of Christian Education of the National Council of Churches of Christ in the United States of America, 1989), while translations of other ancient Jewish and Christian sources derive from the sources below.

Charlesworth, James H., ed. *The Old Testament Pseudepigrapha: Volume 1: Apocalyptic Literature and Testaments*. New York: Doubleday, 1983.

_____, ed. *The Old Testament Pseudepigrapha: Volume 2: Expansions of the "Old Testament" and Legends, Wisdom and Philosophical Literature, Prayers, Psalms and Odes, Fragments of Lost Judeo-Hellenistic Works*. New York: Doubleday, 1985.

Elliott, J. K. *The Apocryphal New Testament*. Oxford: Clarendon, 1993.

García Martínez, Florentino. *The Dead Sea Scrolls Translated: The Qumran Texts in English*. Leiden: Brill, 1994.

General Bibliography

Aland, Kurt, ed.. *Synopsis of the Four Gospels*. Rev. ed. New York: United Bible Societies, 1985.

Alexander, Philip S. "From Son of Man to Second God: Transformations of the Biblical Enoch." Pages 87–122 in *Biblical Figures Outside the Bible*. Edited by Michael E. Stone and Theodore A. Bergen. Harrisburg, Pa.: Trinity Press International, 1998.

Allison, Dale C. *Jesus of Nazareth: Millenarian Prophet*. Minneapolis: Fortress Press, 1998.

_____. "The Eschatology of Jesus." Pages 267–302 in *The Encyclopedia of Apocalypticism: Volume 1: The Origins of Apocalypticism in Judaism and Christianity*. Edited by John J. Collins. New York: Crossroad, 1998.

_____, *The Jesus Tradition in Q*. Harrisburg, Pa.: Trinity Press International, 1997.

Aune, David. *Revelation*. 3 vols. WBC 52. Dallas, Tex.: Word/Nashville: Thomas Nelson, 1997–1998.

_____. "The Social Matrix of the Apocalypse of John." *BR* 26 (1981): 16–33.

Barr, David. *Tales of the End: A Narrative Commentary on the Book of Revelation*. The Storytellers Bible 1. Santa Rosa, Calif.: Polebridge, 1998.

_____. "Towards an Ethical Reading of the Apocalypse: Reflections on John's Use of Power, Violence, and Misogyny." *SBLSP* 36 (1997): 358–74.

Bauckham, Richard. "The Economic Critique of Rome in Revelation 18." Pages 338–83 in *The Climax of Prophecy: Studies on the Book of Revelation*. Edinburgh: T. & T. Clark, 1993.

_____. *The Fate of the Dead: Studies on the Jewish and Christian Apocalypses*. NovTSup 93. Leiden: Brill, 1998.

_____. *The Theology of the Book of Revelation*. New Testament Theology. Cambridge: Cambridge University Press, 1993.

Bauckham, Richard, and Trevor Hart. *Hope against Hope: Christian Eschatology at the Turn of the Millennium*. Grand Rapids, Mich.: Eerdmans, 1999.

Beal, Timothy K. "Intertextuality." Pages 128–30 in *Handbook of Postmodern Biblical Interpretation*. Edited by A. K. M. Adam. St. Louis: Chalice Press, 2000.

Beale, Gregory K. *The Use of Daniel in Jewish Apocalyptic Literature and in the Revelation of St. John*. Lanham, Md.: University Press of America, 1984.

Beard, Mary, John North, and Simon Price. *Religions of Rome: Volume 1: A History*. Cambridge: Cambridge University Press, 1998.

_____. *Religions of Rome: Volume 2: A Sourcebook*. Cambridge: Cambridge University Press, 1998.

Beker, J. Christiaan. *Paul the Apostle: The Triumph of God in Life and Thought*. Philadelphia: Fortress Press, 1980.

Berquist, Jon L. *In Persia's Shadow: A Social and Historical Approach*. Minneapolis: Fortress Press, 1995.

Black, Matthew, in consultation with James C. VanderKam. *The Book of Enoch or 1 Enoch: A New English Edition with Commentary and Textual Notes*. Leiden: Brill, 1985.

_____. "The Messianism of the Parables of Enoch: Their Date and Contributions to Christian Origins." Pages 145–68 in *The Messiah: Developments in Earliest Judaism and Christianity*. Edited by James H. Charlesworth. Minneapolis: Fortress Press, 1992.

Blenkinsopp, Joseph. *Ezekiel*. Interpretation. Louisville: John Knox Press, 1990.

_____. *A History of Prophecy in Israel*. Rev. ed. Louisville: Westminster John Knox Press, 1996.

Bloch, Joshua. *On the Apocalyptic in Judaism*. JQRMS 2. Philadelphia: Dropsie College Press, 1952.

Bloomquist, L. Gregory. "Methodological Criteria for Apocalyptic Rhetoric: A Suggestion for the Expanded Use of Sociorhetorical Analysis." Pages 181–203 in *Vision and Persuasion: Rhetorical Dimensions of Apocalyptic Discourse*. Edited by Greg Carey and L. Gregory Bloomquist. St. Louis: Chalice Press, 1999.

Blount, Brian K. "Reading Revelation Today: Witness as Active Resistance." *Int* 54 (2000): 398–412.

_____. *Then the Whisper Put on Flesh: New Testament Ethics in an African American Context*. Nashville: Abingdon Press, 2001.

Boccaccini, Gabrielle. "Jewish Apocalyptic Tradition: The Contribution of Italian Scholarship." Pages 33–50 in *Mysteries and Revelations: Apocalyptic Studies since the Uppsala Colloquium.* Edited by John J. Collins and James H. Charlesworth. JSPSup 9. Sheffield: JSPT Press, 1991.

Bockmuehl, Markus. *The Epistle to the Philippians.* BNTC. London: A & C Black, 1997.

———. *Revelation and Mystery in Ancient Judaism and Pauline Christianity.* Grand Rapids, Mich.: Eerdmans, 1997.

Boesak, Allan A. *Comfort and Protest: The Apocalypse from a South African Perspective.* Philadelphia: Westminster Press, 1987.

Borg, Marcus J. *Jesus: A New Vision.* San Francisco: Harper & Row, 1987.

———. *Meeting Jesus Again for the First Time: The Historical Jesus and the Heart of Contemporary Faith.* San Francisco: HarperSanFrancisco, 1995.

Boyarin, Daniel. *A Radical Jew: Paul and the Politics of Identity.* Berkeley: University of California Press, 1994.

Boyer, Paul. *When Time Shall Be No More: Prophecy Belief in Modern American Culture.* Cambridge, Mass.: Harvard University Press, 1992.

Brashler, J., and R. A. Bullard. "Apocalypse of Peter (VII, 3)." Pages 372–78 in *The Nag Hammadi Library.* Edited by James M. Robinson. Rev. ed. San Francisco: HarperSanFrancisco, 1990.

Brown, Raymond E. *An Introduction to the New Testament.* ABRL. New York: Doubleday, 1997.

Buchholz, Dennis D. *Your Eyes Will Be Opened: A Study of the Greek (Ethiopic) Apocalypse of Peter.* SBLDS 97. Atlanta: Scholars Press, 1987.

Bultmann, Rudolf. *Jesus Christ and Mythology.* New York: Scribners, 1958.

Burkes, Shannon. "'Life' Redefined: Wisdom and Law in Fourth Ezra and Second Baruch." *CBQ* 63 (2001): 55–71.

Burkett, Delbert. *The Son of Man Debate: A History and Evaluation.* SNTMS 107. Cambridge: Cambridge University Press, 2000.

Cameron, Ron, ed. T*he Other Gospels.* Philadelphia: The Westminster Press, 1982.

Carey, Greg. "Apocalyptic *Ethos.*" *SBLSP* 37/2 (1998): 731–61.

———. "The *Ascension of Isaiah*: Characterization and Conflict." Pages 161–79 in *Vision and Persuasion: Rhetorical Dimensions of Apocalyptic Discourse.* Edited by Greg Carey and L. Gregory Bloomquist. St. Louis: Chalice, 1999.

———. *Elusive Apocalypse: Reading Authority in the Revelation to John.* StABH 15. Macon, Ga.: Mercer University Press, 1999.

———. "Introduction: Apocalyptic Discourse, Apocalyptic Rhetoric." Pages 1–17 in *Vision and Persuasion: Rhetorical Dimensions of Apocalyptic Discourse.* Edited by Greg Carey and L. Gregory Bloomquist. St. Louis: Chalice Press, 1999.

Carey, Greg, and L. Gregory Bloomquist, eds. *Vision and Persuasion: Rhetorical Dimensions of Apocalyptic Discourse.* St. Louis: Chalice Press, 1999.

Charles, R. H. *A Critical and Exegetical Commentary on the Revelation of St. John.* 2 vols. ICC. Edinburgh: Charles Scribner's Sons, 1920.

_____. *The Book of Enoch.* Oxford: Clarendon, 1893.

Collins, John J. *The Apocalyptic Imagination: An Introduction to Jewish Apocalyptic Literature.* 2d ed. The Biblical Resource Series. Grand Rapids, Mich.: Eerdmans, 1998.

_____. *Apocalypticism in the Dead Sea Scrolls.* Literature of the Dead Sea Scrolls. New York: Routledge, 1997.

_____. *Between Athens and Jerusalem: Jewish Identity in the Hellenistic Diaspora.* 2d ed. The Biblical Resource Series. Grand Rapids, Mich.: Eerdmans, 2000.

_____. *Daniel: A Commentary on the Book of Daniel.* Hermeneia. Minneapolis: Fortress Press, 1993.

_____. "The Date and Provenance of the Testament of Moses." Pages 15–32 in *Studies on the Testament of Moses.* Edited by George W. E. Nickelsburg. Septuagint and Cognate Studies 4. Cambridge, Mass.: Society of Biblical Literature, 1973.

_____. "The Expectation of the End in the Dead Sea Scrolls." Pages 74–90 in *Eschatology, Messianism, and the Dead Sea Scrolls.* Edited by Craig A. Evans and Peter W. Flint. Studies in the Dead Sea Scrolls and Related Literature. Grand Rapids, Mich.: Eerdmans, 1997.

_____. "From Prophecy to Apocalypticism: The Expectation of the End." Pages 129–61 in *Encyclopedia of Apocalypticism: Volume 1: The Origins of Apocalypticism in Judaism and Christianity.* Edited by John J. Collins. New York: Continuum, 1998.

_____. "Genre, Ideology, and Social Movements in Jewish Apocalypticism." Pages 11–32 in *Mysteries and Revelations: Apocalyptic Studies since the Uppsala Colloquium.* Edited by John J. Collins and James H. Charlesworth. JSPSup 9. Sheffield: Sheffield Academic Press, 1991.

_____. "Introduction: Towards the Morphology of a Genre." *Semeia* 14 (1979): 9–20.

_____. *Seers, Sibyls and Sages in Hellenistic-Roman Judaism.* JSJSup 54. Leiden: Brill, 1997.

_____. "The Sibylline Oracles." Pages 317–472 in *The Old Testament Pseudepigrapha: Volume 1: Apocalyptic Literature and Testaments.* Edited by James H. Charlesworth. New York: Doubleday, 1983.

_____. *The Sibylline Oracles of Egyptian Judaism.* SBLDS 13. Missoula, Mont.: Scholars Press, 1974.

_____. "Testaments." Pages 325–55 in *Jewish Writings of the Second Temple Period.* Edited by Michael E. Stone. CRINT 2.2; Philadelphia: Fortress Press, 1984.

_____. "Wisdom, Apocalypticism, and Generic Compatibility." Pages 165–85 in *In Search of Wisdom: Essays in Memory of John G. Gammie.* Edited by Leo G. Perdue, Bernard Brandon Scott, and William Johnston Wiseman. Louisville: Westminster John Knox Press, 1993.

Collins, John J., ed. *Apocalypse: The Morphology of a Genre. Semeia* 14 (1979).
_____. *The Encyclopedia of Apocalypticism: Volume 1: The Origins of Apocalypticism in Judaism and Christianity*. New York: Continuum, 1998.
Collins, John J., and James H. Charlesworth, eds. *Mysteries and Revelations: Apocalyptic Studies since the Uppsala Colloquium*. JSPSup 9. Sheffield: Sheffield Academic Press, 1991.
Collins, John J., and Peter W. Flint, eds. *The Book of Daniel: Composition and Reception*. 2 vols. Leiden: Brill, 2001.
Cook, Stephen L. *Prophecy and Apocalypticism: The Postexilic Social Setting*. Minneapolis: Fortress Press, 1995.
Crossan, John Dominic. *The Birth of Christianity*. San Francisco: HarperSanFrancisco, 1998.
_____. *The Historical Jesus: The Life of a Mediterranean Jewish Peasant*. San Francisco: HarperCollins, 1991.
_____. *Jesus: A Revolutionary Biography*. San Francisco: HarperSanFrancisco, 1994.
Daley, Brian E. "Apocalypticism in Early Christian Theology." Pages 3–47 in *The Encyclopedia of Apocalypticism: Volume 2: Apocalypticism in Western History and Culture*. Edited by Bernard McGinn. New York: Continuum, 2000.
Darr, Katheryn Pfisterer. "The Book of Ezekiel." Pages 1073–1607 in *The New Interpreter's Bible: Volume 6*. Nashville: Abingdon Press, 2001.
Davies, Philip R. "The Social World of Apocalyptic Writings." Pages 251–71 in *The World of Ancient Israel: Sociological, Anthropological and Political Perspectives*. Edited by R. E. Clements. Cambridge: Cambridge University Press, 1989.
Davies, W. D., and Dale C. Allison, Jr. *The Gospel according to Saint Matthew*. 3 vols. ICC; Edinburgh: T. & T. Clark, 1991.
de Boer, M. C. "Paul and Apocalyptic Eschatology." Pages 345–83 in *The Encyclopedia of Apocalypticism: Volume 1: The Origins of Apocalypticism in Judaism and Christianity*. Edited by John J. Collins. New York: Continuum, 1998.
deSilva, David A. "Fourth Ezra: Reaffirming Jewish Cultural Values through Apocalyptic Rhetoric." Pages 123–39 in *Vision and Persuasion: Rhetorical Dimensions of Apocalyptic Discourse*. Edited by Greg Carey and L. Gregory Bloomquist. St. Louis: Chalice, 1999.
Dibelius, Martin. "The Shepherd of Hermas." *NTA* 2.642.
Duensing, Hugo, and Aurelio de Santos Otero. "Apocalypse of Paul." Pages 712–48 in *New Testament Apocrypha: Volume 2: Writings Related to the Apostles; Apocalypses and Related Subjects*. Edited by Wilhelm Schneemelcher. Translated by R. McL. Wilson. Rev. ed. Louisville: Westminster John Knox Press, 1992.
Dunn, James D. G. "The Danielic Son of Man in the New Testament." Pages 528–49 in *The Book of Daniel: Composition and Reception*. Vol. 2. Edited by John J. Collins and Peter W. Flint. Leiden: Brill, 2001.

_____. *The Theology of Paul the Apostle*. Grand Rapids, Mich.: Eerdmans, 1998.

Eco, Umberto. *Baudolino*. New York: Harcourt, 2002.

Ehrman, Bart D. *Jesus: Apocalyptic Prophet of the New Millennium*. New York: Oxford University Press, 1999.

_____. *The New Testament: A Historical Introduction to the Early Christian Writings*. 3d ed. New York: Oxford University, 2003.

_____. "The Shepherd of Hermas." Pages 161–473 in *The Apostolic Fathers: Volume 2*. LCL 25. Cambridge, Mass.: Harvard University Press, 2003.

Esler, Philip F. "The Social Function of Fourth Ezra." Pages 110–30 in *The First Christians in Their Social Worlds: Social-Scientific Approaches to New Testament Interpretation*. New York: Routledge, 1994.

Evans, Craig A. "Daniel in the New Testament: Visions of God's Kingdom." Pages 490–527 in *The Book of Daniel: Composition and Reception*. Vol. 2. Edited by John J. Collins and Peter W. Flint. Leiden: Brill, 2001.

_____. *To See and Not Perceive: Isaiah 6:9–10 in Early Jewish and Christian Interpretation*. JSOTSup 64. Sheffield: Sheffield Academic Press, 1989.

Fee, Gordon D. *Paul's Letter to the Philippians*. NICNT. Grand Rapids, Mich.: Eerdmans, 1995.

Ferguson, Everett, ed. *Encyclopedia of Early Christianity*. 2d ed. New York: Garland, 1998.

Fewell, Dana Nolan. *Circle of Sovereignty: Plotting Politics in the Book of Daniel*. Nashville: Abingdon Press, 1991.

Fiensy, David. "*Lex Talionis* in the *Apocalypse of Peter*." *HTR* 76 (1983): 255–58.

Fodor, James, and Stanley Hauerwas. "Performing Faith: The Peaceable Rhetoric of God's Church." Pages 381–414 in *Rhetorical Invention and Religious Inquiry: New Perspectives*. Edited by Walter Jost and Wendy Olmsted. New Haven: Yale University Press, 2000.

Foucault, Michel. *Discipline and Punish: The Birth of the Prison*. New York: Pantheon, 1977.

_____. *The History of Sexuality, Volume 1: An Introduction*. New York: Random House, 1978.

_____. *Madness and Civilization*. New York: Random House, 1965.

_____. *The Order of Things: An Archaeology of the Human Sciences*. New York: Random House, 1970.

_____. *Religion and Culture*. Edited by Jeremy R. Carrette. New York: Routledge, 1999.

Frankfurter, David. "Early Christian Apocalypticism: Literature and Social World." Pages 415–53 in *The Encyclopedia of Apocalypticism: Volume 1: The Origins of Apocalypticism in Judaism and Christianity*. Edited by John J. Collins. New York: Continuum, 1998.

_____. "Jews or Not? Reconstructing the 'Other' in Rev 2:9 and 3:9." *HTR* 94 (2001): 403–25.

Fredriksen, Paula. *Jesus of Nazareth, King of the Jews: A Jewish Life and the Emergence of Christianity.* 2d ed. New Haven, Conn.: Yale University Press, 2000.

_____. "Tyconius and Augustine on the Apocalypse." Pages 20–37 in *The Apocalypse in the Middle Ages.* Edited by Richard K. Emmerson and Bernard McGinn. Ithaca, N.Y.: Cornell University Press, 1992.

Freedman, David Noel, ed. *Anchor Bible Dictionary.* 6 vols. New York: Doubleday, 1992.

_____, ed. *Eerdmans Dictionary of the Bible.* Grand Rapids, Mich.: Eerdmans, 2000.

Friesen, Steven J. *Imperial Cults and the Apocalypse of John: Reading Revelation in the Ruins.* New York: Oxford University Press, 2001.

García Martínez, Florentino. "Apocalypticism in the Dead Sea Scrolls." Pages 162–92 in *The Encyclopedia of Apocalypticism: Volume 1: The Origins of Apocalypticism in Judaism and Christianity.* Edited by John J. Collins. New York: Crossroad, 1998.

Gaylord, H. E., Jr. "3 (Greek Apocalypse of) Baruch." Pages 653–79 in *The Old Testament Pseudepigrapha: Volume 1: Apocalyptic Literature and Testaments.* Edited by James H. Charlesworth. New York: Doubleday, 1983.

Grabbe, Lester L. *Judaism from Cyrus to Hadrian: Volume 1: The Persian and Greek Periods.* Minneapolis: Fortress Press, 1991.

Gray, Patrick. "Abortion, Infanticide, and the Social Rhetoric of the *Apocalypse of Peter.*" *JECS* 9 (2001): 313–37.

Hall, Robert G. "The *Ascension of Isaiah*: Community Situation, Date, and Place in Early Christianity." *JBL* 109 (1990): 289–306.

_____. *Revealed Histories: Techniques for Ancient Jewish and Christian Historiography.* JSPSup 6. Sheffield: Sheffield Academic Press, 1991.

Halpern-Amaru, Betsy. *Rewriting the Bible: Land and Covenant in Postbiblical Jewish Literature.* Valley Forge, Pa.: Trinity Press International, 1994.

Halsell, Grace. *Prophecy and Politics: The Secret Alliance between Israel and the U.S. Christian Right.* Chicago: Lawrence Hill, 1986.

Hanson, Paul D. "Apocalypse, Genre" and "Apocalypticism." *IDBSup* 27–34.

_____. "Apocalypses and Apocalypticism." *ABD*, 1.279–82.

_____. "Apocalyptic Literature." Pages 465–88 in *The Hebrew Bible and Its Modern Interpreters.* Edited by Douglas A. Knight and Gene M. Tucker. Chico, Calif.: Scholars Press, 1985.

_____. *The Dawn of Apocalyptic: The Historical and Sociological Roots of Jewish Apocalyptic Eschatology.* Rev. ed. Philadelphia: Fortress Press, 1979.

_____. "Old Testament Apocalyptic Reexamined." Pages 37–60 in *Visionaries and Their Apocalypses.* Edited by Paul D. Hanson. Issues in Religion and Theology 2. Philadelphia: Fortress Press, 1983.

Hare, D. R. A. "The Lives of the Prophets." Pages 379–99 in *The Old Testament Pseudepigrapha: Volume 2: Expansions of the "Old Testament" and Legends,*

Wisdom and Philosophical Literature, Prayers, Psalms and Odes, Fragments of Lost Judeo-Hellenistic Works. Edited by James H. Charlesworth. New York: Doubleday, 1985.

Harland, Philip A. *Associations, Synagogues, and Congregations: Claiming a Place in Ancient Mediterranean Society.* Minneapolis: Fortress Press, 2003.

Harlow, Daniel. *The Greek Apocalypse of Baruch (3 Baruch) in Hellenistic Judaism and Early Christianity.* SVTP 12. Leiden: Brill, 1996.

Hayes, John H., and Sara R. Mandell. *The Jewish People in Classical Antiquity: From Alexander to Bar Kochba.* Louisville: Westminster John Knox Press, 1998.

Hays, Richard B. "'Why Do You Stand Looking Up toward Heaven?' New Testament Eschatology at the Turn of the Millennium." *Modern Theology* 16 (2000): 115–35.

Hellholm, David., ed. *Apocalypticism in the Mediterranean World and the Near East: Proceedings of the International Colloquium on Apocalypticism, Uppsala, August 12–17, 1979.* Tübingen: Mohr-Siebeck, 1982.

Herzog, William R., II. *Jesus, Justice, and the Reign of God.* Louisville: Westminster John Knox Press, 2000.

Hill, Craig C. *In God's Time: The Bible and the Future.* Grand Rapids, Mich.: Eerdmans, 2002.

Himmelfarb, Martha. *Ascent to Heaven in Jewish and Christian Apocalypses.* Oxford: Oxford University Press, 1993.

_____. *Tours of Hell: An Apocalyptic Form in Jewish and Christian Literature.* Philadelphia: Fortress Press, 1983.

Hollander, H. W., and M. de Jonge. *The Testaments of the Twelve Patriarchs: A Commentary.* SVTP 8. Leiden: Brill, 1985.

Holman, Charles L. *Till Jesus Comes: Origins of Christian Apocalyptic Expectation.* Peabody, Mass.: Hendrickson, 1996.

Holmes, Michael W. *The Apostolic Fathers: Greek Texts and English Translations of Their Writings.* 2d ed. Grand Rapids, Mich.: Baker, 1992.

Horsley, Richard A. "The Kingdom of God and the Renewal of Israel: Synoptic Gospels, Jesus Movements, and Apocalypticism." Pages 303–44 in *The Encyclopedia of Apocalypticism: Volume 1: The Origins of Apocalypticism in Judaism and Christianity.* Edited by John J. Collins. New York: Continuum, 1998.

_____, ed. *Paul and Empire: Religion and Power in Roman Imperial Society.* Philadelphia: Trinity Press International, 1996.

_____. "Popular Messianic Movements around the Time of Jesus." *CBQ* 46 (1984): 471–95.

Humphrey, Edith McEwan. *The Ladies and the Cities: Transformation and Apocalyptic Identity in Joseph and Aseneth, 4 Ezra, the Apocalypse and The Shepherd of Hermas.* JSPSup 17. Sheffield: Sheffield Academic Press, 1995.

Hutcheon, Linda. *The Politics of Postmodernism.* New Accents. New York: Routledge, 1989.

Idel, Moshe. "Jewish Apocalypticism: 670–1670." Pages 204–37 in *The Encyclopedia of Apocalypticism: Volume 2: Apocalypticism in Western History and Culture*. Edited by Bernard McGinn. New York: Continuum, 2000.

Isaac, E. "1 (Ethiopic Apocalypse of) Enoch." Pages 5–89 in *The Old Testament Pseudepigrapha: Volume 1: Apocalyptic Literature and Testaments*. Edited by James H. Charlesworth. New York: Doubleday, 1983.

Jefford, Clayton N. *Reading the Apostolic Fathers: An Introduction*. Peabody, Mass.: Hendrickson, 1996.

Johnson, Luke Timothy. *The Gospel of Luke*. SP 3. Collegeville, Minn.: Michael Glazier, 1991.

_____. The Letter of James. AB 37A. New York: Doubleday, 1995.

Johnstone, Ronald L. *Religion in Society: A Sociology of Religion*. 5th ed. Upper Saddle River, N.J.: Prentice Hall, 1997.

Jonge, M. de. "Christian Influence in the Testaments of the Twelve Patriarchs." Pages 193–246 in *Studies on the Testaments of the Twelve Patriarchs*. Edited by M. de Jonge. SVTP 3. Leiden: Brill, 1975.

_____. "The Interpretation of the Testaments of the Twelve Patriarchs in Recent Years." Pages 183–92 in *Studies on the Testaments of the Twelve Patriarchs*. Edited by M. de Jonge. SVTP 3. Leiden: Brill, 1975.

_____. "Notes on Testament of Levi II-VII." Pages 247–60 in *Studies on the Testaments of the Twelve Patriarchs*. Edited by M. de Jonge. SVTP 3. Leiden: Brill, 1975.

Jung, C. J. *Answer to Job*. Translated by R. F. C. Hull. London: Routledge & Keegan Paul, 1954.

Joy, C. I. David. *Revelation: A Post-Colonial View Point*. Delhi: ISPCK, 2001.

Kaltner, John. "Is Daniel Also among the Prophets? The Rhetoric of Daniel 10–12." Pages 41–59 in *Vision and Persuasion: Rhetorical Dimensions of Apocalyptic Discourse*. Edited by Greg Carey and L. Gregory Bloomquist. St. Louis: Chalice Press, 1999.

Karras, Valerie A. "Eschatology." Pages 243–60 in *The Cambridge Companion to Feminist Theology*. Edited by Susan Frank Parsons. New York: Cambridge University Press, 2002.

Käsemann, Ernst. "The Beginnings of Christian Theology." Pages 82–107 in *New Testament Questions of Today*. Philadelphia: Fortress Press, 1969.

Kee, H. C. "Testaments of the Twelve Patriarchs." Pages 777–828 in *The Old Testament Pseudepigrapha: Volume 1: Apocalyptic Literature and Testaments*. Edited by James H. Charlesworth. New York: Doubleday, 1983.

Keller, Catherine. *Apocalypse Now and Then: A Feminist Guide to the End of the World*. Boston: Beacon, 1996.

_____. "Pneumatic Nudges: The Theology of Moltmann, Feminism, and the Future." Pages 142–53 in *The Future of Theology: Essays in Honor of Jürgen Moltmann*. Edited by Miroslav Volf, Carmen Krieg, and Thomas Kucharz. Grand Rapids, Mich.: Eerdmans, 1996.

Kennedy, George A. *Comparative Rhetoric: An Historical and Cross-Cultural Introduction.* New York: Oxford University Press, 1998.

Khalidi, Tarif. *The Muslim Jesus: Sayings and Stories in Islamic Literature.* Cambridge, Mass.: Harvard University Press, 2001.

King, Martin Luther, Jr. "Where Do We Go from Here?" Pages 555–633 in *A Testament of Hope: The Essential Writings of Martin Luther King, Jr.* Edited by James Melvin Washington. San Francisco: Harper & Row, 1986.

Kittel, G., and G. Friedrich, eds. *Theological Dictionary of the New Testament.* Translated by G. W. Bromiley. 10 vols. Grand Rapids, Mich.: Eerdmans, 1964–1976.

Klassen, William. "Vengeance in the Apocalypse of John." *CBQ* 28 (1966): 300–11.

Klijn, A. F. J. "2 (Syriac Apocalypse of) Baruch." Pages 615–52 in *The Old Testament Pseudepigrapha: Volume 1: Apocalyptic Literature and Testaments.* Edited by James H. Charlesworth. New York: Doubleday, 1983.

Kloppenborg, John S. *The Formation of Q: Trajectories in Ancient Christian Wisdom Collections.* Studies in Antiquity and Christianity. Philadelphia: Fortress Press, 1987.

Knibb, M. A. "Martyrdom and Ascension of Isaiah." Pages 143–76 in *The Old Testament Pseudepigrapha: Volume 2: Expansions of the "Old Testament" and Legends, Wisdom and Philosophical Literature, Prayers, Psalms and Odes, Fragments of Lost Judeo-Hellenistic Works.* Edited by James H. Charlesworth. New York: Doubleday, 1985.

Knight, Jonathan. *The Ascension of Isaiah.* Guides to Apocrypha and Pseudepigrapha. Sheffield: Sheffield Academic Press, 1995.

_____. *Disciples of the Beloved One: The Christology, Social Setting and Theological Context of the Ascension of Isaiah.* JSPSup 18. Sheffield: Sheffield Academic Press, 1996.

Koch, Klaus. "Stages in the Canonization of the Book of Daniel." Pages 421–46 in *The Book of Daniel: Composition and Reception.* Vol. 2. Edited by John J. Collins and Peter W. Flint. Leiden: Brill, 2001.

Koester, Helmut. *History, Culture and Religion of the Hellenistic Age: Volume 1: Introduction to the New Testament.* New York: Walter de Gruyter, 1982.

Krodel, Gerhard A. *Revelation.* ACNT. Minneapolis: Augsburg, 1989.

Kugel, James L. *The Bible as It Was.* Cambridge, Mass.: Harvard University Press, 1997.

Kugler, Robert A. *The Testaments of the Twelve Patriarchs.* Guides to Apocrypha and Pseudepigrapha. Sheffield: Sheffield Academic Press, 2001.

Lawrence, D. H. *Apocalypse.* Harmondsworth, England: Penguin, 1960.

Laws, Sophie. *In the Light of the Lamb: Imagery, Parody, and Theology in the Apocalypse of John.* GNS 31. Wilmington, Del.: Michael Glazer, 1988.

Layton, Bentley. *The Gnostic Scriptures.* ABRL. New York: Doubleday, 1987.

Lindsey, Hal. *The Late Great Planet Earth.* Grand Rapids, Mich.: Zondervan, 1970.

Livingston, James C. *Anatomy of the Sacred: An Introduction to Religion.* 3d ed. Upper Saddle River, N.J.: Prentice Hall, 1998.

Longenecker, Bruce N. *2 Esdras.* Guides to Apocrypha and Pseudepigrapha. Sheffield: Sheffield Academic Press, 1995.

Mack, Burton L. *The Lost Gospel: The Book of Q and Christian Origins.* San Francisco: HarperCollins, 1993.

Malherbe, Abraham J. *Paul and the Popular Philosophers.* Minneapolis: Fortress Press, 1989.

Marsh, Charles. *The Last Days: A Son's Story of Sin and Segregation at the Dawn of a New South.* New York: Basic, 2001.

Marshall, John W. *Parables of War: Reading John's Jewish Apocalypse.* ESCJ 10. Waterloo, Ontario: Wilfrid Laurier University Press, 2001.

Martin, Dale B. *The Corinthian Body.* New Haven, Conn.: Yale University Press, 1995.

_____. "Paul and the Judaism/Hellenism Dichotomy: Toward a Social History of the Question." Pages 29–61 in *Paul Beyond the Judaism/Hellenism Divide.* Edited by Troels Engberg-Pedersen. Louisville: Westminster John Knox Press, 2001.

Martin, Ralph P. *2 Corinthians.* WBC 40. Waco, Tex.: Word, 1986.

Martyn, J. Louis. "The Apocalyptic Gospel in Galatians." *Int* 54 (2000): 246–66.

McGinn, Bernard, ed. *The Encyclopedia of Apocalypticism: Volume 2: Apocalypticism in Western History and Culture.* New York: Continuum, 2000.

Meeks, Wayne A. "Social Functions of Apocalyptic Language in Pauline Christianity." Pages 687–705 in *Apocalypticism in the Mediterranean World and the Near East: Proceedings of the International Colloquium on Apocalypticism, Uppsala, August 12–17, 1979.* Edited by David Hellholm. Tübingen: Mohr-Siebeck, 1982.

Meier, John P. *A Marginal Jew: Rethinking the Historical Jesus: Volume 1: The Roots of the Problem and the Person.* ABRL. New York: Doubleday, 1991.

_____. *A Marginal Jew: Rethinking the Historical Jesus. Volume 2: Mentor, Message, and Miracles.* ABRL. New York: Doubleday, 1991.

Mendel, Arthur P. *Vision and Violence.* Ann Arbor: University of Michigan Press, 1992.

Metzger, Bruce M. *The Canon of the New Testament: Its Origin, Development, and Significance.* New York: Oxford University Press, 1987.

Míguez, Néstor. "Apocalyptic and the Economy: A Reading of Revelation 18 from the Experience of Economic Exclusion." Pages 250–62 in *Reading from This Place: Volume 2: Social Location and Biblical Interpretation in Global Perspective.* Edited by Fernando F. Segovia and Mary Ann Tolbert. Minneapolis: Fortress Press, 1995.

Milik, J. T. *The Books of Enoch: Aramaic Fragments from Qumran Cave 4*. Oxford: Clarendon, 1976.

Moltmann, Jürgen. *The Coming of God: Christian Eschatology*. Translated by Margaret Kohl. Minneapolis: Fortress Press, 1996.

_____. *In the End–the Beginning: The Life of Hope*. Minneapolis: Fortress Press, 2004.

_____. *Theology of Hope: On the Ground and Implications of a Christian Eschatology*. New York: Harper & Row, 1967.

Murphy, Frederick J. "Introduction to Apocalyptic Literature." Pages 1–16 in *The New Interpreter's Bible: Volume 7*. Nashville: Abingdon Press, 1996.

Newman, Carey C., ed. *Jesus and the Restoration of Israel: A Critical Assessment of N. T. Wright's Jesus and the Victory of God*. Downers Grove, Ill.: InterVarsity, 1999.

Newsom, Carol A. "Baruch: Introduction." Pages 1617–18 in *The HarperCollins Study Bible*. Edited by Wayne A. Meeks. San Francisco: HarperCollins, 1993.

Nickelsburg, George W. E. "The Apocalyptic Construction of Reality in *1 Enoch*." Pages 51–64 in *Mysteries and Revelations: Apocalyptic Studies since the Uppsala Colloquium*. Edited by John J. Collins and James H. Charlesworth. JSPSup 9. Sheffield: JSPT Press, 1991.

_____. "The Bible Rewritten and Expanded." Pages 89–156 in *Jewish Writings of the Second Temple Period*. Edited by Michael E. Stone. CRINT 2.2; Philadelphia: Fortress Press, 1984.

_____. *1 Enoch 1: A Commentary on the Book of 1 Enoch, Chapters 1–36; 81–108*. Hermeneia. Minneapolis: Fortress Press, 2001.

_____. *Jewish Literature Between the Bible and the Mishnah*. Philadelphia: Fortress Press, 1981.

_____. "Salvation without and with a Messiah: Developing Beliefs in Writings Ascribed to Enoch." Pages 49–68 in *Judaisms and Their Messiahs at the Turn of the Christian Era*. Edited by Jacob Neusner, William S. Green, and Ernest Frerichs. Cambridge: Cambridge University Press, 1987.

_____, ed. *Studies on the Testament of Moses*. Septuagint and Cognate Studies 4. Cambridge, Mass.: Society of Biblical Literature, 1973.

Nietzsche, Friedrich. *The Birth of Tragedy and the Genealogy of Morals*. New York: Anchor/Doubleday, 1956.

Nogalski, James D., and Marvin A. Sweeney, eds. *Reading and Hearing the Book of the Twelve*. SBLSymS 15. Atlanta: Society of Biblical Literature, 2000.

O'Brien, Julia M. *Nahum-Malachi*. Abingdon Press Old Testament Commentaries. Nashville: Abingdon Press, 2004.

O'Brien, Peter T. *The Epistle to the Philippians: A Commentary on the Greek Text*. NIGTC. Grand Rapids, Mich.: Eerdmans, 1991.

O'Leary, Stephen D. *Arguing the Apocalypse: A Theory of Millennial Rhetoric.*
New York: Oxford University Press, 1994.

Osiek, Carolyn. "Hermas, Shepherd of." *EDB,* 577–79.

_____. *Rich and Poor in the* Shepherd of Hermas*: An Exegetical-Social
Investigation.* CBQMS 15. Washington, D.C.: Catholic Biblical
Association of America, 1983.

_____. *Shepherd of Hermas: A Commentary.* Hermeneia. Minneapolis: Fortress
Press, 1999.

Pagels, Elaine. *Beyond Belief: The Secret Gospel of Thomas.* New York: Random
House, 2003.

Parke, H. W. *Sibyls and Sibylline Prophecy in Classical Antiquity.* Edited by B.
C. McGing. New York: Routledge, 1988.

Patterson, Stephen J. *The Gospel of Thomas and Jesus.* Foundations and Facets.
Sonoma, Calif.: Polebridge, 1993.

_____. "Understanding the Gospel of Thomas Today." Pages 33–75 in *The
Fifth Gospel: The Gospel of Thomas Comes of Age.* By Stephen J. Patterson,
James M. Robinson, and Hans-Gebhard Bethge. Harrisburg, Pa.:
Trinity Press International, 1998.

Patterson, Stephen J., James M. Robinson, and Hans-Gebhard Bethge. *The
Fifth Gospel: The Gospel of Thomas Comes of Age.* Harrisburg, Pa.: Trinity
Press International, 1998.

Perkins, Pheme. "The Gospel of Mark." Pages 507–733 in *The New
Interpreter's Bible: Volume 8.* Nashville: Abingdon Press, 1995.

Pernveden, Lage. *The Concept of the Church in the Shepherd of Hermas.* Studia
theologica Ludensia 27. Lund: Gleerup, 1966.

Pesce, Mauro. *L'Ascensione di Isaiah: Cristologia e profetismo in Siria nei primi
decenni del II secolo.* Studia Patristica Mediolanensia 17. Milan: Vita e
Pensiero, 1989.

_____. "Presupposti per l'utilizzazione storica dell'*Ascensione di Isaiah*: Formazione
e tradizione del testo; genere letterario; cosmologia angelica." Pages
13–76 in *Isaiah: il Diletto e la Chiesa: Visione ed esegesi profetica cristiano-
primitiva nell'*Ascensione di Isaiah. Edited by Mauro Pesce. Testi e
recherche di scienze religiose 20. Brescia: Paideia Editrice, 1983.

Petersen, David L. *Zechariah 9–14 and Malachi.* OTL. Louisville: Westminster
John Knox Press, 1995.

Pippin, Tina. "A Good Apocalypse Is Hard to Find: Crossing the
Apocalyptic Borders of Mark 13." *Semeia* 72 (1995): 153–71.

_____. *Death and Desire: The Rhetoric of Gender in the Apocalypse of John.* Literary
Currents in Biblical Interpretation. Louisville: Westminster/John
Knox Press, 1992.

Polaski, Donald C. "Destruction, Construction, Argumentation: A
Rhetorical Reading of Isaiah 24–27." Pages 19–39 in *Vision and
Persuasion: Rhetorical Dimensions of Apocalyptic Discourse.* Edited by Greg
Carey and L. Gregory Bloomquist. St. Louis: Chalice Press, 1999.

Powell, Mark Allan. *Jesus as a Figure in History: How Modern Historians View the Man from Galilee.* Louisville: Westminster John Knox Press, 1998.

Priest, J. "Testament of Moses." Pages 919–34 in *The Old Testament Pseudepigrapha: Volume 1: Apocalyptic Literature and Testaments.* Edited by James H. Charlesworth. New York: Doubleday, 1983.

Pritchard, James B., ed. *The Ancient Near East: Volume 1: An Anthology of Texts and Pictures.* Princeton, N.J.: Princeton University Press, 1958.

Redditt, Paul L. "Daniel 11 and the Sociohistorical Setting of the Book of Daniel." *CBQ* 60 (1998): 463–74.

Reed, Jeffrey T. "The Epistle." Pages 171–93 in *Handbook of Classical Rhetoric in the Hellenistic Period, 330 B.C.–A.D. 400.* Edited by Stanley E. Porter. Boston: Brill, 2001.

Richard, Pablo. *Apocalypse: A People's Commentary on the Book of Revelation.* Maryknoll, N.Y.: Orbis, 1995.

Robbins, Vernon K. "The Intertexture of Apocalyptic Discourse in the Gospel of Mark." Pages 11–44 in *The Intertexture of Apocalyptic Discourse in the New Testament.* Edited by Duane F. Watson. SBLSymS 14. Atlanta: Society of Biblical Literature, 2002.

_____. *The Tapestry of Early Christian Discourse: Rhetoric, Society, and Ideology.* New York: Routledge, 1996.

Robinson, James M., ed. *The Nag Hammadi Library in English.* 3d ed. San Francisco: HarperCollins, 1988.

Roetzel, Calvin. *Paul: The Man and the Myth.* Studies on the Personalities of the New Testament. Minneapolis: Fortress Press, 1999.

Rowland, Christopher. *The Open Heaven: A Study of Apocalyptic in Judaism and Early Christianity.* New York: Crossroad, 1982.

Ruiten, J. T. A. G. M. van. *Primaeval History Interpreted: The Rewriting of Genesis 1–11 in the Book of Jubilees.* JSJSup 66. Leiden: Brill, 2000.

Said, Edward W. *Orientalism.* New York: Vintage, 1979.

Sanders, E. P. *The Historical Figure of Jesus.* New York: Penguin, 1993.

_____. *Jesus and Judaism.* Philadelphia: Fortress Press, 1985.

_____. *Judaism: Practice and Belief 63 B.C.E.–66 C.E.* Valley Forge, Pa.: Trinity Press International, 1992.

Sandy, D. Brent. *Plowshares & and Pruning Hooks: Rethinking the Language of Biblical Prophecy and Apocalyptic.* Downers Grove, Ill.: InterVarsity, 2002.

Saperstein, Marc, ed. *Essential Papers on Messianic Movements and Personalities in Jewish History.* Essential Papers on Jewish Studies. New York: New York University Press, 1992.

_____. "Introduction." Pages 1–31 in *Essential Papers on Messianic Movements and Personalities in Jewish History.* Edited by Marc Saperstein. Essential Papers on Jewish Studies. New York: New York University Press, 1992.

Sawyer, John F. A. *The Fifth Gospel: Isaiah in the History of Christianity.* Cambridge: Cambridge University Press, 1996.

Sayler, Gwendolyn B. *Have the Promises Failed? A Literary Analysis of 2 Baruch.* SBLDS 72. Chico, Calif.: Scholars Press, 1984.

Schiffman, Lawrence H. *Texts and Traditions: A Source Reader for the Study of Second Temple and Rabbinic Judaism.* Hoboken, N.J.: KTAV, 1998.

Scholem, Gershom. *Judaica: Volume 1.* Frankfurt: Suhrkamp, 1963.

_____. "Sabbatai Sevi: The Mystical Messiah." Pages 289–334 in *Essential Papers on Messianic Movements and Personalities in Jewish History.* Edited by Marc Saperstein. Essential Papers on Jewish Studies. New York: New York University Press, 1992.

Schüssler Fiorenza, Elisabeth. *The Book of Revelation: Justice and Judgment.* 2d ed. Minneapolis: Fortress Press, 1998.

_____. *Revelation: Vision of a Just World.* Proclamation Commentaries. Minneapolis: Fortress Press, 1991.

_____. "The Words of Prophecy: Reading the Apocalypse Theologically." Pages 1–19 in *Studies in the Book of Revelation.* Edited by Steve Moyise. New York: T. &T. Clark, 2001.

Schweid, Eliezer. "Jewish Messianism: Metamorphoses of an Idea." Pages 53–70 in *Essential Papers on Messianic Movements and Personalities in Jewish History.* Edited by Marc Saperstein. Essential Papers on Jewish Studies. New York: New York University Press, 1992.

Schweitzer, Albert. *The Quest of the Historical Jesus.* Translated by James M. Robinson. New York: Macmillan, 1968.

Seely, David Ralph. "Resurrection." *EDB,* 1121.

Segal, Alan F. *Paul the Convert: The Apostolate and Apostasy of Saul the Pharisee.* New Haven, Conn.: Yale University Press, 1990.

_____. *Rebecca's Children: Judaism and Christianity in the Roman World.* Cambridge, Mass.: Harvard University Press, 1986.

Senior, Donald P. "Son of Man." *EDB,* 1242.

Setzer, Claudia J. "The Parousia of Jesus and Jewish Messianic Hopes." Pages 169–83 in *The Return of Jesus in Early Christianity.* By John T. Carroll, Alexandra R. Brown, Claudia J. Setzer, and Jeffrey S. Siker. Peabody, Mass.: Hendrickson, 2000.

Silberman, Neil Asher. *The Hidden Scrolls: Christianity, Judaism, and the War for the Dead Sea Scrolls.* New York: Riverhead, 1994.

Simkins, Ronald A. "Joel, Book of." *EDB,* 720–21.

Smith, D. Moody. *The Theology of the Gospel of John.* New Testament Theology. New York: Cambridge University Press, 1995.

Smith, Jonathan Z., ed. *The HarperCollins Dictionary of Religion.* San Francisco: HarperSanFrancisco, 1995.

_____. "Wisdom and Apocalyptic." Pages 67–87 in *Map Is Not Territory: Studies in the History of Religions.* SJLA 23. Leiden: Brill, 1978.

Snyder, Graydon F. *The Shepherd of Hermas.* The Apostolic Fathers 6. Camden, N.J.: Nelson, 1968.

Soares-Prabhu, George M. "Laughing at Idols: The Dark Side of Biblical Monotheism (an Indian Reading of Isaiah 44:9–20." Pages 109–31 in *Reading from This Place: Volume 2: Social Location and Biblical Interpretation in Global Perspective.* Edited by Fernando F. Segovia and Mary Ann Tolbert. Minneapolis: Fortress Press, 1995.

Sparks, H. F. D., ed. *The Apocryphal Old Testament.* New York: Oxford University Press, 1984.

Stevenson, Kalinda Rose. *The Vision of Transformation: The Territorial Rhetoric of Ezekiel 40–48.* SBLDS 154. Atlanta, Ga.: Scholars, 1996.

Stone, Michael Edward. "Apocalyptic Literature." Pages 383–441 in *Jewish Writings of the Second Temple Period.* Edited by Michael E. Stone. CRINT 2/2. Philadelphia: Fortress Press, 1984.

_____. *4 Ezra.* Hermeneia. Minneapolis: Fortress Press, 1990. Fortress Press

_____. "On Reading an Apocalypse." Pages 65–78 in *Mysteries and Revelations: Apocalyptic Studies Since the Uppsala Colloquium.* Edited by John J. Collins and James H. Charlesworth. JSPS 9. Sheffield: JSOT Press, 1991.

_____, ed. *Jewish Writings of the Second Temple Period.* CRINT 2/2. Philadelphia: Fortress Press, 1984.

Stowers, Stanley K. *Letter Writing in Greco-Roman Antiquity.* LEC 5. Philadelphia: Westminster Press, 1986.

Streete, Gail Corrington. "Discipline and Disclosure: Paul's Apocalyptic Asceticism in 1 Corinthians." Page 82 in *Vision and Persuasion: Rhetorical Dimensions of Apocalyptic Discourse,* ed. Greg Carey and L. Gregory Bloomquist. St. Louis: Chalice Press, 1999.

_____. "Outrageous (Speech) Acts and Everyday (Performative) Rebellions: A Response to Rhetorics of Resistance." *Semeia* 79 (1997): 97–105.

Strozier, Charles B. *Apocalypse: On the Psychology of Fundamentalism in America.* Boston: Beacon, 1994.

Tigchelaar, Eibert J. C. *Prophets of Old and the Day of the End: Zechariah, the Book of the Watchers, and Apocalyptic.* OtSt 35. Leiden: Brill, 1996.

Toorn, Karel van der. "Scholars at the Oriental Court: The Figure of Daniel against Its Mesopotamian Background." Pages 37–54 in *The Book of Daniel: Composition and Reception.* Vol. 1. Edited by John J. Collins and Peter W. Flint. Leiden: Brill, 2001.

Tromp, Johannes. *The Assumption of Moses: A Critical Edition with Commentary.* SVTP 10. Leiden: Brill, 1993.

Tuckett, Christopher M. *Q and the History of Early Christianity: Studies on Q.* Edinburgh: T. & T. Clark, 1996.

Valantasis, Richard. "Constructions of Power in Asceticism." *JAAR* 36 (1995): 775–821.

_____. *The Gospel of Thomas.* New Testament Readings. New York: Routledge, 1997.

VanderKam, James C. "Apocalyptic Tradition in the Dead Sea Scrolls and the Religion of Qumran." Pages 113–34 in *Religion in the Dead Sea*

Scrolls. Edited by John J. Collins and Robert A. Kugler. Studies in the Dead Sea Scrolls and Related Literature. Grand Rapids, Mich.: Eerdmans, 2000.

_____. *The Book of Jubilees*. Guides to Apocrypha and Pseudepigrapha. Sheffield: Sheffield Academic Press, 2001.

_____. *The Dead Sea Scrolls Today*. Grand Rapids, Mich.: Eerdmans, 1994.

_____. *Enoch: A Man for All Generations*. Studies on Personalities of the Old Testament. Columbia: University of South Carolina Press, 1995.

_____. *Enoch and the Growth of an Apocalyptic Tradition*. CBQMS 16. Washington, D.C.: Catholic Biblical Association, 1984.

_____. *An Introduction to Early Judaism*. Grand Rapids, Mich.: Eerdmans, 2001.

_____. "Righteous One, Messiah, Chosen One, and Son of Man in 1 Enoch 37–71." Pages 169–91 in *The Messiah: Developments in Earliest Judaism and Christianity*. Edited by James H. Charlesworth. Minneapolis: Fortress Press, 1992.

_____. *Textual and Historical Studies in the Book of Jubilees*. HSM 14. Missoula, Mont.: Scholars Press, 1977.

Volf, Miroslav, Carmen Krieg, and Thomas Kucharz, eds. *The Future of Theology: Essays in Honor of Jürgen Moltmann*. Grand Rapids, Mich.: Eerdmans, 1996.

Wainwright, Arthur W. *Mysterious Apocalypse: Interpreting the Book of Revelation*. Nashville: Abingdon Press, 1993.

Watson, Duane F., ed. *The Intertexture of Apocalyptic Discourse in the New Testament*. SBLSymS 14. Atlanta: Society of Biblical Literature, 2002.

_____. "Paul's Appropriation of Apocalyptic Discourse: The Rhetorical Strategy of 1 Thessalonians." Pages 61–80 in *Vision and Persuasion: Rhetorical Dimensions of Apocalyptic Discourse*. Edited by Greg Carey and L. Gregory Bloomquist. St. Louis: Chalice Press, 1999.

Weedon, Chris. *Feminist Practice and Poststructuralist Theory*. Cambridge, Mass.: Blackwell, 1987.

Werblowsky, R. J. Zvi. "Messianism in Jewish History." Pages 35–52 in *Essential Papers on Messianic Movements and Personalities in Jewish History*. Edited by Marc Saperstein. Essential Papers on Jewish Studies. New York: New York University Press, 1992.

Whitters, Mark. *The Epistle of Second Baruch: A Study in Form and Message*. JSPS 42. Sheffield: Sheffield Academic Press, 2003.

Wilson, Bryan R. *Magic and the Millennium: A Sociological Study of Religious Movements of Protest Among Tribal and Third-World Peoples*. New York: Harper & Row, 1973.

Wilson, J. Christian. "The Problem of the Domitianic Date of Revelation." *NTS* 39 (1993): 587–605.

Wilson, Stephen G. *Related Strangers: Jews and Christians, 70–170 C.E.* Minneapolis: Fortress Press, 1995.

Wintermute, O. S. "Jubilees." Pages 35–142 in *The Old Testament Pseudepigrapha: Volume 2: Expansions of the "Old Testament" and Legends, Wisdom and Philosophical Literature, Prayers, Psalms and Odes, Fragments of Lost Judeo-Hellenistic Works*. Edited by James H. Charlesworth. New York: Doubleday, 1985.

Witherington, Ben, III. *The Gospel of Mark: A Socio-Rhetorical Commentary*. Grand Rapids, Mich.: Eerdmans, 2001.

Wright, N. T. *Jesus and the Victory of God*. Minneapolis: Fortress Press, 1996.

_____. *The New Testament and the People of God*. Minneapolis: Fortress Press, 1992.

_____. *The Resurrection of the Son of God*. Minneapolis: Fortress Press, 2003.

_____. *What Saint Paul Really Said: Was Paul of Tarsus the Real Founder of Christianity?* Grand Rapids, Mich.: Eerdmans, 1997.

Yarbro Collins, Adela. "The Book of Revelation." Pages 384–414 in *The Encyclopedia of Apocalypticism: Volume 1: The Origins of Apocalypticism in Judaism and Christianity*. Edited by John J. Collins. New York: Crossroad, 1998.

_____. *Crisis and Catharsis: The Power of the Apocalypse*. Louisville: Westminster Press, 1984.

_____, ed. *Early Christian Apocalypticism: Genre and Social Setting*. Semeia 36 (1986).

_____. "Feminine Symbolism in the Book of Revelation." *BibInt* 1 (1993): 20–33.

_____. "The Influence of Daniel on the New Testament." Pages 90–123 in *Daniel: A Commentary on the Book of Daniel*. By John J. Collins. Hermeneia. Minneapolis: Fortress Press, 1993.

_____. "Introduction: Early Christian Apocalypticism." *Semeia* 36 (1986): 7.

_____. "The Political Perspective of the Revelation to John." *JBL* 96 (1977): 241–56.

_____. "The Seven Heavens in Jewish and Christian Apocalypses." Pages 21–54 in *Cosmology and Eschatology in Jewish and Christian Apocalypticism*. JSJSup 50. Leiden: Brill, 1996.